AF870260

Electronic Trading

'TNT'

III

Technical Trading Stuff

JOE ROSS
MARK CHERLIN

Electronic Trading 'TNT' III — Technical Trading Stuff

©

Copyright 1998 by KOATA LTD.

ALL RIGHTS RESERVED

ISBN 976-8108-16-9

Printed in the United States of America

NO PART OF THIS PUBLICATION MAY BE REPRODUCED, STORED IN A RETRIEVAL SYSTEM, OR TRANSMITTED IN ANY FORM OR BY ANY MEANS, ELECTRONIC, MECHANICAL, PHOTOCOPYING, RECORDING OR OTHERWISE, WITHOUT THE PRIOR WRITTEN PERMISSION OF THE PUBLISHER AND THE COPYRIGHT HOLDER EXCEPT IN THE CASE OF BRIEF QUOTATIONS EMBODIED IN CRITICAL ARTICLES AND REVIEWS. ANY PERSON OR ENTITY VIOLATING COPYRIGHT LAWS OR COPYING ANY PART OF THIS BOOK WITHOUT EXPRESS PERMISSION OF THE AUTHORS WILL BE PROSECUTED TO THE FULL EXTENT OF THE LAW. ROSS HOOK™, REVERSE ROSS HOOK,™ TRADER'S TRICK, ™ AND LAW OF CHARTS™ ARE PROPERTIES OF ROSS TRADING INC. THE TITLE ELECTONIC TRADING 'TNT' III — TECHNICAL TRADING STUFF™ AND TRADERS UNIVERSITY™ ARE PROPERTIES OF KOATA LTD.

Distributed by Ross Trading Inc., 1509 Jackson, Cedar Park, TX 78613

Email: ross@rosstrading.com Telephone: 512-249-6930 Fax: 512-249-6931 Order: 800-476-7796 Office hours: 9:00 A.M - 5:00 P.M. CST Visit our Web site: www.rosstrading.com

To our students, past present, and future

DISCLAIMER

NO CLAIM IS MADE BY JOE ROSS, MARK CHERLIN, KOATA LTD., ROSS TRADING (STOCKS) LTD., OR BY ROSS TRADING INCORPORATED THAT THE TRADING METHODS SHOWN HERE WILL RESULT IN PROFITS AND WILL NOT RESULT IN LOSSES. TRADING STOCKS MAY NOT BE SUITABLE FOR ALL RECIPIENTS OF THIS PUBLICATION. ALL COMMENTS, TECHNIQUES, METHODS, SYSTEMS, AND CONCEPTS SHOWN WITHIN THIS MANUAL ARE NOT AND SHOULD NOT BE CONSTRUED AS AN OFFER TO BUY OR SELL ANY OF THE TRADING VEHICLES NAMED HEREIN. THE THOUGHTS EXPRESSED ARE NOT GUARANTEED TO PRODUCE PROFITS. ALL OPINIONS ARE SUBJECT TO CHANGE WITHOUT NOTICE. EACH TRADER IS RESPONSIBLE FOR HIS/HER OWN ACTIONS, IF ANY. PURCHASE OF THIS MANUAL CONSTITUTES YOUR AGREEMENT TO THIS DISCLAIMER AND EXEMPTS THE CREATORS, PUBLISHERS, AND DISTRIBUTORS FROM ANY LIABILITY OR LITIGATION.

Table of Contents

CAUTION

CAUTION: THIS IS A COURSE INTENDED TO HELP TEACH YOU HOW TO TRADE STOCKS, IMPROVE YOUR TRADING SKILLS, OR BOTH. THERE ARE SECTIONS OF THIS COURSE THAT ARE DIFFICULT TO UNDERSTAND UPON FIRST READING. IT IS A MANUAL MEANT TO BE STUDIED. THE CONCEPTS CONTAINED IN THIS COURSE TOOK MANY YEARS TO DEVELOP. MOST TRADERS WILL NOT BE ABLE TO GRASP THESE WITH JUST A CURSORY READING OF THE TEXT. IN THE PAST, MUCH OF THIS MATERIAL WAS RESERVED EXCLUSIVELY FOR PRIVATE SEMINARS WHICH COST $10,000 PER STUDENT.

Books for stock traders by Joe Ross and Mark Cherlin:

- Electronic Trading 'TNT' I — Gorilla Trading Stuff
- Electronic Trading 'TNT' II — How-to-Win Trading Stuff
- Electronic Trading 'TNT' III — Technical Trading Stuff
- Electronic Trading 'TNT' IV — Tips-Tricks and Other Trading Stuff

To the Ladies who are taking this course: We tried to write the manuals in a way that is gender neutral. Ladies, it just didn't work. So please forgive the fact that we used the masculine gender throughout. It is not our intent to offend you in any way.

Foreword

What a surprise it was when I received a call from Joe Ross wondering if I could take the time out from my busy trading schedule to write a brief foreword to a third volume of the course he fondly referred to as "Electronic Trading TNT." He explained that, since I am a great proponent of the proper use of technical analysis and the appropriate use of indicators in combination with common-sense trading, that he and Mark Cherlin would appreciate a candid and straight-forward critique of "Technical Trading Stuff," the third volume in the four part series of their stock trading course. He explained further that if I liked what I read, they would be pleased if I would write a foreword to their work.

If you are reading this, then be most assured that I have read the material contained in this course, and that I give it my heartfelt personal endorsement. You have in your possession one of the finest volumes on the practical implementation of technical trading it has ever been my pleasure to read and put into use.

Not all traders are technically minded, but for those who are, I know that you will enjoy the height, the depth, and the breadth of knowledge presented here. Joe and Mark bring you some of the best "stuff" I have seen in my many years of trading. In fact, I suppose I'm a bit jealous, because some of the concepts contained in these pages took me many years to decipher and master, and I'm not at all sure I would have been as generous and willing to share them as are Joe and Mark. A deep and serious study of their material will put you much ahead of the majority of traders attempting to, as they say, "make it" as professional stock traders.

For example, the presentation on what constitutes congestion followed by what defines a trend is without equal to anything I have ever read. The material is excellent, absolutely splendid "stuff."

The chapter on two ways to use Bollinger Bands to filter trades is without question the finest material you are ever going to see. That chapter alone is worth many times the price of the entire course.

These two professional traders are actually handing you the means of making a living as a trader in the stock markets. Why was there not someone around like Joe and Mark when I was struggling through the earliest years of my own trading career? The truth is that I am not positive that during my beginning years as a trader I would have truly appreciated what is presented here. Take, for instance, the material on "A Word to the Wise," and again "Trade What You See." It quite simply doesn't get much better than what you will learn there. And speaking of letting you in on trading secrets - I have to wonder if these two gents are holding anything back! And, my dear reader, there is more, so very much more. Do enjoy! When you've completed your reading, I'm sure you will be as keen on their work as am I.

Joe and Mark, you have set a new standard in educating traders everywhere and for all time. Congratulations on a most excellent work. I am honored to have been given this opportunity since I had already read and marveled at the first two volumes of this fantastic course in the electronic trading of stocks.

Anthony Barclay, Trader, London, U.K.

Introduction

This is Volume III of a multi-part course in electronic trading.

This part of the course is dedicated to technical charting concepts, and, in particular, those concepts leading to the trading of a price formation which has come to be known as the Ross Hook. Of course, all money, risk, and trade management associated with the Ross Hook is included.

It seems strange to write an entire volume of the course about such a simple formation. Yet, as we tried to put down everything we could about trading Ross Hooks, we realized we could never get it all in writing. There are always new ways to see things, always nuances in the ways to trade.

Ross Hooks are not an entity in and of themselves, but are an integral part of market action. Much of what we see and act upon when trading them involves drawing upon many years of experience trading the Ross Hook in relation to the overall action of the markets.

In the book we try to impart to you, the reader, the essence of that experience.

Our goal is to share with you what has been so profitable for us.

If you are not willing to commit yourself to diligent study of this manual, then you are wasting your time reading it. Conversely, if you are willing to thoroughly study what is present here, you will be richly rewarded. You hold in your hand a treasure trove of information. May you prosper from it.

PLEASE READ THE FOLLOWING

A Special Message from the Authors

There is a different **free gift** offer located within the contents of each of our manuals. The free gift consists of a winning trading strategy that has made substantial profits for those who have used it. Since we feel it is important for you to read the entire manual, we are not going to tell you where it is.

You will have to read the contents to find it.

When you do, please contact Ross Trading Inc. to have it sent to you.

WARNING

This manual has certain critical pages printed in a special ink. The ink is extremely light sensitive. Copying or scanning this manual will result in total destruction of the print on those pages. If you attempt to copy the text, you do so at your own risk. Besides it is illegal. Consider yourself warned. We will not replace or honor the warranty on any books with missing print. We will also prosecute to the full extent of the law any violation of copyright law.

The Authors

JOE ROSS

Joe Ross, trader, author, and educator, has been an active trader since 1957, when he began his trading career in the commodity futures markets. In 1982, when it became possible to daytrade the S&P 500 stock index futures via a live data feed, he successfully made the transition from full-time position trader to full-time daytrader. In 1988 he formed Trading Educators for the purpose of training aspiring traders in the futures, bonds, and currency markets. Since 1988, Joe has written seven major texts on futures trading. All have become classics. An eighth text is distributed only to students who take his private daytrading course. In 1991, in addition to private tutoring, Joe began to give seminars and to write Trader's Notebook, a teaching newsletter. He did this in order to keep his students apprised of new trading techniques, and global situations that can affect all markets. Joe teaches that a trader should be able to live anywhere in the world where he can obtain trading facilities, and be able to trade any market at any time, whether it be stocks, futures, currencies on the Forex, or interest rate contracts. To prove that he means it, Joe moved to the Bahamas. "The phones are lousy, and I can barely get data," Joe says. But he successfully trades from there.

Although Joe's career has centered mostly on the trading of futures, and in recent years more particularly on daytrading the S&P 500 futures, he has also been a successful trader in the stock market. In fact, many active and successful stock market traders have read Joe's books on their way to becoming profitable. As Joe likes to say, "A market is a market, and a chart is a chart. Given those two and a way to enter an order, a trader should be able to make his money."

Joe holds a Bachelor of Science degree in Business Administration from the University of California at Los Angeles. He did his Masters work in Computer Sciences at the George Washington University extension in Norfolk, Virginia.

MARK CHERLIN

Mark Cherlin, trader, money manager, and educator, began trading other people's money immediately after graduation from the renowned A.B. Freeman School of Business at Tulane University.

In addition to owning and operating an investment advisory firm and being trader for a hedge fund, Mark started a day trading firm which quickly became one of the most successful in the country.

Mark is currently the co -founder and president of NexTrend, Inc. the first financial market information provider to create its business and technology specifically to deliver totally integrated market information, professional analysis and trading of securities over the Internet. www.nextrend.com

Mark has been deeply involved with electronic trading and has himself successfully day traded various electronic systems as well as having contributed greatly to the success of scores of day traders.

Mark's other accomplishments are equally impressive. He has been a Vice-President/Investments with both Shearson Lehman Brothers and Oppenheimer & Co., and First Vice-President/Investments with Lehman Brothers.

His articles, views, and accomplishments have been noted or published in such leading journals and periodicals as Investors Business Daily, Barron's, The Houston Business Journal, and Institutional Investors Portfolio Letter, to name but a few. He has made numerous appearances on the national television show Inside Money, and has been mentioned or featured on radio stations around the country. He has also, upon request, written published editorials about trading and investing.

Mark is considered by many to be one of the most energetic and exciting traders / educators in the Electronic Day trading community. He is happy to share with all aspiring traders, both beginners and experts, this, his latest venture, as co-author of this course, Electronic Trading 'TNT.'

Chapter 1

THE PATH

If you follow the simple path mapped out in this part of the course, you will have in your possession a way to accumulate wealth trading in stocks. You will have to work hard. However, your labors will not be where most would expect.

Those who have followed this same path did not spend countless hours backtesting systems. They did not spend weeks and months pretending to trade. Instead, they spent much time, and still do, in perfecting their attitude and approach to trading. They spent great amounts of time in learning the discipline and self-control needed to trade realistically and profitably. As we've repeatedly stated in our other manuals, trading is a business, and it must be treated and managed as a business.

By reversing the way that most traders approach their trading, it is possible to reverse the outcome. Unfortunately, most traders have a disastrous approach.

How can our experiences help you?

Instead of trading with great risk, uncertainty, complexity, and confusion in your trading, it is possible for you to begin to enter trades with a high probability for success. Mathematical, scientific, cyclical, and computerized approaches to the market are totally unnecessary, as are those based on theory. If a high degree of proficiency in mathematics and science were necessary to profitable trading, there would be no way many currently successful traders could have accomplished a winning strategy in the markets.

Winning trades can be yours, and you can consistently pile them up if you will rigorously follow the simple, uncomplicated path we are going to reveal to you.

What we show will be conceptually easy. Yet it may be difficult for you to do. We're not going to promise that you'll have the discipline to implement the techniques shown here. But if you do have the discipline, or can develop it, you will be well on your way towards being a successful trader.

The best part is that trading can be as easy as lifting a finger and turning off the switch of risk and uncertainty, and flicking on the switch of simplicity and inevitable wins. The choice is yours.

You can choose to go from one complicated mathematical concept to another — continuing to lose as you try to force the markets to fit into your preconceived notion of what they should or should not do, or you can learn to simply read a market and let it tell you what it is going to do, and then go along for a profitable journey.

DOES THIS SOUND HARD TO BELIEVE?

Be assured that what we will show in this part of the course is totally genuine, real and true. We have used these concepts, and still are using them. More importantly, others we've taught are successfully using them, right now, perhaps as you are reading this. The concepts you will learn here work!

The technique of the Ross Hook, and the approach to trade selection that is described in this course, are based on sound, time-tested, fundamental rules for successful trading. They are based on the fact that a chart is a chart regardless of whether it is a stock chart, a futures chart, a Forex currency chart, or a chart of some interest bearing financial instrument such as Treasury Bonds. If you long for a way to *simplify* your trading life so that you can concentrate on the important jobs of taking control of your trading and yourself, if you want an exciting fresh start, then pay close attention to the concepts we will be revealing here.

If you desire to be honest with yourself, realizing that you cannot control the markets, and that, when trading, the only thing you can control is yourself, then the methods we teach will work for you.

If you want your trading to start compounding successes in a systematic, ever-growing fashion, but you recoil from risking tons of money on the uncertainty and volatility of stock markets, then perhaps you've finally found the material you've been looking for.

If you never want to painfully look at yourself in the mirror — or confront your spouse and admit with reluctant shame, "Darling, I lost again today," then the ins-and-outs of trading the Ross Hook may be the answer for which you've searched.

And if you hunger for the kind of money and leverage you can find in the stock markets, yet you still want to be relatively *safe and secure* in how your margin account grows, then this approach will change your life as a trader. Our approach has already helped many of our students to become more successful. What we will be showing you is a better, safer, more relaxed way to trade combining basic chart reading with the most simple of technical indicators.

This part of the course, then, is our way of sharing with you the Ross Hook and how almost anyone can achieve wonderful results trading in the stock markets by using it properly. You will learn in great detail how you can apply the marvelous concept of the Ross Hook to your trading. Along with the technique of the Ross Hook, we will be showing you numerous ways to filter your trading so that your trade selection will be vastly improved. Trading the Ross Hook, together with fastidious trade selection, should bring a substantial improvement in your success as a trader.

This part of the course is not intended for the raw beginner. First and foremost, it assumes that by either experience or reading and study you already know the concepts we have presented in ELECTRONIC TRADING 'TNT' I — GORILLA TRADING STUFF. It also assumes that by either experience or reading and study that you know and understand how to run your electronic trading business in a thoroughly business-like manner as presented in ELECTRONIC TRADING 'TNT' II — HOW-TO-WIN TRADING STUFF. As a result of the materials presented in those volumes of this course, it is assumed that you have at least a basic knowledge of how to place orders, using electronic order entry. It is assumed that you know how to read a bar chart, and have a basic understanding of what the markets are, and how and why people trade in them. It is assumed that you have at least paper traded stocks, and you've seen or suffered the inevitable losses that are the nemesis of so many traders.

THE BOTTOM LINE IN TRADING

The bottom line in trading is **love and hate**. We've gone out on a limb with that statement. We've gone against the conventional wisdom. **Although profit and loss are the financial bottom line for trading, profit and loss are not what trading is about!** Profit and loss are important, but they are only secondary. They are a measure of your ability as a trader, but they are not ***the* bottom line.**

It's ***love*** and ***hate*** that drive the markets and control your trading destiny. This will take some explanation. Be assured, the rewards of understanding this will make it *well* worth your while to continue reading.

WHY DO YOU TRADE?

Ask yourself, "Why do I trade?"

The reason you trade is because you ***enjoy*** the results a winning trade can achieve. Wise trading can *make you rich*, multiplying your wealth many times more than if you simply keep your money in the bank, CD's, or mutual funds. Let's face it, inflation and taxes constantly gnaw at and erode your wealth. The leverage available in trading the stock markets gives your trading one of the highest profit potentials of any money making vehicle available. The results of winning can be spectacular, and you love the idea and excitement of trading as well as the outcome. You thrive on the anticipation of the "big" win.

You also like the notion that your money can work for you like a tireless machine, piling up riches day after day for as long as you trade, making you richer and your life easier.

And while friends and relatives may lose their jobs, and professional and business prospects may diminish considerably, your trading prowess will always be there for you, an ever-loyal skill that can add immeasurable security and comfort to your life.

You relish the thought that one day the yearly income you earn from your trading can even surpass the income you earn from your work, which may have become tedious humdrum, and when that happens, you will never have to work another day in your life except at the thing you love the most — trading. And your trading ability will enable you to keep on enjoying your efforts as a trader, making the big money so *you* can have the good, easy life.

Or, you may delight in the thought of enhancing your retirement income, leisurely trading and bringing in additional funds in the relaxed and enjoyable pastime you perceive trading to be.

You love the *excitement* of seeing a trade you've chosen zoom by scores of points, rolling up perhaps a year's worth of income on a single position. Few experiences in life can surpass the thrill of watching your net worth soar higher so fast — and with so little effort.

And while money certainly isn't everything, you cherish the freedom that wealth affords — the ability to treat yourself and your family to the better things of life: a fine home, a prestigious car, travel, and entertainment. You take pleasure in the thought of being able to give to those in need, and to feel surrounded by financial security, knowing you can always afford the finest medical care for you and those you love, and you look forward to a retirement marked by complete financial independence so you can enjoy your restful years free of financial anxiety.

Such rich rewards make smart trading *extremely* important to your future, don't they?

But following close behind your love for trading are the things you **dislike**. You detest the risk of loss and the awful *emotions* that losses trigger. You detest the anger and self-blame you feel for making a wrong trading decision. *"How can I be so stupid?"* is a trader's most painful complaint. "*When will I ever learn to do it right?*" These are questions that will haunt you over and over again, never allowing you to forget that your hard-earned money is lost.

You may be uncomfortable with the reality of the dozens of trading choices all shouting out to be taken, all holding out the promise that ***this*** *is the one to take*. Faced with so many possibilities, you feel overwhelmed and certain you're not going to pick the right one(s). Worse than that, you may try to take them all.

You don't like not having anyone you can really *trust* for objective counsel. With brokers, you always wonder, *"Are they urging me to buy or sell for* ***my*** *benefit, or so they can make a commission today?"* With advisers, you always wonder, *"Is this going to be a winning trade, or is this one a loser?"* You wonder if you can take the heat of the adviser's stop loss, or conversely you wonder why the stop is so close to the price action, and you would like to give the trade more room, or why is the stop so far and you want to give it less room.

You hate the wild, unpredictable volatility which can occur in all markets. You sometimes find yourself wasting so much mental energy wondering, *"Where should I place the entry?"* *"Should I be increasing my position?"* *"Should I take some profits now, or give this trade a little more room, or should I be getting completely out NOW!?"* Those decisions are not easily made. They make you uncomfortable. They challenge and test you, and put your trading fortitude on the line.

You sense from the depth of your soul that whatever you decide, the market will almost certainly do *exactly the opposite*, as if it takes a personal and perverse pleasure in trying to make you feel like a fool. And all this goes against the grain of an achiever like yourself. In almost every other area of life you can feel in *charge* and *successful*. But when it comes to trading, you wonder *"Will I ever get it right? Does anyone ever get it right?"*

All these feelings add to your anxiety, often paralyzing your ability to reach decisions, and making trading an exasperating mix of feelings you love and feelings you hate. *Is there any way out?*

What if you could experience ***mostly*** what you ***love*** and avoid what you ***hate***? What if you could feel comfortable with your trading? What if you could feel reasonably sure that the trades you are entering are the right ones? What if you knew where to place your stop on every trade? What if you could pick a high percentage of winners?

What if you could actually achieve the dream of letting your winners run while keeping your losses small?

There are great *emotional* stakes at risk for most traders. Because of that, it is necessary to design a personal approach to trading that will consistently give you only the experiences you *want* while shielding you against the experiences you *loathe*.

Can such a thing be done? If so, how?

Actually it is simple, once you experience a tremendously important insight.

Between the two emotions that continuously grapple for your trading soul (*your love of gain versus your hatred for loss*), **it is the hatred of loss to which you have to pay the greatest attention**.

To understand why, all you have to do is realize a rule we will describe as...

THE TRUE WEALTH PRINCIPLE

This principle simply states that if you can consistently avoid big losses, you will not only feel much better, more comfortable and in control of your trading, but you will also *automatically and inevitably grow richer.* How can it be any other way?

You see, trading money is rarely static. The money you trade with proper selection works ceaselessly while in that trade, minute after minute, even days or weeks at times, to multiply itself and make you wealthier. In fact, the only way you can *stop* money from multiplying itself and relentlessly making you richer while in a trade, is to ***lose*** that money.

Losing, invariably, is what most traders manage to do. That is when the entire magnificent and automatic process of building wealth breaks down — and it's why the majority of traders never really succeed at trading.

So this great principle of wealth teaches that the most important secret of building a trading account is to *avoid losses*. If you do, your money will automatically and inevitably multiply. It cannot do anything else.

So what? You've always known that, right? But sometimes the simplest truths are the most profound. And this truth does have profound implications for how you should trade, as you'll soon see.

This approach will enable you to trade with very low risk, often much lower than you might imagine. As you'll see in the remaining pages, it's an approach that raises avoidance of loss to the highest pinnacle of decision making. It's an approach whose chief characteristic is avoidance of overtrading and an almost fanatical avoidance of loss of capital. Perhaps most surprising of all, this approach, which can keep you very safe in the markets, has also been profitable year in and year out.

Trading the Ross Hook using the filtering processes we will show you, accompanied by the money management techniques we use, all in conjunction with the right mental attitude, will let you experience mostly the things you ***love***, and very little of the things you ***hate***. It is a safety-first style of trading that allows us to sleep comfortably.

You might be wondering, *"How can this be possible? How can any style of trading give me what I love about trading and eliminate what I hate about it?"* We'll be sharing with you how we employ the true principle of wealth to do just what we've said. Here are some of the things you will be doing if you learn to properly trade the Ross Hook:

- You will learn to protect your capital.

- You will greatly simplify your trading life.

- You will not keep all your money in your margin account.

- You will never again have to worry about what a market is going to do.

- You will enter trades when they have the highest probability of being correct. You will be eclectic in your trading, learning to take the best of the best, and profit by so doing.

- You will learn to read the market in such a way as to be able to profit from the emotional drives of other traders.

- You will trade like the wise owner of a profitable business — one who knows how to make a profit, and take it when it is available.

- You will be able to utilize the Ross Hook for daytrading, position trading, or both. The time frame you choose will be up to you.

LET'S SET THE STAGE

At various points we will refer to floor traders, specialists, market makers and market movers, as "operators," or "insiders." By this we mean traders apart from the public. Some brokers are also insiders. We always refer to the public as "outsiders." For the most part, that's us, and anyone who is not usually a significant force in the market.

MANAGEMENT

This may sound strange to some, but it is proper management techniques that have made successful the methods you will learn.

Some individuals thrive on variety. Some become bored with trading one method for very long periods of time.

Yet, the discipline that can be developed by sticking to a single methodology may firmly cement in place the self-control needed for successful trading. Once developed you can always go back to it in the event you fail with other methods or with experimentation. Your roots should be firmly grounded in at least one successful way to trade. You will then have anchored your trading career so that you can continue trading and trying out new ideas.

It is possible to successfully trade many methods. Although the methods may vary considerably one from the other, sound management techniques have hardly changed at all since trading first began.

We teach the concept of dividing your position. The reason for this is to use part of your position for cost covering plus a small amount of profit, and then allow the rest of your position to ride to greater profit levels if the market will grant that. Your objective should always be to get paid to trade — gather some profit for the effort expended.

We teach that you should never try to take from the market, only to accept what it so graciously gives you.

This differs considerably from the mindset of most traders who are driven by greed to attempt squeezing every last penny from each and every trade.

As profits are earned, an exit point is trailed according to any one of a number of acceptable methods. The exit point is never allowed to do any worse than breakeven.

This management technique derives from a different attitude towards the markets than is commonly taught and practiced by the majority.

We have heard and read that a trader should learn to "love small losses."

Such an attitude is pure nonsense. Our philosophy of trading is to learn to detest losses and reluctantly settle for break-even.

While it's true that trading brings many losses, and although we must accept the fact of losses, learning to detest them yields a totally different result from learning to love losses.

The trader who learns to love small losses expects to get them, and so he does.

Conversely, the trader who learns to love to win, and at worst to break even, begins to manage his trades, risk, money, and self in such a manner as to ***not lose***.

There are two sides to the human brain. One side responds to positive suggestion, the other to suggestions phrased in the negative.

A part of every trader's plan should be to program himself to win. "*I will win*" programs one side of the brain with the mindset needed to win.

"*I will not lose*" establishes the opposite side of the brain with the mindset needed to not lose.

The human mind is a goal seeking mechanism. Once programmed correctly, it will strive day and night, awake or asleep, in an attempt to bring about fulfillment of the goals with which it has been programmed.

In ELECTRONIC TRADING 'TNT' II — HOW-TO-WIN TRADING STUFF, we show you how to deal with every aspect of your life that might affect your trading. The course deals with the "**Life Index™**" and "**Charting Your Equity"** to help you gain control over yourself so that you can trade properly.

As a trader, you can control only one thing — yourself. You cannot control the market. One of the reasons most people fail in the market is because they try to control it.

Most people who trade are of above average intelligence. They solve problems by controlling their environment. Often, they are part of the solution.

Unfortunately, when trading stocks in front of a screen or from a set of printed charts, you cannot control the environment. This calls for an entirely different approach to problem solving from that which most people employ throughout their entire lifetimes.

We strongly recommend reading and studying ELECTRONIC TRADING 'TNT' II — HOW TO WIN TRADING STUFF. You will need all the ammunition you can get to begin to change the way you think and the way you behave when trading in the markets.

CAPITALIZATION

We receive phone calls from far too many aspiring traders who are tremendously undercapitalized.

The undercapitalized trader, unless he accidentally and immediately encounters a runaway successful trade and good fortune, cannot in reality hope to be a winner.

The undercapitalized trader has all his eggs in one basket. His one trading decision must see him through not only cost covering, but must also deliver a sizable profit.

People call to ask if they can succeed by trading a round lot (100 shares). The answer is "yes," if you get very lucky, or you are an investor with lots of time to wait for the next Microsoft. It has been done, but the winners are few and far between. The odds are tremendously against the trader with a puny margin account. For most, it amounts to nothing more than gambling.

LOT SIZE

Once a trader can go beyond a couple of round lots, he should trade in multiples of 100 shares. That would be five hundred shares, a thousand shares, and more. If he chooses to go beyond the limit of some electronic trading systems, he can always trade using an ECN. There is no limit to the amount of shares you can trade using an ECN.

ORDERS

This course advocates the use of electronic order entry. All examples are based upon the ability of the trader to enter his orders via some sort of electronic trading system. It is assumed that all orders are entered at a specific price or as a market order except when working with a broker. These methods will also work if you prefer to call your order in to a broker.

We will include more of these matters as they come up in context and at the correct places throughout the course. However, you cannot really begin to study this part of the course without a basic understanding of how to manage your affairs as a trader.

Here is one way we suggest you manage your affairs as a trader:

Try to enter each trade with a share amount that you are comfortable with. Assuming the trade goes your way within a short time, as soon as you can, cover immediate costs (commissions), and as the system allows, cash in a portion of those shares. This will make you immediately profitable.

As soon as possible, set your exit point on any remaining shares to breakeven. This can be immediately or after a short time. There is no way to know in advance just how soon. Each trade is different and must be adjusted in accordance with the price action.

At breakeven (the original price of entry, and whenever possible the original entry price plus costs), expect to have to exit 7-8 out of 10 attempts. The other 2 or 3 tries may result in medium to very large wins.

What if the trade does not go your way immediately, or after a short time? Then get out. Something is wrong! If your entry does not result in immediate, or almost immediate success, exit. A more specific way to handle fast exits, called the "violation method," is fully explained in ELECTRONIC TRADING 'TNT' I — GORILLA TRADING STUFF.

Taking small losses is inexpensive compared with the losses most traders suffer because they lack the discipline to quickly extract themselves from a trade.

The problem with most traders is that they view each trade as though it were the 'be all' to 'end all'. This is simply a wrong view. Trades must be viewed as a series of events, many of which will earn money for you if you have the discipline to follow a managed plan of action.

Once a method, system, or style of trading has been proven to work profitably, then the rest becomes simply a matter of discipline and proper trade, risk, and money management.

PHILOSOPHY

Try variety in your trading. Try to trade a variety of stocks and a variety of time-frames. You need to find a best fit for your trading style and comfort zone.

Many have strong feelings regarding daytrading. They want to trade a single exchange, using only one system. More than that is involved. When you specialize in a single exchange using only one system, what do you do when the Exchange discontinues or greatly alters that system? Be a trader. You want to be able to trade from anywhere at any time.

There is strong agreement among professionals that you should trade only extremely liquid stocks and only those with good price action, especially when daytrading. This is especially true when you trade as a chartist or technical analyst. We agree with that wholeheartedly.

With the exception of relatively short term trades designed specifically to scalp a quick profit, we believe the only way to trade as an "outsider" is to "position trade," even if it means position trading a five minute chart. **By "position trade" we mean taking a position in any trade designed to keep one in the market as long as possible relative to the time frame traded.**

Whereas a scalp trade may be designed with a short term targeted price zone for exiting all shares, a position trade has no such targeted price zone. Instead, it is a trade designed to stay with a trend in the market for as long as possible with at least some portion of shares, even to the point of transcending the current shorter term trend in favor of matriculating to an overall longer term trend.

We have heard many daytraders say that the reason they daytrade is because in position trading the daily charts they leave too much money on the table.

While that may be true for some, it is certainly not true for all. We've tried it both ways, and can honestly tell you that in all too many cases it is the pure daytrader who may be leaving most of the money on the table.

We have seen daytraders lose scads of money in markets that were trending beautifully on the daily chart. The daily-chart position traders were picking up big profits by holding their position, while the daytraders were fighting their way into the market every single day and losing on the intraday action. We're giving you this information because it is important that you find the kind of trading with which you are the most comfortable.

There are a great many bugaboos and false beliefs about trading that have been propagated throughout the years.

TIME FRAME

For instance, who says that a weekly chart needs to consist of five trading days? Why not make three day charts and obtain different trading signals from everyone else?

Why do daytraders think they have to use five, fifteen, thirty, or sixty minute charts? Why not use a six minute chart and trade from a completely different set of signals?

Try to sometimes use twelve minute charts and nine minute charts. Doing that enables you to see the chart form somewhat differently from the way others see it.

You might try trading some stocks from a 120 minute chart. Such trading separates you when you do not want to go along with the pack. Learn to be a contrarian.

We strongly believe you should trade where you feel most comfortable. Don't be afraid to take a trade in virtually any stock, if a good opportunity arises. Simply lengthen the time frame so that the chart forms up in the way that you prefer to see a chart.

Certain stocks may reveal a thin market on a daily basis, but what about trading them from a weekly chart?

Refuse to be rigid in your trading. But be as rigid as you can be about self-discipline and self-control. Determine now that you will put up with no nonsense from yourself in those areas.

Many try and fail to succeed because they think that by being rigid in their trading, they are being disciplined traders. But that is the wrong place to be rigid.

If you are going to be rigid about anything in your trading, it must concern your work habits and mental outlook. Be rigid in determining to not lose. Be rigid in setting your heart to win. Be rigid in keeping good records and statistics about your trading that will enable you to be a better planner and executor of your trades.

If you are comfortable with variety, trade a variety of stocks on different exchanges and in a variety of time frames. Be eclectic. Smell all the flowers, not just one. Sample every market sector, not just one.

Learn to trade where you're comfortable. Learn to take only the best of the best trades. Place stops where you are comfortable with them. Insist on being a happy trader. If trading ever becomes like work, perhaps it's time to find something else to do.

CONCLUSION

A final thought in this introductory chapter is that there is something at the table for everyone. Daytraders can daytrade exclusively if that's what they desire. Daily-chart position traders can trade the daily charts to their heart's content.

Others can combine both, and in varying ways. We won't all do it the same. We will trade in different markets, and with varying degrees of success. It's always been that way, and will continue to be that way.

The notion that if we reveal any trading secrets, everyone will begin doing what we do, which would spoil our methods for everyone, is the height of naivete. You will never trade exactly as anyone else does, even if you purchase and follow a mechanical trading system, nor will anyone else trade exactly as you do. To even make the attempt would be foolish. We are wonderfully and individually different. No one can be you, and you cannot be anyone other than yourself.

The best action you can take with the material in this course is to integrate the methods you like into your own style of trading. You must be yourself in the markets. You trade within your own frame of reference and your own comfort level. Trading must make sense to you or you will not have the confidence — the courage of conviction that you need to be a winner.

There are many different trading methods presented in this third volume of the four volume 'TNT' course, but most of what will be taught in this volume revolves around the Ross Hook, a powerful formation found on price charts in virtually any time frame.

When trading, one method is not necessarily any better than the next. Each method is only as good as it meets with your needs and only if you are able to execute it satisfactorily.

Some will ask, "Which one do you recommend now?" The answer to that is that you should be willing to do any one of them as the mood suits you.

All the methods shown work, and all are derived from real life experiences. Some traders can relate best to highly technical methods, others to pure chart trading with no technical studies at all. As a trader, you must be eclectic; pick and choose among those techniques which most appeal to you and which give you the most success.

One way to use technical analysis and indicators is to use them ***indirectly.*** We have studied and are very much cognizant of how others use them. We will use such studies against those who use them blindly, not fully understanding what those indicators are revealing to them. If we detect that an indicator or study has become popular and that a large number of traders are using that particular study or indicator, then we will adjust our trading accordingly in order to take advantage of those traders who are ignorant of their proper use and use their lack of knowledge against them. There is great danger in trading along with the crowd, so let the trader beware!

We try to not close off our options to change, because markets change and exchange rules change. The Ross Hook is for use with trending prices. Many stocks have years when they don't trend. That is when we look for the stocks that do trend. What will a daytrader do if the liquid NASDAQ stocks are not trending? It is our hope that this course will teach you to be a trader, a total and complete trader able to trade anything that has prices that can be formed on a chart.

We have daytrading students who tell us that they trade multiple hooks all day in dozens of different stocks and time frames and then we have students who have waited patiently for as much as two weeks in certain stocks, using a daily chart to trade Hooks in combination with the filters they are using. It's totally up to you to decide which time frames are best for you to trade.

This has been a rather long first chapter. We felt it necessary to share with you some sort of foundation upon which we can build. Now it's time to begin learning the content of this part of the course.

Chapter 2

LET'S GET STARTED

The tools reviewed in this chapter are one and the same with those shown in <u>ELECTRONIC TRADING 'TNT' I — GORILLA TRADING STUFF</u>. They are repeated here for your convenience and edification, and as a reminder for those who have already completed the above mentioned first part of this trading course. By now, though, you are ready to understand the "why's" of these formations.

1-2-3 HIGHS AND LOWS

We suppose we can never cease showing this most basic and essential of formations in the market. **IN VIEW, THE 1-2-3 HIGH OR LOW IS THE BUTTRESS OF ALMOST EVERY GREAT MOVE EVER MADE IN A STOCK. WHY? BECAUSE VIRTUALLY EVERY TREND, GREAT OR NOT SO GREAT, CAN START FROM IT.**

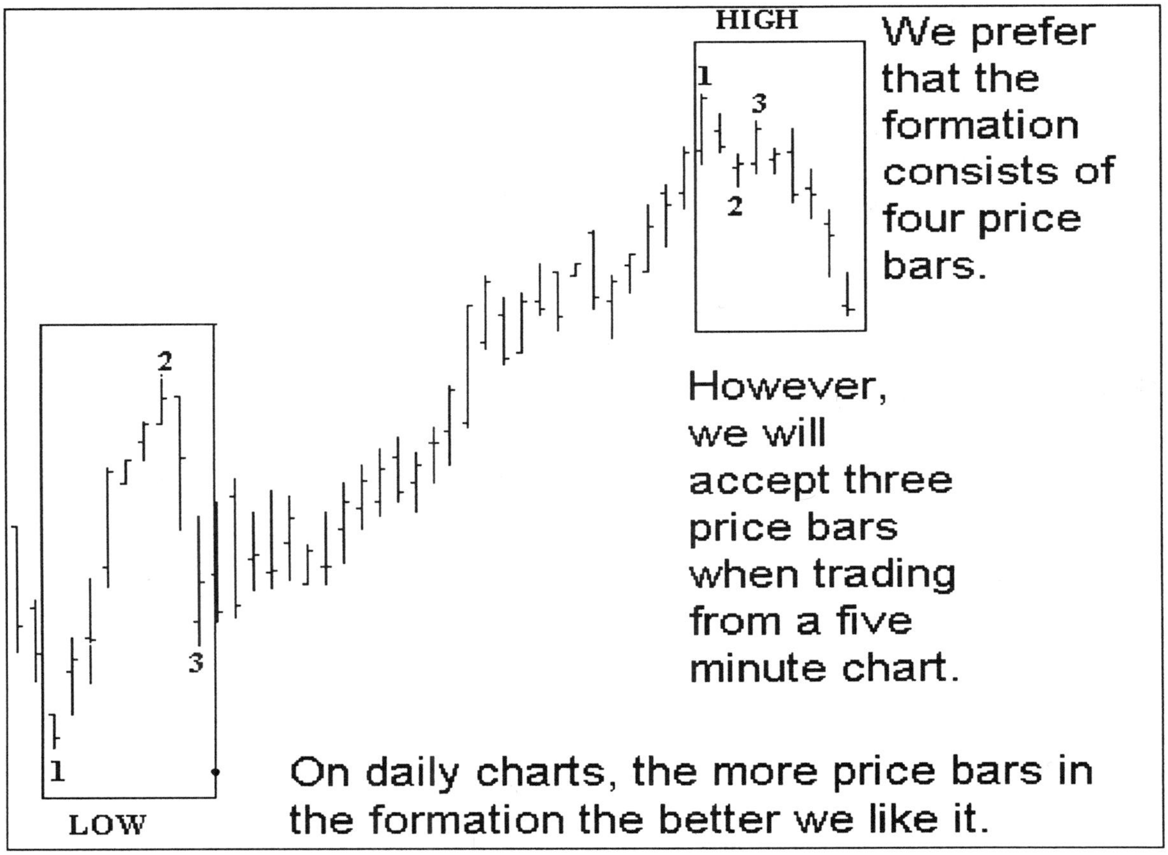

The 1-2-3 high or low formation not only initiates trends, but defines them as well. They occur at major and intermediate highs and lows in a market. Of course, what constitutes a major or intermediate high or low is somewhat interpretive — one of those things that is in the eye of the beholder. We're sorry about that, but whoever said that trading is a science? There is nothing more foolish than to attempt to apply *scientific* principles to the *art* of trading.

The sooner we learn the lesson that there is nothing scientific about the actions and interactions of markets, the better off we are. Market action is not mathematical, geometrical, cyclical, statistical, or theoretical. The markets move based upon the perceptions of those who trade them. Therefore, markets are emotional, at times bordering on hysteria.

For the most part, money is made in markets by those who most correctly read and act upon the perceptions of the masses who trade them.

Notice that we said, "for the most part."

Often market moves are initiated by those who have an interest in, and the ability to, engineer such moves. Many moves, particularly short term intraday moves, are totally contrived.

Nevertheless, it is our perception of market action, and our expectations for a profit, that trigger the buy/sell orders that almost continually cause markets to tick up and down.

The emotions and human behavior driving the markets can be seen in the price action as revealed on a simple bar chart showing the open, high, low, and close of any given time period. This is true whether time be measured in seconds, minutes, hours, days, weeks, months, or years.

The more adept we are at reading the finer points of a price chart, the closer to the reality of what is actually happening in the markets we become. The ability to read the finer points of a price chart greatly increases the probability of our success in trading.

In a moment we'll review the 1-2-3 and how it can evolve into an established trend. The 1-2-3 is a gateway to the practical use of momentum. Momentum is created by the emotional drives of human nature as they affect the various markets. Remember, we are dealing here with human emotion as expressed through human action taken based upon human perception of market direction. There is nothing exact about it apart from the definition.

1-2-3's look like this:

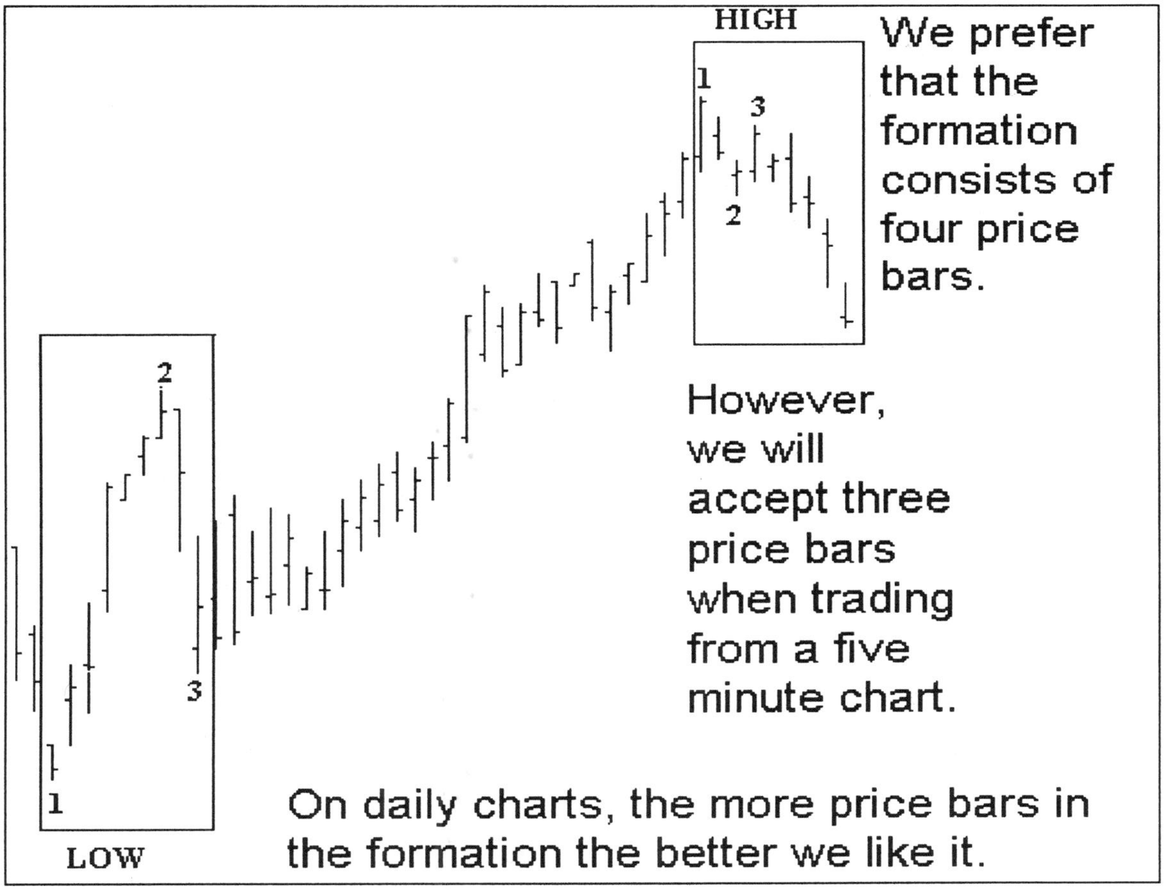

The usual objective with 1-2-3 highs and lows is to enter a market prior to a breakout of the number 2 point using a trick we call "The Trader's Trick". That is an overly simplified view of 1-2-3's and how they are traded, but it will suffice for now. The main thing is to recognize what they are.

Let's review the anatomy of 1-2-3's.

1-2-3 LOWS

A 1-2-3 low is characterized by prices reaching a major or intermediate low. This is the shown by the first boxed off area on the chart below. The low is evidenced by prices then making an up leg away from the low. The low is the first number 1 point marked on the chart. This up leg is immediately followed by a correction as the market moves briefly back towards the low.

The move back towards the low leaves behind a high which can be labeled as the number 2 point. If the correction is such that it reaches or exceeds the former low (number 1 point), the 1-2-3 low is nullified in favor of anticipating that prices will make a further downside move or form a congestion area. If the correction fails to reach the low and then begins to move upward, it leaves behind a somewhat higher low which can be labeled as the number 3 point.

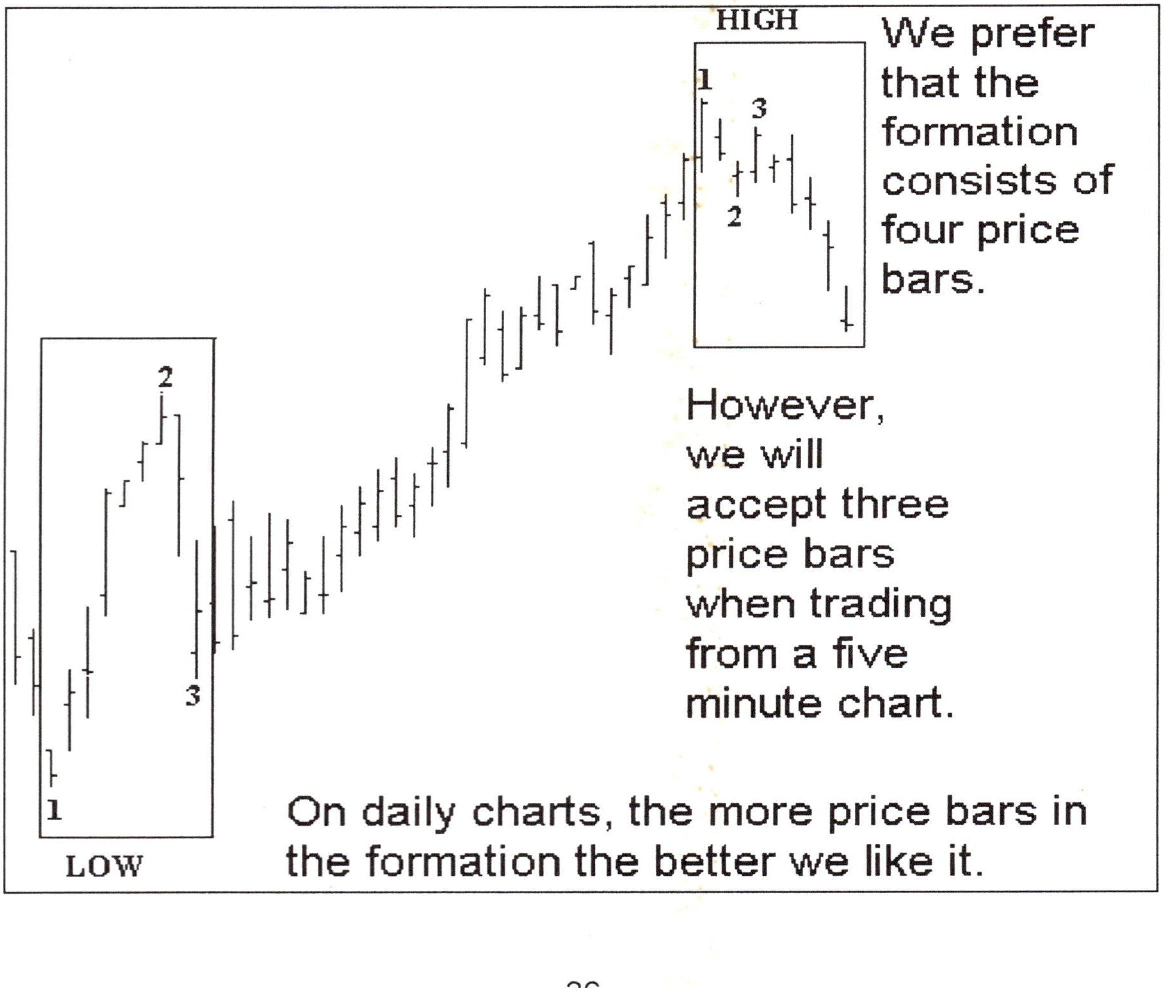

THE MEANING OF A 1-2-3 LOW

Since 1-2-3 lows can come at the end of a downtrend (at the inception of a period of consolidation or the inception of a V shaped bottom), or at the end of consolidation, it is reasonable to ask what is taking place in the market to cause this formation to occur.

When a 1-2-3 low occurs at the end of a downtrend, the number 1 point is brought about by the following events:

First, there simply are no longer an abundance of willing sellers in the market. Prices have been pushed as low as they can go. At that point, supply shifts from too much to too little, and prices begin to move up. When those market participants who were short, and had been pushing prices down, realize that prices have started to move up, they buy back their short positions in order to take profits. Their buying in order to liquidate their short positions causes the market to move up. Would-be longs who have been sitting on the sidelines waiting for these short bears to finish having their fun, then begin to buy, adding to the upward price movement. Prices are then driven upward from point 1 to point 2.

Soon those early longs, especially those with a short term view, begin to take profits by selling out at least a part of their long position. This tends to drive prices downward again away from the number 2 point towards the number three point. This downward move or correction is aided by those bears who think the market is going to go down forever. They perceive the upward move as a bear market rally, and move to establish or re-establish their short positions in hopes of a continuation of the downward trend.

If they are correct, prices will go down and take out the number 1 point, thereby nullifying any new uptrend. Prices may then plunge as hoped for by the shorts, or it may simply violate the number 1 point and then enter a period of congestions and sideways movement. If the shorts are wrong, and prices will not be pushed lower, new buying will come into the market and drive prices back away from the number 3 point and towards the number 2 point. If prices then take out the number 2 point, a new trend may be in the making, and may be in the process of being established. When the number 2 point is violated we have a "defined" trend. How long it will last or how far it will go remains to be seen.

It is of the utmost importance that we understand this scenario. It has everything to do with the money management plan that will be used for our trading of stocks.

It is entirely possible that the breakout of the number 2 point will go nowhere as the bulls and bears battle the market into a consolidation phase. This consolidation may represent accumulation prior to a later move upward, or it may represent distribution resulting in a later continuation of the downtrend. Only time will tell.

If a consolidation phase does occur, a 1-2-3 low may form from **within** the price structure of the resulting congestion area we call a Trading Range.

When a 1-2-3 low formation occurs at the end of a Trading Range, the reasons are quite different from those that exist when a 1-2-3 low occurs at the end of a trend.

During the period of a Trading Range, the underlying stock has been in a state of accumulation at what is considered to be a relatively fair value. The stock is changing hands between those who no longer want to hold it and those who want to acquire it. At the end of an accumulation period, the availability of the stock at what was formerly considered to be fair value prices dries up, and prices form a 1-2-3 low just prior to moving higher.

Prices will break out to the upside if the consolidation was indeed an accumulation phase. Once the supply of the stock is gobbled up at the lower prices, there will be a shortage of supply, and prices will rise according to the amount of demand in relation to the shrinking supply.

A 1-2-3 low breakout to the upside often signals that the battle is over and the bulls have won.

THE MEANING OF A 1-2-3 HIGH

1-2-3 highs can come at the end of an uptrend (at the inception of a period of consolidation or the inception of a V top), or at the end of consolidation. It is reasonable to ask what is taking place in the market to cause this formation to occur.

When a 1-2-3 high occurs at the end of an uptrend, the number 1 point is brought about by the following events:

1-2-3 HIGHS

A 1-2-3 high is caused by the exact opposite phenomena of the 1-2-3 low. See the second boxed off area in the chart below. When there is a lack of willing buyers in the market, and prices refuse to rise to any greater heights, prices begin to stabilize or even to drop. The bulls, sensing that for the time being the upward move is over, begin to liquidate their long positions in order to take profits.

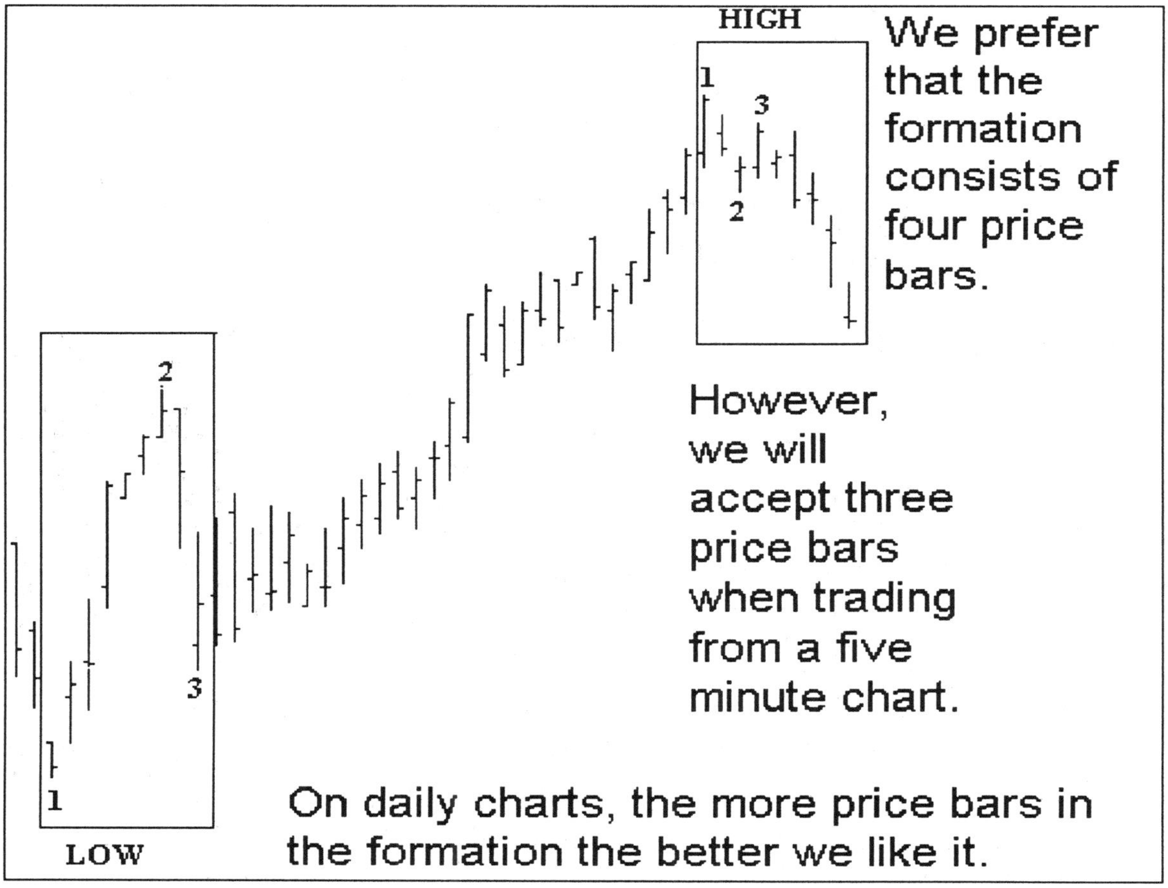

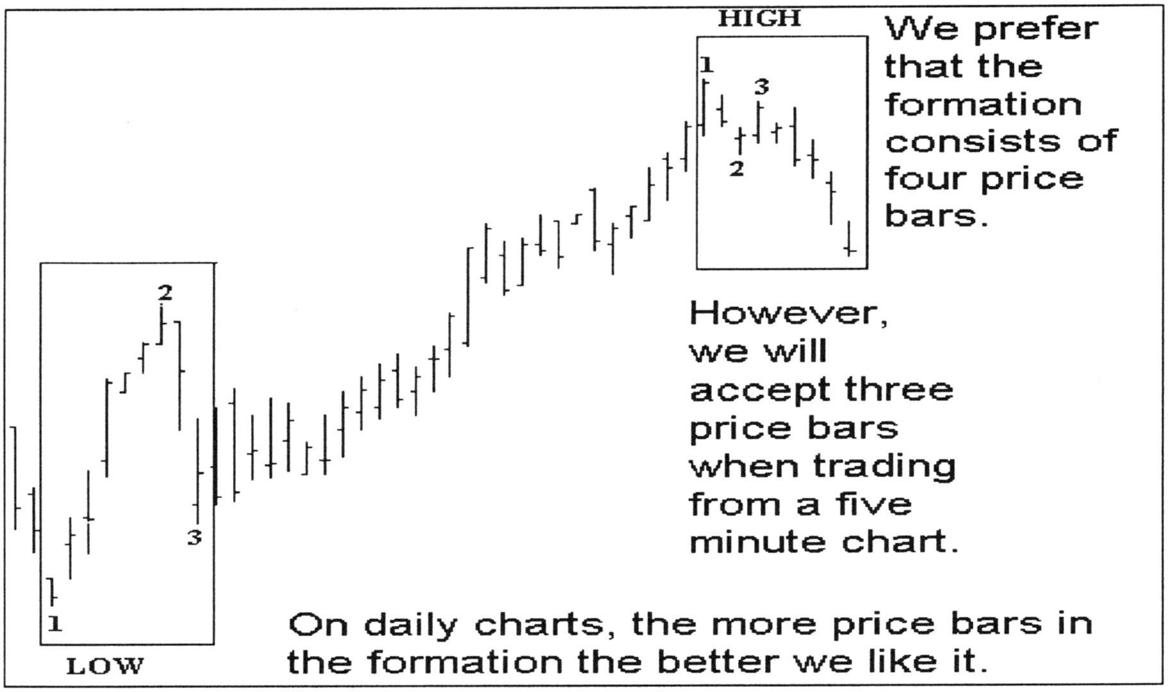

The bulls liquidate their long positions by selling what they have bought. This tends to drive prices down even more, and a number 1 point is formed. This downward action attracts the bears who are looking for an opportunity to enter the market from the short side. Their entry pushes prices down even further. Prices move away from the number 1 high and toward what will become the number 2 point. Soon the early bears begin to liquidate at least a portion of their position by buying back their shorts.

Their buying action drives prices back towards the number 1 point, leaving behind a low that can be marked as the number 2 point. Eager bulls, and those anticipating even higher prices, jump on the bandwagon and buy, expecting new highs. They view the downward move as a bull market reaction. This drives prices even higher. If prices come all the way back and take out the number 1 point, the 1-2-3 high is nullified and the uptrend is still intact. The bulls have won. If prices fail to take out the number 1 point, prices will begin to move downward again, leaving behind a number 3 point. Longs will want to cover their positions by selling. This action, coupled with the bear's jumping on the wagon to go short, may cause prices to take out the number 2 point. The taking out of the number 2 point to the downside "defines" the downtrend.

When a 1-2-3 high formation occurs at the end of a Trading Range, the reasons are quite different from those that exist when a 1-2-3 high occurs at the end of a trend.

During the period of a Trading Range, the underlying stock has been in a state of distribution at what is considered to be a relatively fair value. The stock is changing hands between those who no longer want to hold it and those who want to acquire it. At the end of an accumulation period, the availability of the stock at what was formerly considered to be fair value prices becomes too great, and prices form a 1-2-3 high just prior to moving lower.

Prices will break out to the downside if the consolidation was indeed a distribution phase. Once the demand for the stock at the higher prices dries up, there will be an overage of supply, and prices will fall according to the amount of supply in relation to the shrinking demand.

Whether or not prices will continue to slide cannot be known. Prices may go into a consolidation phase. If this happens, we have come full circle, as we've already explained the possible breakouts from the trading range surrounding the consolidation.

A 1-2-3 high breakout to the downside often signals that the battle is over and the bears have won. Many downtrends in markets are preceded by the formation of a 1-2-3 high. 1-2-3 highs tend to be larger in size from top to bottom than 1-2-3 lows. This is because stock prices generally fall faster than they rise. In the previous example and the one that follows, you can see that once prices began to fall (left side), it took only 2 bars to wipe out most of the gains made by the previous 5 bars. On the right side of the chart, once prices began to drop, i.e., after the breakout of the point labeled "2" on the chart, it took only four bars to erase most of the gains made by the previous 14 bars. Even counting the four bars subsequent to the bar labeled "1," it required only 8 bars to erase all of the gains made by the previous 14 bars.

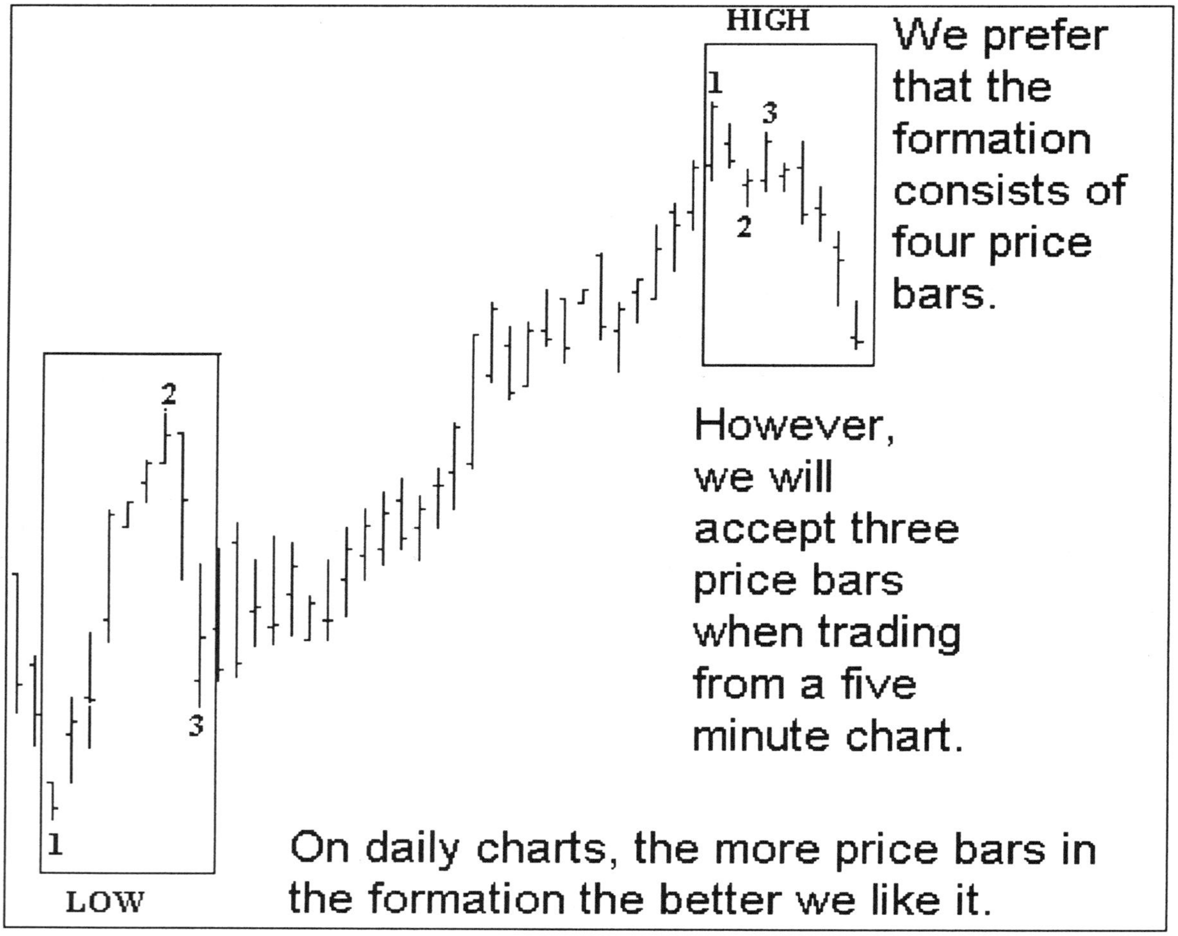

The 1-2-3 formation is an especially good trading signal for day traders, as the momentum needed to carry through the number 2 point on the daily chart generally gives enough thrust to cover costs and yield a profit provided the trader enters via the Trader's Trick. The Trader's Trick Entry (TTE) was explained in **ELECTRONIC TRADING 'TNT' I — GORILLA TRADING STUFF**, but for the sake of convenience, and because it is extremely important, we will take a brief detour in Chapter 4 to make sure you know what it is and how to trade it.

On the following pages we have summarized the essentials of the 1-2-3 formation. It is essential that you fully understand these formations to take advantage of what follows.

YOU MAY RECALL FROM VOLUME I THIS IS PART OF THE LAW OF CHARTS (TLOC)

1-2-3 HIGHS AND LOWS

A typical 1-2-3 high is formed at the end of an uptrending market. Typically, prices will make a final high (1), proceed downward to point (2) where an upward correction begins; then proceed upward to a point where they resume a downward movement, thereby creating the pivot (3). There can be more than one bar in the movement from point 1 to point 2, and again from point 2 to point 3. There must be a full correction before points 2 or 3 can be defined.

A number 1 high is created when a previous up-move has ended and prices have begun to move down.

The number 1 point is identified as the last bar to have made a new high in the most recent up-leg of the latest swing.

The number 2 point of a 1-2-3 high is created when a *full* correction takes place. Full correction means that as prices move up from the potential ***number 2 point***, there must be either a single bar that makes both a higher high and a higher low than the preceding bar *or* a combination of ***up to three bars*** creating both the higher high and the higher low. The higher high and the higher low may occur in any order. Subsequent to three bars we have congestion. Congestion will be explained in depth later on in this volume of the course. It is possible for both the number 1 and number 2 points to occur on the same bar.

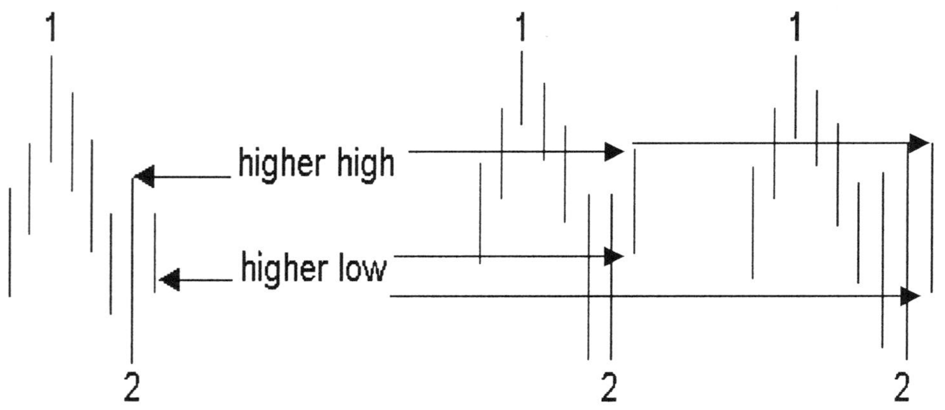

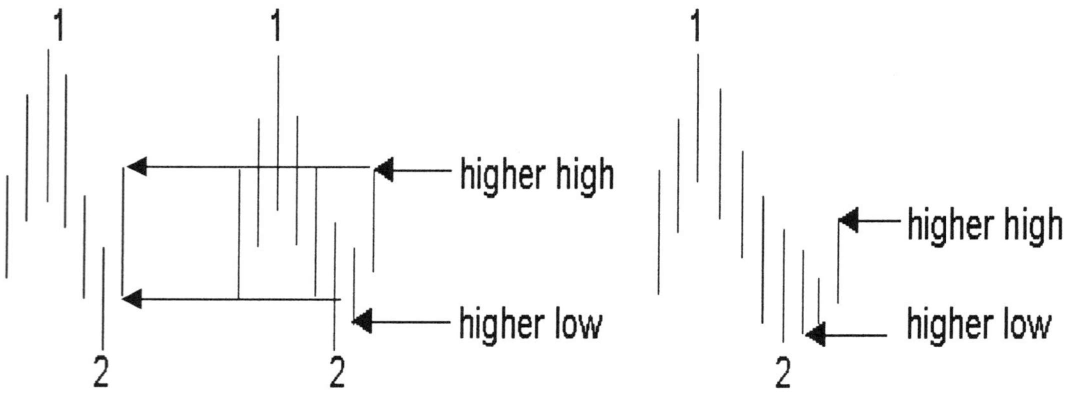

The number 3 point of a 1-2-3 high is created when a full correction takes place. A full correction means that as prices move down from the potential number 3 point, there must be either a single bar that makes a lower low and a lower high than the preceding bar, *or* a combination of ***up to three bars*** creating both the lower low and the lower high. It is possible for both the number 2 and number 3 points to occur on the same bar.

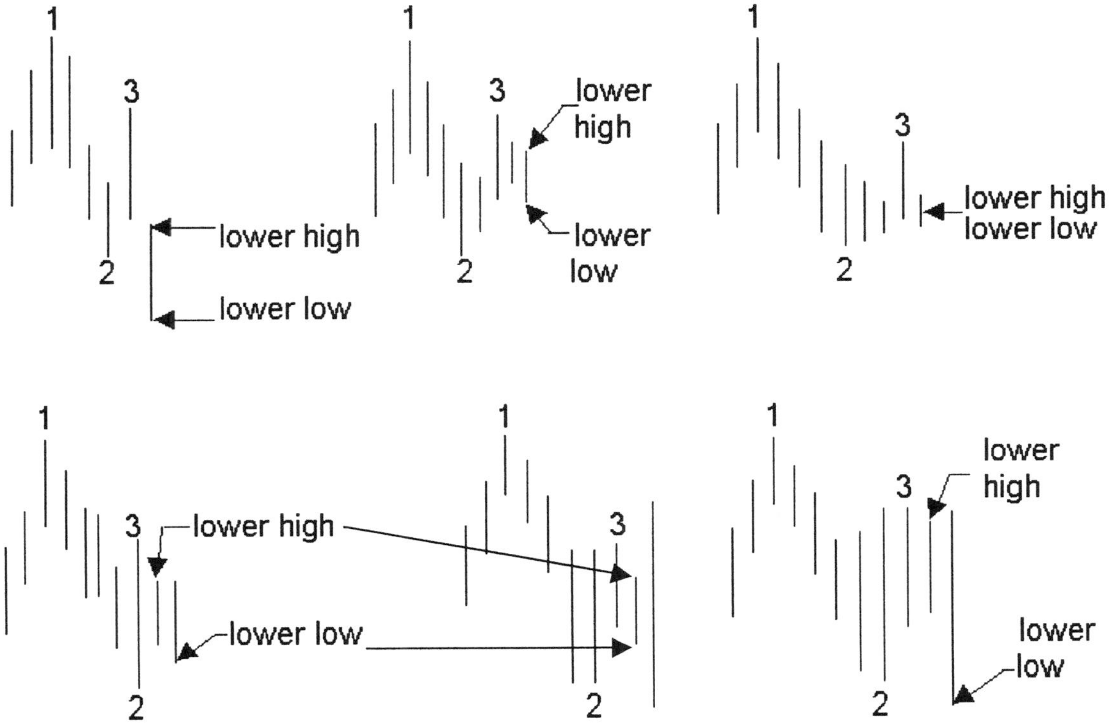

Now, let's look at a 1-2-3 low.

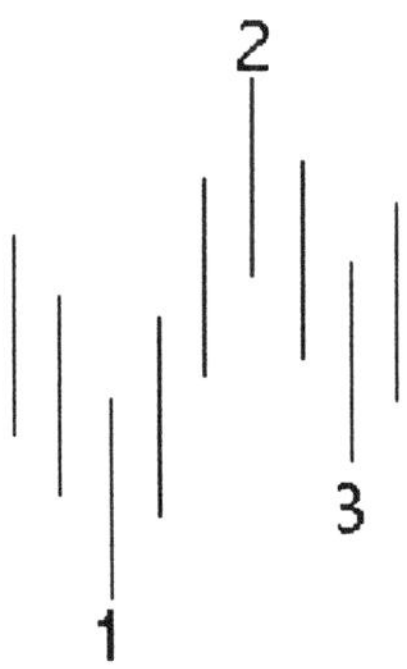

A typical 1-2-3 low is formed at the end of an downtrending market. Typically, prices will make a final low (1); proceed upward to point (2) where an downward correction begins; then proceed downward to a point where they resume an upward movement, thereby creating the pivot (3). There can be more than one bar in the movement from point 1 to point 2, and again from point 2 to point 3. There must be a full correction before points 2 or 3 can be defined.

A number 1 low is created when a previous down-move has ended and prices have begun to move up. The number 1 point is identified as the last bar to have made a new low in the most recent down-leg of the latest swing.

The number 2 point of a 1-2-3 low is created when a *full* correction takes place. Full correction means that as prices move down from the ***potential number 2*** point, there must be either a single bar that makes both a lower high and a lower low than the preceding bar, *or* a combination of ***up to three bars*** creating both the lower high and the lower low. The lower high and the lower low may occur in any order. Subsequent to three bars we have congestion. It is possible for both the number 1 and number 2 points to occur on the same bar.

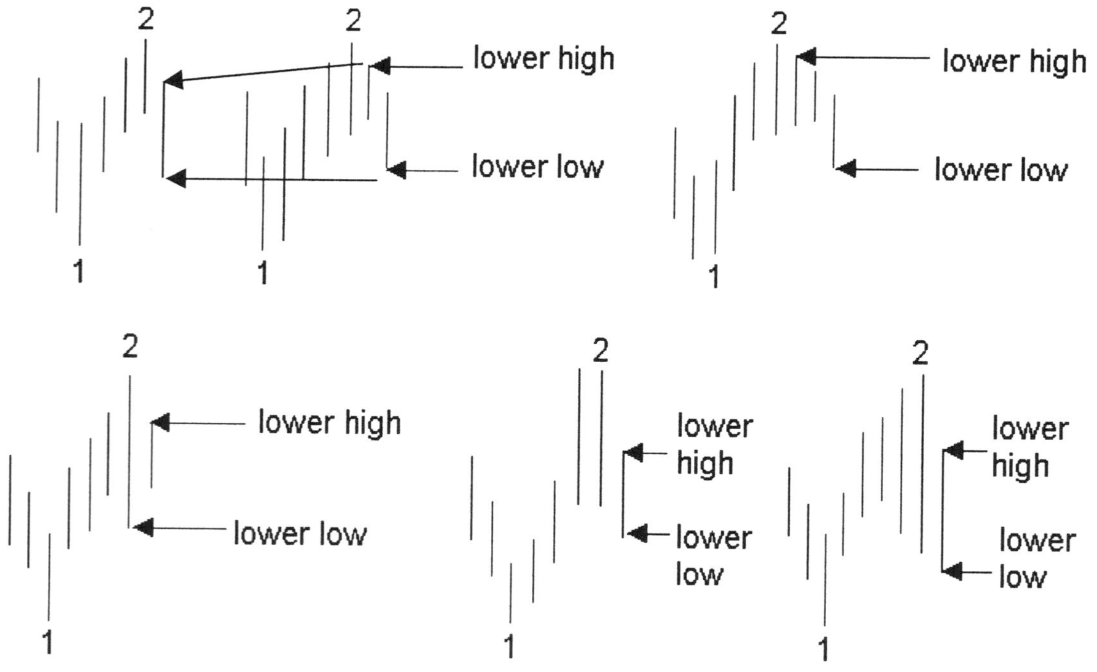

The number 3 point of a 1-2-3 low exists when a full correction takes place. A full correction means that as prices move up from the potential number 3 point, there must be either a single bar that makes a higher low and a higher high than the preceding bar, *or* a combination of ***up to three bars*** creating both the higher low and the higher high. It is possible for both the number 2 and number 3 points to occur on the same bar.

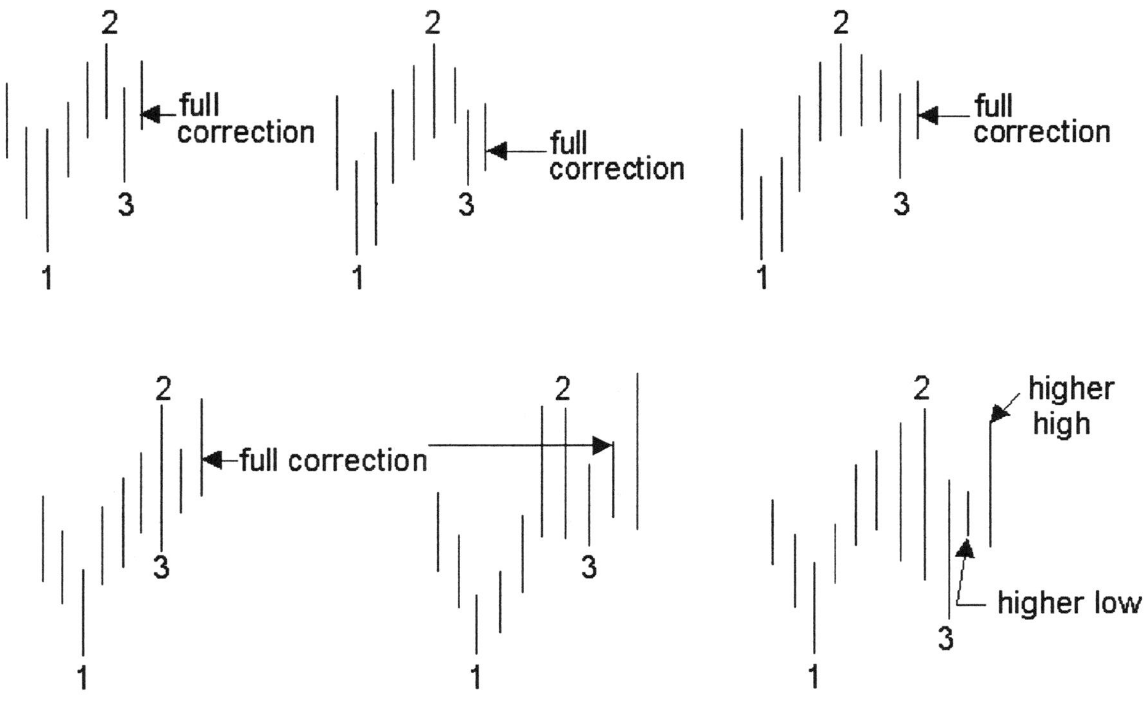

The entire 1-2-3 high or low is nullified when any price bar moves prices equal to or beyond the number 1 point.

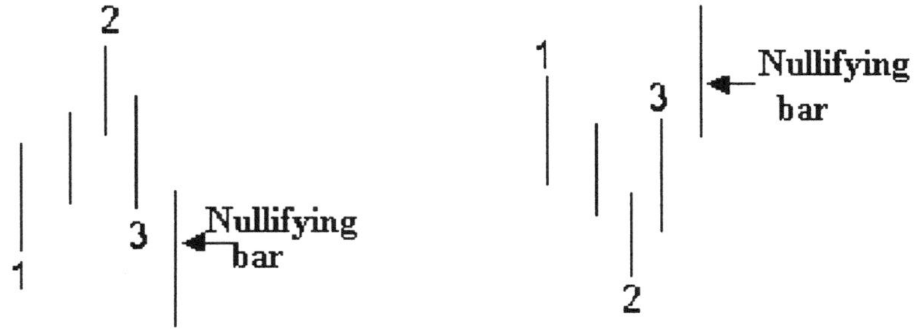

Chapter 3

THE ROSS HOOK

This chapter is a very important review of some of the material presented in <u>ELECTRONIC TRADING 'TNT' I — GORILLA TRADING STUFF</u>, plus additional concepts. For the sake of variety, the material is presented in a somewhat different fashion.

A Ross Hook is created by:

1. The first correction following the breakout of a 1-2-3 high or low.
2. The first correction following the breakout of a Ledge.
3. The first correction following the breakout of a Trading Range.

In an uptrending market, after the breakout of a 1-2-3 low, the first instance of the failure of a price bar to make a new high creates a Ross Hook. (A double high/double top also creates a Ross Hook).

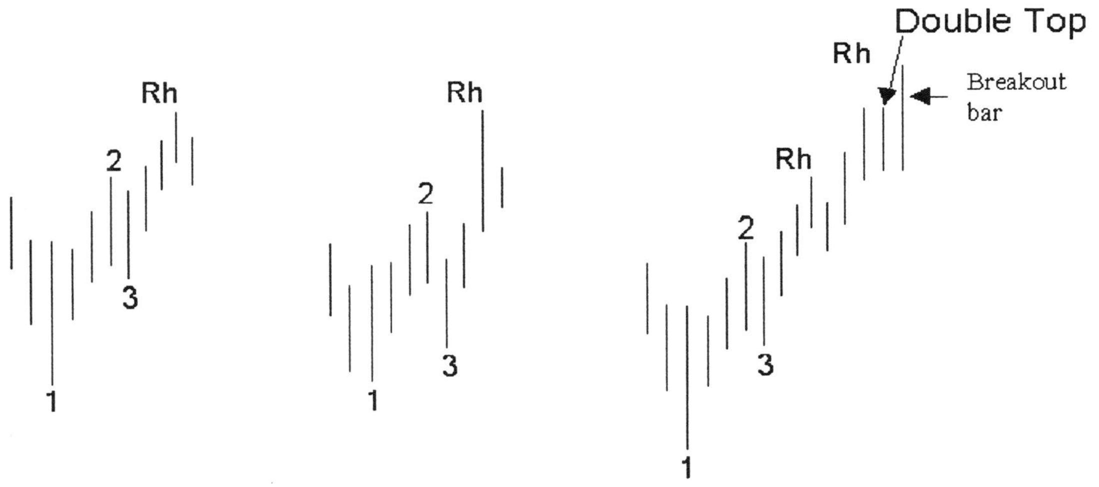

In a downtrending market, after the breakout of a 1-2-3 high, the first instance of the failure of a price bar to make a new low creates a Ross Hook. (A double low/double bottom also equals a Ross Hook).

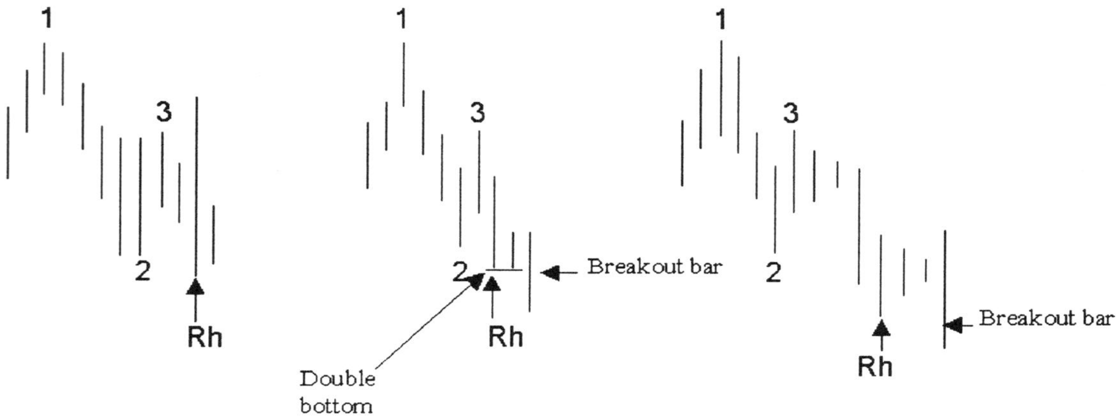

IF PRICES BREAKOUT TO THE UPSIDE OF A LEDGE OR A TRADING RANGE FORMATION, THE FIRST INSTANCE OF THE FAILURE BY A PRICE BAR TO MAKE A NEW HIGH CREATES A ROSS HOOK. IF PRICES BREAKOUT TO THE DOWNSIDE OF A LEDGE OR TRADING RANGE FORMATION, THE FIRST INSTANCE OF THE FAILURE BY A PRICE BAR TO MAKE A NEW LOW CREATES A ROSS HOOK (A DOUBLE HIGH OR LOW ALSO CREATES A ROSS HOOK).

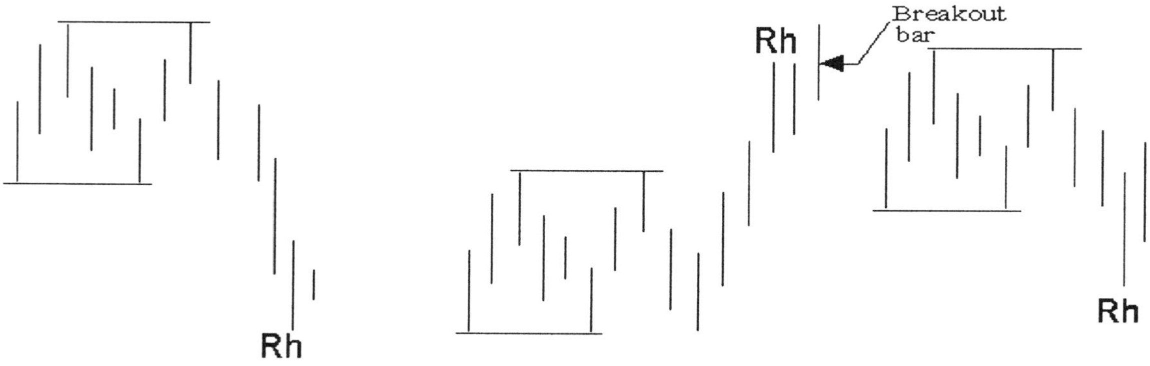

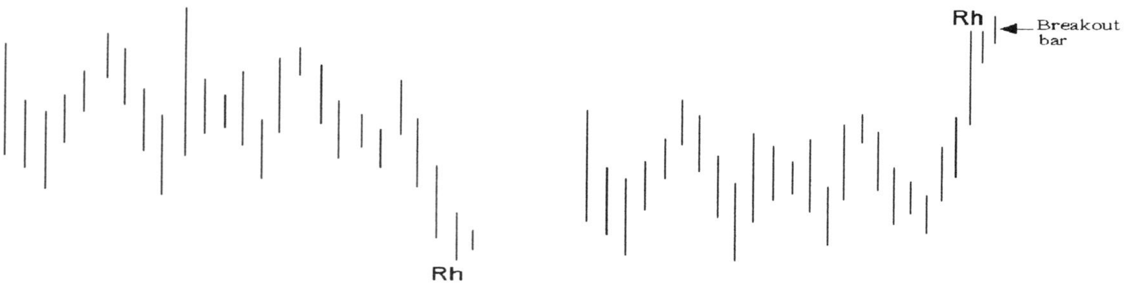

Sometimes Ross Hooks appear to be 1-2-3 formations that occur subsequent to the initial 1-2-3 formations that take place at lows and highs. Indeed, many of them are formed at the intermediate and minor lows and highs that occur in trending markets. But to call them all 1-2-3's would be to present an erroneous picture. Not all Ross Hooks are identifiable as 1-2-3 formations, and many of them occur as the first retracement subsequent to the breakout from a Ledge or a Trading Range.

1-2-3 formations are the direct result of certain market forces at work. These were described in Chapter 2. Ross Hooks are the result of a different market phenomenon. Then, too, there are **Reverse Ross Hooks, which are a bit more difficult to see, identify, and trade. The number two point of a 1-2-3 is often a reverse Ross Hook as will be explained further on.**

Before this volume of the course is finished, you will know how to identify and trade Ross Hooks, reverse Ross Hooks, double bottom Ross Hooks, and double top Ross Hooks. But before we go any further, we need to show you what these Hooks look like, and also show you how they relate to, and often derive from, the basic and fundamental 1-2-3 formation.

Keep the following in mind: We must know how to identify a trend. We must know what constitutes a 1-2-3 high or low. We must know how to identify congestion, and finally we must know how to identify a Ross Hook.

We must also know the five functions of a manager, but these were discussed in ELECTRONIC TRADING 'TNT' II — HOW-TO-WIN TRADING STUFF.

The following chart shows a number of things relative to Ross Hooks. At the extreme left of the chart we see that prices have formed a 1-2-3 low. Following that, prices have moved to their highest level. You see that highest level with two labels: First of all it is a Ross Hook (Rh). Secondly, it is the number 1 point of what became a 1-2-3 high. **NOTE: EVERY ROSS HOOK IS A POTENTIAL NUMBER 1 POINT AND AN OPPORTUNITY FOR PRICES TO MOVE IN THE OPPOSITE DIRECTION.**

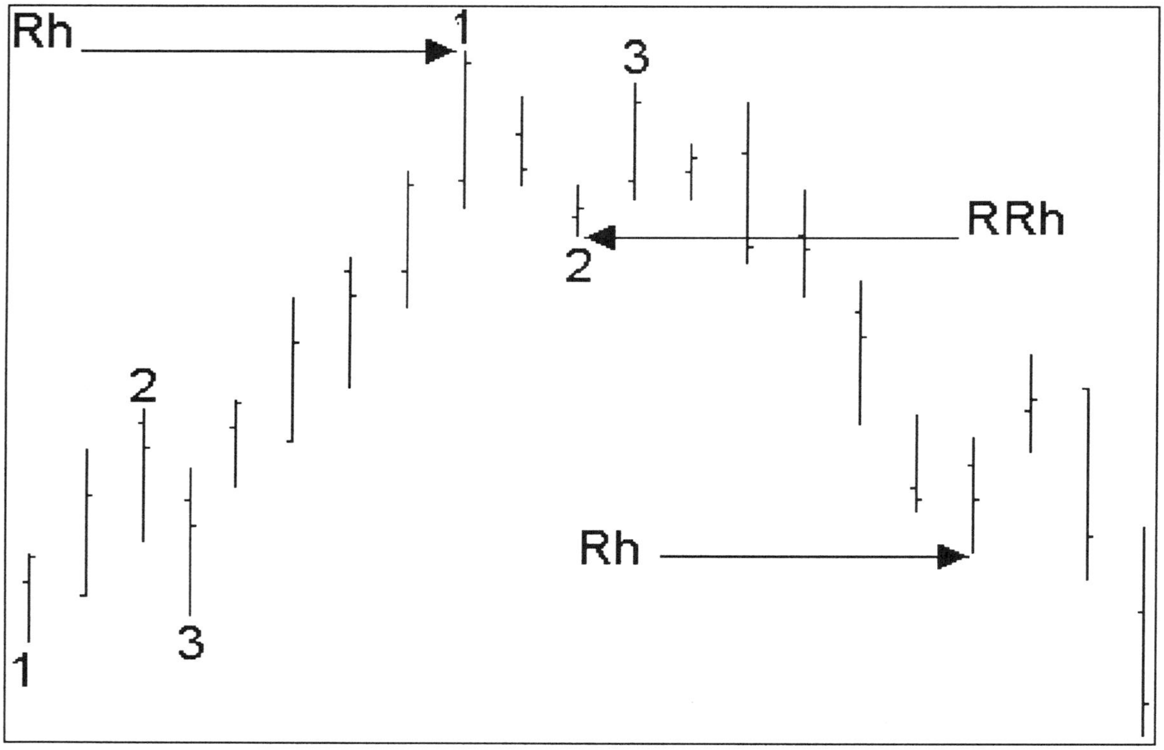

On the chart above, the highest high became a Ross Hook by virtue of the fact that prices on the bar following the highest high failed to exceed the highest high and move higher. As soon as prices fail to move higher in an uptrend, you have a Ross Hook.

NOTE: THE BREAKOUT OF THE 1-2-3 LOW FORMATION DEFINED THE TREND. BUT IT WOULD HAVE REQUIRED A BREAKOUT OF THE ROSS HOOK TO ESTABLISH THE TREND.

Instead, we see that prices failed to go higher and, in fact, formed a 1-2-3 high formation.

Following the 1-2-3 high formation we see a breakout of the number 2 point. The number 2 point is labeled as a Reverse Ross Hook (RRh).

Now lets go back to the second #1 point, the high on the chart above. You can see that the market topped out at that point. That's when prices were higher than what any additional buyers were willing to pay. At this point, there was too much supply and not enough demand.

Longs taking profits drove the price down to the number 2 point. They were aided and abetted by bears seeking to establish a short position.

Since the number 1 high was itself a Ross Hook (Rh), then the number 2 point can be termed a Reverse Ross Hook (RRh). More of that later.

Shorts took profits by buying at the number 2 point. Renewed buying comes into the market by virtue of bullish traders who treated the pull-back to number 2 as a bull market correction. The pullback created the number 3 point on the chart.

There were not enough traders willing to buy at the high prices, so the attempt to continue the upward trend failed. The market took out the number 2 point (RRh) of the 1-2-3 high formation, and a new downtrend was defined.

After prices moved down for awhile, a correction took place. This correction was caused by shorts taking profits. To cover their positions, they bought, thereby causing the market to rally. At this time, other buying may come into the market by those who think the down move is about over. They may feel that prices are at support. Buying may also come in to the market by technical traders and retracement traders who think *"this is the time to buy."*

The rally left behind a minor or intermediate low which we will call the point of the Ross Hook. This is the last Rh shown on the previous chart. The shaft of the Hook is the defined down trend.

The Hook itself, the remainder of the formation, consists of the rally also known as a correction or reaction. It is this correction, the move opposite to the trend, that leaves behind a "pointy" place on the chart. The correction can be from one to many bars in length. At times it can occur in a much more subtle way by having the correction **and** low occur in the same bar. Other nuances can occur and will be shown as we progress. For now, the important thing is to understand what a Hook is and how it looks. It is the breakout of the Hook that "establishes" the trend and can earn us a great deal of money, provided we get in ahead of the violation.

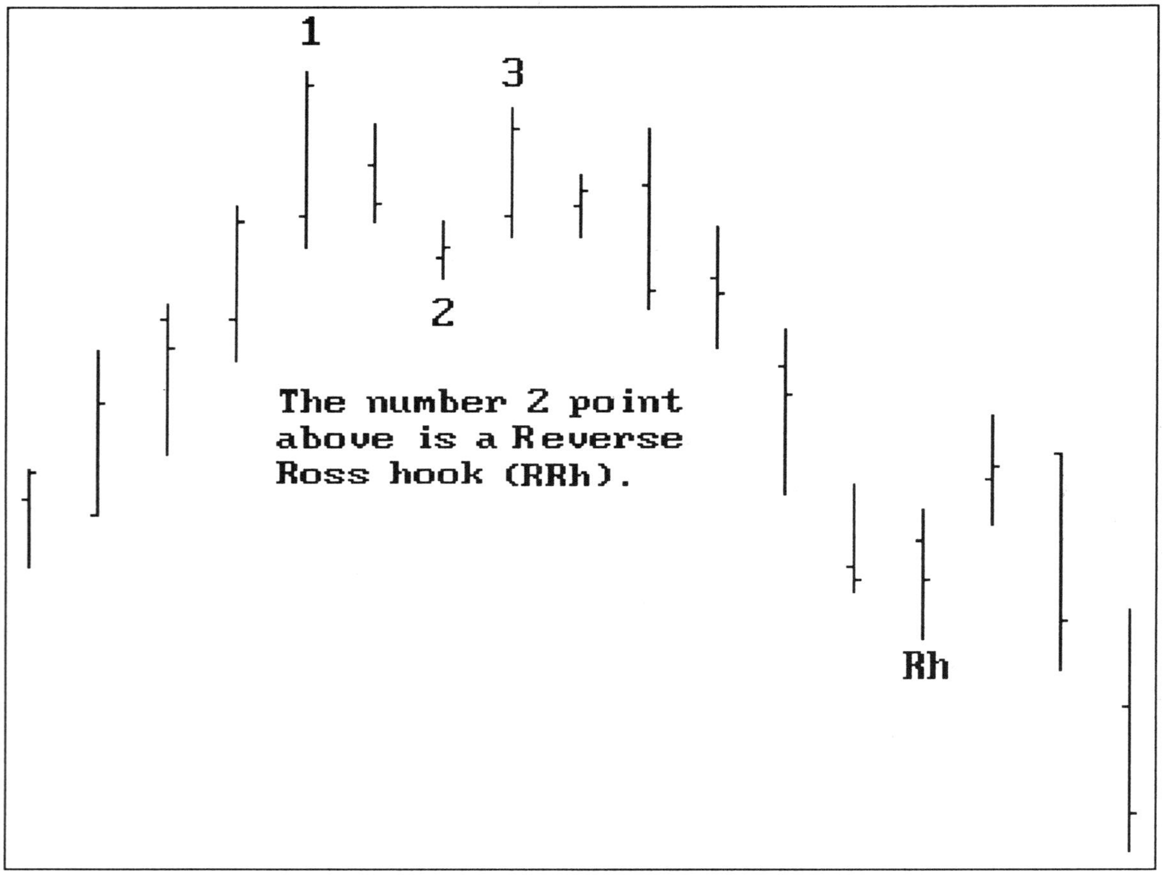

The preceding chart demonstrated a 1-2-3 high chart formation, a breakout of the number 2 (RRh) point of that formation which defined a downtrend. A further falling of prices led to a Ross Hook which was formed when prices temporarily failed to move lower, and ultimately to a breakout (violation) of the Hook, which event established the downtrend.

Next, let's look at a series of Ross Hooks that began with a 1-2-3 low.

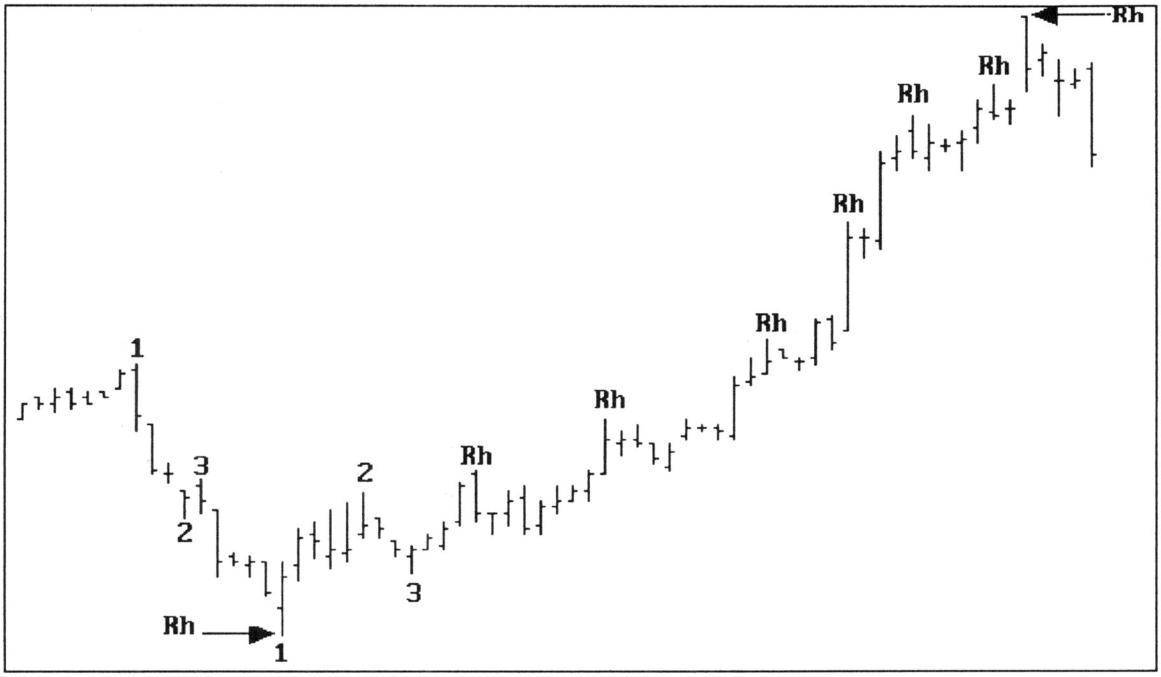

On the chart above we see that near the extreme left of the chart a 1-2-3 high formed out of congestion. The number 2 point of the 1-2-3 formation was violated thereby defining a downtrend.

An end to selling came, which was the low at (Rh) point 1. As prices started to rise, shorts began to cover in order to take profits. Their buying, aided and abetted by the entry of longs who thought this was the bottom, caused prices to rise to the number 2 point of the 1-2-3 low formation. Some traders who went long, looking for a quick profit, began to sell. They were joined by traders who felt that what they were seeing was a bear market rally. Prices headed back down to the number 3 point.

However, there was simply not enough supply at these low prices to warrant continued selling. Prices refused to take out, or go as low as, the number 1 point of the 1-2-3 low formation. Instead, demand took over the market and bargain hunters, who thought that prices would move even higher, began to buy. The demand was strong enough to overcome the number 2 point and thereby defined a new upward trend.

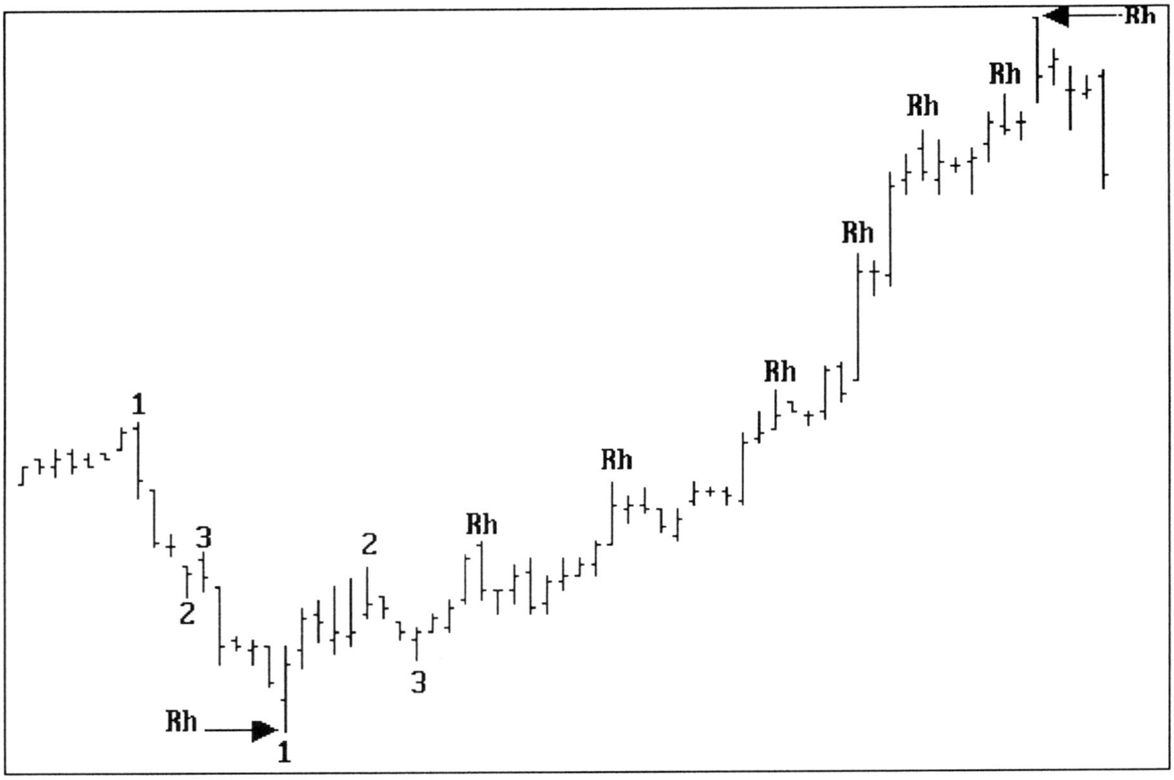

As prices rose, the second Rh on the chart above, selling came into the market as some longs liquidated all or part of their position. This selling, joined by those who felt it was time to get short, drove prices back down in what was viewed as a pull-back, a retracement, a reaction, or a correction, take your pick. Prices move down in reaction to this selling.

But demand is still greater than supply, and it appears prices are not yet too high to keep buyers away. The market moves up, taking out the points labeled as Rh. This process is repeated several times, until eventually we see what may prove to be a market top, the last Rh on the chart above.

The Ross Hooks made subsequent to the initial breakout of the 1-2-3 low are a frequently occurring event. Sometimes the distance between what might be labeled as a number 1 point and what might be labeled as a number 2 point is considerable.

THE IMPORTANT THING TO REMEMBER ABOUT ROSS HOOKS IS THAT THE FORMATION ALWAYS OCCURS IN A TRENDING MARKET, UNLESS IT IS THE RESULT OF THE FIRST CORRECTION SUBSEQUENT TO A BREAKOUT FROM A LEDGE OR A TRADING RANGE.

Within reason, the stronger the trend the better. There are also times when caution overrules all other considerations. More of that in a later chapter.

What is best about the concept of trading Hooks is that they represent truth in the market. A breakout represents a truth in the market. Once prices have broken through the point of the Hook, they have broken out. Even if the breakout should prove to be a false breakout, the immutable fact is that prices have broken out — generally with sufficient force to afford the opportunity to at least cover costs and allow the remaining time in the trade to be "free." But remember, we want to enter a trade prior to the actual violation of the Hook, just as we want to enter a trade prior to the violation of a number two point of a 1-2-3 formation. To do that, we must use a concept known as the Trader's Trick.

The next question may seem overly simplistic, but we have to ask ourselves...

"WHAT CAUSES A ROSS HOOK?"

Obviously these "pointy places" are different from the number two points of 1-2-3 formations. It should be obvious that they have nothing to do with supply and demand.

If that is the case, there are only two things that could be causing them. One is obvious — the Hooks are caused by profit taking. Whenever the market had moved sufficiently to satisfy a majority of traders, or those holding the majority of shares, profit taking causes the market to begin to move counter-trend.

The other reason is not so obvious, but it has to do with the phenomenon people have come to call "the technical indicator trader."

In classical technical analysis which involves learning how people trade various price formations known as heads and shoulders, megaphones, pennants, flags, speed lines, etc., no consideration is given to the effect that technical indicator trading has on price action.

A good chart watcher can generally spot an engineered move by large operators and can choose to participate or not. But chart watching doesn't tell you when and what the technical indicator trader is going to do.

There are a number of technical indicators used by all too many traders to tell them what has happened in the market. Sadly, they fail to realize that what they need to know is not what has happened, but what is happening — ***now!***

You may have heard of some of these technical indicators: "Percent R," "Moving Average Convergence and Divergence" (MACD), "Relative Strength Index" (RSI), "ADX," "CCI," "DEMA," "Keltner Channels," "Bollinger Bands," "Stochastics," etc.

We have nothing against the proper use of any of these, and in fact, this manual will present a number of them. They are good only to the extent that their limitations and their behavior are thoroughly understood. Their names are not always descriptive of what they truly represent. For instance, the RSI indicator does not truly indicate relative strength in the market in the traditional sense that relative strength is used.

If you look up the word stochastic in a dictionary, you will readily see that the term stochastic is a misnomer relative to the indicator it purports to be describing.

The **New World Dictionary of the American Language** says, "**sto-chas-tic** (sto kas'tik)**adj.** **[**<Gr.*stochastikos*, proceeding by guesswork, lit., skillful in aiming <*stochazesthai,*to aim at < *stochos*, a target: for IE. base hastikos*, proceeding by guesswork, lit., skillful in aiming* <stochazesthai*,to aim at* < stochos*, a target: for IE. base see STING]* ***1.*** *of, pertaining to, or arising from chance; involving* *probability; random* **2. Math.** *designating a process having an infinite progression of jointly distributed random variables.*

We will not argue with anyone against the fact that ***markets*** are an infinite progression of jointly distributed random variables. But the study which has wrongly been named stochastics is not the market, but rather a mathematical attempt to measure, on a fixed scale, momentum, divergence, and an idiotic concept called "overbought" and "oversold." The concept of the indicator is that it is always relative. It asks the question, where is the closing price today relative to where closing prices were previously? This is precisely why the so-called Stochastics falls apart in a trending market, where it can stay "overbought" or "oversold" for many time periods beyond where the market was supposedly in the "overbought" or "oversold" condition.

What you just read about the Stochastics indicator being relative is also true of the RSI indicator and Percent R, and is mostly true of may other indicators in use in the markets today.

To conclude the thought started earlier about the causes of Ross Hooks: it is sometimes trading by technicians using technical indicators that in part causes the market corrections that result in Ross Hooks.

More than that, it is the **incorrect** use of these oscillators and indicators that, in part, cause the corrections that result in Ross Hooks. Technical traders, erroneously thinking the market is in an overbought or oversold condition, are entering the market the wrong way, and adding to the momentum of the correction by profit takers.

With the advent (or should we say the re-invention) of Fibonacci trading, corrections often became more pronounced, as Fibonacci traders blindly buy or sell at their predetermined "magic" Fibonacci ratios, where the market is supposed to stop going one way and begin going another.

Add to this the more recent, illogical notion that markets are supposed to turn on moon dates, and you will know exactly how to fade these moves and stick a huge chunk of money in your pocket.

ROSS HOOK DEFINITION RECAP FOR TRENDING PRICES

WHENEVER A MARKET TREND IS INTERRUPTED BY A FAILURE TO CONTINUE IN THE DIRECTION IN WHICH IT WAS TRENDING, NO MATTER HOW SLIGHT THE INTERRUPTION, IT WILL LEAVE BEHIND A ROSS HOOK.

IN A DOWNWARD TRENDING MARKET, A FAILURE BY PRICE TO MAKE A NEW LOW CONSTITUTES A ROSS HOOK.

IN AN UPWARD TRENDING MARKET, FAILURE BY PRICE TO MAKE A NEW HIGH CONSTITUTES A ROSS HOOK.

IN A DOWNWARD TRENDING MARKET, IF PRICES MAKE AN EQUAL LOW, REVEALING A DOUBLE "SUPPORT" POINT ON THE CHART, THE MARKET HAS MADE A ROSS HOOK.

IN AN UPWARD TRENDING MARKET, IF PRICES MAKE AN EQUAL HIGH, REVEALING A DOUBLE "RESISTANCE" POINT ON THE CHART, THE MARKET HAS MADE A ROSS HOOK.

This means that in a down trending market, a double low (two consecutive equal lows) followed by a higher low creates a Ross Hook. In an uptrending market, a double high (two consecutive equal highs), followed by a lower high, also constitute a Ross Hook.

In ELECTRONIC TRADING 'TNT' I — GORILLA TRADING STUFF, we saw that Ross Hooks occur only in trending markets. We saw several ways to define a trend. Once a trend is defined, the very next correction that occurs results in a Ross Hook.

What will be shown in this part of the course is in no way in conflict with what was shown in ELECTRONIC TRADING 'TNT' I — GORILLA TRADING STUFF. By definition, Ross Hooks occur in trending markets, unless they are the result of the first correction to occur subsequent to the breakout of a Ledge or a Trading Range. For our purposes, we will consider a trend as being defined upon any breakout, whether gradual, or by explosion or meltdown from Ledges or Trading Ranges. To further explain, a Ross hook can occur in one of three ways:

- The first correction (i.e., retracement) after the breakout of the number two point of a 1-2-3 formation.
- The first correction (i.e., retracement) after the breakout of a Trading Range,
- The first correction (i.e., retracement) after the breakout of a Ledge.

In this part of the course, we will see that a trend can be ***defined*** by a 1-2-3 formation.

WHEN ROSS HOOKS OCCUR IN A TRENDING MARKET, REGARDLESS OF HOW YOU DEFINE THE TREND, THE ROSS HOOK CAN OCCUR ONLY AFTER A TREND HAS BEEN DEFINED. A TAKING OUT OF THE FIRST HOOK TO OCCUR *ESTABLISHES* THAT TREND. EACH SUBSEQUENT BREAKOUT OF A ROSS HOOK SERVES ONLY AS ADDITIONAL CONFIRMATION OF THE TREND, UNTIL SUCH TIME AS THE TREND IS EXHAUSTED.

ROSS HOOK DEFINITION RECAP FOR NON-TRENDING PRICES

We stated earlier that a Ross Hook can also be formed as the first correction following the breakout of a Ledge or Trading Range. Following is a summarization of what we mean by Ledges and Trading Ranges.

LEDGES

A LEDGE CONSISTS OF A MINIMUM OF FOUR PRICE BARS. IT MUST HAVE TWO MATCHING LOWS AND TWO MATCHING HIGHS. THE MATCHING HIGHS MUST BE SEPARATED BY AT LEAST ONE PRICE BAR, AND THE MATCHING LOWS MUST BE SEPARATED BY AT LEAST ONE PRICE BAR.

The matches need not be exact, but should not differ by more than three minimum tick fluctuations. If there are more than two matching highs and two matching lows, then it is optional whether to take an entry signal from either the latest price matches in the series (Match 'A') or those that represent the highest and lowest prices of the series (Match 'B'). [See below]

A LEDGE CANNOT CONTAIN MORE THAN 10 PRICE BARS. A LEDGE MUST EXIST WITHIN A TREND. The market must have trended up to the Ledge or down to the Ledge. The Ledge represents a resting point for prices, therefore you would expect the trend to continue subsequent to a Ledge breakout.

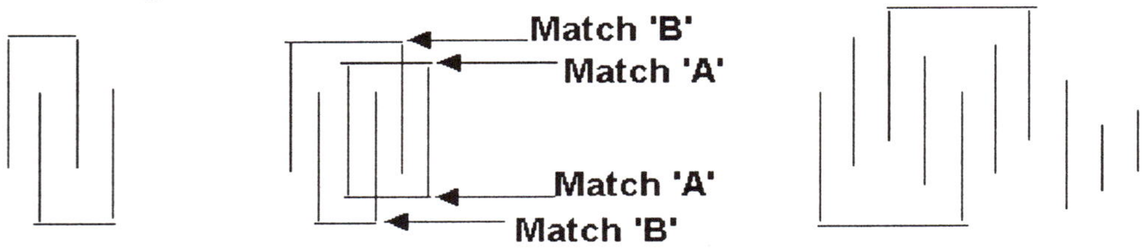

TRADING RANGES

A Trading Range is similar to a Ledge, but must consist of more than ten price bars. The bars between ten and twenty are of little consequence. Usually, between bars 20 and 30, i.e., bars 21-29, there will be a breakout to the high or low of the Trading Range established by those bars prior to the breakout.

It becomes crucial, then, to know when we are in a trending market and when we are in congestion Therefore, we must learn a most elementary way to identify a trend. However, before we do, we need to reintroduce you to the Trader's Trick.

Chapter 4

THE TRADER'S TRICK

The purpose of the Trader's Trick entry (TTE) is to get us into a trade prior to entry by other traders.

Let's be realistic. Trading is a business in which the more knowledgeable have the advantage over the less knowledgeable. Knowledge of and ability to use the Trader's Trick give you a distinct edge in the markets.

What we are trying to avoid with the Trader's Trick is the damage that can be done by trading from a false breakout.

Typically, there will be many orders bunched just beyond the point of a Ross hook. This is also true of the number two point of a 1-2-3 formation.

The insiders are very much aware of the bunching of orders at those points, and if they can make it happen, they will move prices to where they see the orders bunched together, and then a little past that point in order to liquidate as much of their own position as possible.

Unless the buying or selling pressure from the outsiders (us) is sufficient to carry the market to a new level (either high or low), the breakout will prove to be false.

The Trader's Trick is designed to beat the insiders at their own game by taking advantage of their moves, or at the very least to create a level playing field from which we can trade. When trading Ross Hooks, we want to get in ahead of the actual breakout of the point of the Hook. If the breakout is not false, the result will be significant profits. If the breakout is false, we will have at least covered our costs and taken some profit for our effort.

Insiders will often engineer moves aimed at precisely those points where they realize orders are bunched. It is exactly that kind of engineering that makes the Trader's Trick possible.

The best way to explain the engineering by the insiders is to give an example. Ask and answer the following question: If you were a large operator able to move prices, and you wanted to make the market move sufficiently for you to take a fat profit out of the market and know that you could liquidate easily at a higher level than where the market now is because of the orders bunched there, how would you engineer such a move?

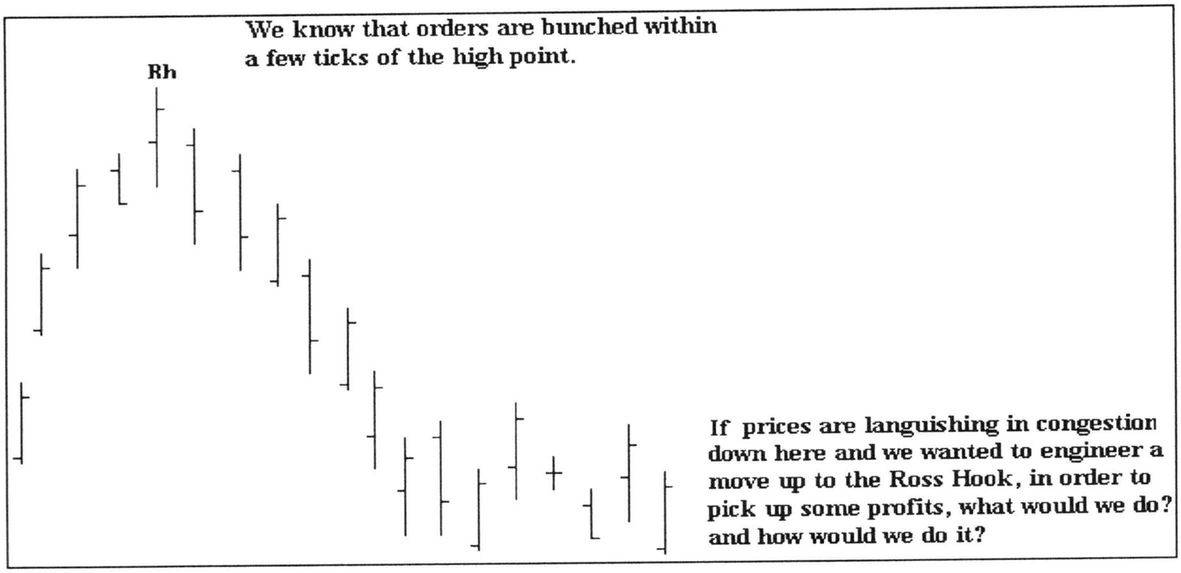

You would begin by bidding slightly above the market.

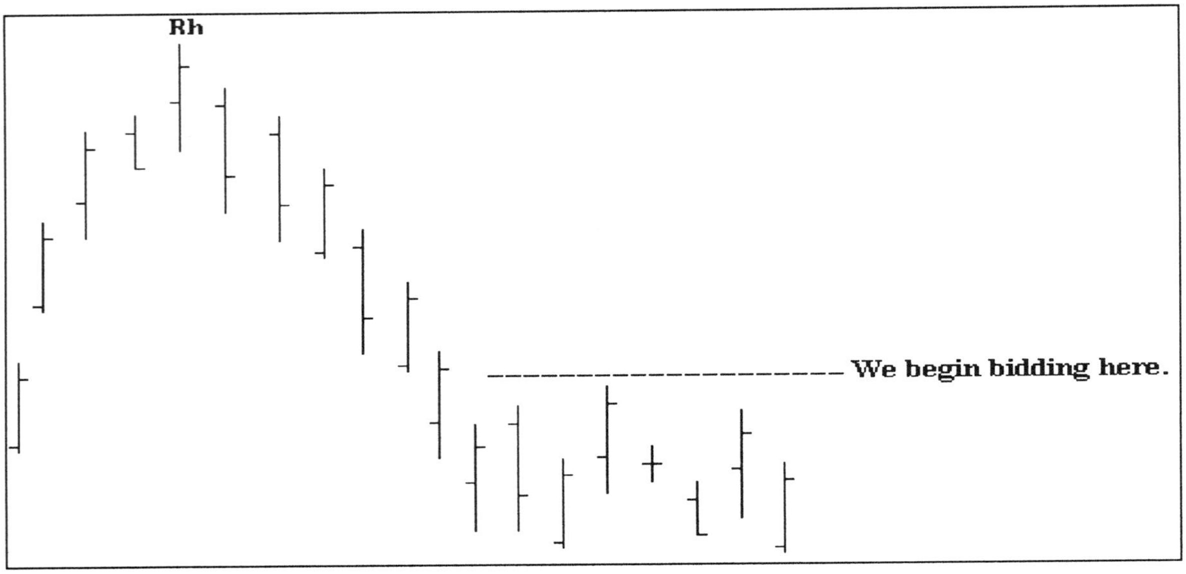

By bidding a large number of shares above the market, prices would quickly move up to your price level.

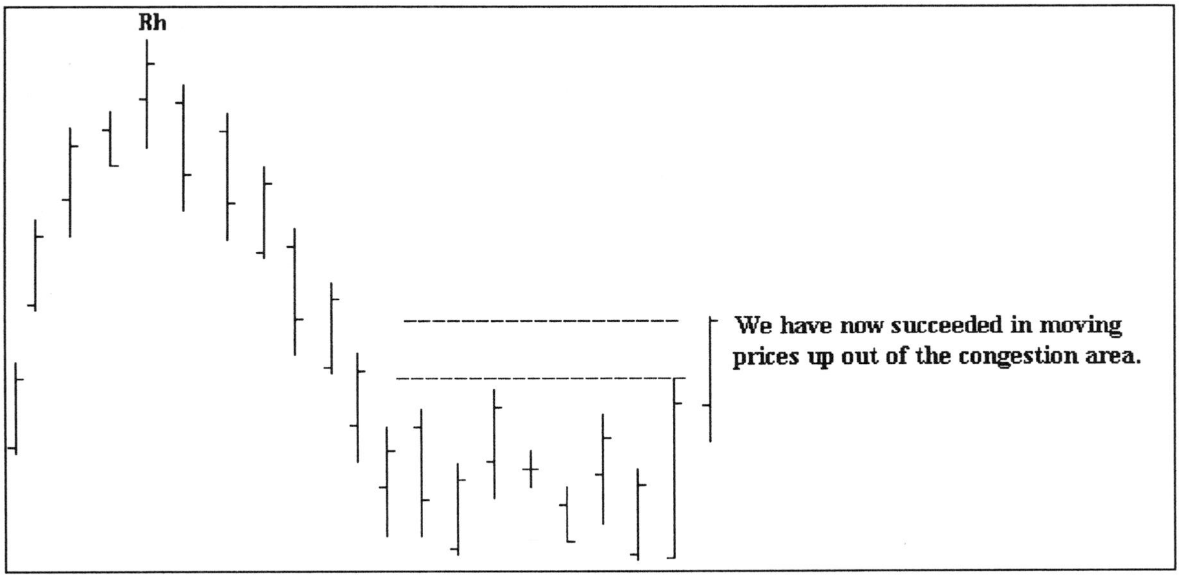

Once again by bidding a large number of contracts at a higher level, prices would move up to that next level.

The sudden movement up by price, to meet our large-order overpriced-bid, will cause others to take notice. The others are daytraders trading from a screen, and even other insiders.

Their buy orders will help in moving the market upward towards where the stops are bunched. It doesn't matter whether this is a daily chart or an intraday chart, the principle is the same.

In order to maintain the momentum, you may have to place a few more buy orders above the market, but you don't mind. You know there are plenty of orders bunched above the high point. These buy orders will help you fill your liquidating sell orders when it's time for you to make a hasty exit.

Who has placed the buy orders above the market? The outsiders, of course. They are made up of two groups. One group are those who went short sometime after the high was made, and feel that above the high point is all they are willing to risk. The other group are those outsiders who feel that if the market takes out that high, they want to be long.

Because of the action of our above-the-market bidding, accompanied by the action of other inside traders and daytraders, the market begins to make a strong move up. The move up attracts the attention of others, and the market begins to move up even more because of new buying coming into the market.

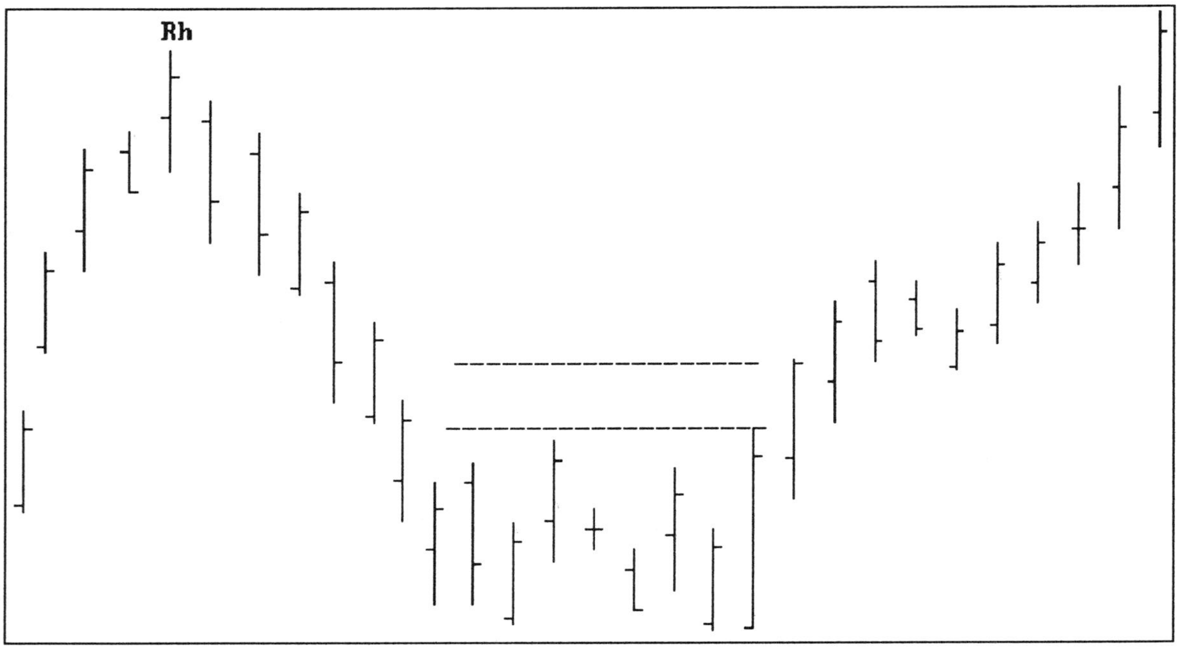

This kind of move has nothing whatsoever to do with supply and demand. It is purely contrived and engineered.

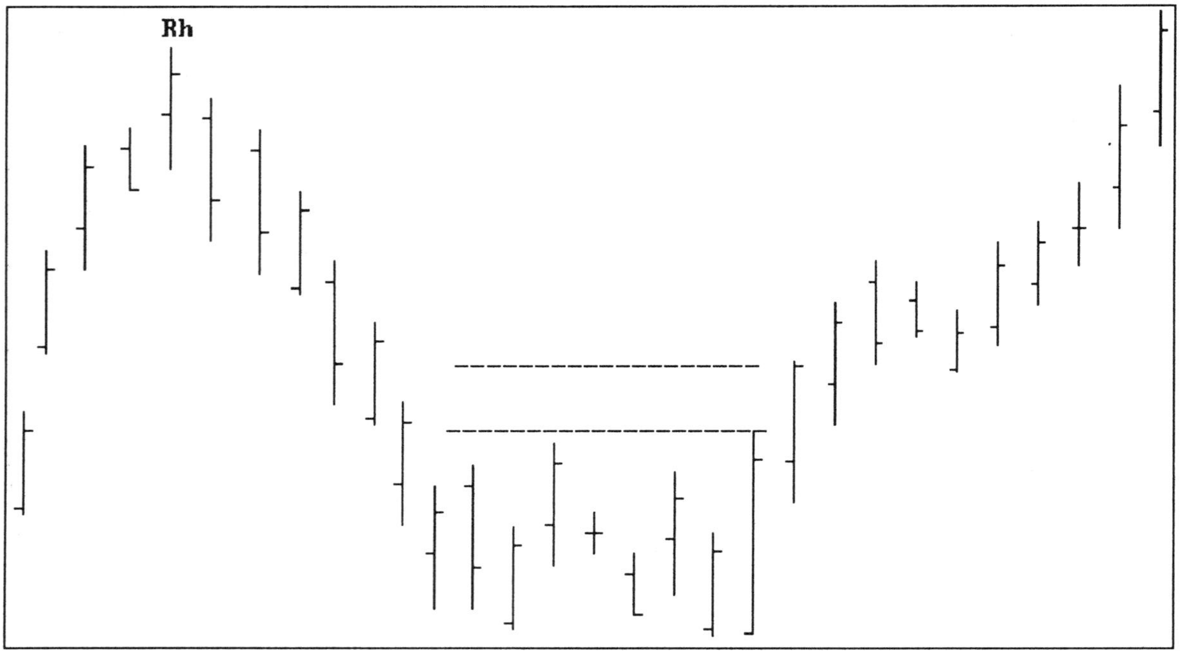

Once the market nears the high, practically everyone wants in on this "miraculous" move in the market. Unless there is strong buying by the outsiders, the market will fail at or shortly after reaching the high. This is known as a buying climax.

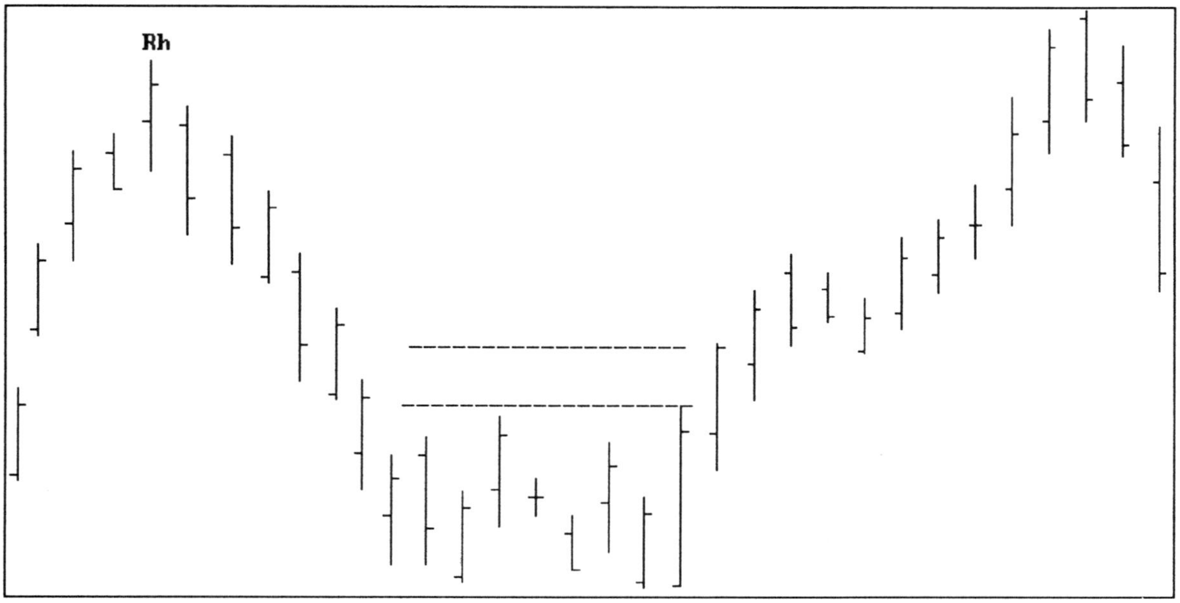

What will cause this failure? Selling. By whom? By you as a big operator, and all the other insiders who are anxious to take profits. At the very least, the market will make some sort of intraday hesitation shortly after the high is reached.

If there is enough buying to overcome all the selling, the market will continue up. If not, the insiders will have a wonderful time selling the market short, especially those who know this was an engineered move.

NOTE: DON'T THINK FOR ONE MOMENT THAT THERE IS NOT COLLUSION BY INSIDERS TO MANIPULATE PRICES.

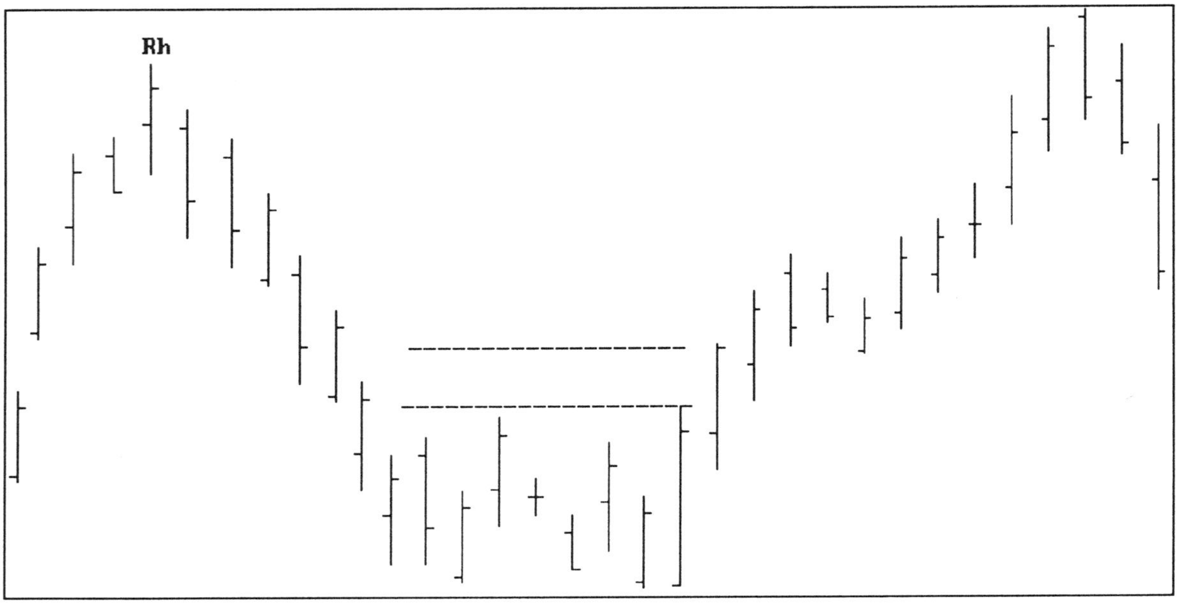

What will happen is that not only will selling be done for purposes of liquidation, but also for purposes of reversing position and going short. This means the selling at the buying climax may be close to triple the amount it would normally be if there were only profit taking.

Why triple? Because if prices were engineered upward by a large operator whose real intention is to sell, he will need to sell one set of shares to liquidate all of his buying, and perhaps double that number in order to get short the amount of shares he originally intended to sell.

For prices to be able to go higher, the buying from the outsiders will have to overcome that additional selling. But unless buying demand is real, prices will not go higher.

Because of that fact, the charts will attest to a false breakout. Of course, the reverse scenario is true of a downside engineered move resulting in a false breakout to the downside.

It is very important to realize what may be happening when a market approaches a Ross Hook after having been in a congestion area for awhile. The prior pages have illustrated this concept.

With the preceding information in mind, let's see how to accomplish the Trader's Trick.

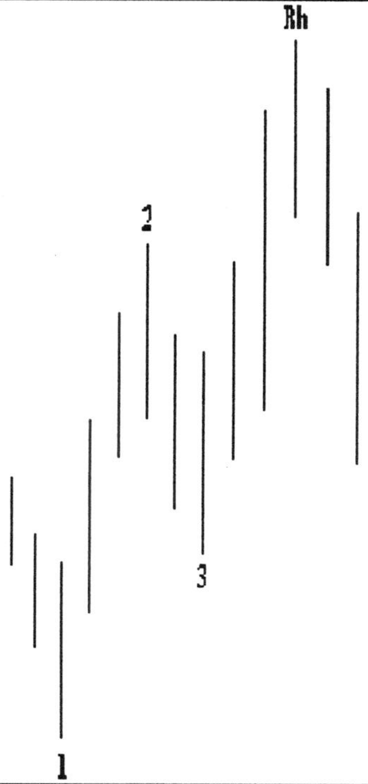

As prices approach the high of the point of an Rh, we buy a breakout of the high of a price bar that is in the correction. We want to make sure that there is sufficient room betwee the entry pont and the Rh so that if all that happens is that prices above the Rh are violated by a few ticks and not more, we can exit still having enjoyed a profitable trade. There is always the possibility that we will get nothing more than a double top or a false breakout. If so, we will have traded for free, having covered transaction costs and taken a small profit as well.

There were two price bars following the high: one is the bar whose failure to move higher created the Hook, and the other is one that simply furthered the depth of the correction.

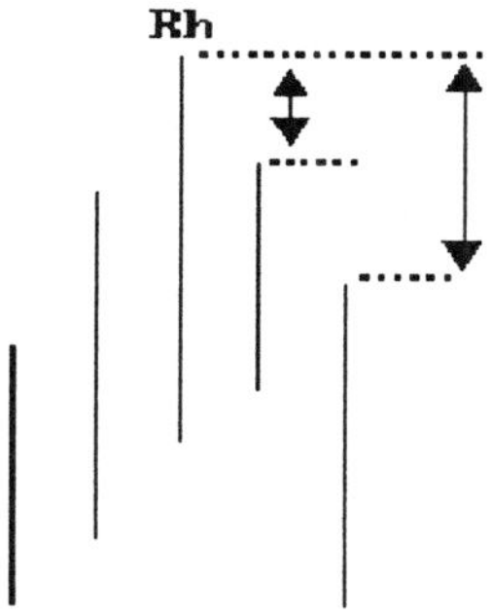

Prior to the second bar of correction, if there is sufficient room to cover costs and take a small profit in the distance between the high of the correcting bar and the point of the Hook, we attempt to buy a breakout of the high of the bar that created the Hook, i.e., the first bar of correction.

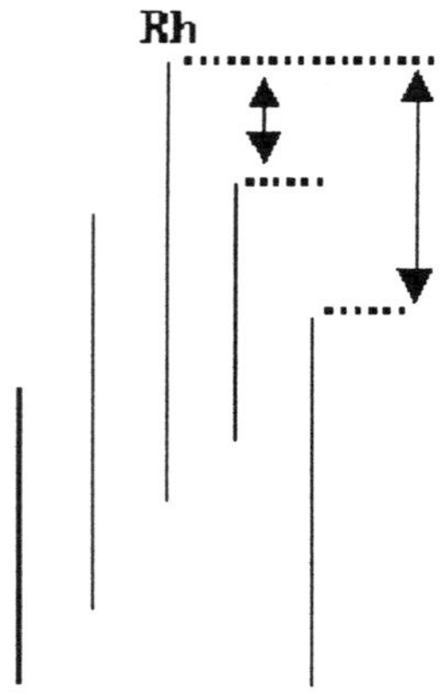

Once the second bar of correction is in place, we attempt to buy a violation of its high, again provided that there is sufficient room to cover costs and take a profit in the distance prices have to travel between our entry point and the point of the Hook. We will repeat our action taken for the second bar of correction, if we get a third bar of correction. Beyond three bars, we will cease in our attempt to buy a breakout of the correction highs.

What if the fourth bar in the correction did as pictured above?

As long as prices are moving back up in the direction of the trend that created the Ross Hook, and as long as there is sufficient room for us to cover costs and take a profit, we will buy a breakout of the high of any three of the previous correction bars. In the example above, if we were able to enter before prices violated the high of the second bar of correction, we would enter on a violation of the high of the second correcting price bar. If not, and there was still room to cover costs and profit from a violation of the first correcting price bar, we would enter there. Additionally, we could choose to enter on a takeout of the high of the latest price bar because it is within the buying range of the buying area. You might ask, "what about the fact that the latest price bar gapped up?" The answer is that we are not suggesting that you trade during the time interval that involves that latest price bar, but rather that it is acceptable to enter on a violation of the latest bar's high because it is occurring within the range of the buying area and by virtue of its moving higher may be an indication of a resumption of the trend.

Risk management is based upon the expectation that prices will go up to at least test the point of the Hook. At that time, we will take, or already have taken, some profit, and have covered costs.

We are now prepared to exit at breakeven at the very worst, on the remaining shares. Barring any horrible slippage, the worst we can do is having to exit the trade with some sort of profit for our efforts.

We usually limit the Trader's Trick to no more than three bars of correction following the high of the bar that is the point of the Hook. However, there is an important exception to this rule. The next chart shows the use of double or triple "support" and "resistance" areas for implementing the Trader's Trick.

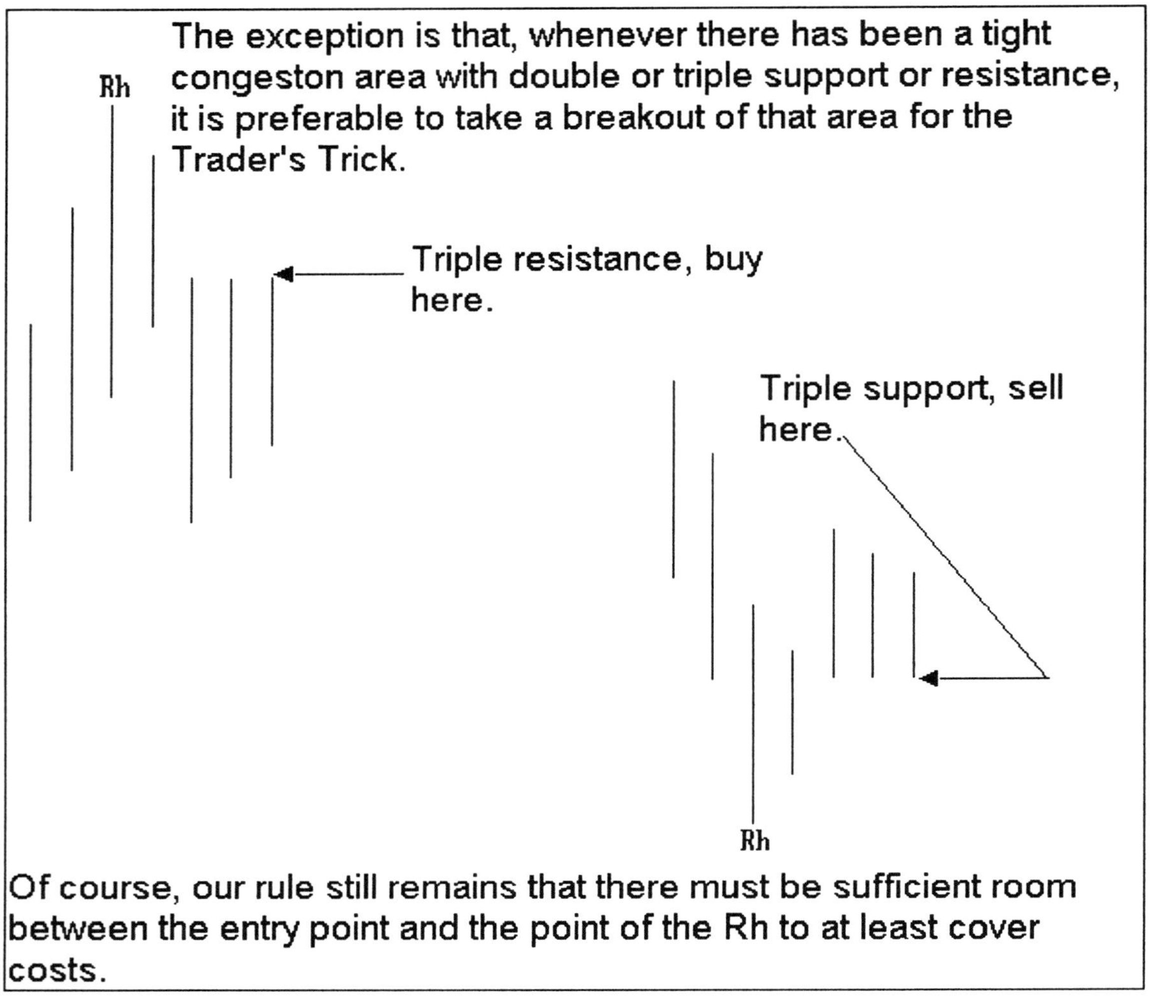

Any time a business can consistently make profits, that business is going to prosper. Add to that profit the huge amount of money made on the trades that take off and never look back, and it's readily apparent that enormous profits are available from trading.

You never want to be filled on a gap opening beyond your entry price. Gap openings more often than not, result in a price correction (retracement). When that happens, you will find yourself on the wrong side of a losing trade.

Can you grasp the logic of that? You have no way of knowing whether a move toward a breakout is real or not. If it is engineered, the market will move forward to the point of taking out the order accumulations and perhaps a few ticks more. Then the market will reverse with no follow through in the direction of the breakout. As long as you have left enough room between your entry point and the point where orders are accumulated to take care of costs and a profit, you will do no worse than breakeven. Usually, you will also have a profit to show for the any remaining shares, however small.

If the move proves to be real (not engineered), then the market will give you a huge reward relative to your risk and costs. Remember, immediate costs are your only real investment in the trade if it goes your way.

The important understanding that we need to have about the Trader's Trick is that by taking entry into a market at the correct point, we can neutralize the effect of, and even take advantage of the action by the insiders. We can be right and earn something for our efforts should the breakout prove to be false because the move is merely engineered.

Some breakouts will be real. The fundamentals of the market ensure that. When those breakouts happen we will be happy, richer traders. With proper money management, we can earn something for our efforts *even if* the breakout proves to be false. Now that you know what the Trader's Trick is all about, we can continue.

We need have only a few rules as pertains to 1-2-3 formations: they should be well defined, and easily seen as a 1-2-3. For the most part, we must insist that the 1-2-3 consist of at least four bars. The more bars, the better, so that the formation really stands out as being a 1-2-3. On five minute charts there must be at least 3 bars. However, this part of the course is not about 1-2-3 formations. It is about the Ross Hook. It is via the 1-2-3 that the Ross Hook was derived. It was recognizing what takes place at the number 2 point that led to the further pursuit in the search for viable trading situations.

DISCOVERING THE HOOK

The discovery of the Ross Hook is somewhat akin to Newton's discovery of the law of gravity. The law of gravity was there all the time. It wasn't really discovered by Newton.

And so it was with Ross Hooks. They were there all along. They've been there since the first bar chartist drew a bar chart. It is through publicizing them in writings and seminars that they have become known as Ross Hooks. We have come to call those who trade them "Hookers."

The discovery of them came as with many discoveries — in the search for something else.

Newton may have been looking for an explanation of why things fall. The Hooks came by way of looking for a way to enter trending markets.

Training and discipline, had brought about the concept of trading ahead of the number 2 point of the 1-2-3 formation using the Trader's Trick described in the first part of this course.

Listen to the following words taken from Joe's previous writings.

"As I looked over and studied my charts, I noticed there were plenty of 'pointy' places on the chart. Amazingly, I was able to find nothing that indicated that anyone was trading ahead of these 'pointy' places. It was as if everyone were trading only breakouts that went right through them and somehow no one was seeing them. It was as though they were invisible.

"What a find! What a rare treasure! Here were acres of diamonds, and everyone else was stumbling past them, kicking them to the side as they would any ordinary stone.

"I can't say for sure that no one else had ever utilized these 'pointy' places. In fact, I think there must have been plenty of others who used them. There are a good number of secret traders one never hears of. I couldn't find anyone who had ever written about these pointy places. My brokers certainly didn't know about them, and neither did anyone else I had ever spoken with. I felt like the man who has found a pearl of great price. It is only since I began imparting my trading knowledge to others that I've been willing to share what I know about these 'pointy' places on the chart, which I have named the Ross Hook."

A REVELATION

We will see step by step how to use the Ross Hook, how and why it works, and why it will continue to work in the markets. Perhaps, more importantly, we believe that it will work no matter how many people trade it. If enough people do trade it, it may become self-fulfilling.

Next we must learn how to identify congestion.

Chapter 5

IDENTIFYING CONGESTION

One of the concepts every trader **must learn** is how to know when prices are in congestion. There are a few rules for the early discovery of this ever important price action, and they are explained in detail in this chapter.

RULE: ANY TIME PRICES OPEN OR CLOSE ON FOUR CONSECUTIVE BARS, WITHIN THE CONFINES OF THE RANGE OF A "MEASURING BAR," YOU HAVE CONGESTION. THIS IS REGARDLESS OF WHERE THE HIGHS AND LOWS MAY BE LOCATED. A "MEASURING BAR" BECOMES SUCH BY VIRTUE OF ITS PRICE RANGE CONTAINING THE OPENS OR CLOSES OF AT LEAST 3 OF 4 SUBSEQUENT PRICE BARS.

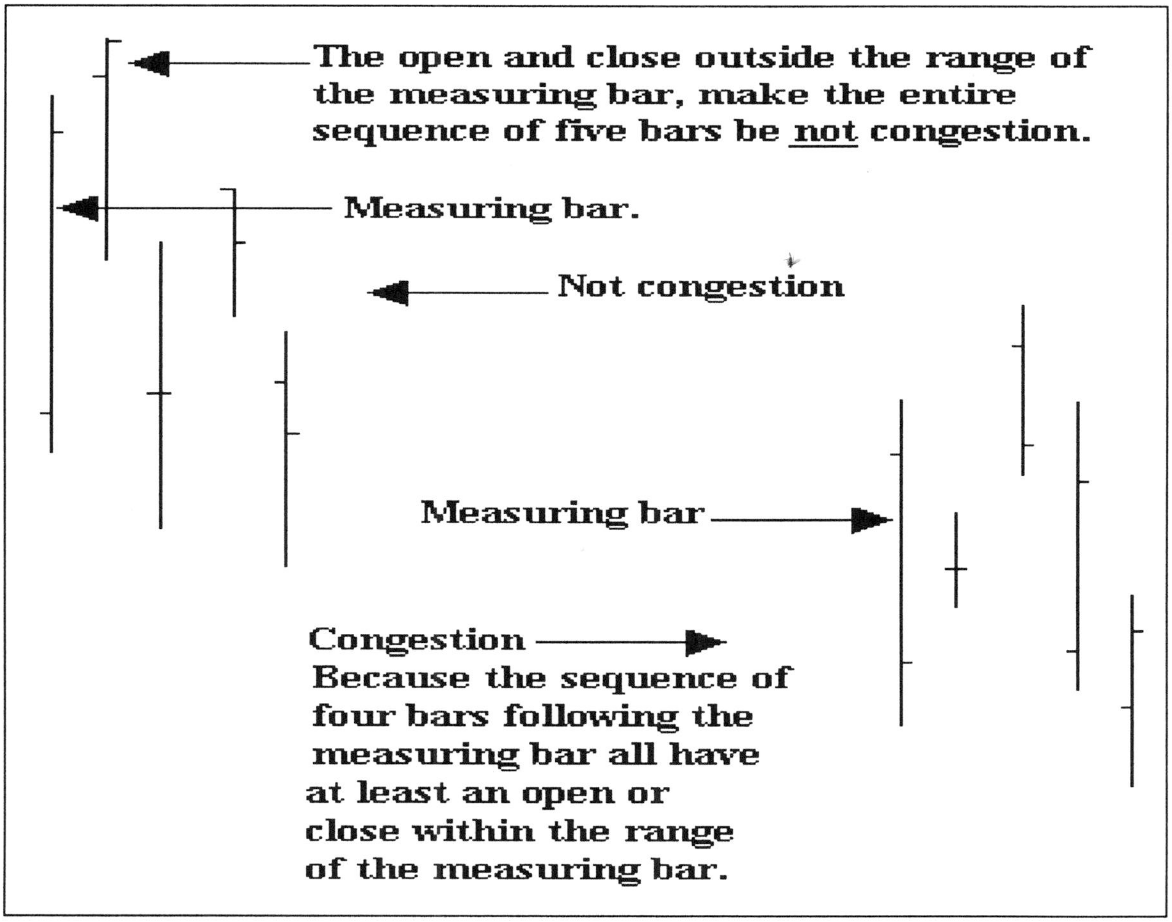

Closely and carefully study this chart again. Congestion can be very subtle in appearance. Often the difference between congestion or trend is the positioning of a single open or close.

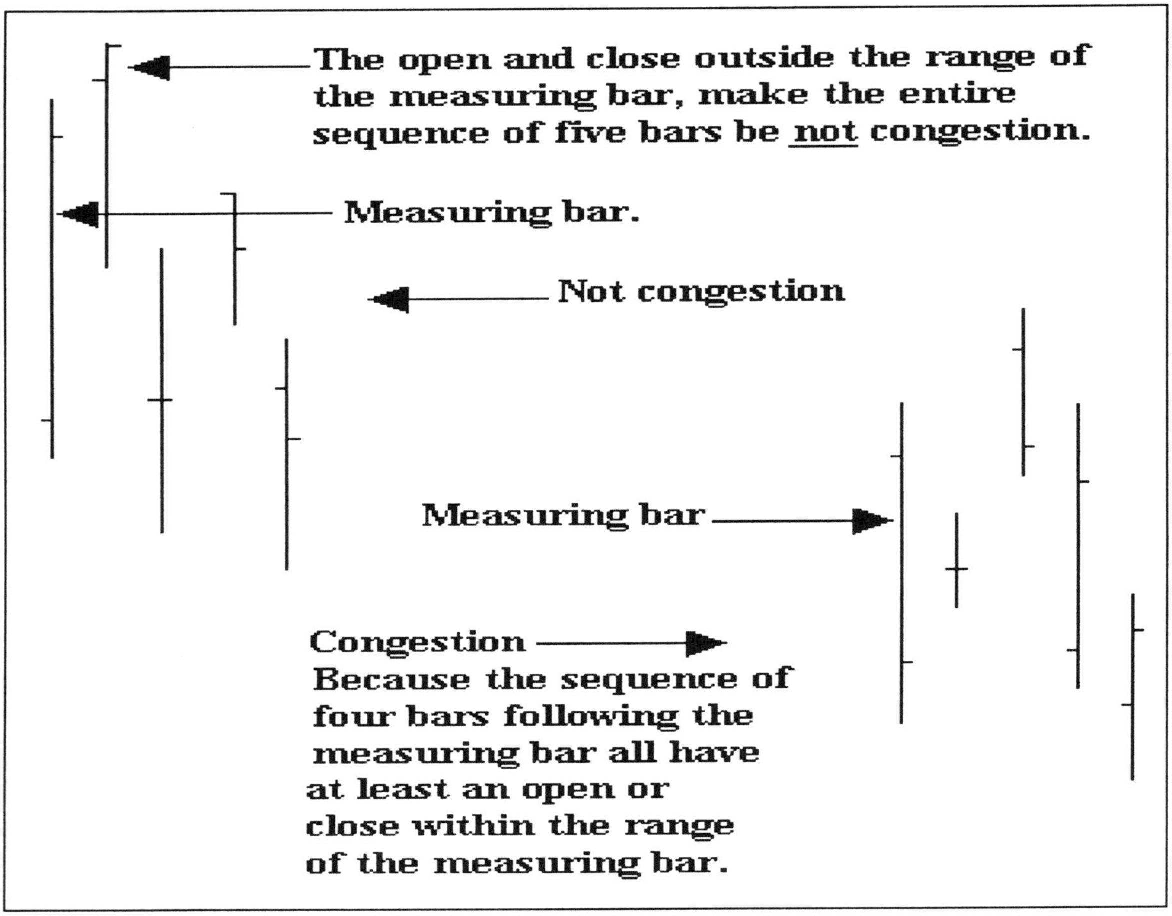

To further demonstrate this concept, let's first look at the combination of points "K" through "M" on the chart below. Even though "M" closed below the range of the measuring bar "J," the fact that "L" made a new high and then closed, dropping back into the Trading Range of "J", tells us that prices are still in congestion. This will be explained on the following pages. In addition, we now have congestion by virtue of alternating bars, which will also be discussed next.

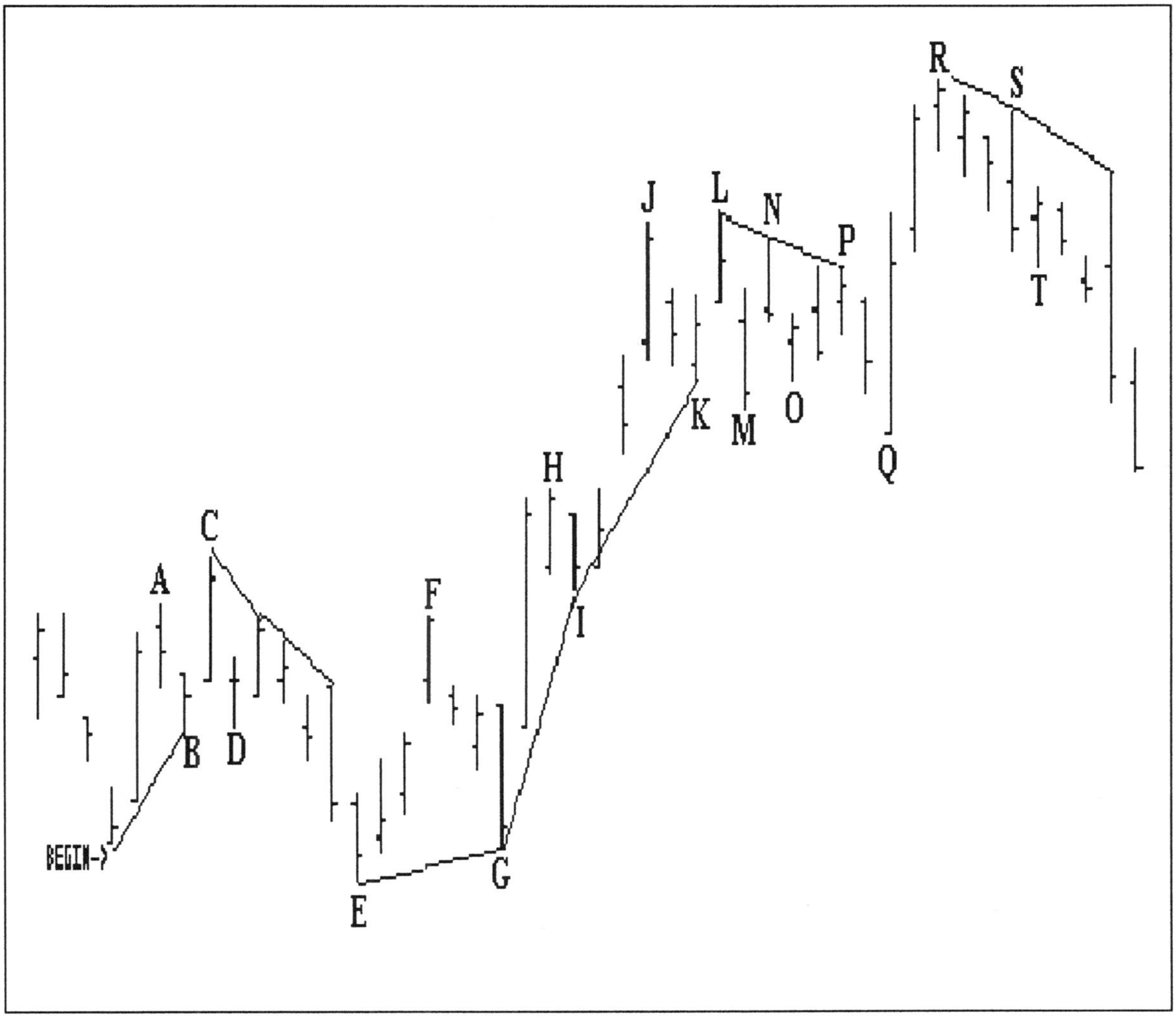

ANY TIME PRICES ARE NOT MAKING HIGHER HIGHS AND HIGHER LOWS, OR LOWER HIGHS AND LOWER LOWS, AND WE CAN SEE FOUR ALTERNATING BARS, AT TIMES COUPLED WITH INSIDE BARS AND AT TIMES COUPLED WITH DOJIS, WE HAVE CONGESTION.

ALTERNATING BARS ARE ONES WHERE PRICES OPEN LOWER AND CLOSE HIGHER ON ONE BAR, AND OPEN HIGHER AND CLOSE LOWER ON THE NEXT.

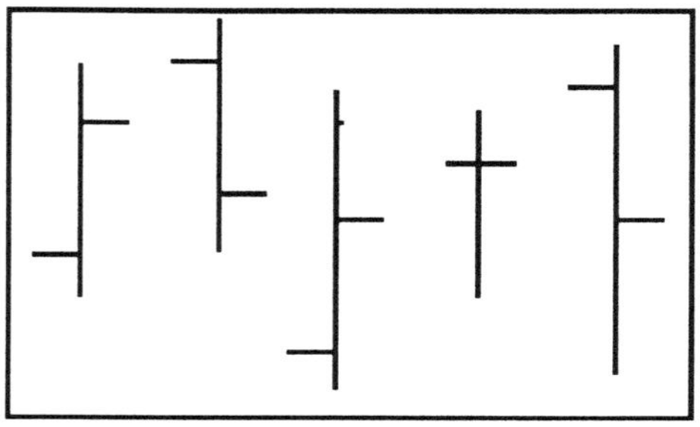

Inside bars look like this:

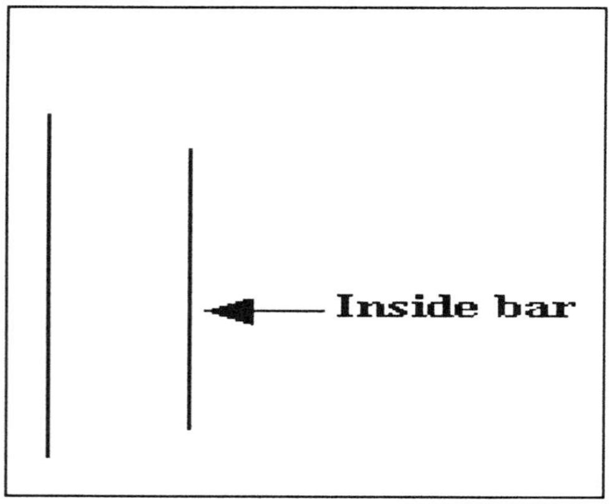

Doji Bars look like this:

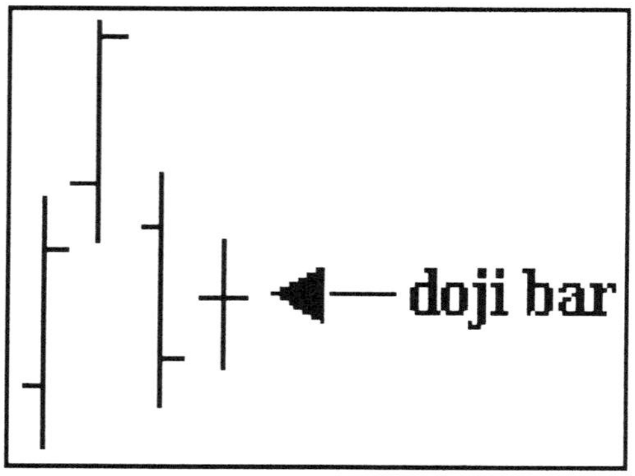

Below are more Doji bars. The open and close are at the same price or very near to the same price, yielding a bar that looks like this:

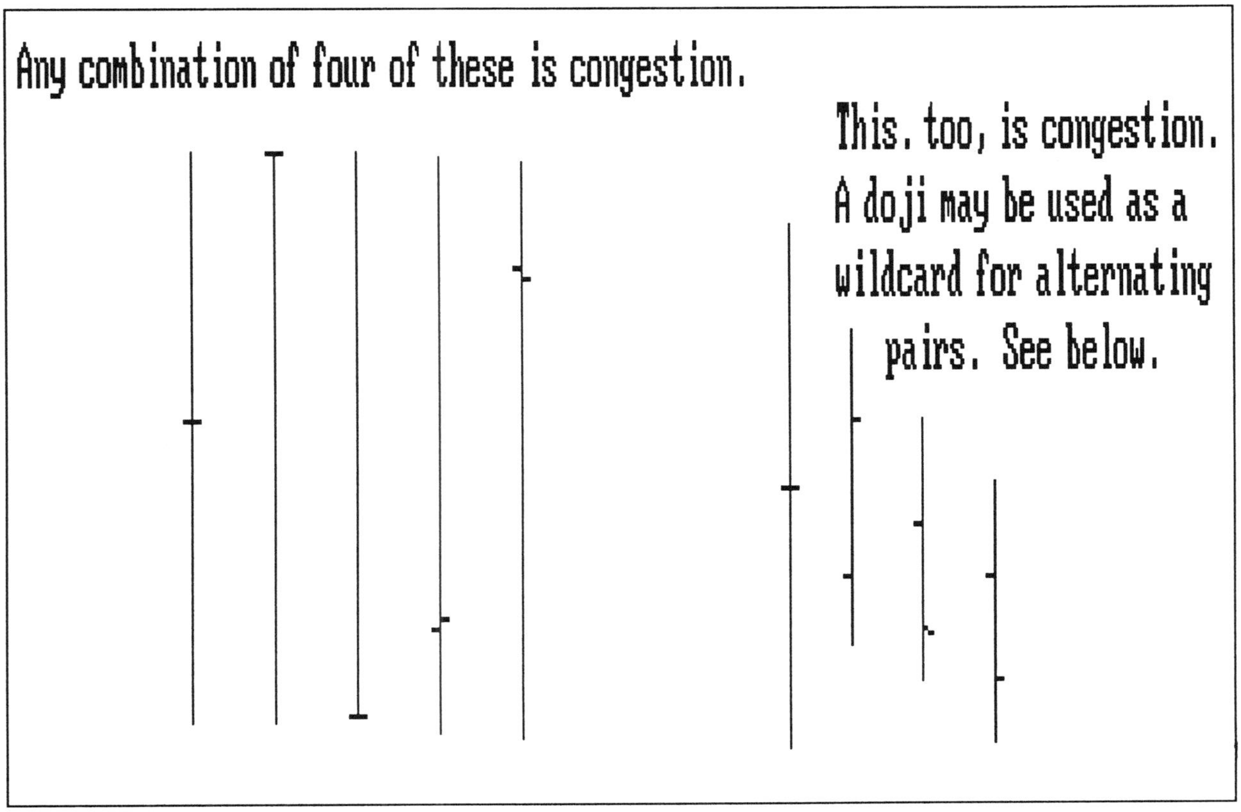

A combination of alternate closing high-low, low-high pairs is congestion.

"Pointy" places made when the market is in congestion are ***not*** Ross Hooks. If a trend has been defined within congestion you now have a trend and any subsequent point place is a Ross Hook.

The first bar of the congestion may very well be the last bar of what had been a trend. A congestion may look similar to any of the following, as long as it consists of four or more bars. Study these formations carefully:

CONGESTIONS:

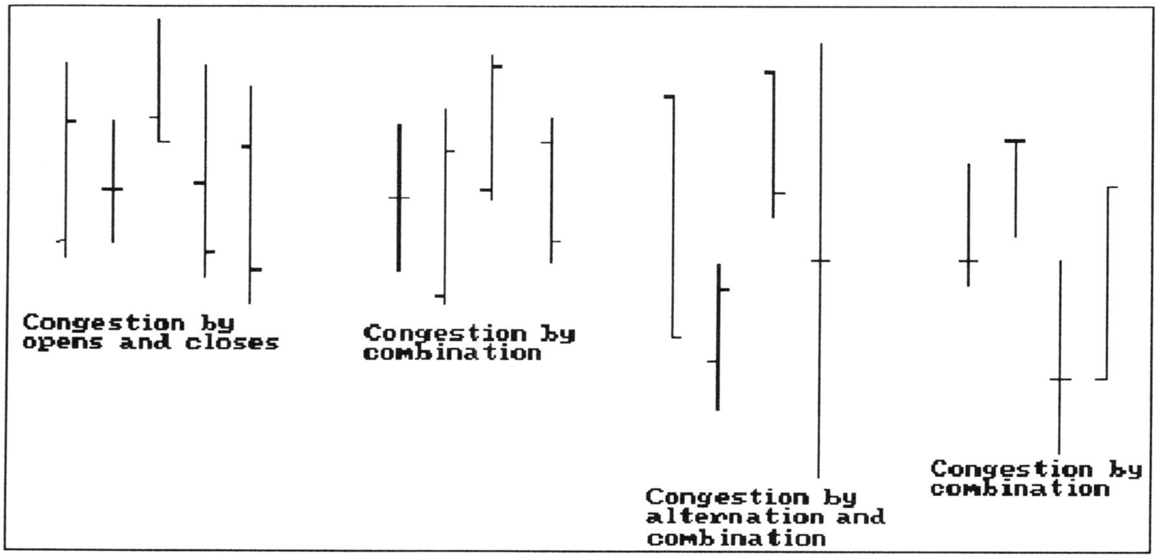

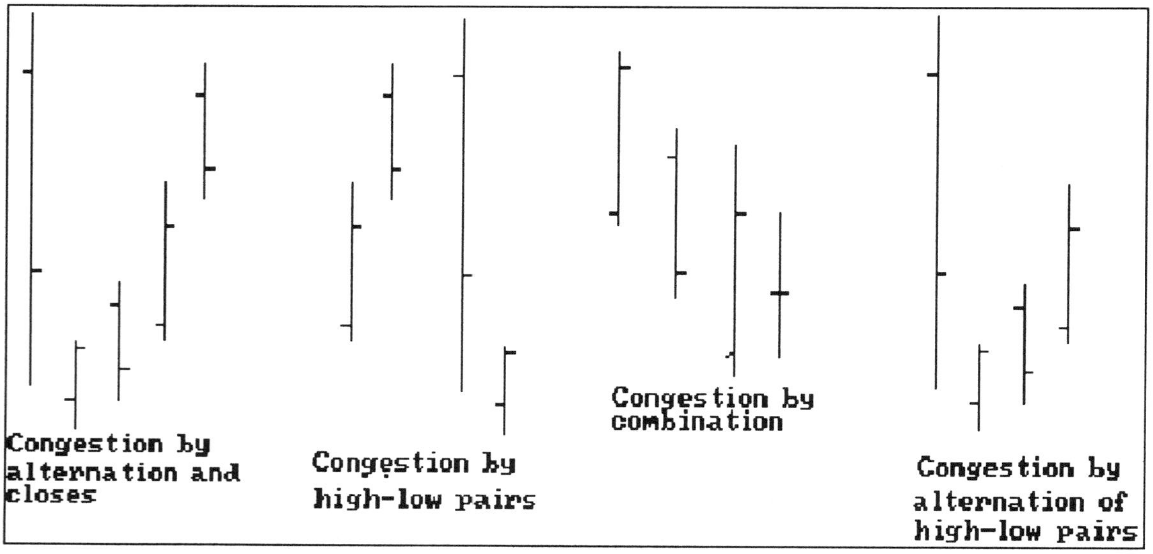

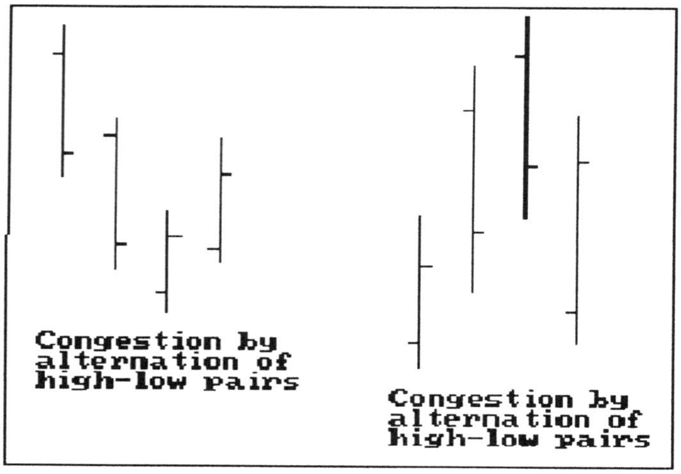

Frequently congestion will start or end with a doji. Frequently congestion will begin or end with a long bar move, or a gap.

Another way to identify congestion is when you see /\/\ or \/\/ on the chart.

The smallest possible number of bars that can make up this formation is four. Let's see how this can be done.

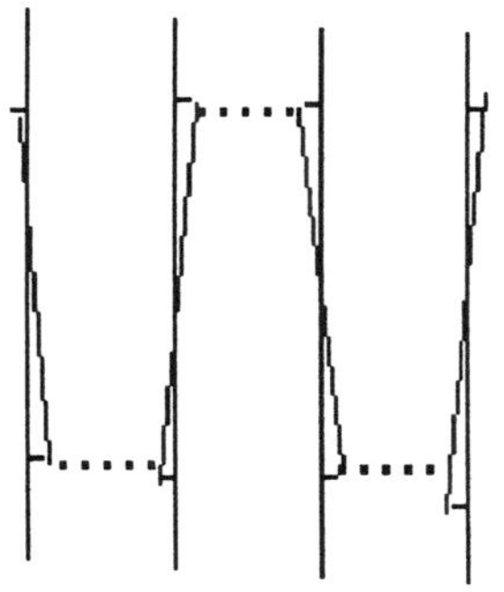

What we have here is an open higher close lower, followed by an open lower close higher, followed by an open higher close lower, followed by an open lower close higher sequence This forms a \/\/.

Idealized \/\/'s and /\/\'s

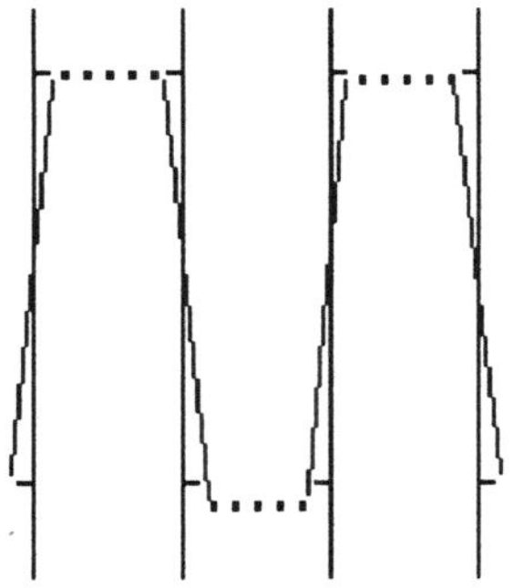

Here we have an open lower close higher, followed by an open higher close lower, followed by an open lower close higher, followed by an open higher close lower sequence. This forms an /\/\.

In reality, we may get something that looks more like the following:

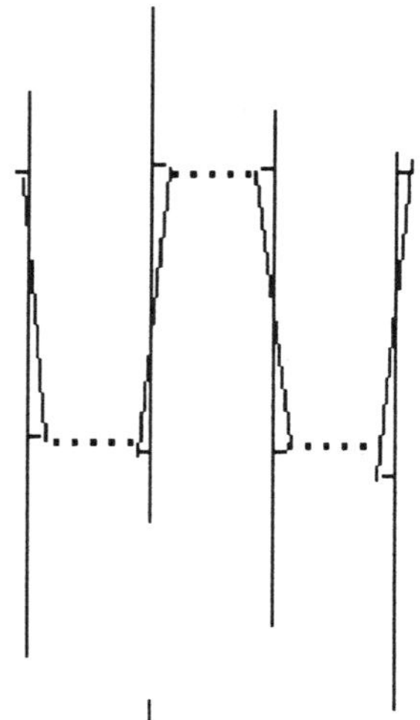

What we have here is an open higher close lower, followed by an open lower close higher, followed by an open higher close lower, followed by an open lower close higher sequence This forms a \/\/.

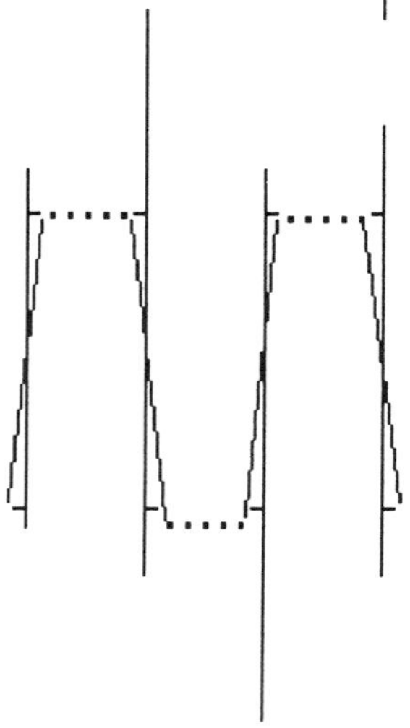

Here we have an open lower close higher, followed by an open higher close lower, followed by an open lower close higher, followed by an open higher close lower sequence. This forms an /\/\.

If we were to get a formation that looked like the following, the Ross Hook would be as marked. If that Hook is taken out, we would want to be long prior to the violation. Notice that the bar that created the Ross Hook was the last bar of the trend and the first bar of the congestion.

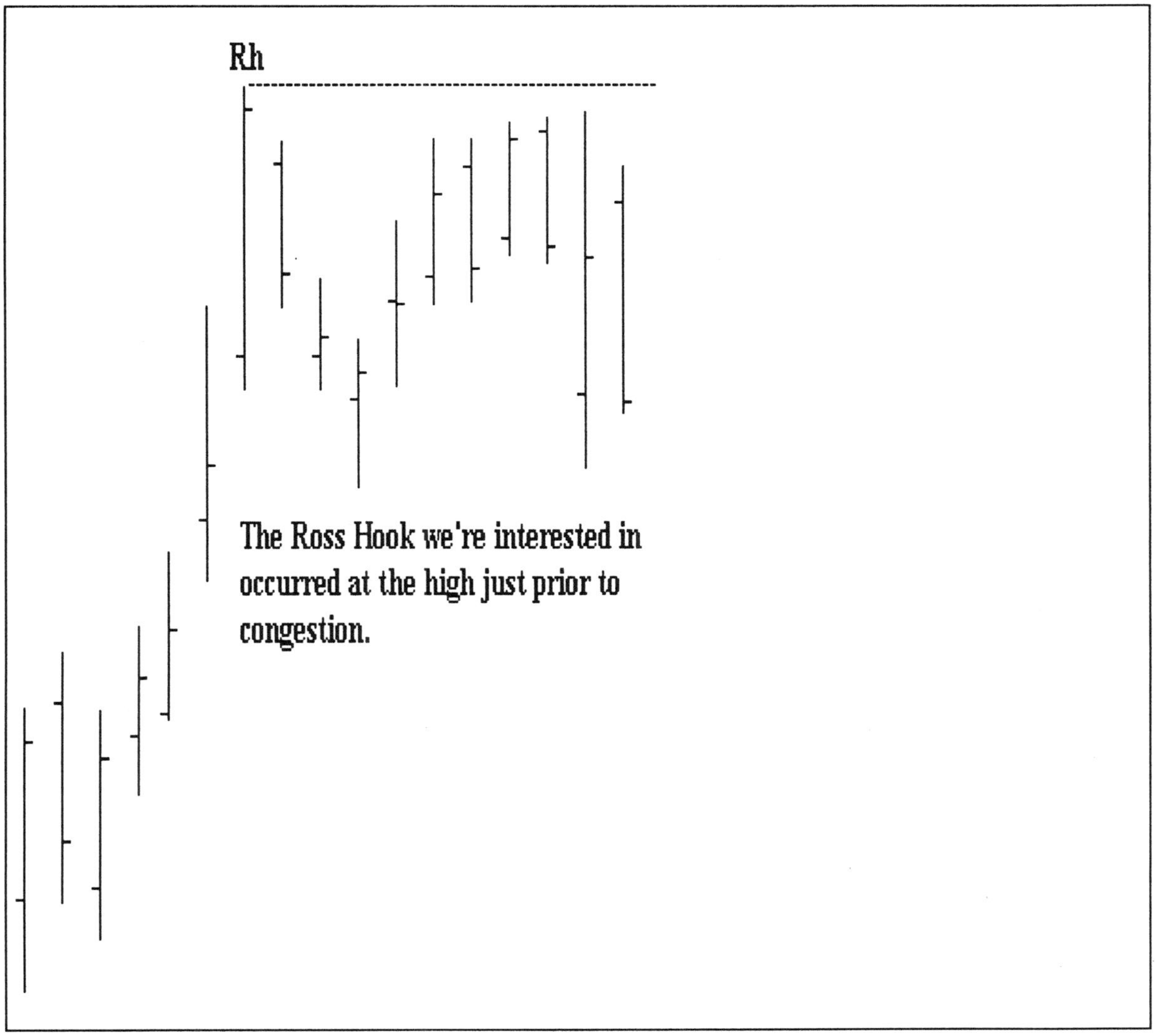

Now, let's see if you're really getting this. Assume that an established trend is in effect, with prices having trended up from much lower. We've changed the chart a bit, so pay attention.

The Ross Hook is as marked below.

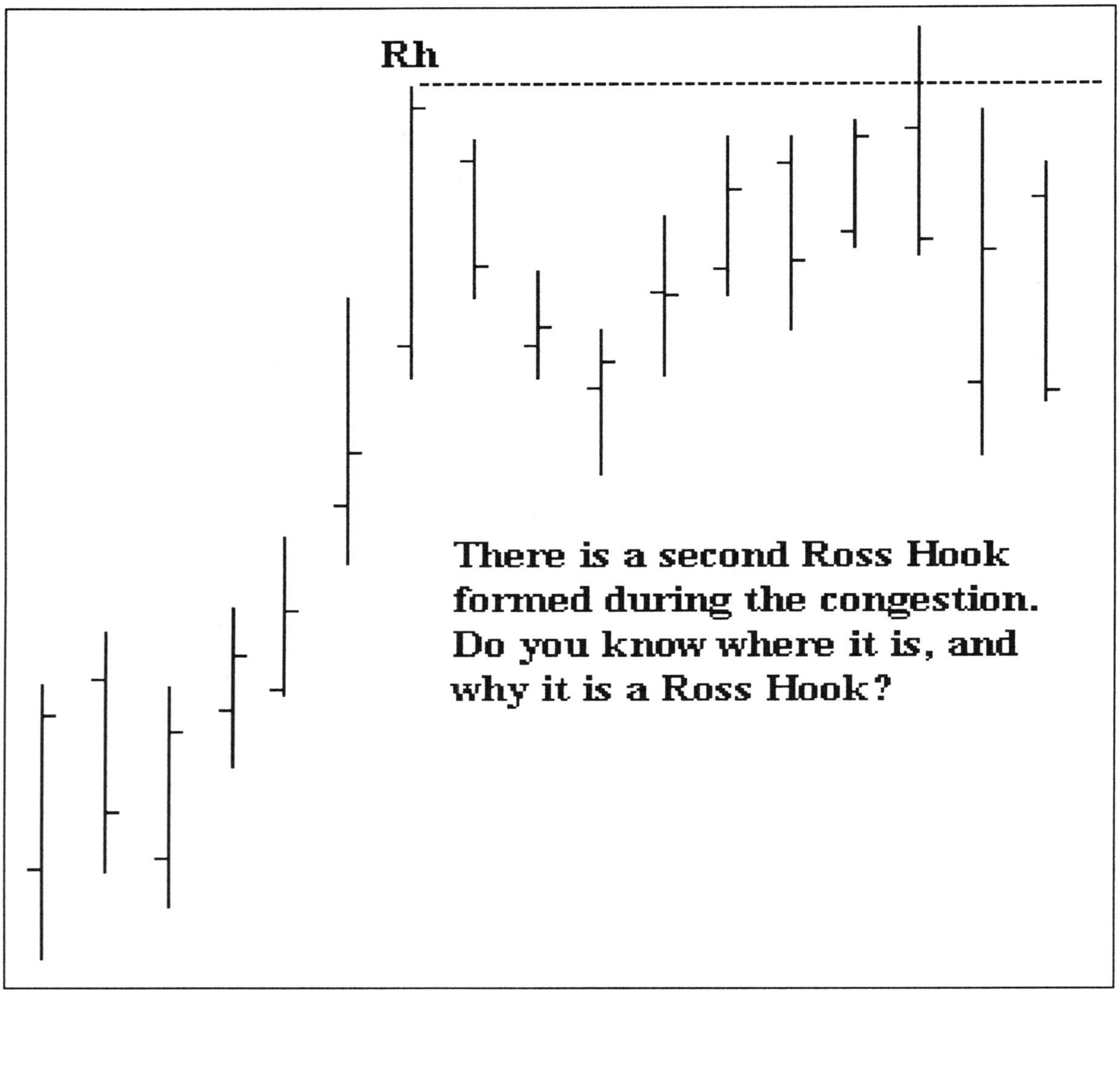

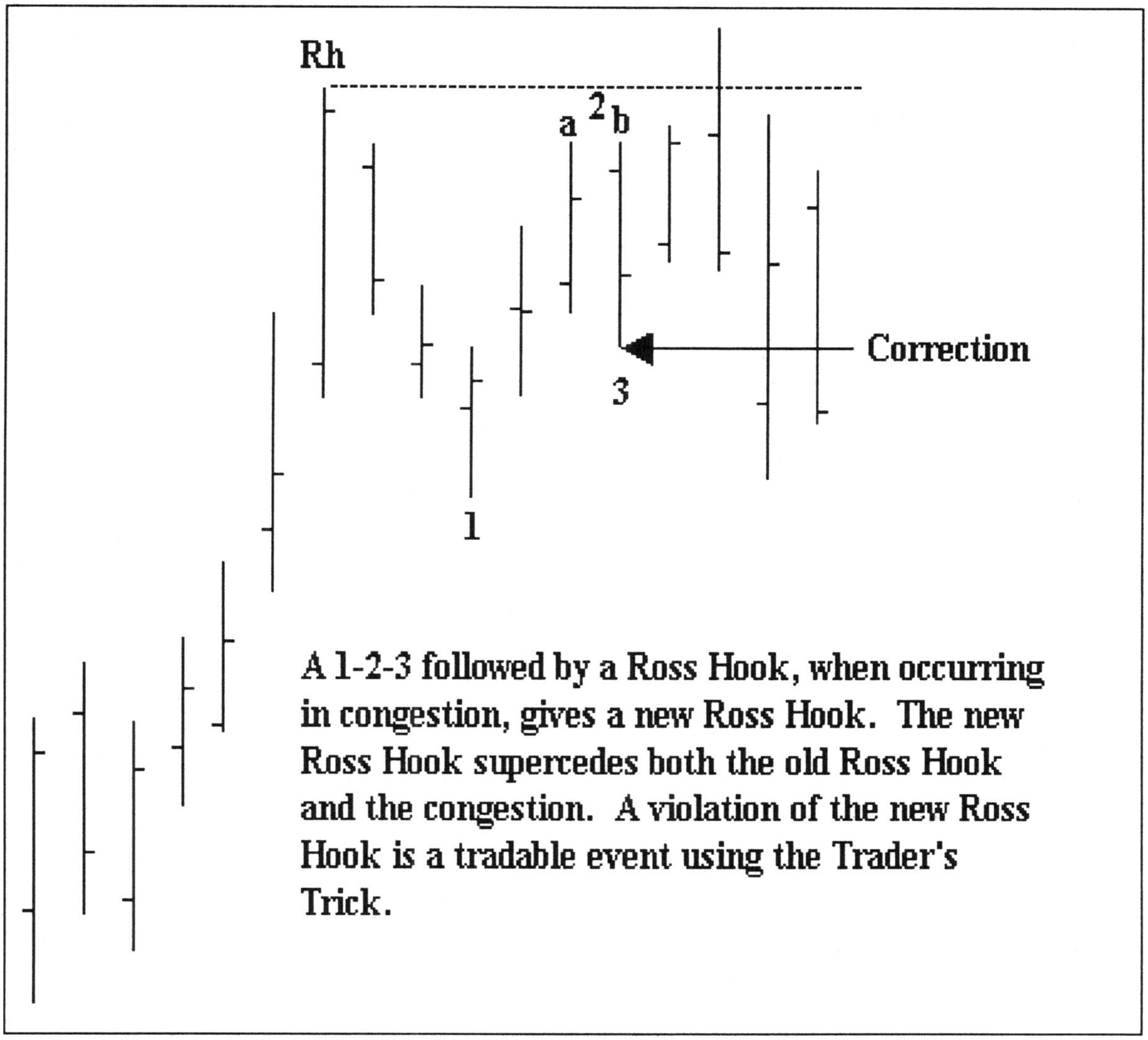

Note: A **1-2-3** FOLLOWED BY A BREAKOUT OF THE **#2** POINT, THAT SUBSEQUENTLY RESULTS IN A ROSS HOOK, SUPERCEDES ANY CONGESTION OR PREVIOUS ROSS HOOK. QUITE OFTEN, SUCH A SERIES OF PRICE BAR OCCURRENCES WILL BE THE WAY PRICES EXIT A CONGESTION AREA, I.E, A **1-2-3** FORMATION WITHIN A CONGESTION AREA, A BREAKOUT OF THE **#2** POINT, FOLLOWED BY A ROSS HOOK .

The price bar labeled "b" made a new local low. The take out by prices of the local double resistance, "a" and "b" is a significant event. "a" and "b", together, constitute the number two point of a 1-2-3 low occurring in congestion. The low of bar "b" is also a #3 point, and two bars later we get the highest high of the congestion, which is also an Rh.

The new Ross Hook represents an even more significant breakout point. Combined with the old Rh, there is significant resistance. Within a few ticks of each other, the two constitute a double top. If prices take them both out, we would normally expect a relatively longer term, strong move up.

We use the term "relatively" here, because the intensity and the duration of the move would be relative to the time frame in which the price bars were made. Obviously such a move on a one minute chart would hardly compare with an equivalent move on a daily chart. While we are looking at the chart, there is something else of importance to notice. Prices retreated from the resistance point, thereby creating the second Ross Hook. This represented a failure to break out. This failure is why Reverse Ross hooks are important. When prices retreat from a resistance point and move towards a RRh, it may indicate that the only reason the resistance point was challenged or even violated was because prices were "engineered" in that direction by some party or parties capable of moving prices for their own benefit. The anticipation is that prices next may move in the opposite direction toward a violation of the RRh.

Now, go through a brief review of the various congestions. All of the three following conditions that define congestion must occur without consistently making higher highs or lower lows.

Congestion by Opens/Closes: Four consecutive closes or opens within the range of a measuring bar. If opens are used, there can be no correcting bars ***before*** or ***coincident*** with the bar in which the open is used.

Congestion by Combination: A series of four consecutive dojis, or at least one doji and any three alternating bars. The doji is a wild card and can be used to alternate with any other bar. If there are three non-doji bars, one of them must alternate high-to-low with the other two non-doji bars.

Congestion by Alternation: A series of four consecutive alternating open high - close low, open low - close high bars in any sequence. This definition includes Congestion by High/Low pairs.

Chapter 6

IDENTIFYING THE TREND

We need a tool with which to clearly identify a trend. Such a tool allows us to lock onto definite rules. Either the market is trending or it is not, according to the rules. Let's take a look at the rules. Is there some sort of magic about them? Definitely not. Their value lies in the fact that they afford a concrete definition of what constitutes a trend. As long as we follow the rules, we can safely assume that prices are trending.

Do the rules work one-hundred percent of the time? No! No one has yet found a perfect way of trading. The rules work most of the time, and that is sufficient.

THE RULES

- **WITH THE EXCEPTION OF WHEN THEY MATERIALIZE AT THE FIRST CORRECTION SUBSEQUENT TO A BREAKOUT FROM A LEDGE OR A TRADING RANGE, ROSS HOOKS OCCUR ONLY IN TRENDING MARKETS.** There are plenty of "pointy" places on a bar chart, but not all of them are Ross Hooks. It is essential to trading them that we understand this.

- **THOSE HOOKS WHICH OCCUR IN TRENDING MARKETS WILL REMAIN AS VALID HOOKS. OFTEN, THEY MAY BE VIOLATED, I.E., TAKEN OUT MORE THAN ONCE.**

- At times prices are both in congestion and trending. Because of this enigma, there must be a rule: **IF PRICES ARE IN CONGESTION AND A TREND CAN BE DEFINED, THEN TREND ALWAYS SUPERCEDES CONGESTION. A TREND IS "DEFINED" UPON THE TAKING OUT OF THE NUMBER 2 POINT OF A 1-2-3 FORMATION, EVEN IF THAT FORMATION ARISES WITHIN AN AREA OF CONGESTION.**

- **IF PRICES HAVE BEEN TRENDING, AND THEY MOVE INTO CONGESTION, THEN PRICES REMAIN IN CONGESTION UNTIL A TREND CAN BE DEFINED.**

- PRICES HAVE TO MOVE IN A SINGLE DIRECTION, FOR INSTANCE *UP*, FROM A LOW TO A HIGH, OR *DOWN*, FROM A HIGH TO A LOW.

  ONCE PRICES ARE IN MOTION, THEY THEN MUST REACT, OR CORRECT SUFFICIENTLY TO GIVE US A CONNECTING POINT FOR A TREND LINE.

  THIS CONNECTING LINE WILL HAVE ITS INCEPTION AT THE ORIGINAL HIGH OR LOW, AND ITS TERMINUS WILL BE AT THE END OF THE REACTION HIGH OR LOW. THIS CONCEPT IS BEST SHOWN BY ILLUSTRATION.

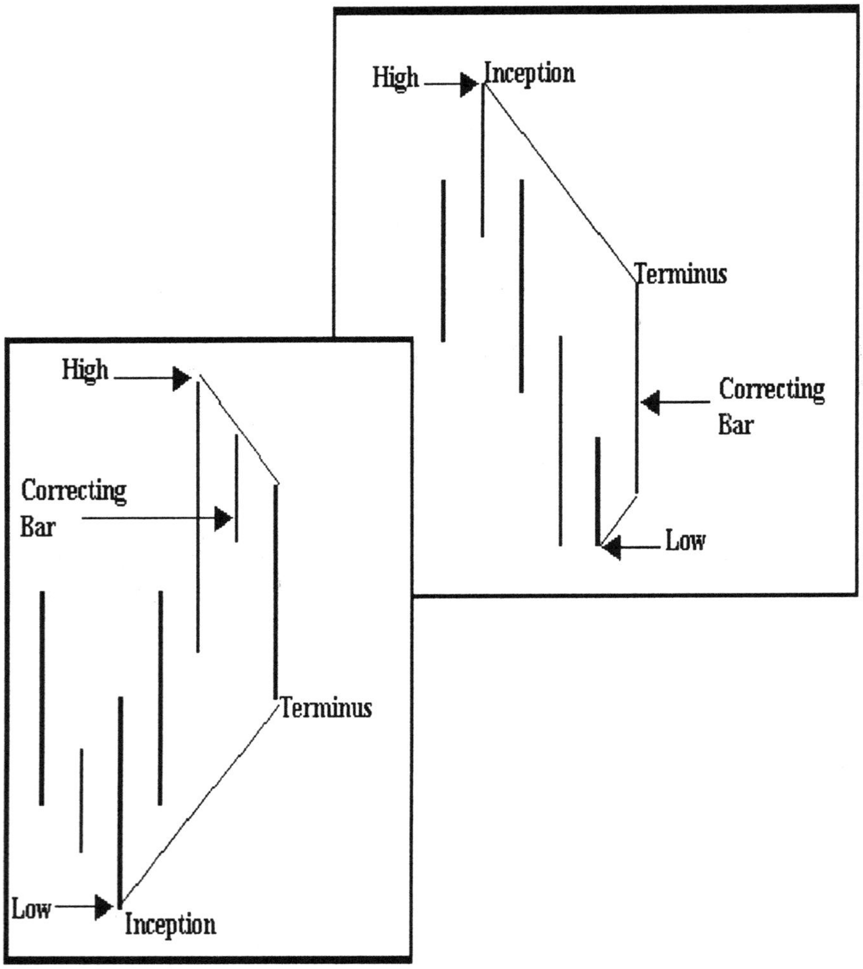

WHEN PRICES TAKE OUT THE EXTREME OF THE LOW BAR IN THE DIRECTION OF THE TREND LINE AS SHOWN BELOW, WE ASSUME A TREND HAS BEGUN.

As stated, this is not a perfect method for identifying a trend, but it is one we can use when we want to exclusively trade Ross Hooks.

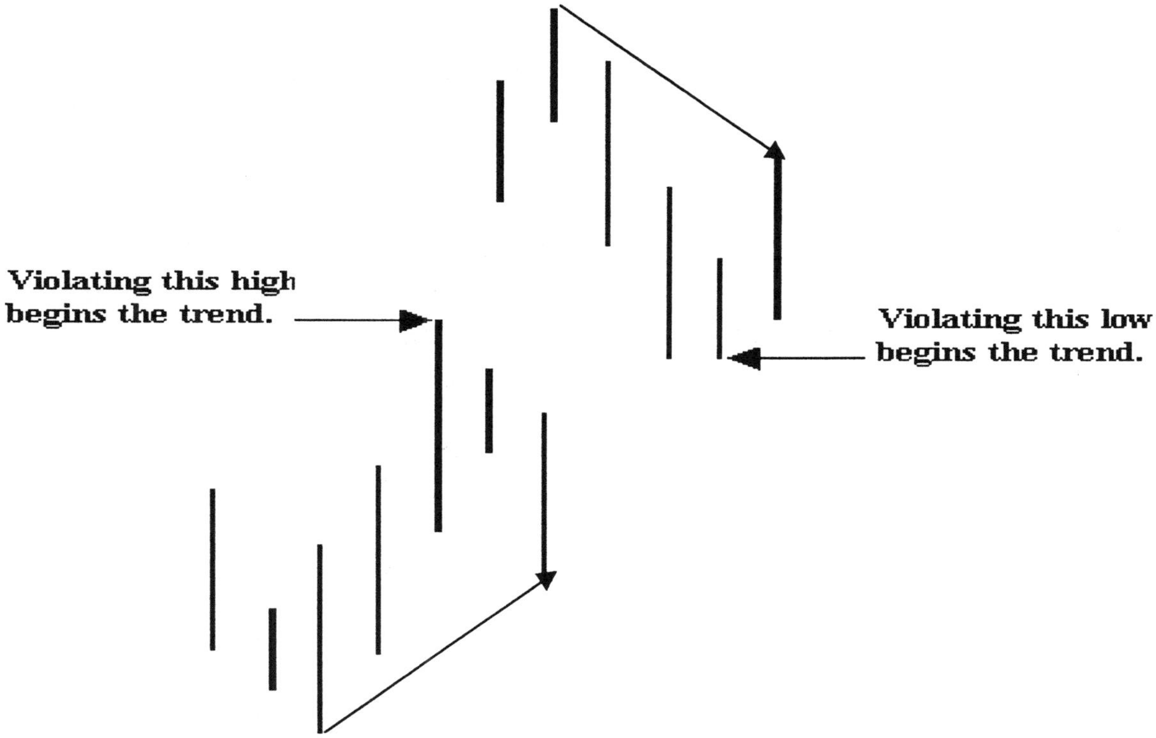

Over the years, this has proved to be an adequate and excellent way to determine and define trends.

Before you are tempted to race out and start trading this way, please realize there is more to this concept than what we've just seen. Money management and some filters need to be applied. For now, you simply must begin grasping the concept and the terminology that will be used.

Once the trend has begun via the rules, you can begin looking for and trading Ross Hooks.

The Hooks come only **after** the trend is defined and in effect.

AN IMPORTANT CONCEPT

Now, let's look at the difference between a Ross Hook and any other "pointy" places in a market. Remember, **ROSS HOOKS CAN OCCUR ONLY *AFTER* THE DEFINED TREND HAS BEGUN, OR *AFTER* A BREAKOUT FROM A LEDGE OR TRADING RANGE. PLEASE RECALL THAT A DEFINED TREND IS CREATED BY A VIOLATION OF THE #2 POINT OF A 1-2-3 FORMATION.**

The price chart chosen has some very difficult areas to define. Each letter labeling a particular price bar is placed there because, at the time that bar was made, it was a pointy place on the chart.

The lines drawn connect either a high or a low to a correction. The pointy places were either local highs or local lows at the time they were made. A local high or low is the high or low closest to the current price action.

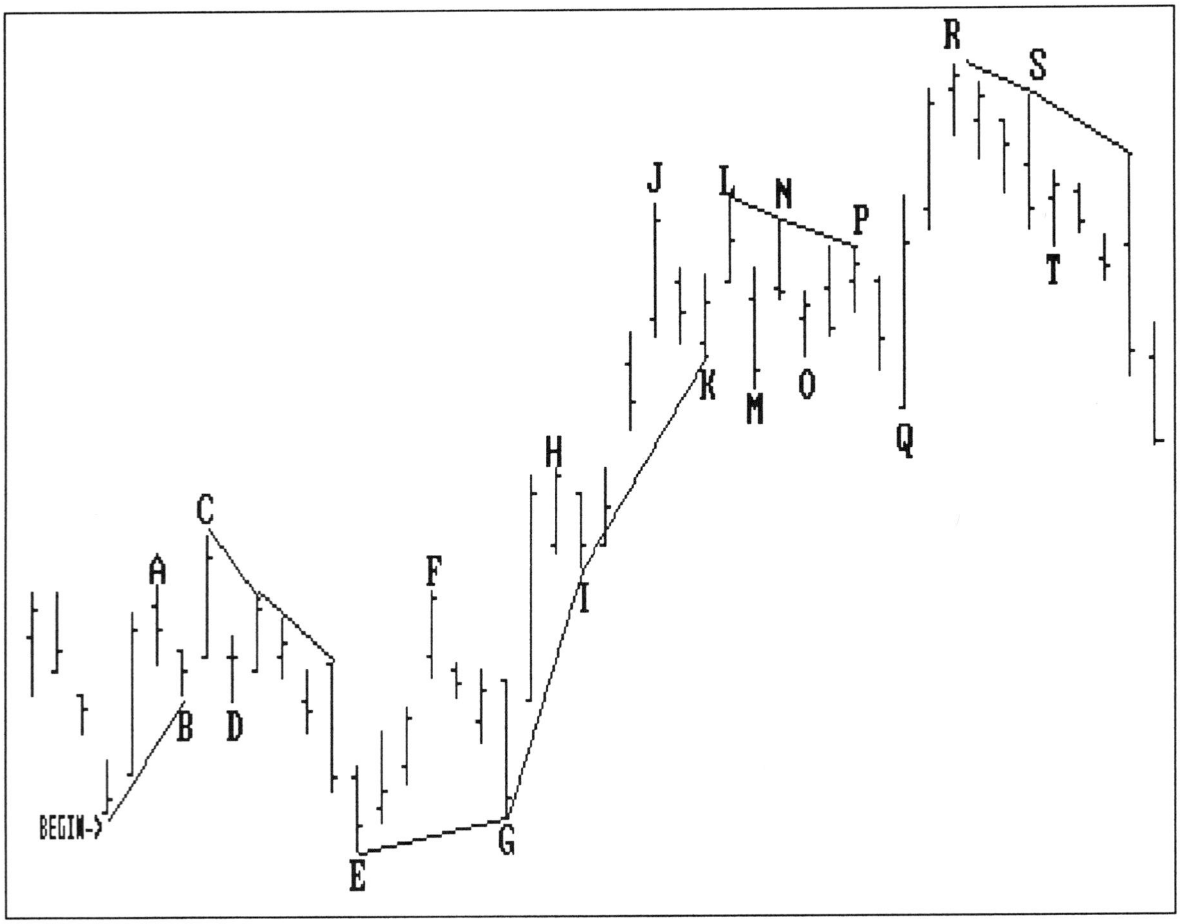

As an exercise in understanding the material presented so far, using the entire chart from the first bar where it says "BEGIN," to the last bar on the chart, mark those points at which you think a Ross Hook is in place. As you are doing so:

- Mark any 1-2-3's you encounter.
- Explain any Ledges or Trading Ranges you perceive.
- Give reasons for everything you see and note.

Feel free to use anything you learned in <u>ELECTRONIC TRADING 'TNT' I — GORILLA TRADING STUFF</u> in carrying out this assignment. There is more than one way to interpret this chart. In part, what is there is in the eye of the beholder. That is why we must come to realize that trading is an art form. There is nothing scientific or mathematical about it.

Our own answers begin with the next page. Good luck!!

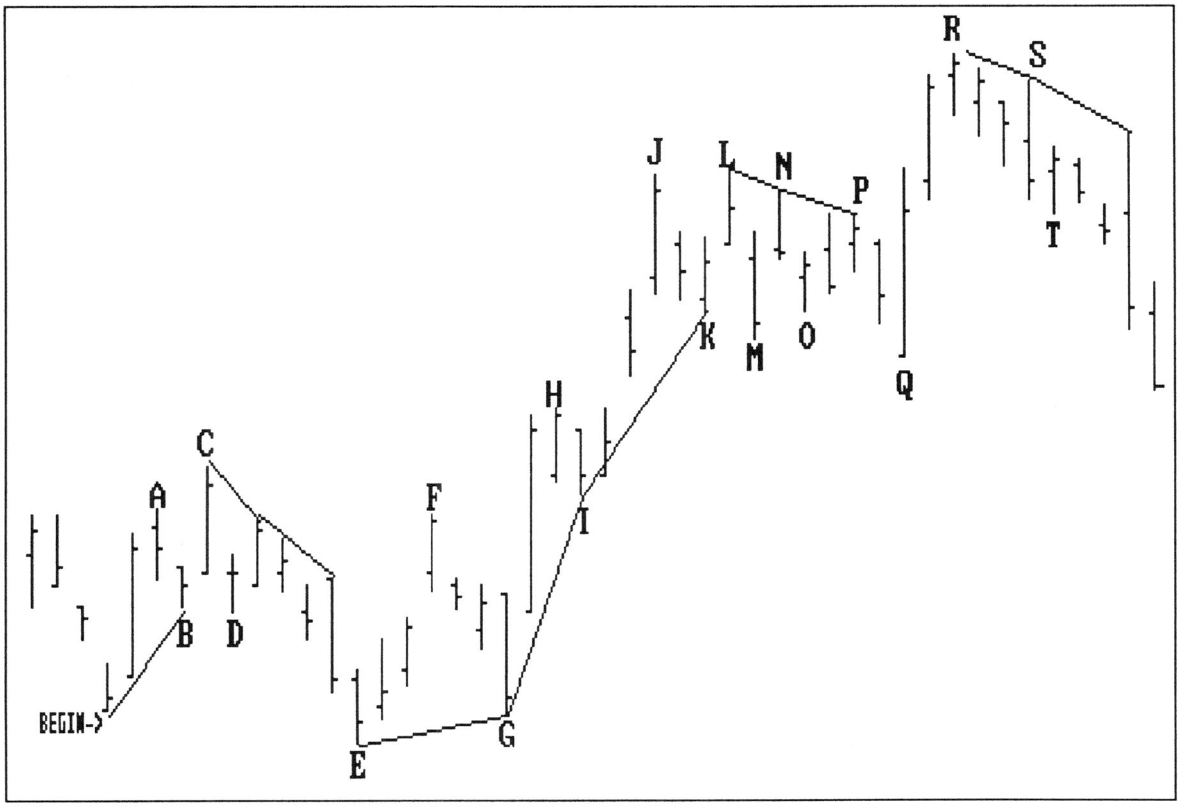

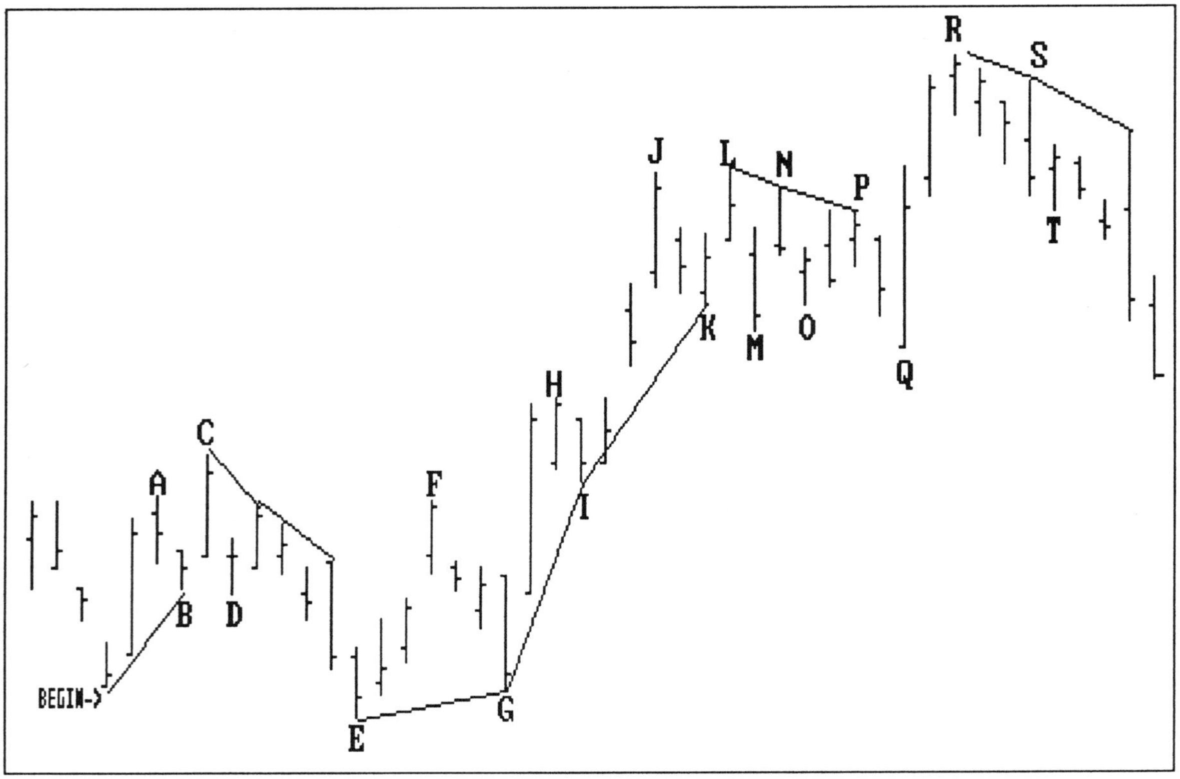

Our answers will incorporate the material shown at the beginning of this chapter, but will also incorporate concepts shown in ELECTRONIC TRADING 'TNT' I — GORILLA TRADING STUFF.

We begin two bars prior to **point "A,"** which was a pointy place on the chart. It was not a Ross Hook. Why? Because as far back as we can see, until point "A" is violated by price action, there is no trend.

Point "B" constitutes the low, a #3 of a correction from a 1-2-3 low formation (i.e., BEGIN TO "A," AND THEN TO "B"). Since there is also no visible downtrend in effect, point "B" cannot be considered to be a Ross Hook to the downside. As it turns out, "B" is nothing more than a correction.

Point "C" is a Ross Hook. Why? By definition of the material presented in the first pages of this chapter, "C" is the result of the trend that had begun by virtue of the move up — the correction bar and the violation of point "A," the # 2 point of a 1-2-3. Point "C" is also a Ross Hook because it exists as the result of the first correction after the breakout of a 1-2-3 formation. From the inception low (BEGIN) to point "A" and then over to point "B" we have a 1-2-3 formation. You may have wanted to be a buyer using the Trader's Trick entry to gain early entry, if prices took out the high of point D. Prices did break the point D high but look again. Isn't that congestion by our previous definitions? If you have doubt about a trade do not take it.

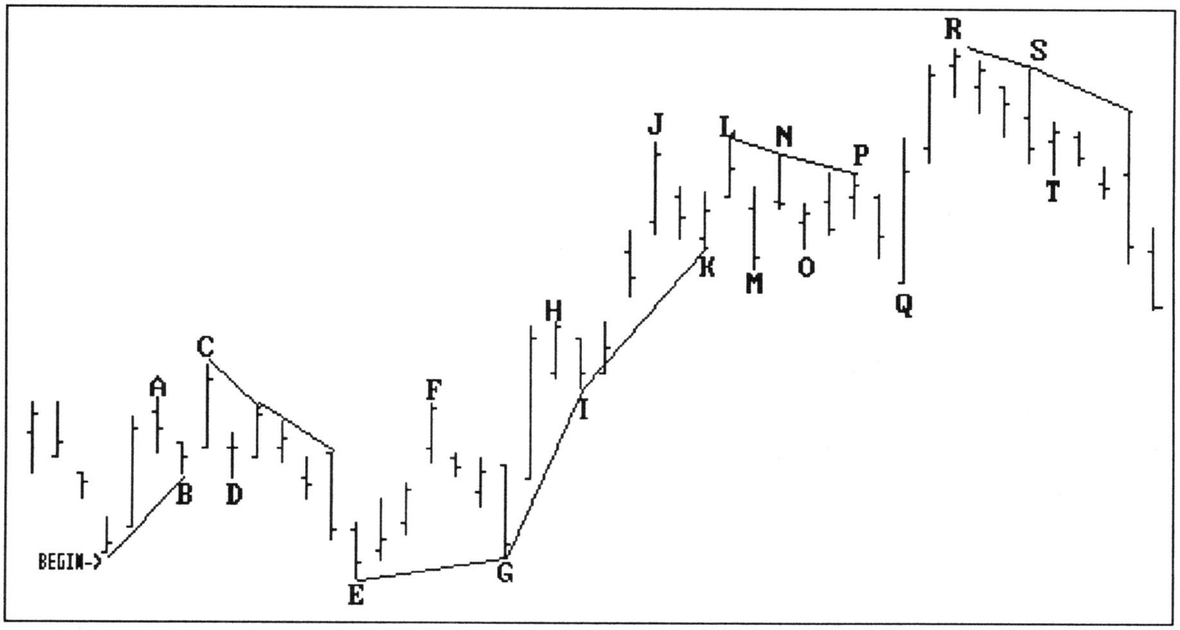

Point "D" ***is*** a Reverse Ross Hook. When bar "C" violated point "A" a trend was defined, therefore "D" became a Reverse Ross Hook. At the same time "C" became a #1 point of a 1-2-3 high that went from "C" to "D" to the bar following "D."

Point "D" has further importance, because it, together with point "B," constitute a double "support" point. If Point "D" is violated, it would be an event worth notice.

There is another choice for point "D." It is possible to see it as not being a Reverse Ross Hook. Why? Because point "D" also fits the scenario for having occurred in congestion. It is the fourth consecutive bar having either an open or a close within the range of a measuring bar, "A." We feel the better choice is the that it was a Reverse Ross Hook because we were able to define a trend. And when you have both trend and congestion, trend supercedes congestion. Another rule is: **WHEN YOU ARE NOT SURE, STAND ASIDE.**

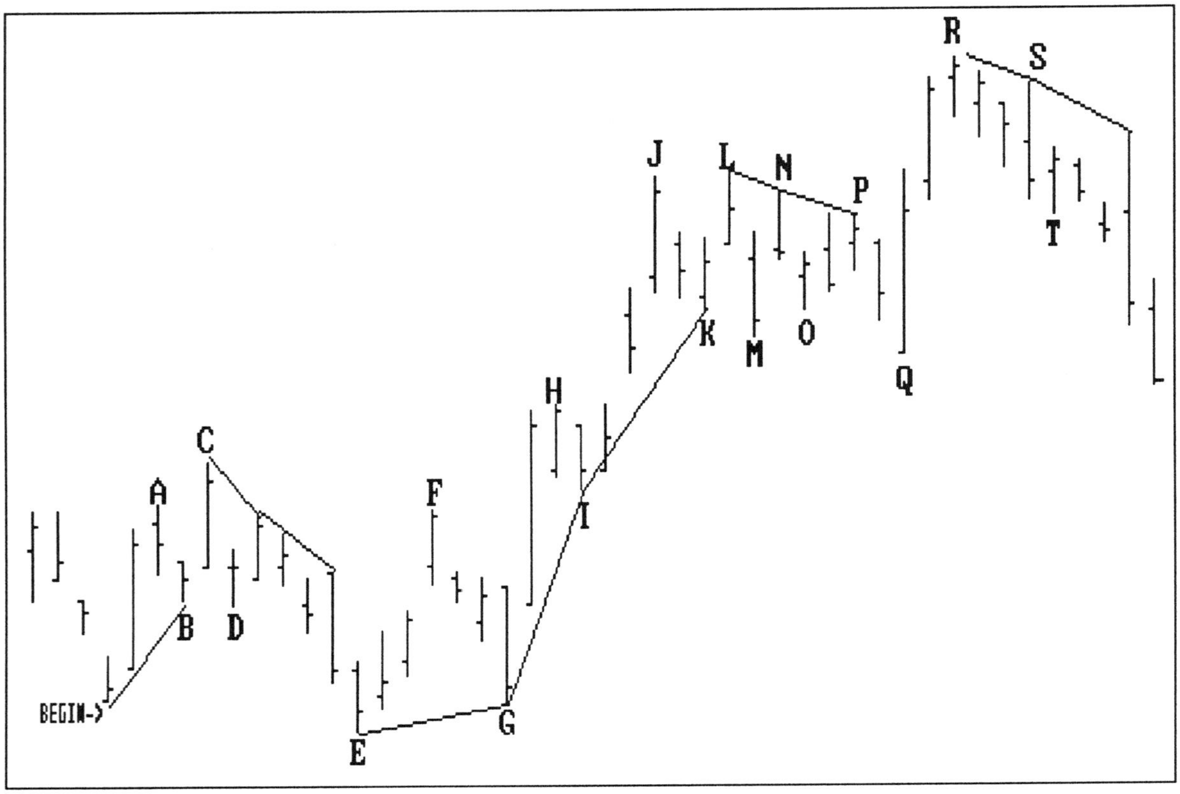

Point "E" is a Ross Hook. Why? It is made in a defined trend to the downside. Keep in mind that Rh's are also potential #1 points. Notice that from "C" to the bar following "D," we have a 1-2-3 high. When "D" is violated, we have a defined trend to the downside. If "E" is taken out, we would want to be a seller on any available Trader's Trick entry subsequent to "E."

Point "F" is not a Ross Hook. Why? Because until prices violate it, there is no uptrend in effect. In that respect, "F" is like "A."

Point "G" is not a Ross Hook. Why? Because it does not occur in a trend. If point "G" is taken out it could, if prices go far enough, constitute a breakout of a Trading Range whose low is "E." A Ross Hook would come into effect on the first correction subsequent to such a breakout. Until then, it is simply the flip-side of points "A" and "F." In that sense, "G" is the equivalent of "B."

However, point “G” is important because it results in a connecting point for the trend line from “E”.

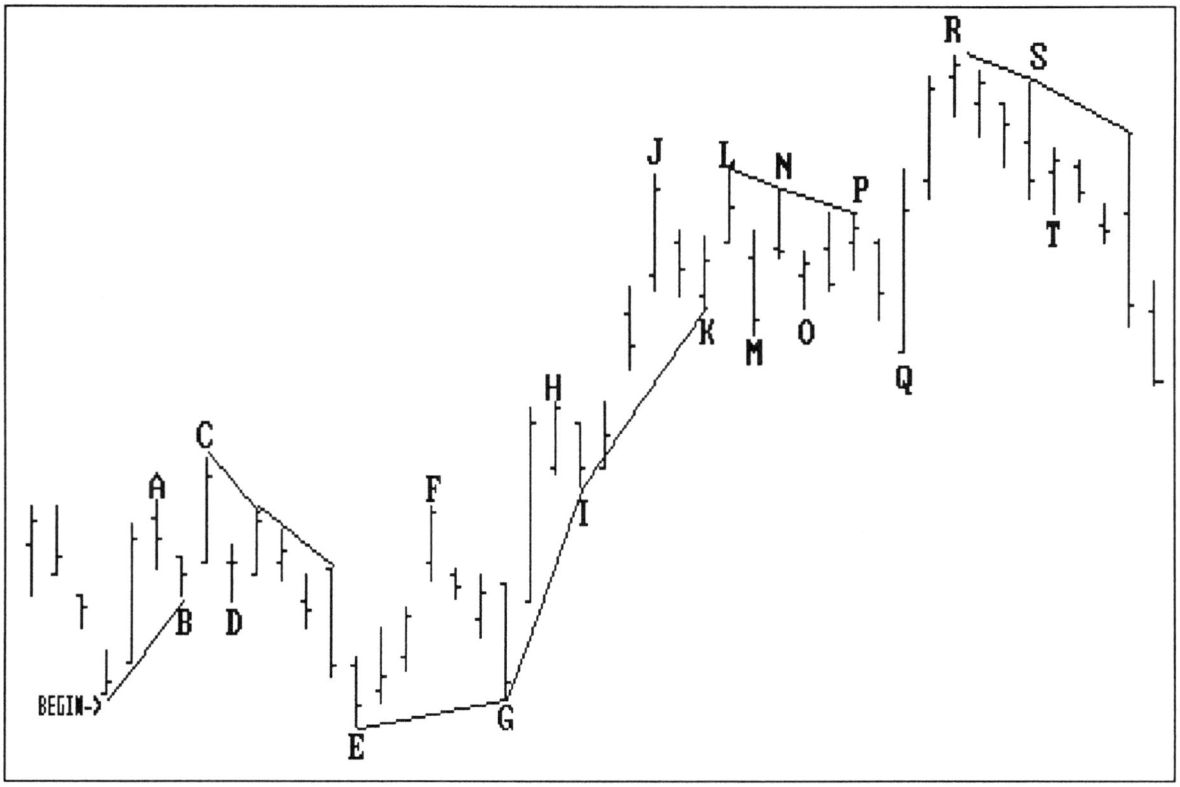

Point “H” is a Ross Hook. Why? It occurs in a defined trend. The trend came into effect when the bar preceding bar “H” violated the high at point “F. It is also the result of the first correction subsequent to the breakout of a Trading Range whose high was “C.”

Please note that as prices move to “H,” the Hook at point C is violated. Once a Hook is in place, it remains a Hook. We want to be in the market before any breakout of “H.” A violation of “H” will give us an ***established*** trend.

Point “I” is a Reverse Ross Hook. Why? Because it is made in a trending market, in this case an uptrend. The trend came into effect when the bar preceding bar “H” violated the high at point “F”. “I” gives us a connecting point for the trend line from “G.”

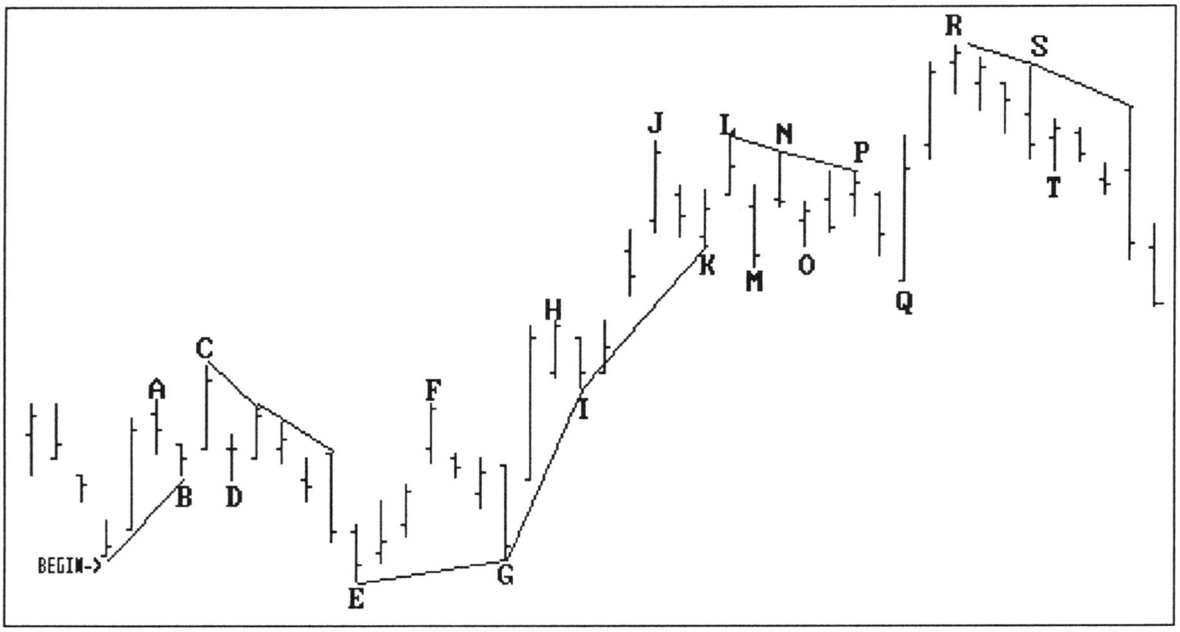

Point "J" is a Ross Hook. Why? It occurs in an established uptrend. The established trend was the result of a violation of "H."

Point "K" is a Reverse Ross Hook. Why? It is made in an established trend. It gives us a connecting point on the trend line from point "I."

Point "L" is a Ross Hook. Why? Because it occurs in an established uptrend.

Point "M" is not a Ross Hook. Why? Because it is not made in a trend. It is made in congestion.

Point "N" is not a Ross Hook. Why? Because it is the sixth bar of a congestion area. However, point "N" gives us a connecting point from point "L."

Point "O" is not a Ross Hook. Why? Because it is the seventh bar of a congestion area.

Point "P" is not a Ross Hook. Why? Because it is the ninth bar of a congestion area. However, point "P" gives us a connection from "N".

Point "Q" is a Ross Hook. Why? Because it is made in a defined downtrend. L-M-N constitute a 1-2-3 high. "Q" violates the number 2 point at "M." Q defines a trend. A violation of "Q" establishes the trend.

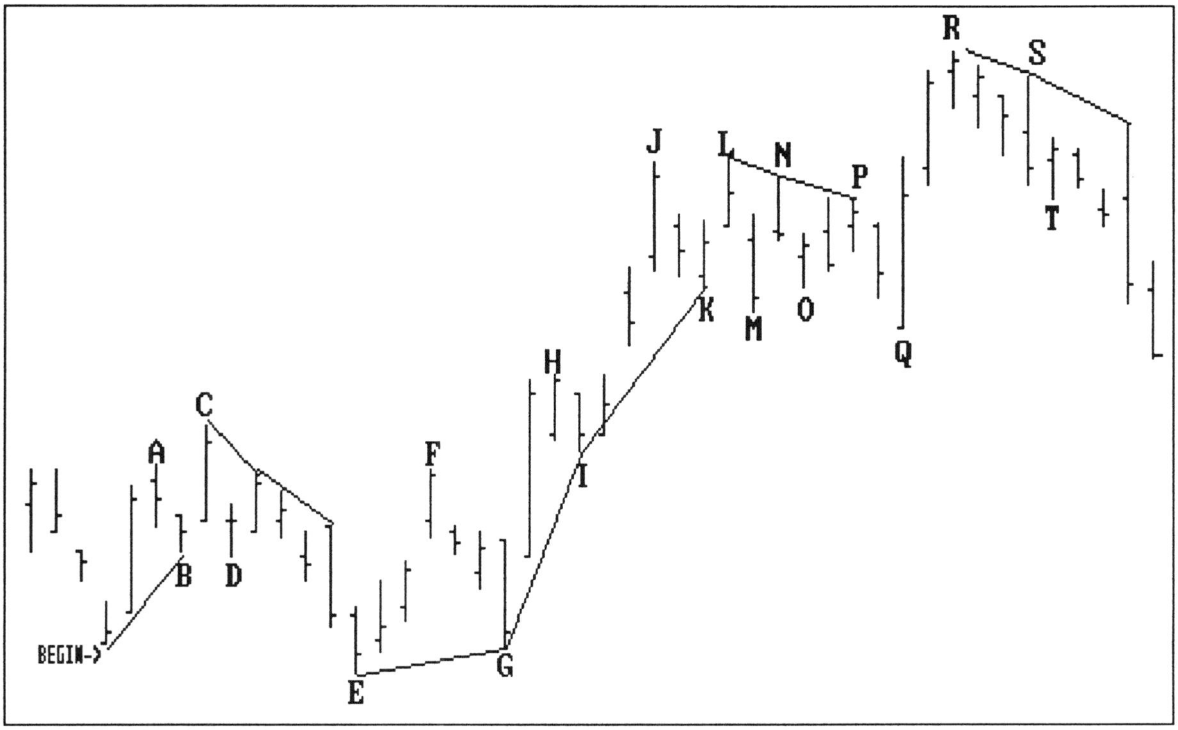

Point "R" is a Ross Hook. Why? Because it is created by the first reaction to a breakout from a Ledge. The Ledge comprises bars "K"-"Q."

Point "S" made a higher high, taking out the high of the previous day. That gives us a connecting point from "R," and, in actuality, became a Trader's Trick Entry.

Point "T," by definition in this chapter, is a Ross Hook. Why? Because it is made in a defined downtrend. Another way to see it is that from "R" to the low of "S" back to the high of "S" constitutes a 1-2-3 high. The bar subsequent to "T" fails to make an equal or lower low than "T," thereby creating the Rh. **IN A DEFINED TREND, ANY TIME A NEW LOW (HIGH) IS MADE AND THE FOLLOWING BAR FAILS TO MAKE A NEW LOW (HIGH), YOU HAVE A ROSS HOOK.**

Chapter 7

TREND REVERSALS

The Reverse Ross Hook always has the potential of becoming the beginning of a true trend reversal. A Reverse Ross Hook is always the number 2 point of what *may* become a new 1-2-3 formation in the direction opposite to the most recent trend.

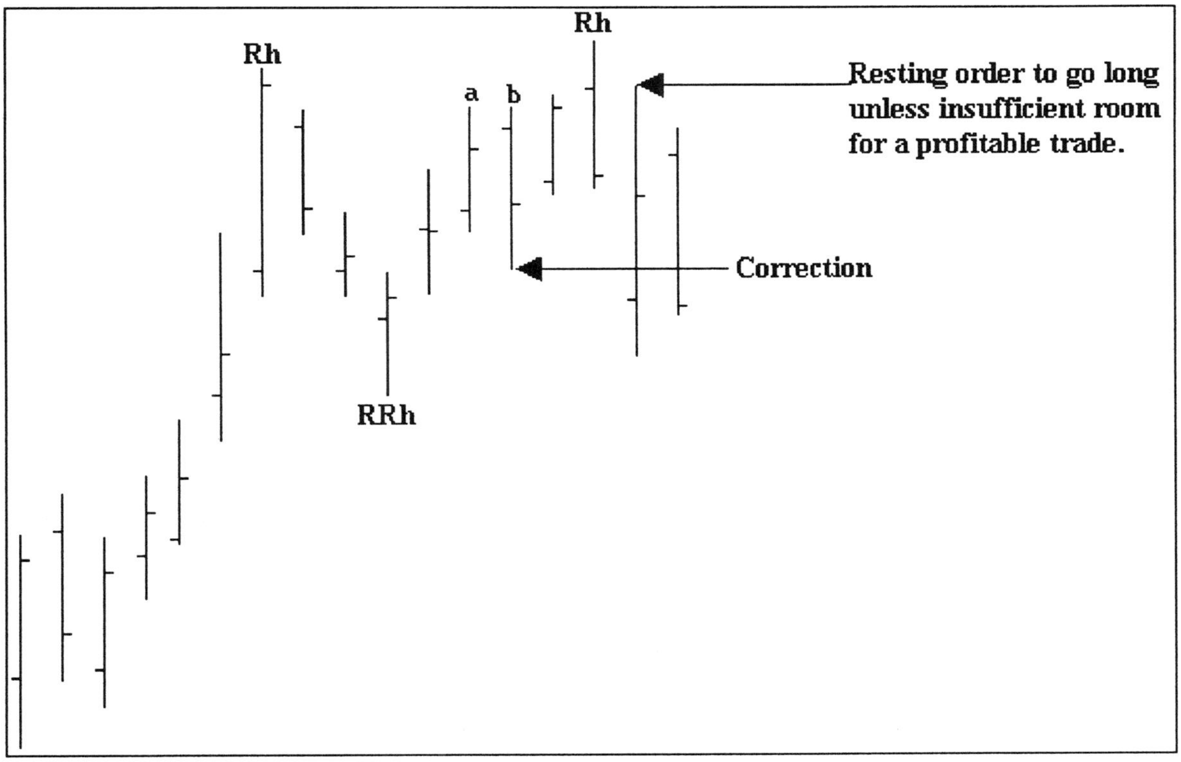

On the chart above, a Reverse Ross Hook (RRh) is labeled on the third bar after the first Rh bar on the left side of the chart.

Moving from left to right, the Rh became a number 1 point when prices failed to move higher. The RRh became a number 2 point when prices on the bar following the RRh failed to make both lower low and a lower high.

The subsequent bar to the RRh bar was a fourth bar having its close within the range of a measuring bar, in this case the Rh bar.

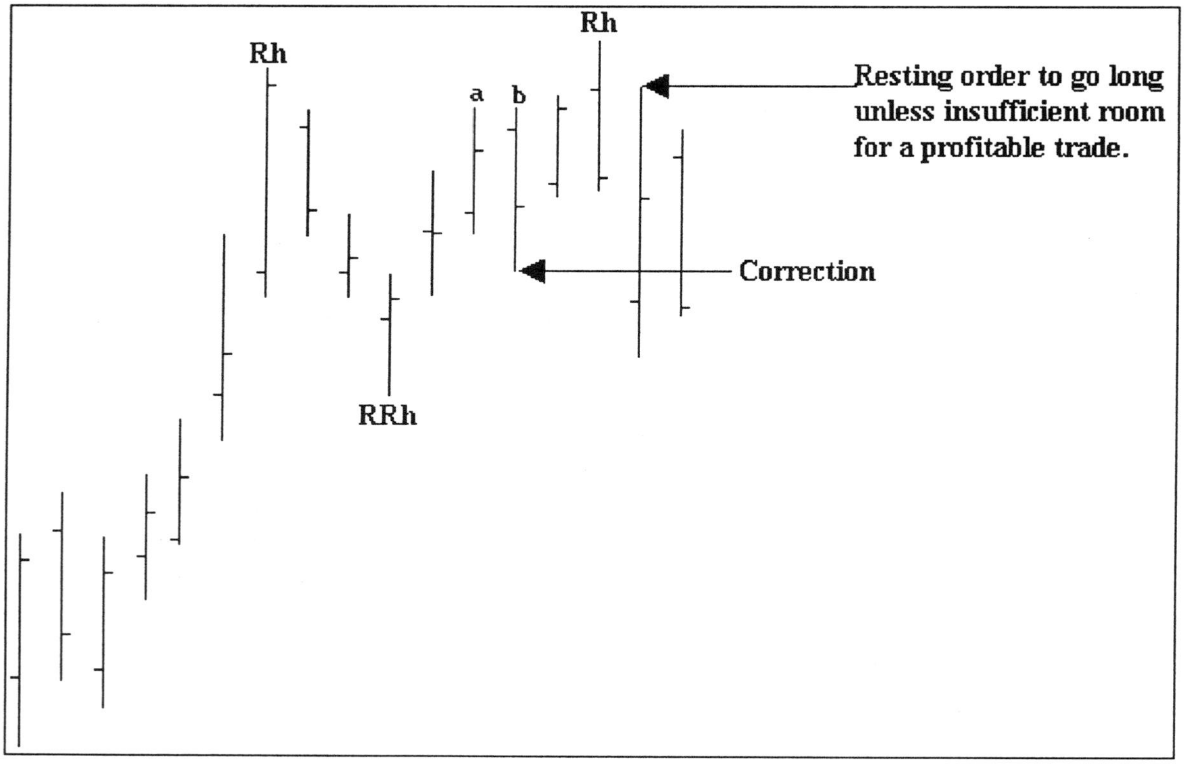

The bar that ended up being the point of the first Rh also qualified to become the beginning of congestion, as a measuring bar, because the four bars following it have closes within its price range. The bar subsequent to the RRh qualifies as having established that congestion because it ***is*** the fourth bar to have its close within the price range of a measuring bar. Therefore, at the time the price bar following the RRh completed, prices were by, definition, in congestion.

RRh's are important in spotting trend reversals. ***Some*** RRh's occur in the correction that follows a market top. When that happens, we have the following scenario having taken place:

Demand has been sufficient to take prices to new highs. Then profit takers sell into the strength of the rally to the top, pushing prices back down to what is to become the point of the RRh.

Then the remaining bulls step in again to push prices up to the next, but not necessarily higher, high. Usually volume is thin compared

with the previous up legs. Thin volume as prices move to new highs is a clue to what is happening and may be used as a filter.
Finally, one last sell-off follows on heavy volume, pushing prices down through the RRh.

It is when you see prices approach a previously made Rh on lower than previous volume, and then fail to take it out, that you have one signal that prices may be ready to reverse. Such an event ***is*** a first clue as to what the market may be saying.

Then, when prices drop down and take out the bar labeled RRh, we have a second signal to indicate a trend reversal is in the making. At this point, we do not blindly take a breakout of that RRh. There must be a filtering process. The filtering process will give us the third signal that a trend reversal is taking place. We will look a step at a time at a chart that demonstrates this concept, but first we want you to learn a few facts about offset moving averages.

DISPLACED MOVING AVERAGE OF THE CLOSE (DMAC)

A moving average is like any other indicator, lagging, because it is always computed on history. Unfortunately, all of the things that we can compute in trading are based upon what has already happened. No one has ever been able to figure out what tomorrow's numbers will be other than by inconsistent approximation and just plain guessing. Yet it is possible for us to be forward-looking in our thinking. That is where the displaced moving average comes into play. Although it is still a lagging indicator, it is "forward-looking." Keep reading, you will see what we are talking about.

For the sake of ease, we will compute a three-day moving average of the close and displace it three days in time (3x3 DMAC). Here is how we compute it, and it is quite simple:

Close Day 1 + Close Day 2 + Close Day 3 = Total of three closes.

Total of three closes divided by 3 = 3 MAC.

3 MAC is then moved to Day 6 to become a 3x3 DMAC

Note the table on the following page:

Day 1 Close	50	3 MAC	0	3X3 DMAC	0
Day 2 Close	49	3 MAC	0	3X3 DMAC	0
Day 3 Close	48	3 MAC	49	3X3 DMAC	0
Day 4 Close	47	3 MAC	48	3X3 DMAC	0
Day 5 Close	46	3 MAC	47	3X3 DMAC	0
Day 6 Close	45	3 MAC	46	3X3 DMAC	49

What we've done is to take the 3 MAC from Day 3 and place it as the 3x3 DMAC for Day 6.

A displaced moving average has a number of benefits over that of a non-displaced moving average. The main benefit is that it does a better job of ***visual*** containment. Buy and sell signals can be taken from price penetration, but only with great caution. Penetration should be treated as you would a gap, it is an alert. **A double penetration of the moving average by the price is an especially strong signal of a failure of the trend to continue.** Finally, a displaced moving average keeps us much closer to the price action than a non-displaced moving average, because it is projected forward in time. You have a rough idea of the extreme at which prices will be at the next price bar. This is true only in the absence of any unusual price action.

The 3 bar moving average displaced by 3 bars can be used when a market is moving steeply. If the closing price of a price bar penetrates the moving average, it may be a signal of imminent change. If the closing price then turns around and re-penetrates in the opposite direction, then an extra strong signal is given to trade in the direction of the close. If the market is moving less steeply, we want to lengthen either the number of bars used, or the amount of the displacement. Please, do not think for a moment that there is anything magic about a 3 x 3 DMAC. It is primarily a visual aid which can be used in any time frame.

FILTERING A TRADE WITH A 3 X 3 DMAC

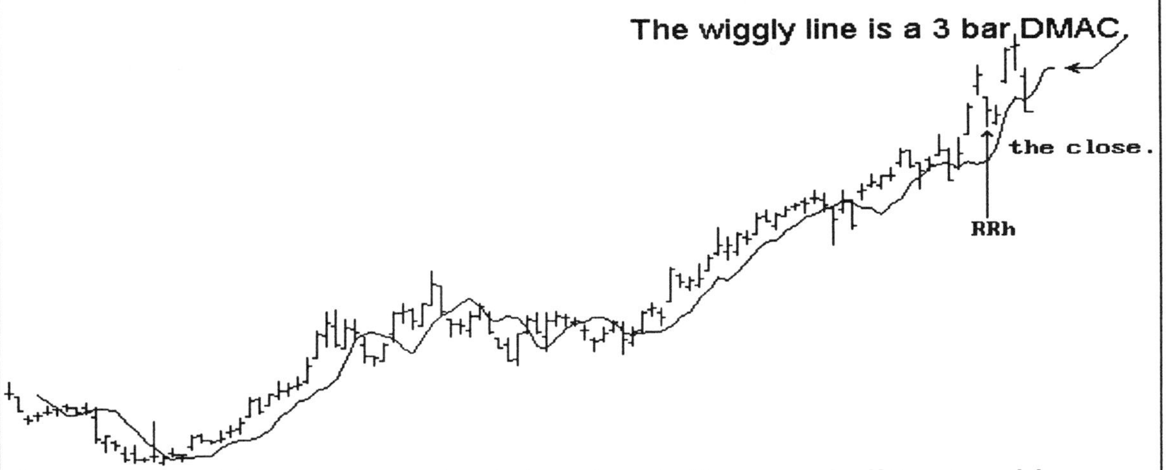

The 3 x 3 DMAC will be our third signal for telling us whether or not to trade a violation of the RRh. Watch it closely!

On the graph above, we do not want to trade a violation of the RRh because the 3 x 3 DMAC has not yet turned over. We would want to see it turn over as shown in the next chart, before we would consider entry.

If the 3 x 3 DMAC turns over before the RRh is taken out, you would take the trade. That gives us two parameters for taking a RRh, lower volume during the making of the point of the RRh, and a turning over of the 3 x 3 DMAC.

It can be argued that looking ahead, we can see that a violation of the RRh would cause the 3 x 3 DMAC to turn over. This is true, and is a more refined, advanced way to trade, one that has made considerable money. However, in any instance where we are trading from a chart, if a turnover by the 3 x 3 DMAC is anticipated, we must be prepared to daytrade any violation of the RRh, as the trade may be only short lived. In other words, if we are trying to trade the anticipation as a position trader using a daily chart, we must be prepared to take a short term scalp by having a short term objective stop. Violations of RRh's are often false. We have to keep that firmly in mind when we trade them. RRh's are not nearly as high percentage trades as are Rh's preceded by 1-2-3's and capable of entry via the Trader's Trick. We also need to realize that because we often do not have time or space to trade RRh's using the Trader's Trick, we can use the 3 x 3 DMAC as our signal to get in early ahead of an RRh being violated.

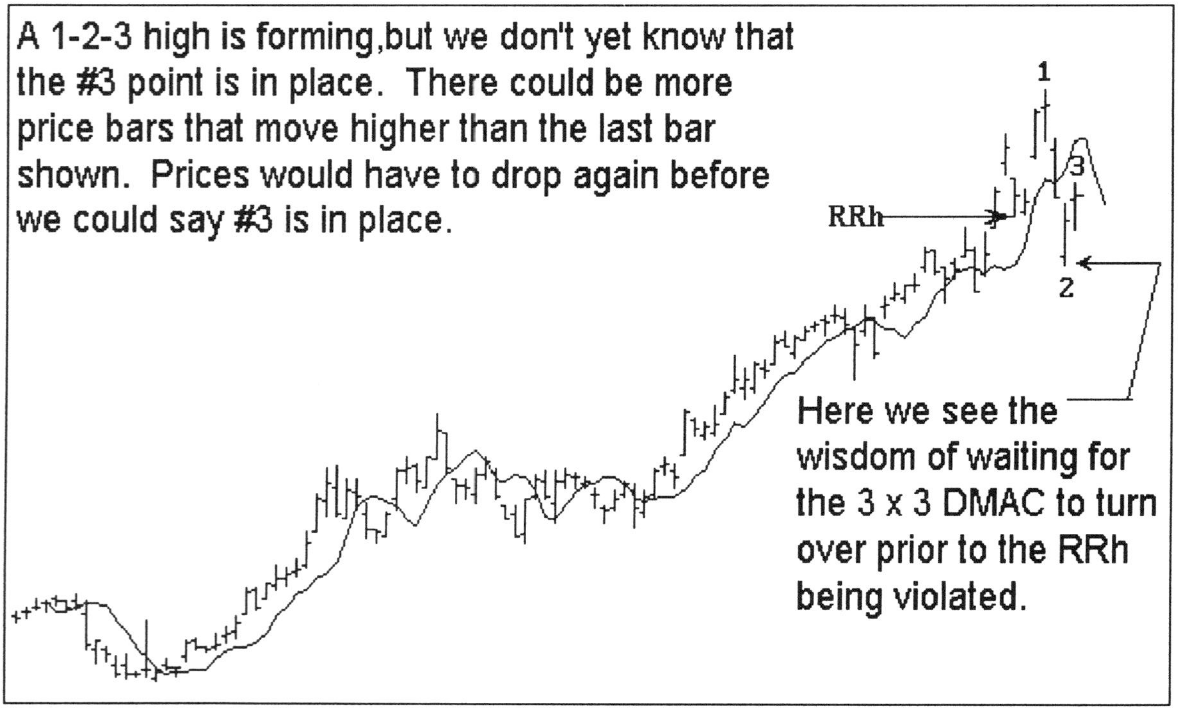

If we had taken a violation of the RRh without the 3 x 3 DMAC having turned over, our entry would have almost immediately gone against us.

Care must be taken as prices approach a RRh. Hold back any trade entries until the 3 x3 DMAC turns over, and prices show a more definite commitment as to direction. We want to be sure as to whether or not prices may be moving into a Trading Range after the violent blow-off at the top.

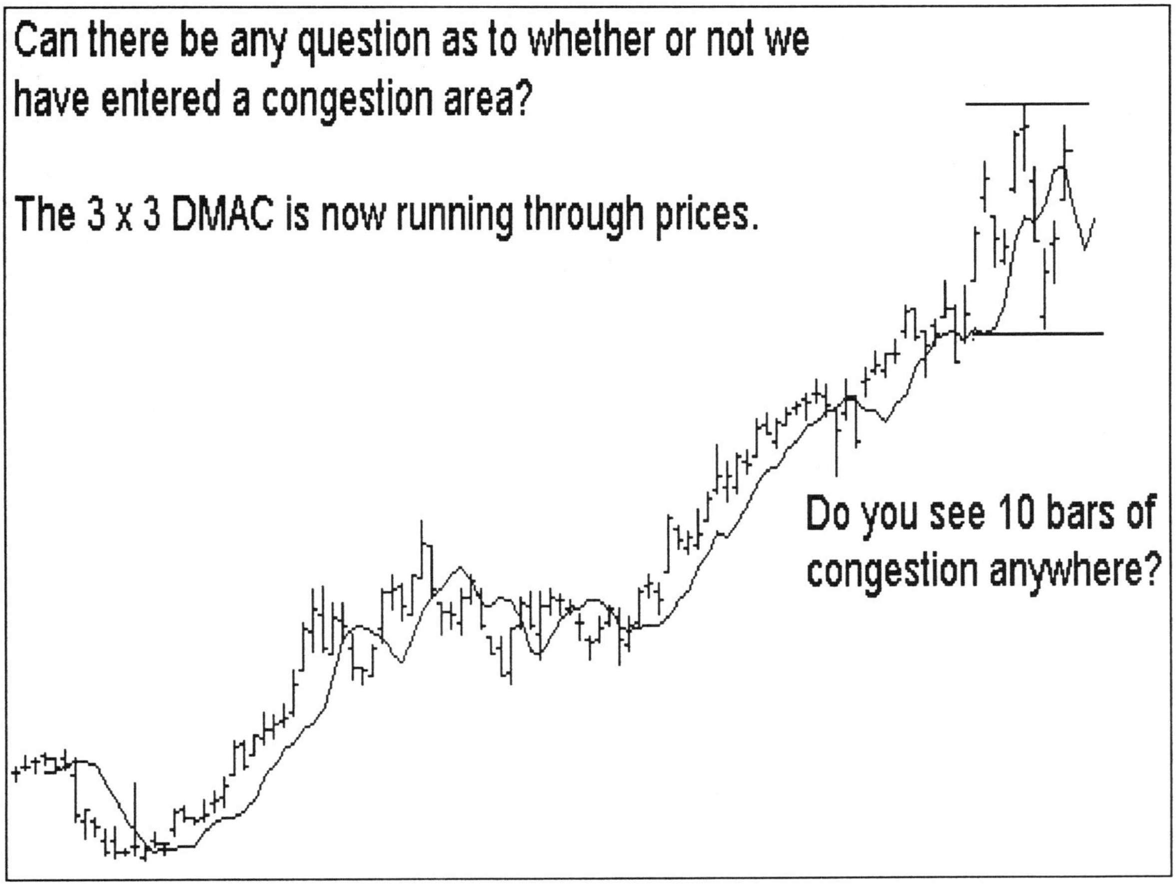

In fact, by our definition of congestion and the flip-flopping of prices, we are now seeing congestion on the chart. If we include the last price bar and count backward nine additional bars, we can see that we have had sets of reversing bars, and two bars which are very close to being defined as doji bars.

Prices next form a double resistance, minor top. If prices go no higher, and in fact move lower, the number 3 point of a 1-2-3 high will be in place.

A double resistance point provides a relatively low risk entry point, if you want to trade within the congestion. Trading within congestion is a topic that goes beyond the scope of this manual but is covered in ELECTRONIC TRADING 'TNT' IV — TIPS-TRICKS AND OTHER TRADING STUFF. Here we are covering only the trading of trends and trend reversals.

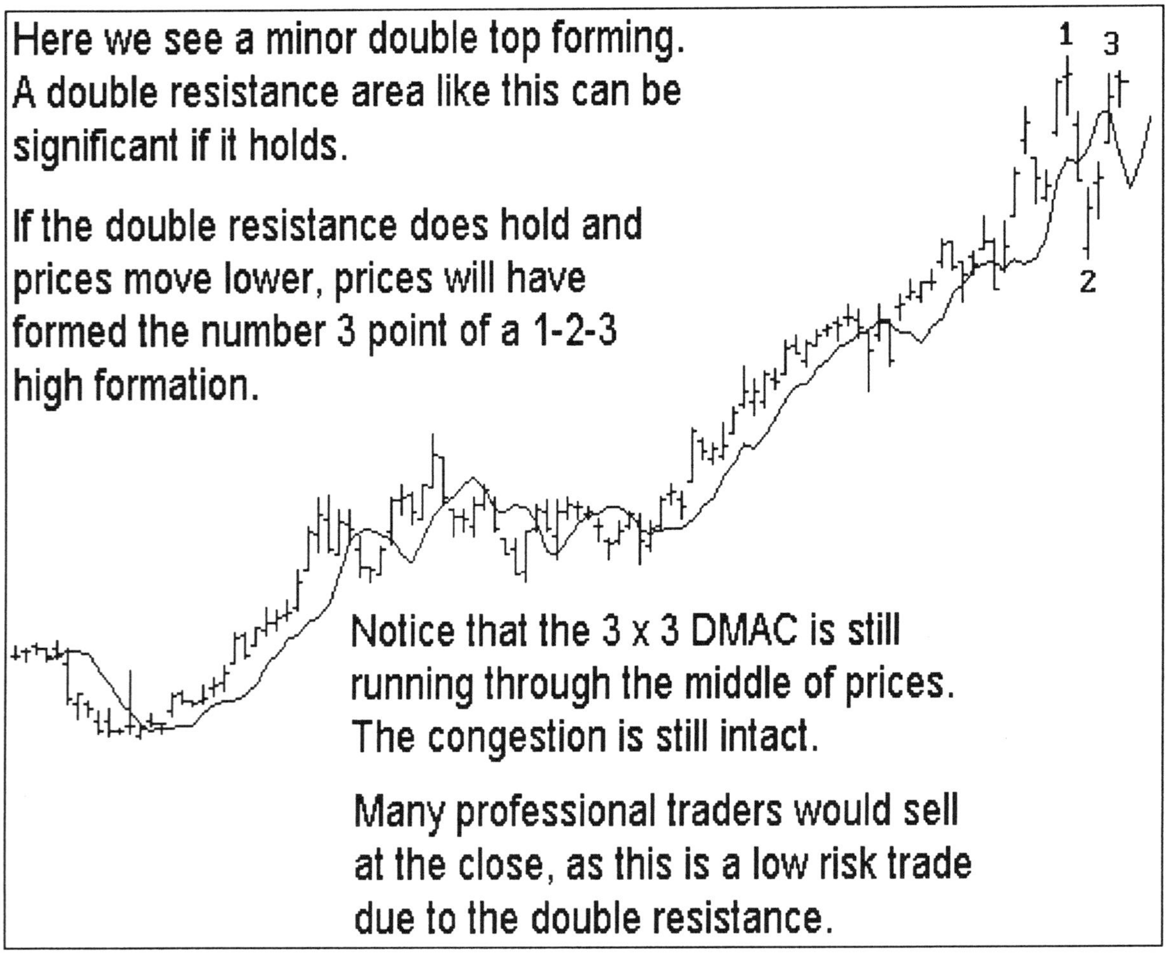

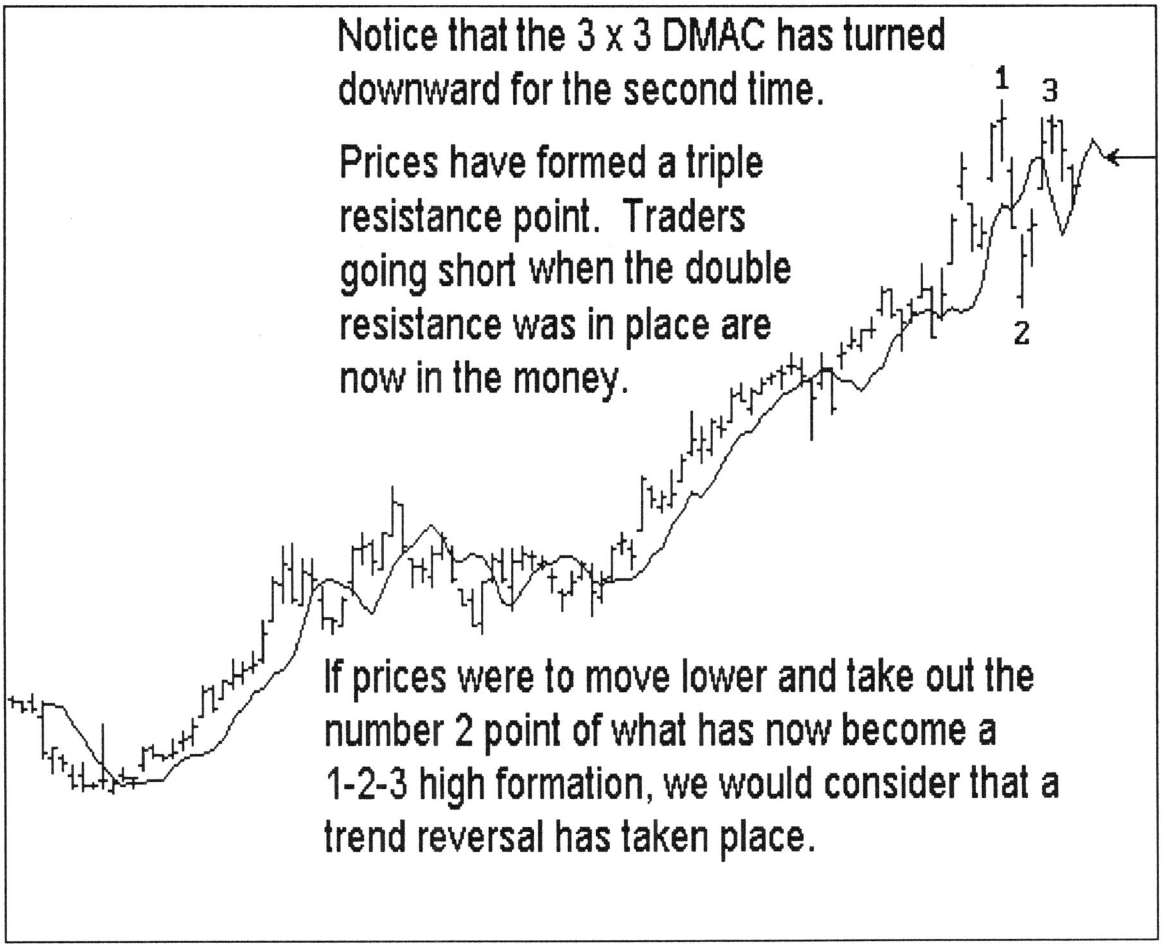

With the 3 x 3 DMAC having now turned over twice, we have an excellent chance of a winning trade if we enter ahead of a violation of the # 2 point, a RRh. In fact, entry based on a violation of the low of the last bar on the chart has the same probability of producing a winning trader as if we were able to enter the market based on a Trader's Trick entry, as long as there is enough room between the entry point and the number 2 point to allow us to cover costs and take a small profit.

Do keep in mind that, until the # 2 point is taken out, we will not, by definition, have a defined trend.

It is the combination of three things that determine that a trend reversal has indeed taken place. Let's review them here, noting that numbers 2 and 3, as well as 2 and 4, may reverse the order of their occurrence:

1. A failure to take out a Ross Hook on lower volume at the end of a trend, signifying weakness in the market.

2. A move in prices strong enough to violate the point of an RRh.

3. The 3 x 3 DMAC turning down ahead of the violation of an RRh which occurs when prices fail to move to a new high.

4. The 3 x 3 DMAC turning down ahead of the violation of the #2 point of a new 1-2-3 high when prices have moved to a new high as part of a congestion area following an Rh, as in the example just shown. Later on, in the chapter on plain vanilla trading, we'll see how you can know, without any indicators, whether or not to take an RRh trade.

We've shown the beginning of a trend reversal at a market top. If you want to see what such a reversal looks like at a market bottom, simply turn the page upside down and hold it up to a mirror. This works really well, try it.

When there is a test of an extreme followed by a failure, be aware that you may be looking at a trend reversal. However, be cautious. Before the trend reversal goes into full force, there may be a trading range or congestion area. Congestions at a trend reversal are far more common then total and absolute reversals.

Such a trading range can be indicative of accumulation or distribution. We cannot be sure which. We want to be sure to wait for definite commitment by the price action before beginning to look for Ross Hooks. Such commitment can be seen in the form of a 1-2-3 breakout, followed by the forming of a Ross Hook.

Yes, we will miss a part of the move, but we will, if we follow what has been shown, trade most of the time in a trending market. Since most of the money to be made by us, the outsiders, occurs when prices are trending, this represents a conservative and effective way to trade.

We've now seen something of trends, trend reversals, and Reverse Ross Hooks.

We've seen that the RRh in itself is one signal that helps us to suspect a trend reversal may be imminent. We regard every correction in a trend as suspicious.

We've also seen that a filtering process is necessary in combination with the RRh for determining the plausibility of entering a trade based solely on the fact of the RRh being there.

The RRh as a signal must be filtered. In the case shown previously, we used the 3 x 3 DMAC as our filter for the RRh.

In the chapters ahead we will be looking at various ways to filter Ross Hooks and Reverse Ross Hooks, as well as nuances, concepts, and intricacies that will help you. These will add new strategies and techniques that undoubtedly will add to your success in trading.

Chapter 8

CONCEPTUAL PROCESSES

ANTICIPATING HOOKS

In the previous chapter we learned that, "It can be argued that looking ahead, we can see that taking out the RRh would cause the 3 x 3 DMAC to turn over."

The key point was that a signal can be based upon "looking ahead". We call such a concept "anticipatory trading."

Here's how it works. When we see a market in an established trend, we can anticipate that every bar in the direction of the trend has the potential of becoming a Ross Hook.

Let's look at a picture of what we mean.

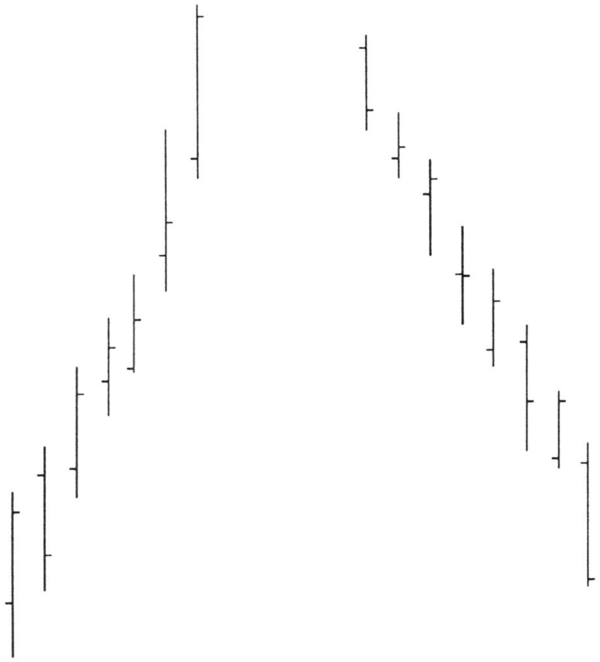

In the above illustration we see pictured two trend segments, one up and the other down. Let's assume that somewhere earlier they had become established trends.

What if we change a single bar in each of the two trends?

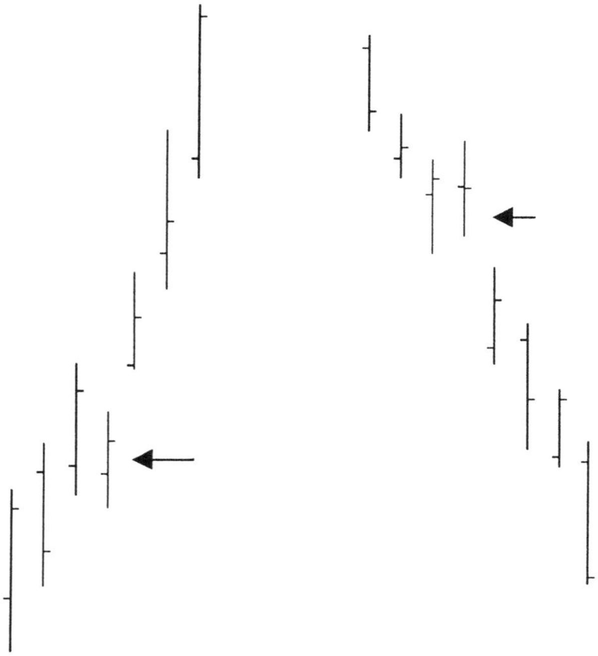

We then have a Ross Hook in each trend. Let's say we want a resting entry stop above the high of the correcting bar that created the Hook in the uptrend and below the low of the correcting bar that created the Hook in the downtrend.

The idea that the extreme of any correcting price bar may become an entry point ahead of a Hook gives rise to the following trading signal:

IN AN ESTABLISHED UPTREND, BUY A BREAKOUT OF THE HIGH OF ANY CORRECTING PRICE BAR. IN AN ESTABLISHED DOWNTREND, SELL A BREAKOUT OF THE LOW OF ANY CORRECTING PRICE BAR.

DO EITHER, PROVIDED THAT THERE IS ROOM BETWEEN THE ENTRY PRICE AND THE PRICE AT THE POINT OF THE ROSS HOOK TO COVER TRANSACTION COSTS AND TAKE AT LEAST SOME PROFIT.

Why? Because that is what we would have wanted to do if a violation of that correcting price bar resulted in the continuation of the trend by moving past the point of the Hook; or resulted, at the very least, in prices moving as far as to challenge the point of the Hook if such challenge resulted in the chance to cover transaction costs and earn some profit.

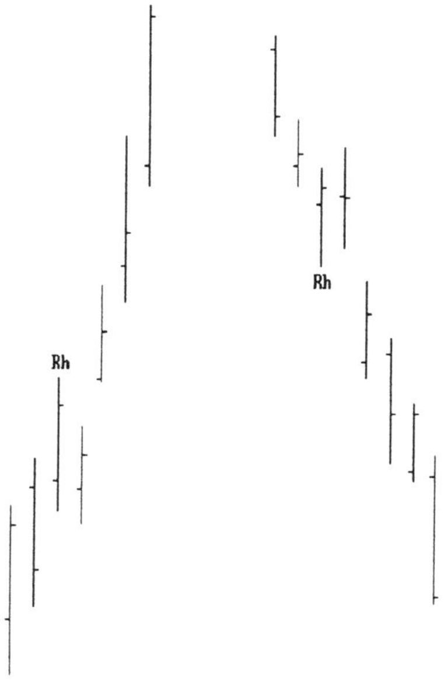

The anticipation here is that you can jump in front of the market and it will take you along for the ride to a distance where prices at least challenge the point of the Hook.

However, we can use some filters with this method.

- **DO NOT ENTER ON A GAP OPENING BEYOND THE PRICE RANGE OF THE CORRECTING BAR.**

Wait to see if there is a move opposite to the gap. If so, and there is still room to enter via the Trader's Trick, enter then.

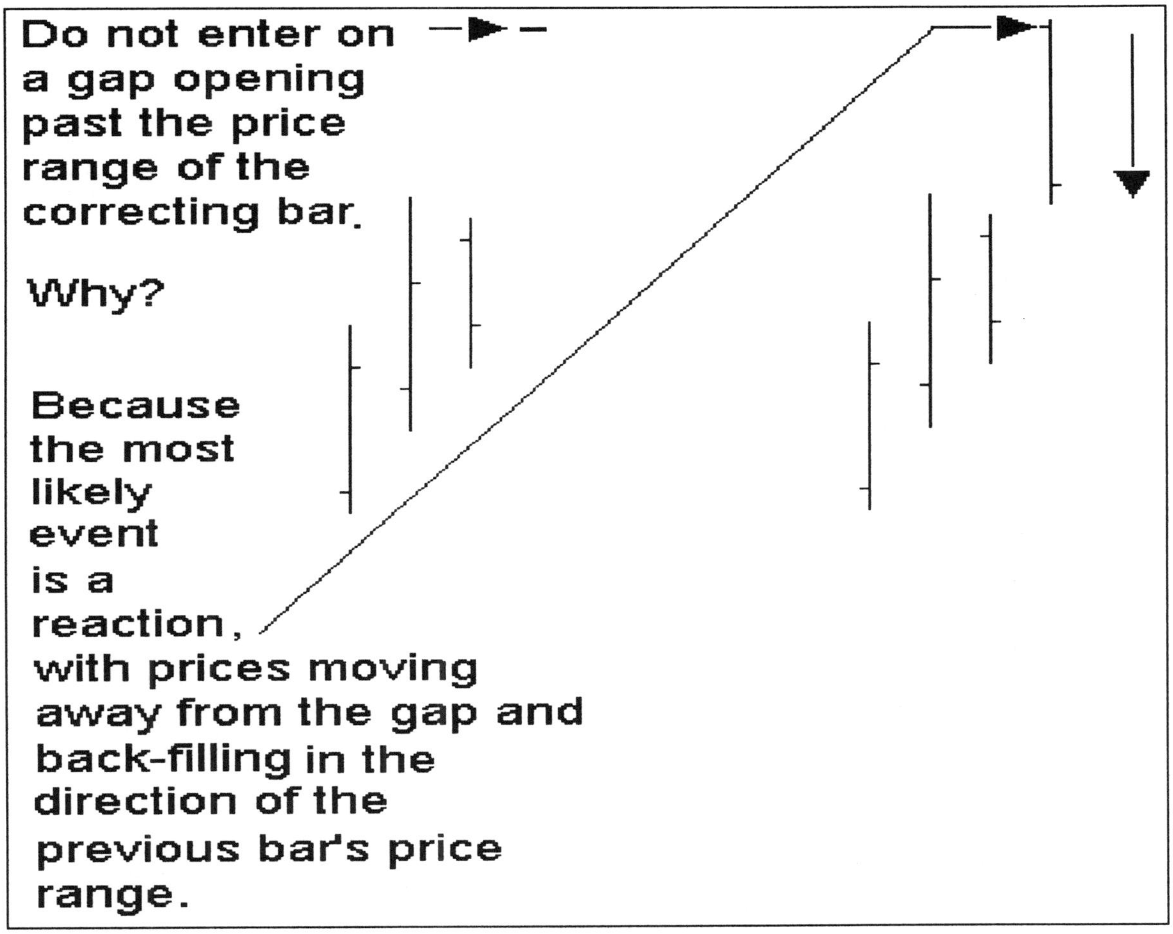

Day traders, with quick reactions and instantaneous execution, can fade the gap opening much as do the market makers and insiders.

The probabilities favor a reaction, with prices moving opposite to the direction of a gap opening that is outside the price range of the previous bar.

Let's look at another no-no situation.

DO NOT ENTER ON THE BREAKOUT OF THE EXTREME OF A LONG BAR MOVE THAT TOOK PRICES FAR BEYOND THE EXTREME OF THE CORRECTING BAR THAT CREATED THE ROSS HOOK.

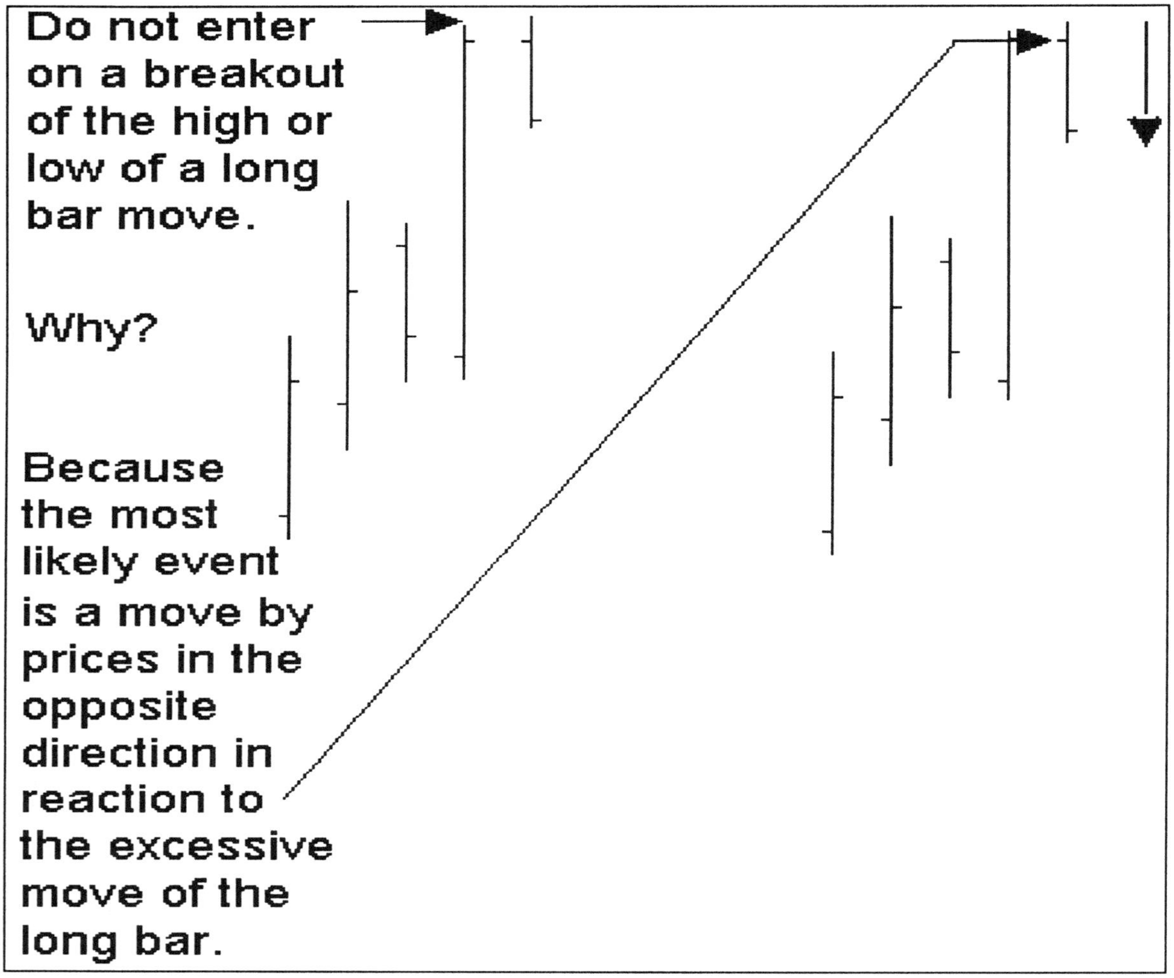

Once again, day traders with quick reactions and instant execution can fade the breakout of a price bar that violates the high of a long bar move that went past the extreme of the correcting bar which created the Ross Hook.

This type of trading should normally be limited to day traders, because a hasty retreat may become necessary. Daily chart position traders who cannot sit and watch all day can take such trades provided they are able to give explicit instructions to their broker with an assuredness that such instructions will be carried out. This means the position trader must have the ability to give a set of contingency or standing orders.

- **IF PRICES ARE TRENDING, AND THERE HAVE BEEN THREE OR MORE SUCCESSIVE BARS IN THE SAME DIRECTION, DO NOT ATTEMPT TO JUMP IN FRONT OF THE MARKET; ON A PERCENTAGE BASIS, A CORRECTION IS USUALLY IMMINENT AND A BETTER ENTRY WILL BE OBTAINABLE. THERE IS AN IMPORTANT DIFFERENCE HERE FROM WHAT WE SHOWED IN ELECTRONIC TRADING 'TNT' I — GORILLA TRADING STUFF, AS EXPLAINED BELOW.**

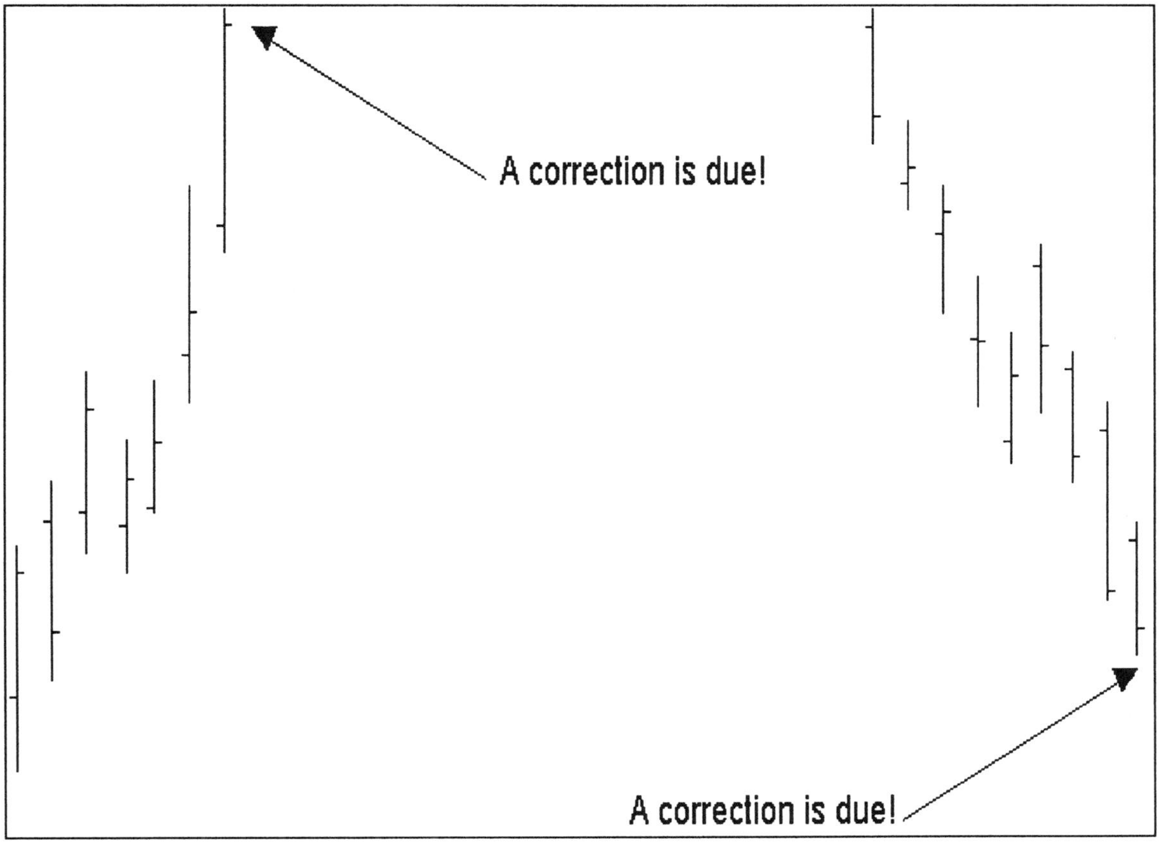

ANTICIPATING CORRECTION

Because most moves in the direction of an existing trend average a duration of four bars, we want to be conservative. We do not attempt to jump in front of a market after three consecutive price bars in the direction of an existing trend as we do when we are trying to discover the ***beginnings*** of a trend during a period of congestion as was discussed in ELECTRONIC TRADING 'TNT' I — GORILLA TRADING STUFF.

After three to five consecutive price bars in the direction of the trend, a correction will normally take place, giving an opportunity to either take a position in the trend or add a new position to an existing position.

ANTICIPATING CORRECTION LENGTH

Most corrections last from one to three price bars moving opposite to the trend. It is here that we have a safe entry opportunity with relatively low risk. It is at such times that we attempt entry with the Trader's Trick.

ANTICIPATING TREND RESUMPTION

In most cases, a trend, if it's going to resume, will do so after one to three price bars of correction. Anticipation of the trend resumption is an important factor in trading Ross Hooks using the Trader's Trick.

TRADING ANTICIPATION

Now, let's put our anticipations together, and taking it one step at a time, see how we might have traded a trending market.

As each chart sequence unfolds (Chart Sequences A-D), we are looking for an opportune and relatively safe point from which to gain entry to the market. See charts on the following pages.

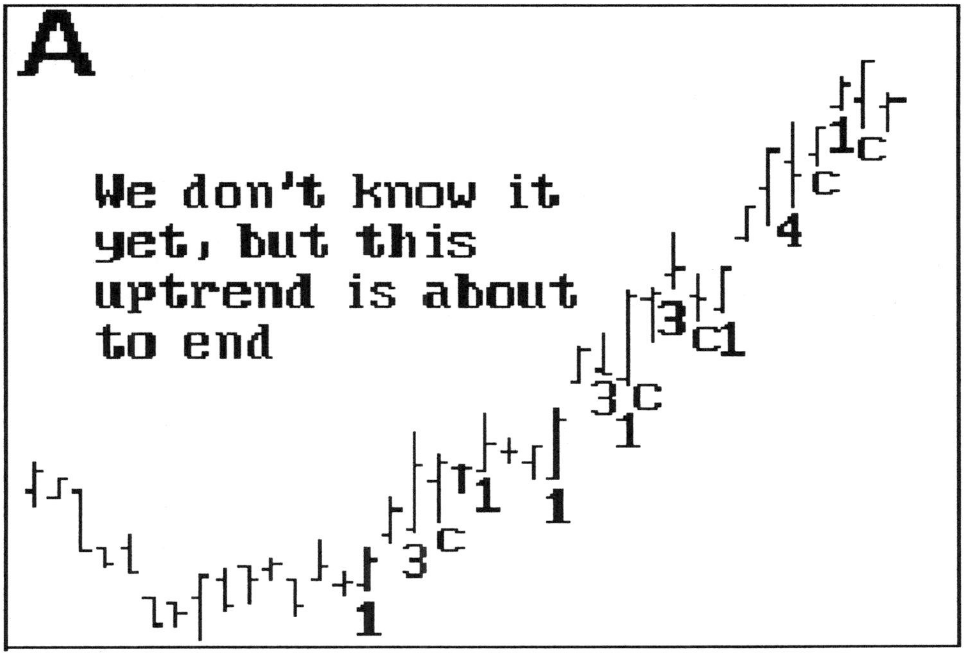

In Chart Sequence A, we've marked a cadence count. Follow along, moving from the bottom of Chart Sequence A to the top of Chart Sequence A, then over to Chart Sequences B, C, and D in that order. Charts B, C, and D will follow.

1 - Prices take out the high of a small doji bar.

3 - Prices have made 3 higher highs.

c - Prices fail to make a new high.

(MOVE TO THE SECOND #1) Prices make a new high, but notice there is no follow-through at the next price bar. This is a warning of either a trend reversal to follow, or that we are entering a congestion area.

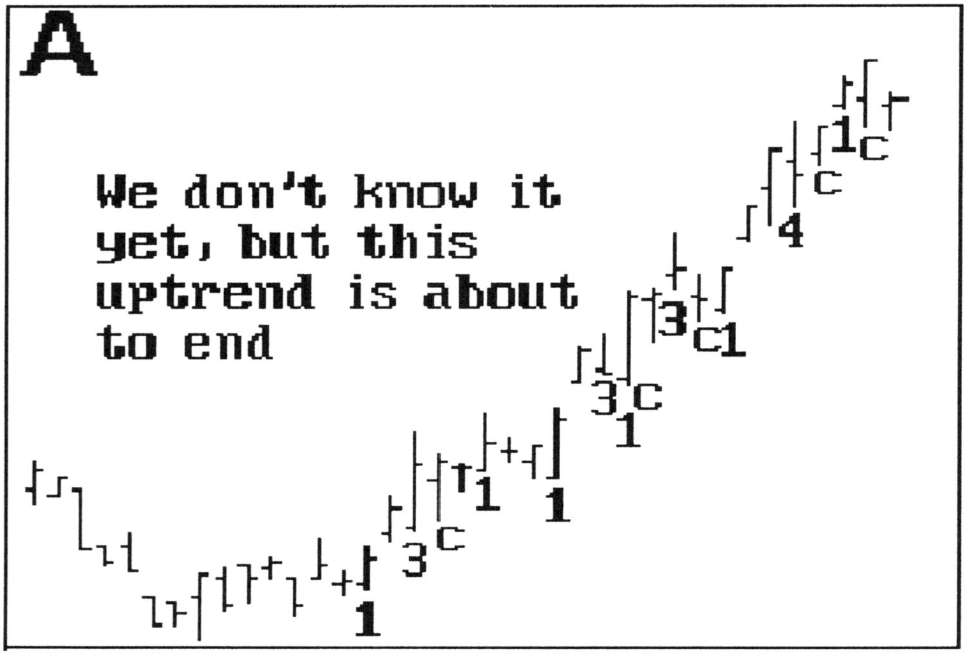

Continuing in Chart Sequence A:

Prices do little for two days. (MOVE TO THE THIRD #1)

1 - Prices make a high, moving out of the congestion area.

3 - Prices have made three higher highs.

c - A correction occurs. Prices gap lower at the open and trade down before moving up to give a new high. This bar is both a correction and a (MOVE TO THE FOURTH #1) 1 count.

3 - Prices have made three higher highs.

c - A correction occurs. On a gap lower opening doji bar, we fail to make a new high.

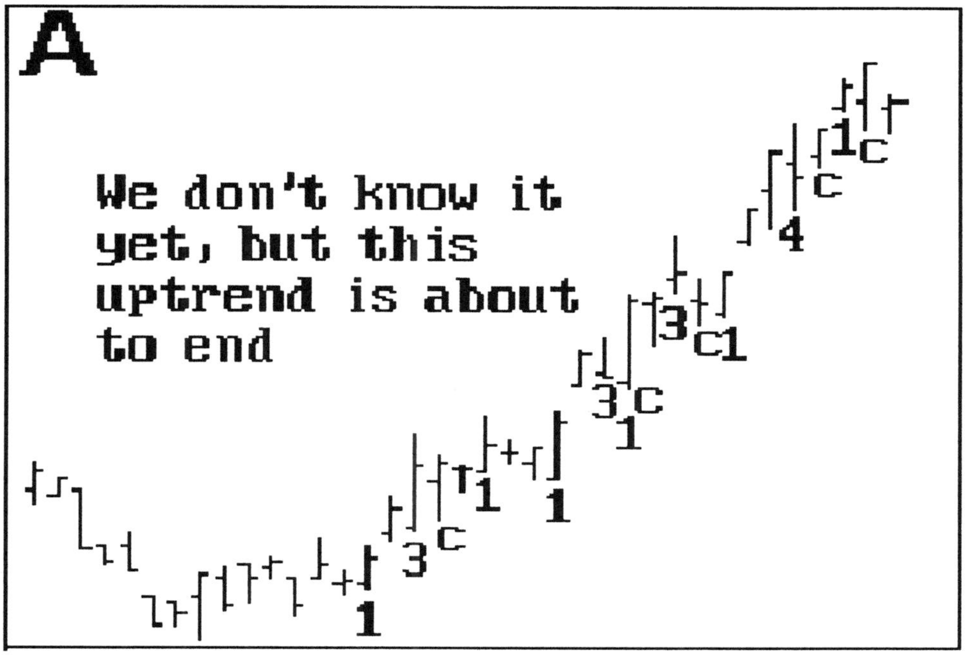

Continuing with Chart Sequence A:

1 - Prices make a high taking out the high of the doji bar.

4 - Prices have made four higher highs.

c - Prices fail to make a new high on an inside bar.

1 - Prices make a high gapping up at the open. Last # 1 on the chart above.

c - A correction occurs, after only a one count. This is important. While a trend is moving strongly we expect three to five bars in the same direction prior to a correction. WHEN CORRECTIONS COME FREQUENTLY AND NOT FAR APART, WE CAN ANTICIPATE THAT AT LEAST IN THE SHORT TERM THE MOVE IS ABOUT TO END. We must suspect either a trend reversal is ahead, or that a congestion area is coming. Throughout Chart Sequence A, there was never a really good place from which to enter a trade. [End of Chart Sequence A]

Charts Sequences B - D need little further explanation. You should be able to follow them pretty much as labeled.

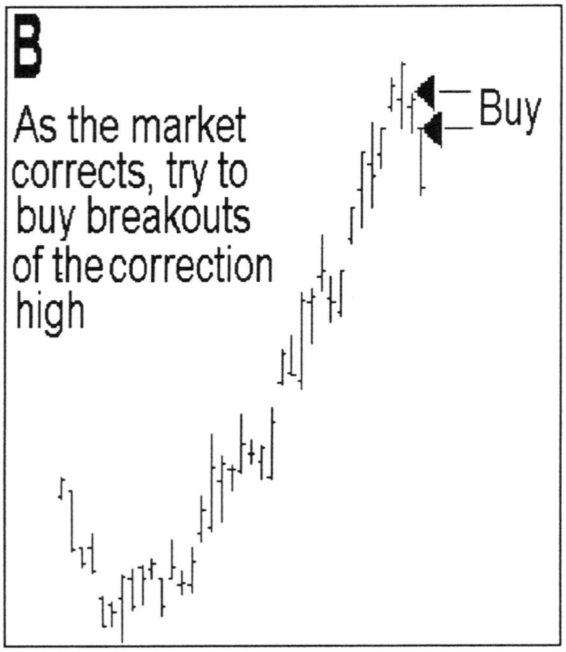

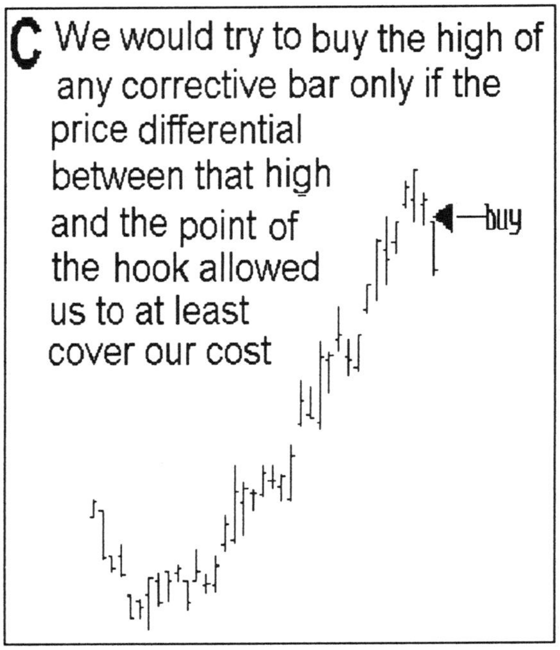

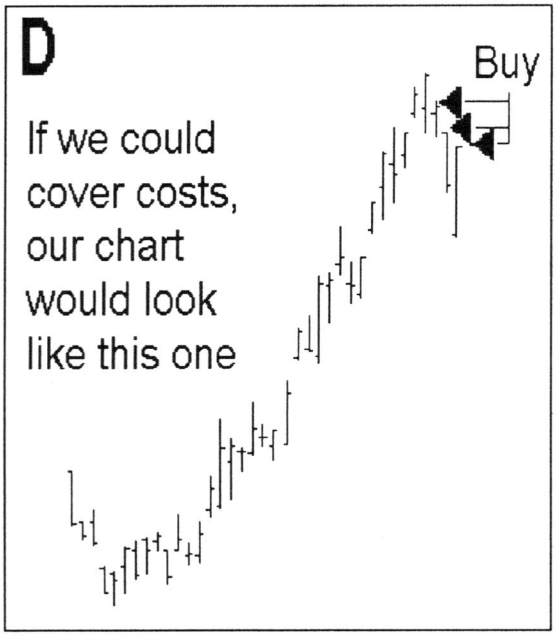

Now lets look at chart sequence E - H.

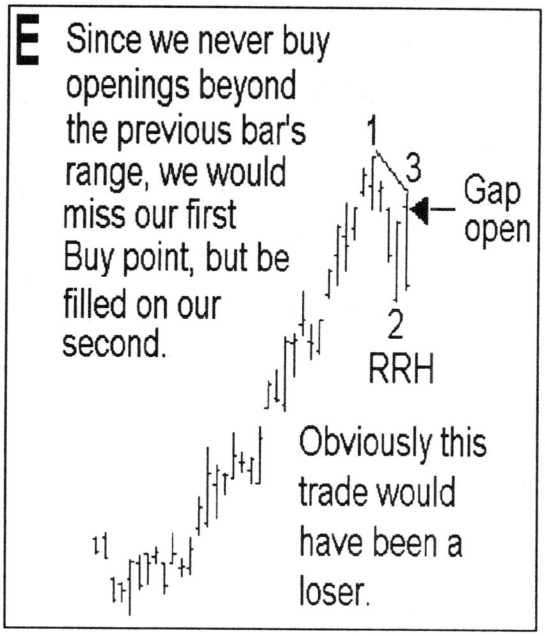

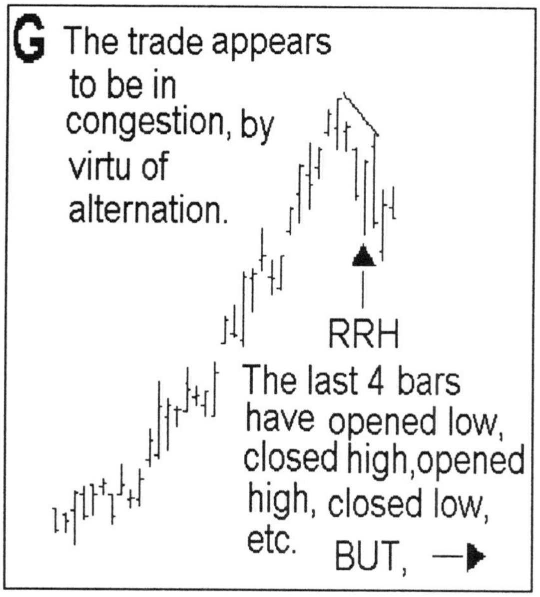

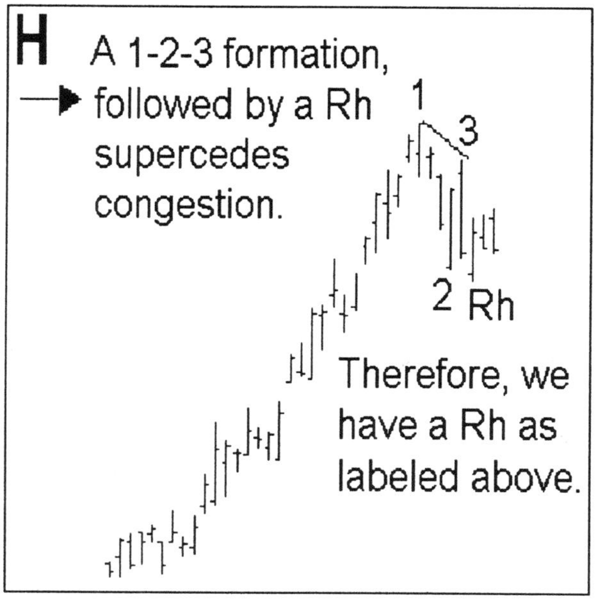

The loss taken on chart E would probably have been less for a daytrader than for a position trader. A daytrader could have gotten out more quickly when there was a failure to at least cover costs. Depending on intraday price action, a day trader might have been able to reverse and go short, thereby making a profit.

You need to know that getting in early is the best way to enter breakouts, which is why we use the Trader's Trick.

It's time now to give some serious thought to stop placement. The next topic will be quite lengthy. If you feel that you would like to read it completely through, this might be a good place to stop for a break. Get something to eat, take a nap, or do some exercise.

When you come back get ready for some in-depth material about stops. Then we will get back in to more technical trading stuff.

Chapter 9

STOPS

WHERE DO YOU PLACE THE STOP?

Stop placement appears to be a topic that is on every trader's mind. Where ***do*** you place the stop?

In this chapter, we will consider several situations for using stops:

1. Mechanical Stops: As dictated by mechanized trading systems.

2. Protective Stops: To protect against loss, or to protect profits.

3. Objective Stops: To cover costs.

4. Entry Stops: To initiate a trade.

5. Exit Stops: To terminate a trade.

GENERAL CONSIDERATIONS

At various times you will hear or read material from someone who tells you where to place a protective stop.

Of course, if you are following an adviser and taking that adviser's trades, you must utilize the adviser's stop placement. Why? Because when you follow an adviser, you are trading a mechanical system. The adviser is your system, and you must follow the adviser mechanically. You cannot possibly expect to achieve success until and unless you do exactly as the adviser dictates. In addition, you also need to do a lot of praying. Pray that the adviser will have a good year in the markets.

The same consideration is true if you follow a computerized mechanical system. If you expect to get the results you paid for when you purchased the system, you must place your stops as the system dictates. At times, the draw down against your margin will be virtually intolerable. That's the price you have to pay for trading a mechanical system.

There are few traders who can maintain the discipline needed to exactly follow a mechanical system, whether it be computer generated or derived from an advisory of some sort.

We will see more about trading mechanical systems a bit further ahead.

There are a number of questions that come up relative to stops and their placement. Should you place a stop at a certain number of points distant from current price action? Should you place a stop at a certain percentage distant from current price action? Or, should you place a stop a fixed money amount distant from current price action? Any or all of these may be an incorrect way to place stops.

We are thoroughly convinced that no one on earth can tell ***you*** where to put ***your*** stop.

The truth is, only you can decide. Unless you are trading a mechanical system or following an adviser, the responsibility is yours. If you are calling your own trades, there is no way you can pass that responsibility to anyone else.

Since proper stop placement is such an important responsibility, let's take a few minutes to reflect on some of the items that must be taken into consideration when placing stops. We will return to these individually later on and view them in the context of whether we are using the stop to protect against loss, protect profits, or seek an objective.

Keep in mind that if you are a daytrader, you may want to use mental stops. Stops for a daytrader are usually one and the same with exit points.

SPECIFIC CONSIDERATIONS FOR STOPS

- **The size of the margin account**. Certainly, the size of your margin account will affect where you are able to place stops. It will even affect the selection of stocks in which you are able to trade.

- **Your individual psychological and emotional tolerance for pain, that is, your individual comfort level**, greatly affects stop placement. Provided you can afford to trade in the stock you have chosen, this is probably the most important factor in setting stops. You might have a $100,000 account, but if taking a $500 hit will devastate you psychologically, then you cannot set your stop that far away.

- **Your economic tolerance for loss**. Being willing to lose a certain amount of money, even though you can afford it, affects your stop placement. If you are stopped out with a loss often enough, you will reach the point where you will no longer have money to lose. Therefore, you must have a rational approach to stop placement.

- **The number of existing open positions already held**. If you are already positioned in other trades, you may not be able to set your stop properly in any new trades. In that case you may be forced to miss a good opportunity, or to set stops too close.

- **Market volatility**. This is a market generated criteria for setting stops. Prices may be too volatile, causing you to set a stop beyond your affordability or psychological comfort level. Conversely, using a market-generated criteria, volatility may be not sufficient to even warrant entering a market, let alone placing an effective stop. The stop would be too close to the price action and virtually certain to be hit.

- **The rate of trading**. Whether prices are moving fast or slow affects stop placement. If a market is moving quite fast, you may have to set a stop further away than is affordable or comfortable.

- **Tick size**. Usually, when prices are fast, or a stock is highly volatile, the tick size will also increase. That means your usual and normal stop will not suffice.

- **Participants in the market**. When an order for a large number of shares, enters the trading arena, prices may begin to do strange things. These large orders are placed in the market by traders who are able to handle considerable "size." They often have the resources to move prices. They may move a market up quickly so they can go short from a higher price. They may sell it down quickly so they can go long from a lower price. Whatever their reasons, knowing who is in the market can affect where you place your stop, or even whether you should enter a trade.

- **Liquidity**. Whether a market is liquid or illiquid affects successful stop placement. Thin markets tend to be much more volatile than liquid markets. The operators in thin markets can "run" prices up and down more easily than operators in liquid markets. This volatility can greatly affect where you have to place a stop. In addition, operators can more easily run stops in thin markets.

- **Turnaround time**. Your reaction time, in part, dictates stop placement. How long does it take you to see and react to a situation? If you are slow, plan on needing larger stops. Your order turnaround time also dictates stop placement. If your orders are slow in gaining entry, you will need to use larger stops. There can be considerable lag time with an order entry placed through some electronic trading or Internet trading systems. Time is money. Markets can move quickly. The longer the time you spend in taking care of business, the more you will have to risk in stop placement.

- **Your overall objectives and strategy for the trade**. For instance, if you expect to make a long term trade, you would probably place your stop a lot further back than if you were anticipating a short term trade.

In view of the preceding points, how can a trader expect someone else to tell him where to place a protective stop? You, and only you, are in a position to know all of these things. And while someone else may know some of these things, only you can know your comfort level.

Also, in view of the considerations we've presented, isn't it a bit ludicrous to set loss protection stops at a fixed number of points, a set money amount, a previously determined percentage away from the price action, or based upon the dictates of a mechanical trading system?

None of these methods has anything to do with the reality of price action in the market, or the trader's economic, mental, or emotional condition, or any of the other conditions mentioned.

Stop placement is truly the arena in which the mature trader is separated from the less mature trader.

MECHANICAL SYSTEMS

No discussion that concerns separating knowledgeable traders from less knowledgeable traders would be complete without mentioning mechanical trading systems. Therefore, before going on with a discussion of stop placement for loss protection, let's digress a bit in order to peer into the concept of mechanical systems. It seems as if many feel this is the solution to stop placement.

It is said that imitation is the highest form of compliment. Some of the people who have come to our seminars have paid us that highest form of compliment — they want to learn to think as we do. While we feel humble in light of such high praise, there is no doubt more to this concept than you might imagine.

At a recent seminar we shared a thought with those attending. It's a thought we don't mind repeating and sharing with others. It has to do with computers and mechanical systems. More importantly, it has to do with discipline.

Over the years we have seen numerous intellectual individuals who have tried to automate trading. They have tried to turn trading into mechanized systems. We have never personally met anyone who succeeded at this, but we feel that our statement needs to be qualified.

We have known professional traders trading managed money who were able to use models in their trading. Notice the plurality of the word models.

These traders run several models. They have models for trading in congestion, and they have models for trading in a trend. They have models for trading based on fair value. These models run simultaneously for those stocks they desire for trading. The model producing the best result in a trending market is traded in a trending market. The model producing the best result in congestion is traded in congestion. All other models are constantly fine tuned so that they can be adjusted to current market conditions.

By continuously fine tuning, optimizing, and adjusting, there is always a model from which to choose. One or the other of the models generally outperforms the others.

This type of automated trading is very expensive and time consuming. It is far beyond the reach, in both time and money, of the average trader. The amazing thing is that it rarely does better than a good individual trader who knows what he is doing.

In addition to systems conceived in-house, many purchased systems have also been employed. The conclusion of the matter has been that no mechanical system attempted to date has been able to outperform the professional trader himself. No stone has been left unturned — no expense spared in trying to find an easier or better way than what can be done by the human factor. The money spent has been in vain.

Experts in artificial intelligence have attempted to computer emulate top notch traders. There are simply too many details, nuances, and variations in market action. What can be seen by the human eye and interpreted by the human brain is beyond the ability of any programmer to translate into a computer program. However, with that said, and an overwhelming request list from technically minded traders, we have employed some top notch programmers to fill your requests and computerize many of the indicators taught in this course.

THE NEED FOR AUTOMATION

Is there a need for automation? Yes, there is. But in an area you might not immediately consider. **What you must do to become a successful trader is to *automate* yourself**.

Yes, learn to automate **your** behavior in the market. Discipline **yourself** to act and react in certain ways to various market conditions.

When you see a trending market pause to correct, leaving behind a Hook, and when your filters all indicate a market entry, then condition yourself to take that opportunity.

Do not waiver. Do not hem and haw. Your actions must be automatic, but based upon an intelligent deployment of the knowledge within your possession.

In this regard, trading is like the martial arts. You must be so well trained and conditioned that you act automatically and appropriately to market stimuli.

If the trade is not going your way, exit immediately. No wavering. No wondering. You get out. You do it now!

If a developing opportunity gives you any pause for thought, refuse that trade. It must be your trade by fitting your parameters for what constitutes a tradable event. It must happen your way, when you are ready for it. There can be no "but's", no "maybe's." If an entry opportunity does not have your criteria associated with it, leave it alone.

If you have placed an order in the market and it is not filled, and the market goes on to make what would have been a wonderful trade for you, there can be no regrets. You cannot afford to stop to mourn over trades missed. You must be looking to the next trade, to the next opportunity. Above all, you must not change what you are doing simply to accommodate the missed trade. That kind of thinking can be disastrous. Drill yourself to stay with what you know works for you.

You cannot automate the market action anymore than you can control prices. Just as your actions and reactions are the only thing in the market which you can control, so it is with automation. You can only automate yourself.

Stop and think about it. To successfully trade a mechanical system, you must develop the discipline to follow it religiously. That means blindly following the dictates of some algorithm that may or may not fit in with your personality, your margin account, or your trading style.

If you're going to blindly follow a system, why not blindly follow your own reason, based upon the best computer that has ever been available — the human brain?

Unlike what many would have you believe, trading a mechanical system does not remove the emotional strain of trading. It does not get rid of the suffering so many experience. The emotional strain remains. It is only relocated to another area. You are forced to agonize under the terrible draw-downs associated with mechanical systems. You have to trade not knowing exactly why you are doing what you are doing. You have made a mechanism your god. You must bow to its dictates. If you are trading a system that uses daily charts, there are still the same sleepless nights when you get in trouble. If you are daytrading, there is still the same gut wrenching agony of seeing the trade go against you.

You still have to grit your teeth and hang on. You dare not get out, even in the face of disaster. The moment you take any initiative and act apart from the system, you have broken the system.

Is there any virtue in sitting still while your mechanical system destroys you financially? Probably not. The very same discipline that you must exercise to withstand the withering heat of mechanical trading could be harnessed to work for you if you are determined to make it so. It is much more difficult and it takes a great deal more discipline to blindly follow a mechanical trading system than to follow your own human reason.

We all have a computer. It's our own brain. No mechanical monstrosity has ever come close to the marvel you carry around in your own head.

Your job is to learn to act upon what your human computer is telling you. Isn't it easier to develop that kind of discipline than to force yourself to become the slave of a piece of software written by someone who may never him/herself have traded successfully?

Is there any better computer than the one housed between your ears? No!

It is not one bit harder to follow the dictates of human reason than it is to follow a mechanical trading system. Both require a discipline and faith that is tantamount to religion.

Seldom, if ever, can an electronic computer relate the myriad of variables needed to make a trading decision any better or faster than your brain. The computer simply cannot see all the relationships in any manner approaching the adeptness with which you can see it with your own eyes.

Most traders confuse their inability to control their emotions, their human behavior, with their ability to know what is going on in the markets.

You know what to do. You simply do not act appropriately to what you see.

The computer is not going to see any better than you do. Therefore, if you can determine to follow a mechanical system, you can equally determine to follow a system based upon your own human logic and reason. After all, a mechanical system is not going to be any better than your own or someone else's logic and reason transferred into the computer via a programming language.

Learn how to trade. Learn to read what a market is showing you, and then discipline yourself to follow the dictates of the best system you can have for you, the one based upon your own observations and knowledge.

Look at it this way, here are two computers:

Each gives buy and sell signals. One is a personal computer programmed to follow certain linear relationships in the market. The other is the human brain, trained and educated to see complex relationships in the market. PC can view the market only serially. PC cannot multiplex ideas. No matter how carefully it is programmed, it cannot possibly reason or take into account the myriad combinations that occur in the market.

HB can view the market in a multiplexed fashion. It sees numerous relationships within moments. It is able to comprehend the big picture in context, relative to everything else that is going on in the market. While it may not register every combination of events, it is able to take into account multiple combinations that do occur in the market. It can spot formations even though they do not exactly conform to a specific definition of what those formations are supposed to be.

For instance, HB can spot an intermediate high or low in the market, and judge it to be that in relation to all other highs and lows in the market. It can see /V\ and VV formations in every imaginable way they can occur, along with heads and shoulders, pennants, flags, megaphones, etc. In fact, it is the ability of HB to make judgments that sets it so far above PC that the gulf between them is immeasurable.

As mentioned previously, both these computers give buy and sell signals.

Is it any more difficult to develop a discipline surrounding the signals from HB than it is to develop a discipline surrounding the signals from PC? Probably not! It takes no more discipline, determination, and mind set to state, "I will follow the signals from HB," than it does to state, "I will follow the signals from PC." In fact, it is harder to blindly follow the signals from PC — it takes more discipline.

Is there any virtue in attaining to the greater discipline required to follow PC? No! But because it may appear that way, many choose it, thinking that somehow the market is going to reward them for doing so.

It is the decision to blindly follow signals that makes a system mechanical. The act of blindly following invokes the faith and discipline involved in successful trading. Once you have a method or system that gives more money won than money lost, all that is necessary is to develop the mind set, diligence, and determination to follow that method or system.

Notice, we said a method or system that gives more money won than money lost. It does not have to give more winning trades than losing trades. It's the end result that counts. The plus dollars have to exceed the minus dollars.

Once you have a vehicle that gives that kind of result, it does not matter which computer gives you the signals. However, because of the ability to make judgments, personally we'll take the signals from HB any time over those from PC.

As previously stated, stop placement is where you separate the knowledgeable mature trader from the amateur trader who still does not know how, when, or where to place stops or exit points in the market. Knowing when and where to exit is far more important than knowing how to enter.

PLACING A LOSS PROTECTION STOP

Of the many stop-loss placement techniques we have seen, only two have proven continuously successful over the years. Only two have made any sense at all. One method uses **natural support** and **natural resistance** for placing stops. The other uses **market volatility** to dictate stop placement. In both cases, we allow the market to tell us where to put the stop. We then filter that knowledge through our financial, mental, and emotional condition.

If the market is telling us where to place a stop and that stop is too far away for comfort, then we do not take the trade. Or, if placing the stop where the market indicates would create too great a financial risk, we refrain from taking the trade.

USING NATURAL SUPPORT AND RESISTANCE

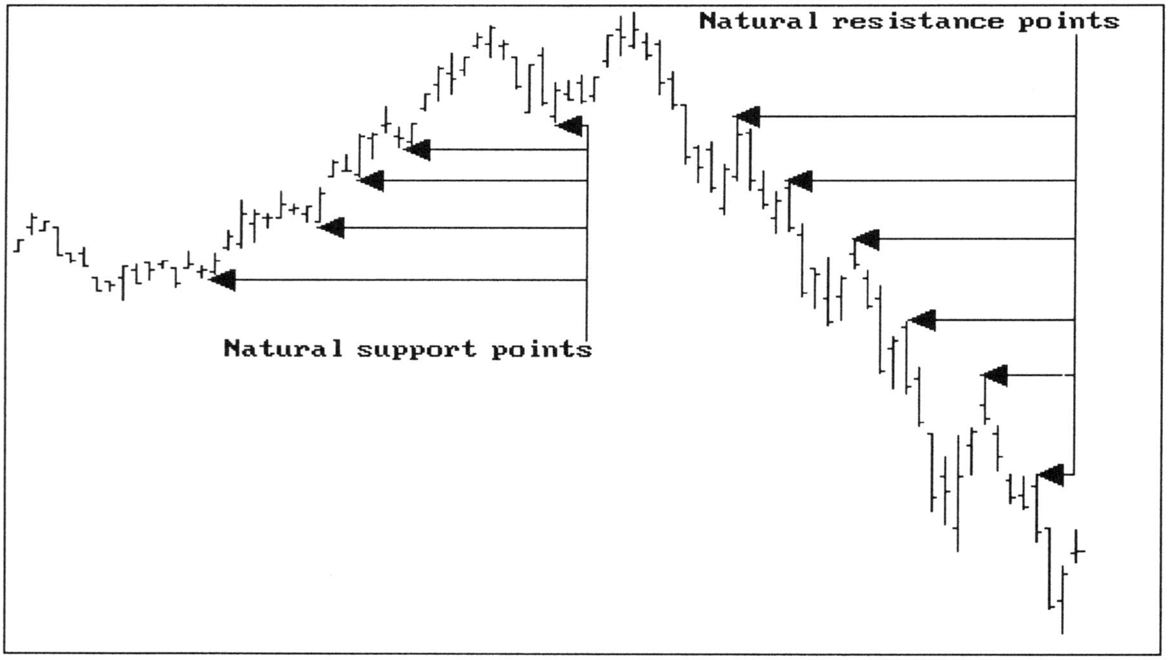

Let's look now at what is meant by "natural" support and resistance. Let's look at a nicely trending price chart.

Natural support and resistance points are those places in a trend where prices either move sideways for a brief period or where prices make some sort of correction by moving counter-trend for a few bars.

These stops usually work because price action in the market has previously held at those levels. If the recent price was too high or too low at that level, the price will probably be considered too high or too low at that level in the near future. These stops take advantage of the natural support and resistance in the market.

If prices at a natural point of resistance or support do not hold, then the probabilities are that we have been wrong in our estimation of market action, and we are better off being stopped out of the trade.

It has been useful to use natural support and resistance points when planning a longer term trade for the time frame in which the trade is taking place. The next chart will illustrate this concept. The essence of this method for stop placement is to set the stop with respect to objectives and strategy.

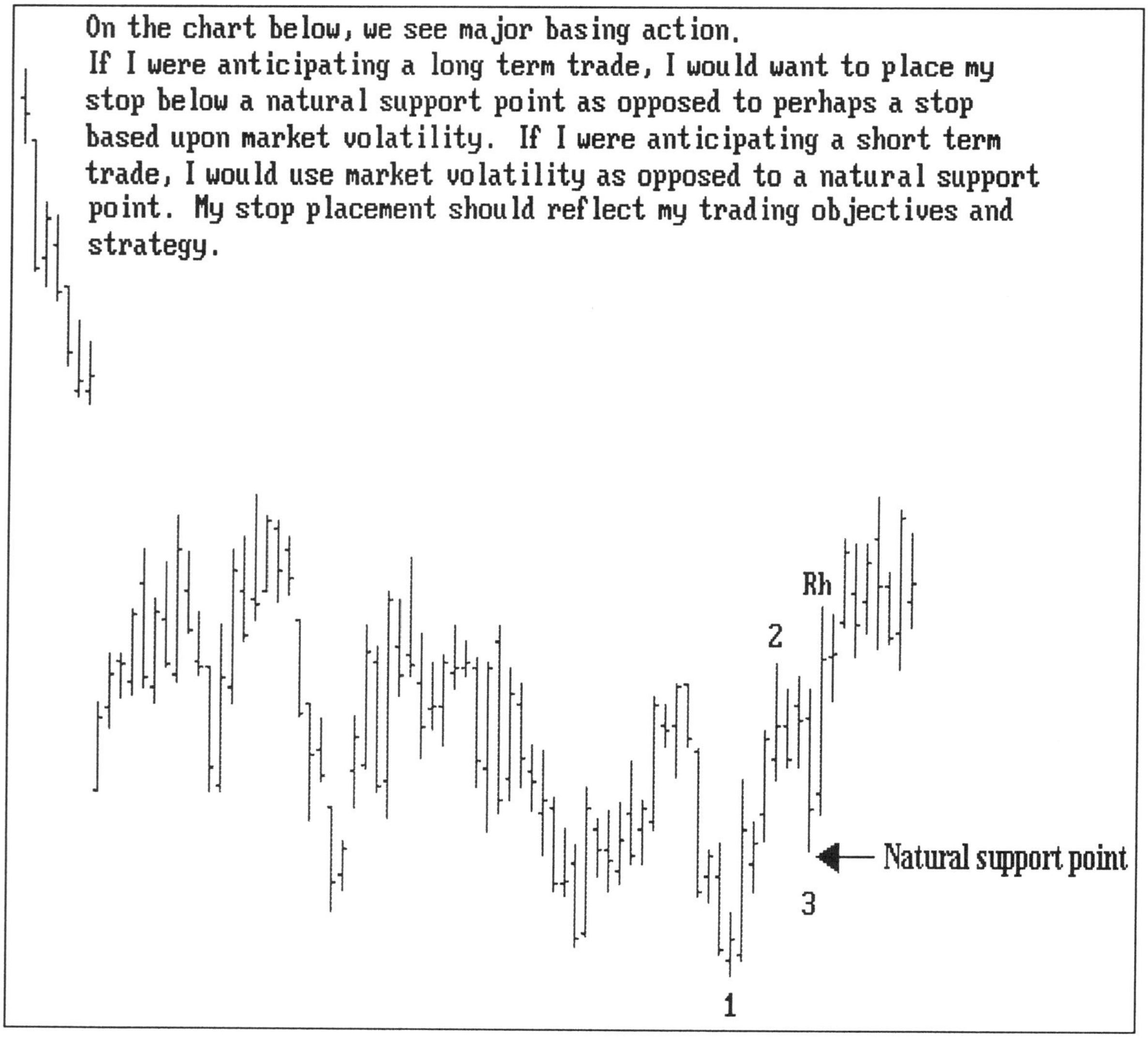

Depending on the direction of a trend, tops and bottoms of Ledges and tops and bottoms of corrective retracements yield natural support and resistance point.

ADVANTAGES AND DISADVANTAGES OF NATURAL STOPS

The single greatest disadvantage to using natural stops is at one and the same time its greatest advantage: Prices may be too far removed from the current price action, thereby increasing risk beyond the financial, psychological, or emotional tolerance zone.

Natural stops are easy to see on a chart once prices move away from them, and in a trending market prove to be remarkably safe. They tend to keep you in a trade for a long time.

A big disadvantage to using natural stops is that at times, when we wait until they are hit, we may see a rather nice gain turn into a loss.

NATURAL STOPS ARE OF LITTLE OR NO USE IN NON-TRENDING MARKETS.

The next chart gives you an idea of what is meant by a natural support point being too far removed from the current price action.

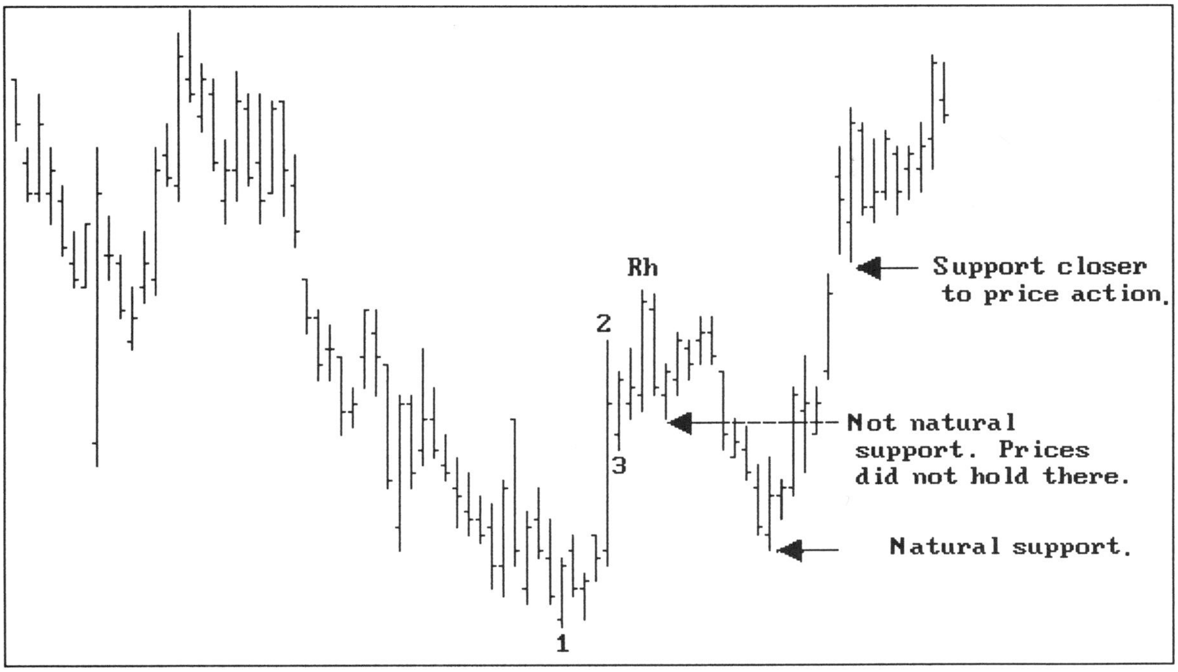

Anticipating a bull move technically supported by the strong basing action on the chart, we would want to use a natural support point. However, if we took the most natural support point, we would have a stop substantially away from current prices.

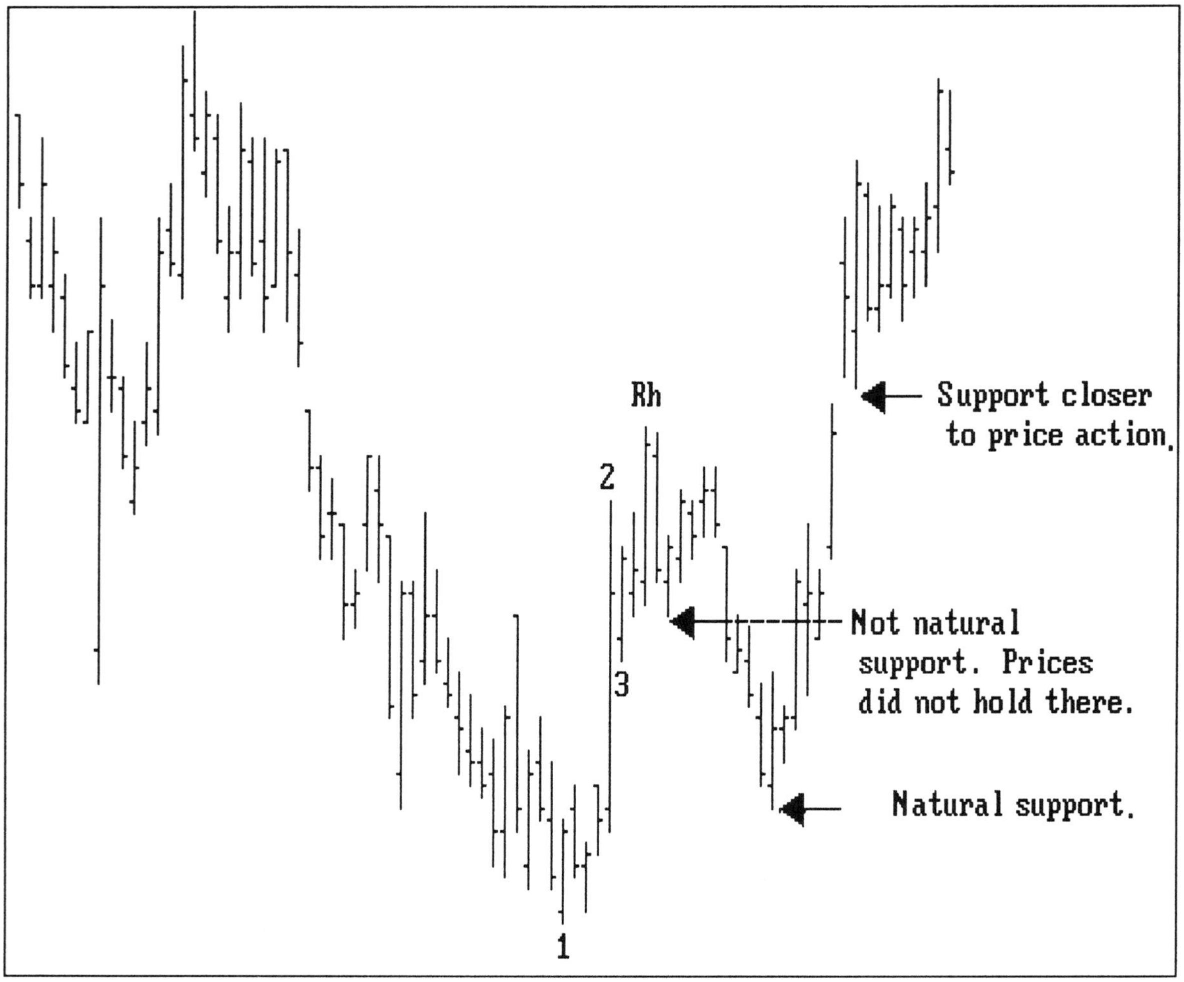

The alternative stop placement point we can use is shown closer to the price action. Notice the arrow pointing to "Not natural support." At the time that low was made it was natural support, but subsequently, because that low was violated, it lost its status as a natural support point.

VOLATILITY STOPS

Experience has shown that, other than natural support and resistance points, the market has only one other factor to aid in stop placement. That factor is volatility.

To understand how to use volatility, we first need to understand the concept of volatility.

The ***distance*** between a price bar's high price and low price is that price bar's trading range. The arithmetic ***difference*** between a price bar's high price and low price is that price bar's volatility.

We can use the high and low of a week to get a weekly trading range, or we can go intraday to look at hourly, 15 minute, or the trading range of any time period. We simply look at the distance between the low and the high for that period.

Similarly, we can subtract the low from the high for a given period, and the difference represents volatility. When we look at any bar chart, the length of each bar, from high to low, represents that price bar's (or period's) trading range and the arithmetic difference represents volatility.

Once we have the arithmetic difference for one period, we can do the same calculation for any number of sequential periods, and then take an average. If you want to look at volatility over a five bar period, we subtract the low from the high of each bar, and after five bars we add up all five individual bars' differences, then divide by five to get the five bar average volatility. However, there's a complication.

Let's say that we have a gap up opening, and the low for the current bar ends up being higher than the previous bar's close. If we assume volatility to be the high of a price bar minus the low of that price bar, then what happens to the gap, the distance that the market moved between the previous bar's close and the current low?

True volatility must include not only the gap, but the distance from the previous bar's close to the current bar's high. Conversely, when there is a down gap, and the current bar's high is lower than the previous bar's close, true volatility is equal to the difference between the previous bar's close and the current bar's low.

There is yet another complicated consideration. What do we do about stocks that trade elsewhere, or are affected by trading elsewhere, and the result is often a large gap opening due to the price action that has taken place overnight, or at a different exchange?

We must decide for ourselves whether or not to take that kind of gap into consideration in our calculation of volatility.

Once we know how to calculate a bar's true range with gap considerations, we can take an average over any selected number of days to come up with true average volatility.

True average movement of price is a direct measurement of a stock's volatility. When price movements expand, we are seeing increased volatility come into the market. When price movements decrease, so does volatility.

If prices are very volatile, an exit point based upon that same volatility will give a good indication of where to place the stop.

There are a number of ways to compute a volatility stop or volatility exit point. In each case, we must first come up with a volatility figure.

A way that has been satisfactory much of the time is to use average volatility for the last five price bars, provided they are reasonably the same in size relative to one another. If there is an abnormally large, or an abnormally small price bar, we may need to compute average volatility for the last ten bars. As much as possible, we want to eliminate any aberrations in the price movement. When prices are displaying lots of gaps, we may use ten or more price bars.

To compute average volatility for any number of price bars, N, we take the sum of the differences between the high and the low for N days, and divide by N. We then have the average volatility for the last N days.

It's important to notice that there is a flaw in the above method of computing volatility. There's something missing, and we mentioned it a few paragraphs back.

Gaps are missing from this calculation. In fast moving markets, on the daily chart especially, this leaves a lot of the market missing from the calculation.

The truth is that on a gap day, prices have moved from where we see the close today to where we see the open the following day.

There are two sides to the argument. One says that regardless of the gaps, prices are only volatile to the extent that we see the market move each day during the hours we trade. The other side says that to compute true volatility, you must include the ***net*** amount of the gap. In an up market the net amount of the gap would be the distance from today's close to tomorrow's open. In a down market the net amount of the gap would be the distance from today's close to tomorrow's open. On intraday charts it doesn't really matter.

We should try to calculate volatility both ways and see which method suits us best. If the gaps are left out, we need to be aware that they are there, and they may be more important in some time frames and some stocks than in others. On daily charts that contain many gaps, if the gaps are left out, we need to compute a 10-20 bar volatility.

THE VOLATILITY STOP STUDY

One of the more interesting ways to set stops using volatility is to utilize the study called the Volatility Stop.

We can adjust this study to our own liking by occasionally removing the multiplier that is normally a part of the study. However, the multiplier can be used effectively in a more volatile market to curve fit the study to the greater volatility occurring in that market. To use the Volatility Stop study, simply compute average volatility and then add the figure to the lowest close of the last N days, and subtract it from the highest close of the last N days.

This will yield two prices, one for upper volatility and one for lower volatility. Typically, one of the figures will be a price that is within the range of prices we see on the chart for the last N days. The other figure will be either above or below the range of prices we see on the chart. We want to use the price that is furthest away from the range of prices for our stop.

Rather than try to explain further, let's view a picture of the Volatility Stop study. If you have such a study available (some software will have it or allow you to program it), simply set the multiplier to 1 to put it out of commission, or experiment with the multiplier until you get a plot that shows containment of the move.

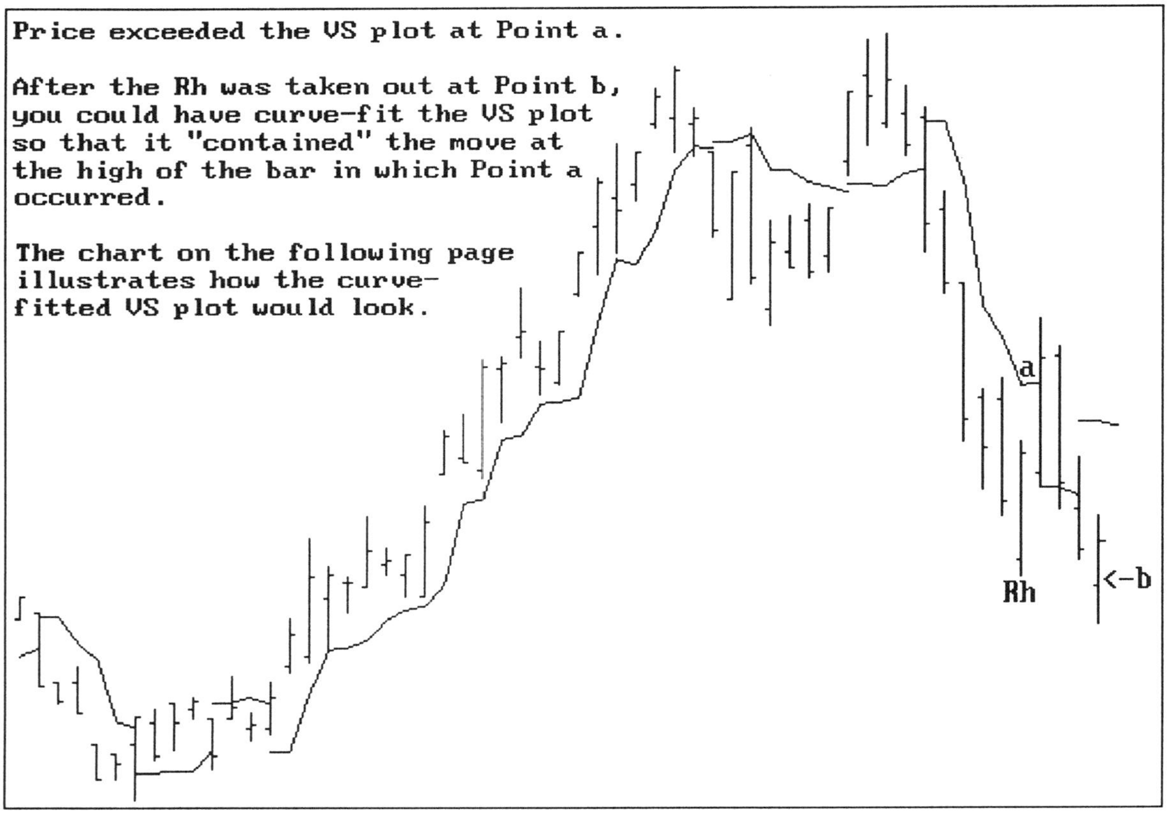

Volatility for the study above was set at 5,1. The 1 takes away any multiplier but because we did not use the multiplier we did not get containment. Had we used the multiplier here, we could have gotten containment of the downtrend.

An interesting thing about the Volatility Stop study is that it is computed and plotted at the completion of each bar such that you know where the stop is for the next bar. It is displayed as a forward displacement. On the preceding chart you see it above the next to the last bar on the chart, but sticking out past the last bar on the chart.

When Average Volatility (AV) is running through the price range, it is a sign to avoid entry into the market, unless, of course, you want to trade in the congestion.

Here is an interesting way to use the Volatility Stop (VS) study.

Since a setting of 5,1 contained the upmove, you would leave that setting in place for the down move. But when you did not get containment of the down move, you would change the multiplier as shown on the next chart to 5,1.7.

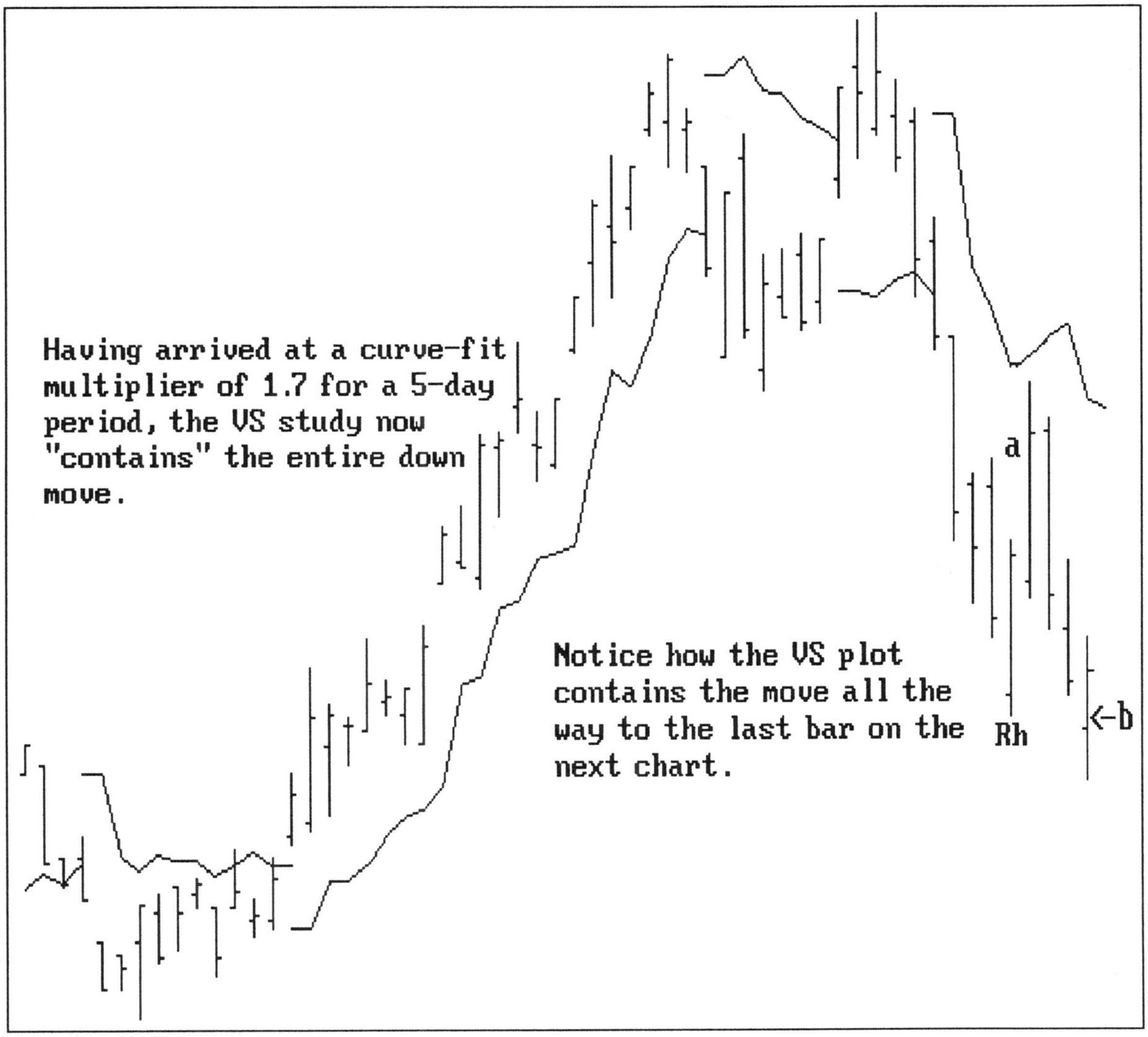

Here's how it looks once you've done it.

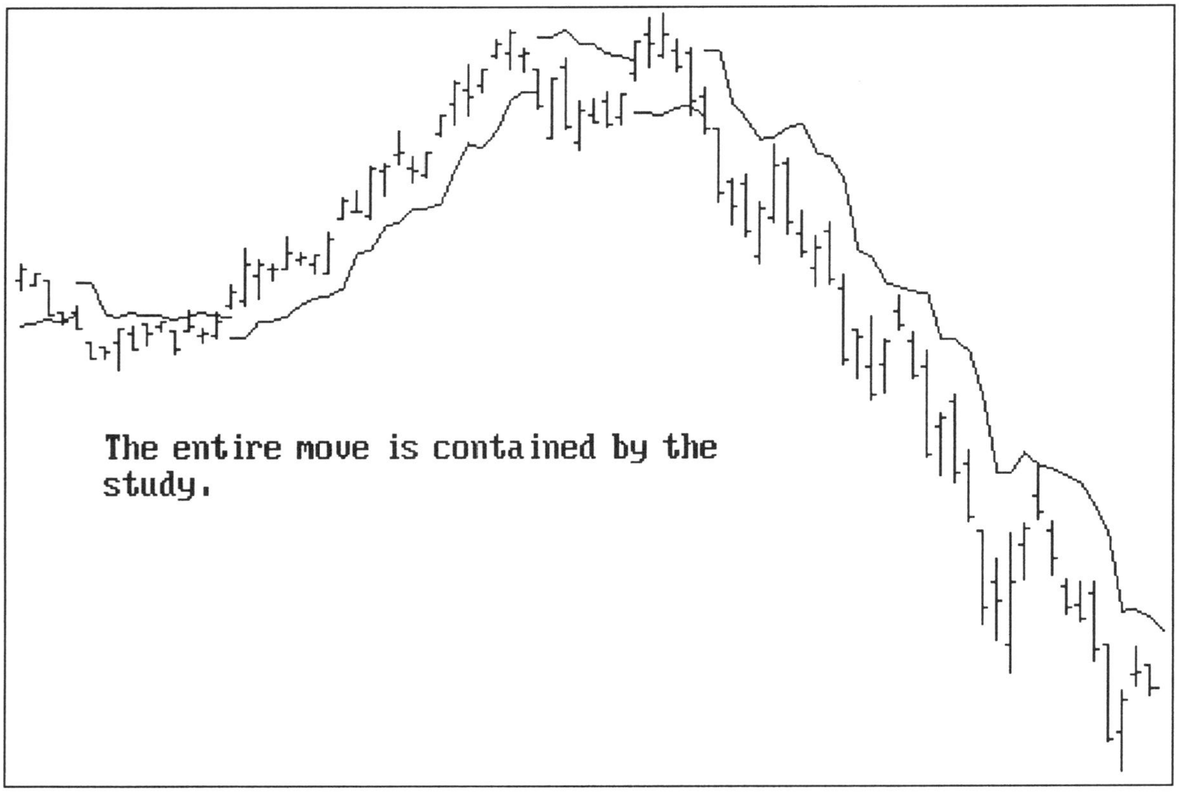

We want to cooperate with the market. If the volatility is such that a 5,1 VS study is not able to contain price action, then set up a study that will contain it, in this case with a multiplier of 5,1.7. The market is always right, the only ones wrong are us! We must adjust to what the market is doing, not what we want to force it to do. However, realize that whenever we use the multiplier, we risk a greater loss if we are wrong. The chart above shows containment all the way down because we curve fit the multiplier.

We like to see a little room between the highs of the price bars and the VS study. But remember that if the stop is too far away, we don't have to trade. No one is twisting our arms to make us take the trade.

It might be preferable to fit the study to prices when we have made some profits. Then it's our decision whether or not we want to risk those profits.

A good rule of thumb is that if the VS study would cause us to lose more than we've made, then it might be better to chip away at the market until we do have enough to risk the amount dictated by the study.

Would you agree that this a much more intelligent way to set stops than to just use some fixed number of points, dollars, or percentages that have no real meaning?

Once we see that the market is in an established trend, we simply ride that trend. The concept here is to wait for commitment by the market. Once we have it, we hang on for the ride.

Our own students have proved this type of trading to be a lot better than jumping in and out all the time. We are letting the market tell us how far away to place the stop.

Since this is a chapter on stops, let's realize that one way to get stopped out of a market is to be purely a day trader. When we make the decision to day trade exclusively, we have made the decision to stop ourselves out of the market. Sometimes, however, this is tantamount to closing a toy store in the month of December.

Each trader has to find his own comfort level. Daytrading has advantages, and daily position trading has advantages. It's entirely a personal decision based on experience as to how to trade

The chart we've been viewing using the Volatility Stop is a daily price chart in a very heavily traded and liquid market. Let's take a look at how that same chart looked on an intraday basis using a 5 minute chart. We will then be able to see how difficult it would have been to have entered this market as a day trader, all while scads of money were being made by the daily position traders. There were plenty of days that, on an intraday basis, looked like the following chart.

The chart shown below is that of a market that was trending, actually gapping up, from day to day.

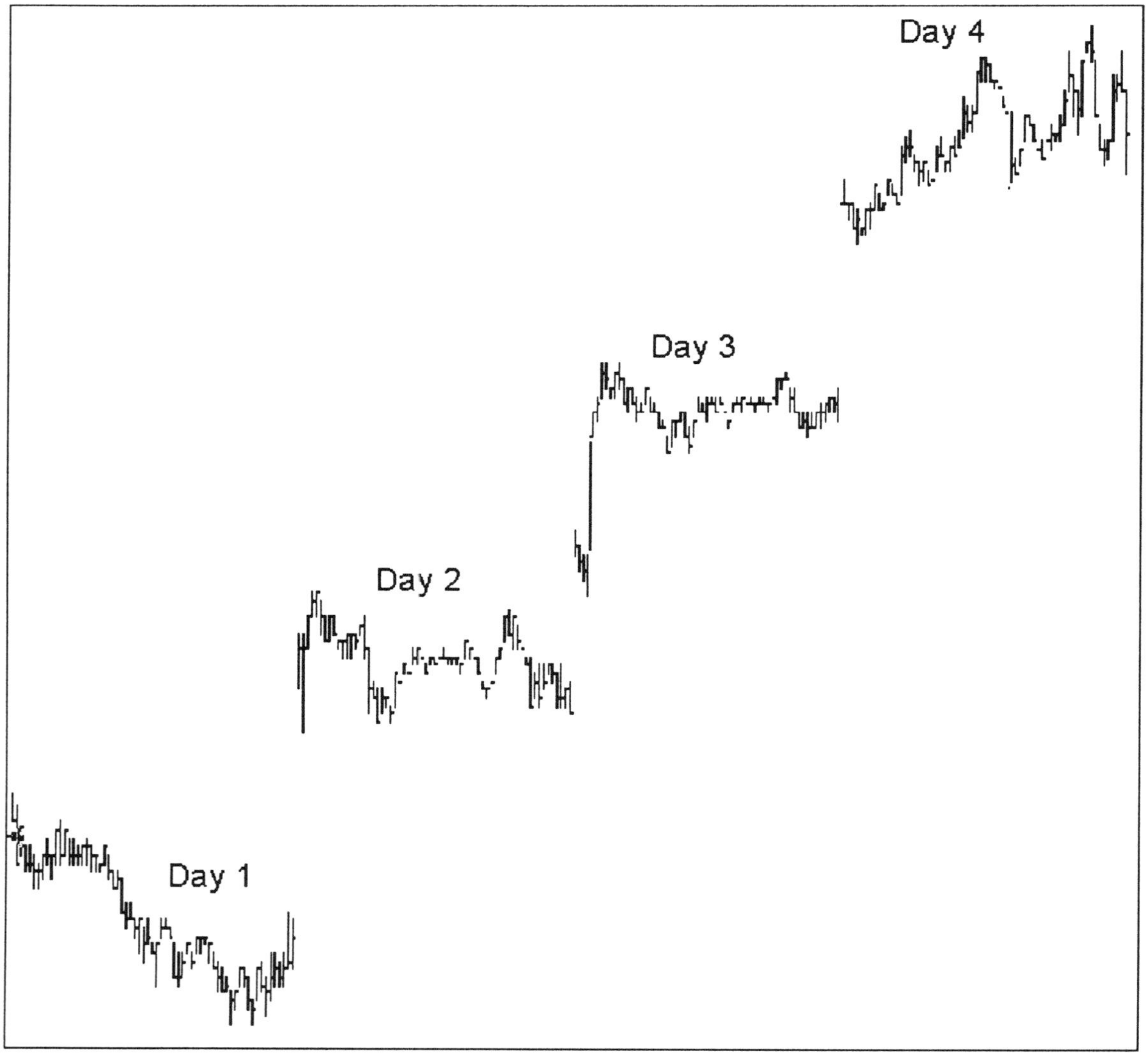

Yet day traders were not participating in the trend at all. Instead, on the first day, they may very well have lost money trying to go long. On the second day prices were flat. On the third day, it they missed the very early price action, they were faced with a very tight market in which they no doubt would have been whipsawed. The fourth day was not a picnic, that's for sure.

The chart below is that of a market that was trending, actually gapping down, from day to day.

One drawback of daytrading is that many traders end up stopping themselves out of a market when there is no need to do that.

This course teaches a balanced approach to trading. Every time we enter a trade, we are going into business. When we get stopped out or have to exit, we are out of business. It's bad enough that we are put out of business more often than we care to be. Taking ourselves out of a market that is making us money may not be the wisest choice we can make. Making that choice displays a type of rigidity that has nothing to do with good trading. If we don't get the big wins, how can we ever make up for the small losses?

Probably the oldest saying in the business is to let your winners run. If we stop ourselves out of the market, we are ignoring this most basic of principles.

Of course, there may be an overriding reason to be strictly a day trader. In that case, by all means you should restrict all trading so that you are out by the close.

Chapter 10

OBJECTIVE EXITS

Good planning dictates that we should have some sort of objective for at least a part of our position. In this section of the course we teach a step approach to exiting at objectives.

We can choose to take full profits by the violation method taught in ELECTRONIC TRADING 'TNT' I — GORILLA TRADING STUFF.

WE EXIT WHEN WE SEE TWO REVERSAL BARS, OR WHEN A PRICE BAR VIOLATES THE LOW OF THE PREVIOUS PRICE BAR IN AN UPTREND, OR WHEN A PRICE BAR VIOLATES THE HIGH OF THE PREVIOUS PRICE BAR IN A DOWNTREND. YOU MAY ALSO CHOOSE ONE OF THE FOLLOWING:

COST COVERING EXIT

This course stresses the importance of grasping the concept of covering costs. It's not that costs for trading stocks are terribly expensive when you consider the actual cost per share that it is possible to pay as electronic traders. Rather, this single, simple idea has been one of the most important concepts for success that we have taught to so many of our students who are now successful traders.

THE OBJECTIVE IS TO GET INTO THE HABIT OF TAKING SOMETHING OUT OF THE MARKET IN RETURN FOR UNDERTAKING RISK. IT'S THE IDEA THAT YOU SHOULD BE PAID TO TRADE.

We never allow ourselves the luxury of counting profits until we have covered costs. As long as we take care of that one detail, the profits seem to take care of themselves.

By "covering costs," we mean liquidating enough shares that by doing so we take care not only of the immediate costs of the trade — commissions and fees — but that we also earn a small profit as well.

We can do this in conjunction with market volatility. We use a rule that states:

VOLATILITY MUST BE EQUAL TO AT LEAST TWICE OUR IMMEDIATE COSTS, OR WE DO NOT TRADE.

This means unless we have a chance to cover costs and take a profit with no more than average volatility, we simply do not take the trade.

Look at the following chart:

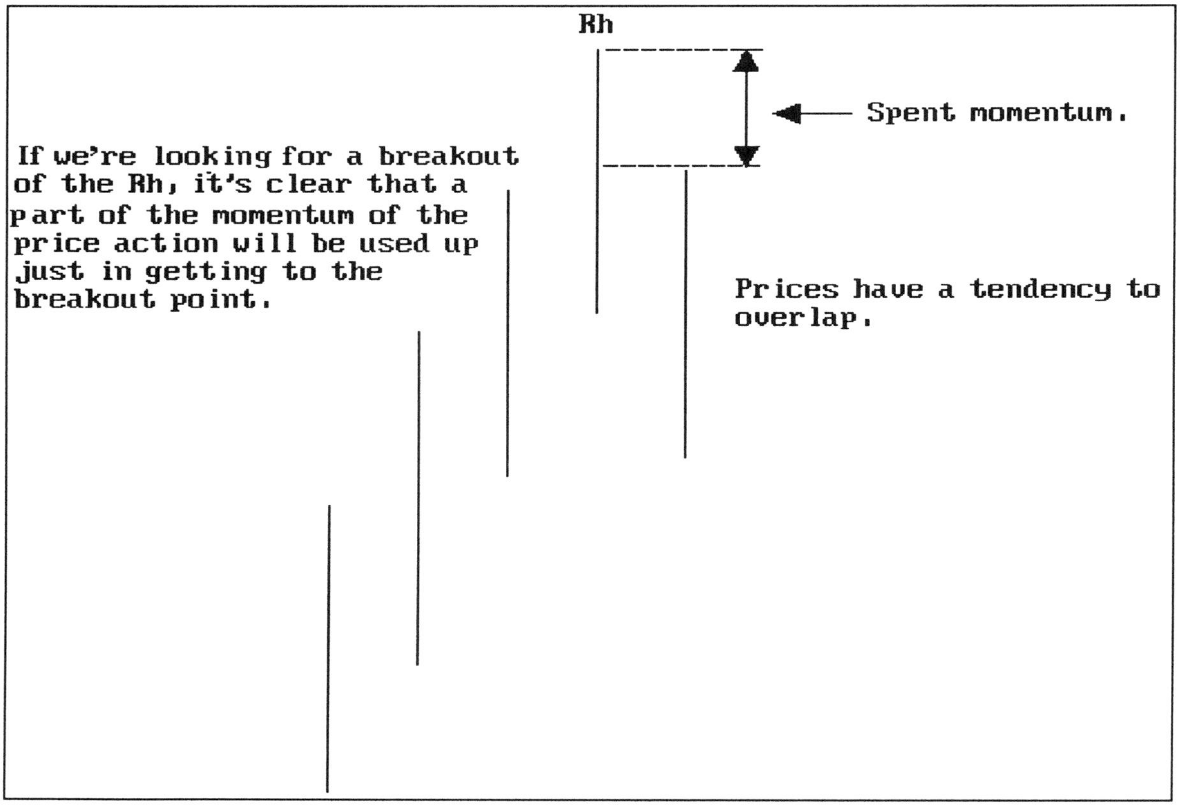

By using twice the volatility as the least amount of volatility with which we are willing to enter a trade, we increase our chances of reaching an objective of covering our costs.

SMALL PROFIT OBJECTIVE

SMALL PROFIT OBJECTIVE EXIT

We take a small profit at the same price at which we cover costs. The point of this strategy is to avoid a situation in which we have no profit to show for our having taken the risk of market entry.

FULL PROFIT OBJECTIVE

FULL PROFIT OBJECTIVE EXIT

Once we have covered costs and gathered in a small profit, our next objective is to capture as much of the move as the market will allow. This can be done with a trailing exit price in mind. In other words, our objective is to exit or be stopped out at some point where we have at least as much profit as we earned previously, and certainly an exit at not less than breakeven. There are two considerations here:

- Until we are satisfied in our mind that the market is now trending, or is going to trend strongly, we will trail a 50% exit stop. By 50% trailing stop we mean that you are protecting at least half of the unrealized paper profit that has existed since the inception of the trade you are presently in. (When we are convinced we are in a strong trend, then we can do a number of things which will be covered in the next section under trailing stops.)

- When we are satisfied that we've made a nice profit, and feel there is no way we can be terribly hurt, we lift our 50% trailing stop in favor of giving the market all the room we are comfortable in allowing. That may be in the form of a subsequent violation of support or resistance at a point that still enables us to profit from the trade, or in the form of a profit taking volatility stop.

TRAILING STOPS

As stated previously, we trail a 50% stop until we feel as though we can take a chance on allowing prices a lot of room.

There are at least three ways we can do this, and we use them in accordance with our comfort level. A fourth way exists, which will be revealed in ELECTRONIC TRADING 'TNT' IV — TIPS-TRICKS AND OTHER TRADING STUFF. However, these three ways are all excellent and we can use them according to our perception of the price action.

- Natural Support and Resistance. We've already seen this, but in a different context. Natural support and resistance points are superb stop placement points in steeply trending markets. The use of them is a judgment call — we have to look at the market anatomy and see if they have been working for this stock, both in past trends and in the current trend. If they have been working well, we use them. This is the simplest, least complicated way of trailing a stop. It requires that you know a bit about the previous price action of the stock in which you are trading. You come to "know" it by studying its chart history. You can also use the following:

- The Volatility Stop study, which is available in some trading programs, and which can easily be computed by hand. The Volatility Stop study and how to compute it was covered earlier.

- Curve fitting a moving average to a trend. This is done in the same manner as we showed for curve fitting the Volatility Stop Study. Study the charts that follow. There are some important lessons to be learned.

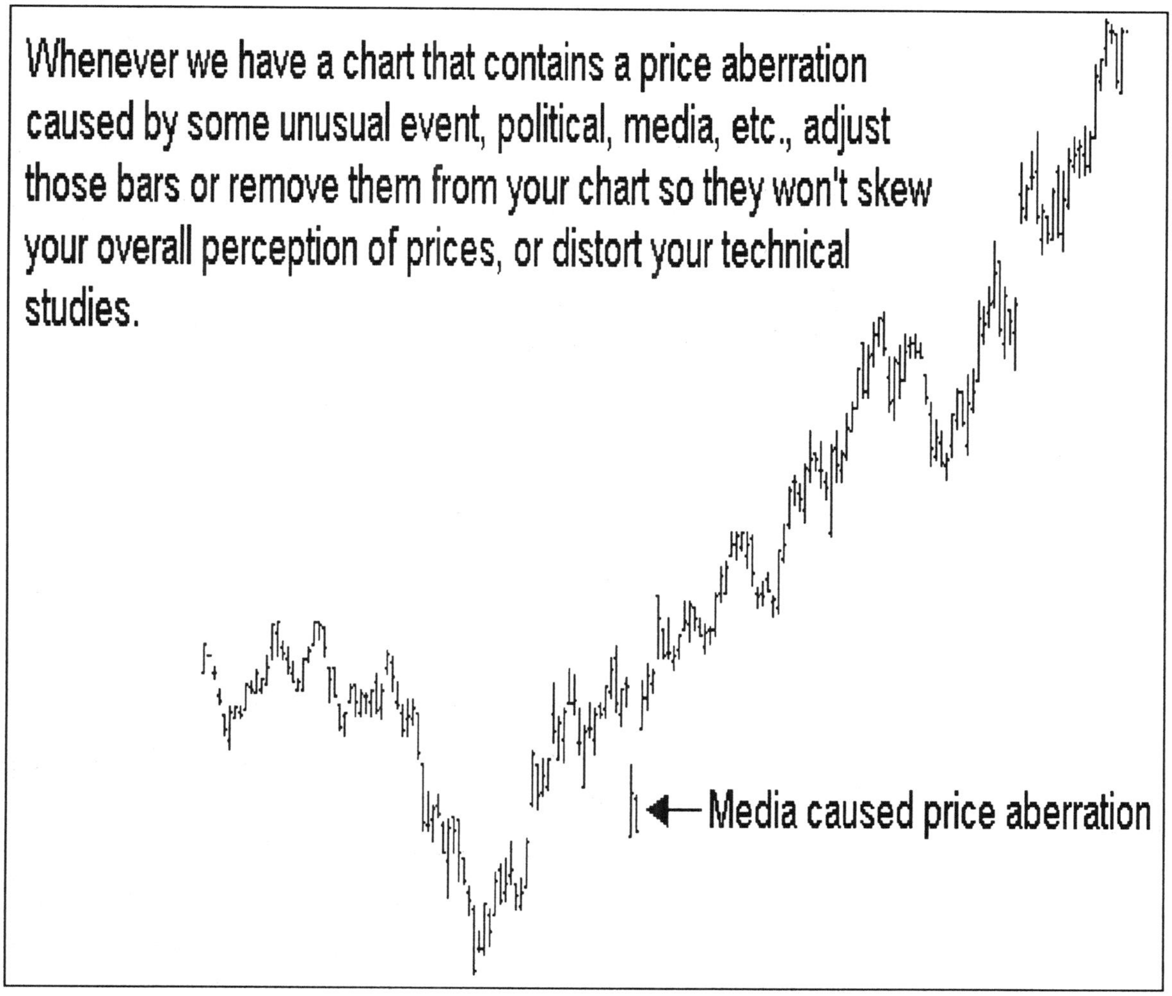

You may adjust the offending bars or remove them from your chart. Although they do reflect the short term price action at the time they occurred, they do not reflect the overall price action and they will give false readings to any technical indicator studies you may have on your chart, as well as skew your overall perception of prices.

In the charts that follow, notice that we have done exactly that — we removed them.

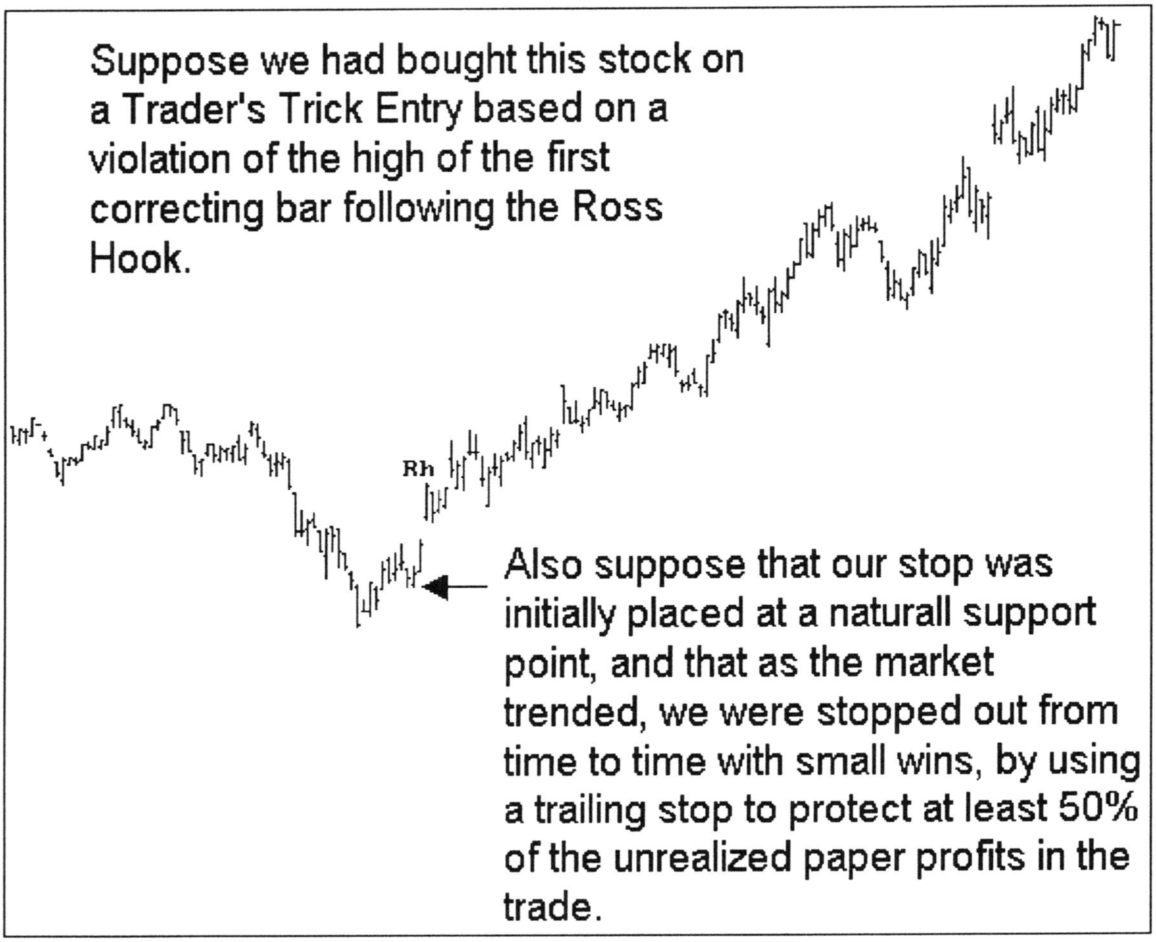

In the above situation, prices are trending steadily. Although we might have used an initial stop set at a natural support point, the price action, as best we can decide (judgment), dictates that a 50% trailing stop be used. Note: By judgment, we see that prices are not exactly running away. They're trending nicely, but with plenty of anxiety spots and sizable retracements.

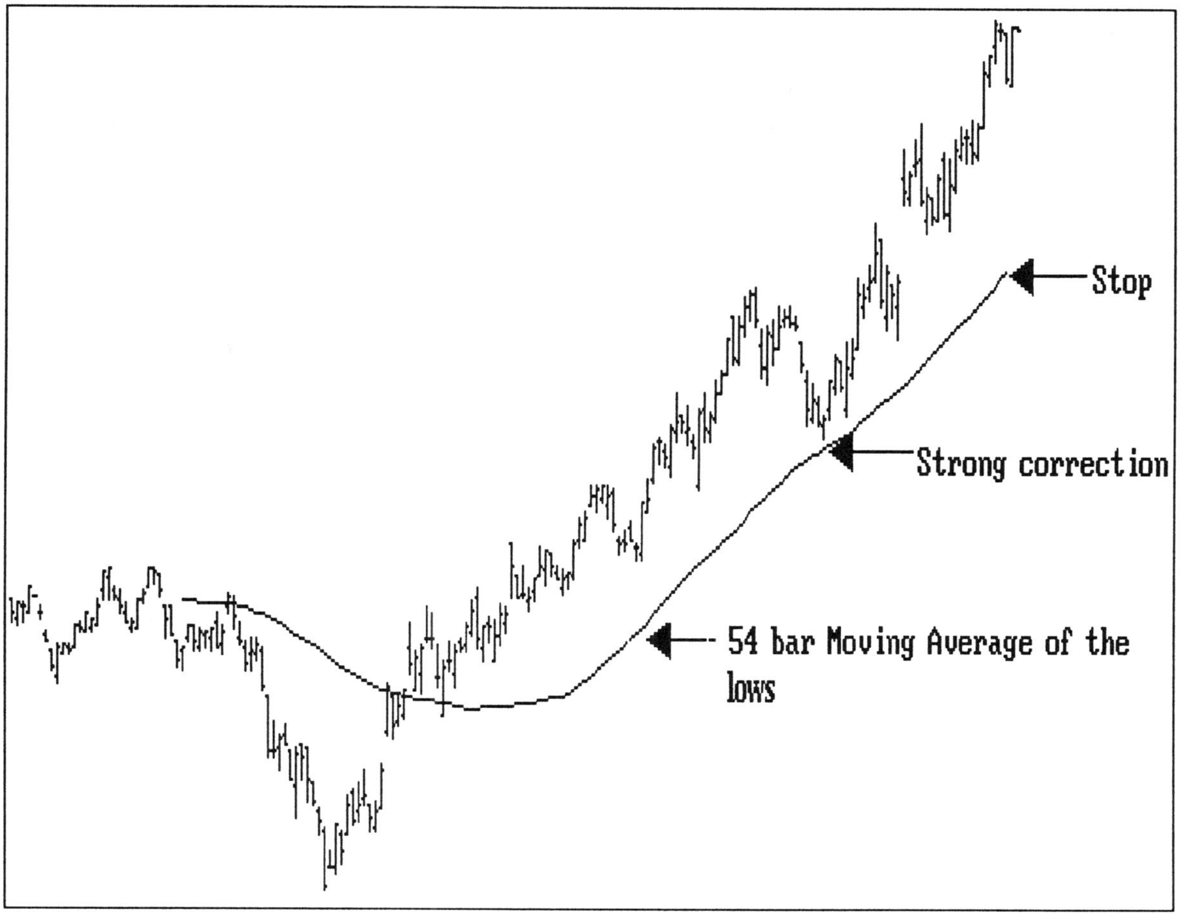

After awhile, we may have built up substantial profits. Eventually prices make a rather strong correction, and begin to move up once again. If we were trading this chart, and not previously stopped out of all portions of our position, and if we were willing to risk some of the profits we've already made, we could curve fit a simple moving average of the lows to the major correction low, and set a trailing stop just beyond the price level of the moving average.

Although the chart shows a 54 bar simple moving average of the lows, there are a number of other moving averages that would have given similar results: for instance, a simple moving average of the closes, or an exponential moving average of the lows or closes. Since this is an uptrend, it seems appropriate to use the lows as a base for the moving average . If it had been a downtrend, we could have used a simple moving average of the highs. This is also a study found in most charting packages.

There's no magic in these moving averages. We use them only to show containment of a trend.

Perhaps, we could have used a volatility stop with a large multiplier to show this containment. Offset Moving Averages could have been used. We might even have drawn an old fashioned trend line!

OTHER CONSIDERATIONS

PROFIT OBJECTIVES USING POINTS

If prices reach the point where we are able to cover costs with one-half of our position, we may then decide to take profits based on making a certain number of points. For instance, if we have made one point to cover costs and taken a small profit on an intraday trade, we may decide to take our remaining profits by liquidating the balance of our position when see another three points.

Some trades are designed as short term scalps. For such trades we may decide to have a profit objective based upon points.

Point objectives may be adjusted upward as the time interval for each price bar is increased, but keep in mind the volatility of prices within the time frame in which you are trading. You wouldn't expect an objective of 10 points on a stock with an average volatility of 1-1/2 points per 30 minute price bar.

USING FIBONACCI EXPANSION OBJECTIVES

The use of this type of objective has been pretty much hammered to death in recent years. It has been written up repeatedly.

We can use Fibonacci objectives to project the expansion from a trading range. They can also be used in trending markets. Objective stops can be set at these objective points because they tend to be self-fulfilling when enough people use them in a market.

That in itself is a reason to know where they are. When enough people are using them, you will know where to expect reactions.

If you can spot a heavily traded liquid stock where traders are using Fibonacci expansions, you can pretty much tell where these traders will be looking for profits. If you see a stock that regularly expands in accordance with Fibonacci expansion ratios, and then retreats, you can use these ratios to your own advantage. You will be able to forecast market moves with fairly good accuracy. Not only can you take profits at the expansion ratios, but you can make good counter-trend, short-term scalps by going in the opposite direction at those expansion levels.

Here's how to do it.

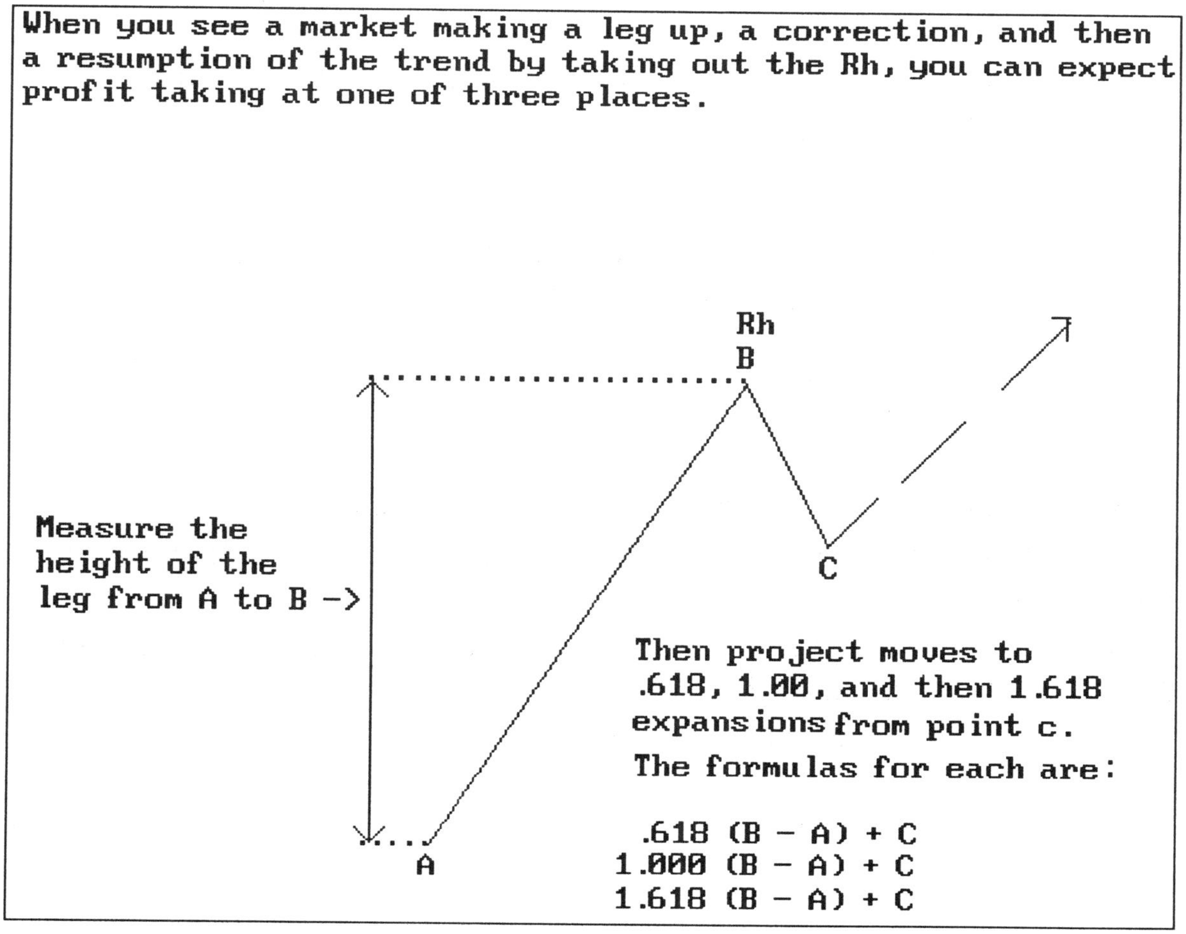

We want to avoid using money objectives. It's psychologically important for most traders to think of their trades in terms of points. When we do that, the money takes care of itself. It is defeating to count your money before the trade is over.

We avoid using percentage objectives. It's rather foolish to attempt to dictate to a market that it must move a certain percentage. However, if Fibonacci ratios can be deemed to be percentages, we can take advantage of those ratios by scalping into them in markets where we have determined that many other traders are using them.

DETERMINING A PROFIT PROTECTING EXIT

Taking profits from a market while they are there to be had is a very important part of money management.

Any of the trailing stop methods can be used. The idea is to make sure you get out with a profit. By determining a profit protection exit point, we avoid the trap of seeing the profit in a trade disappear and turn into a loss. By trailing a 50% stop in the early stages of a trade, we will make a decent profit on most of your trades and, at the very least, avoid huge losses.

There is a time to lift the 50% trailing stop. One instance is when we decide to let the market run, and place a stop far back using one of the trailing stop methods we've already seen. The other is when we decide to get out before our 50% stop is hit because of the price action we are seeing in the market. The decision to get out early is normally made during a short to intermediate term phase of the trade.

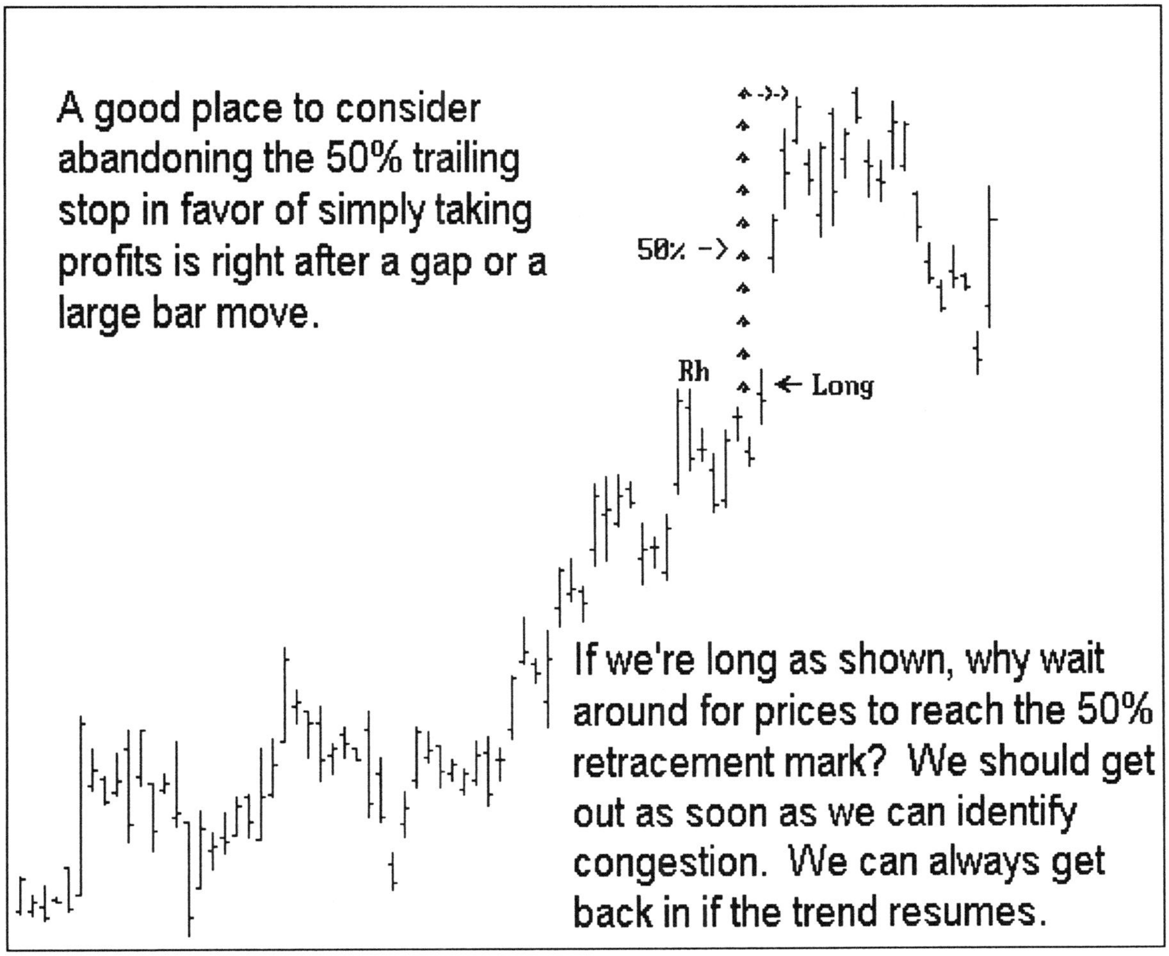

In other words, in the early or intermediate stages of a trade, be aware of the market's going into congestion, point A on chart above. At the end of the congestion, or even at some point during the congestion, prices may move to the 50% stop, and we will have given up more than necessary.

Don't feel "honor bound", or in any way compelled to stay with a trailing exit point if it doesn't seem to make sense. Take profits!

Winning traders learn to take profits when they are available! Do not let greed keep you in a trade when you see the position beginning to crumble. Do not allow false hopes for the "big" win keep you from grabbing profits while they are there. You have earned them. Be sure to take them.

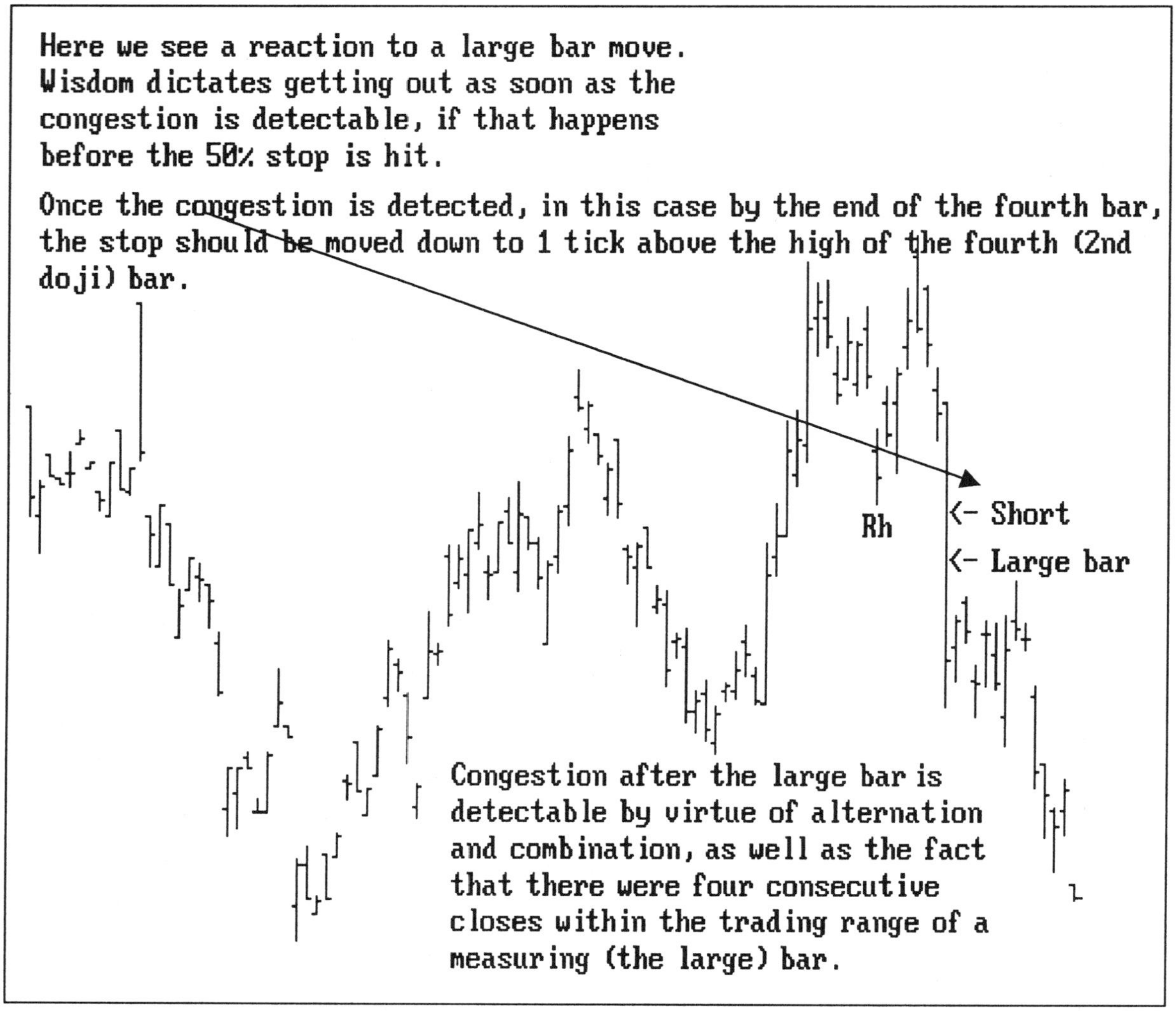

Another important realization to consider when setting a 50% trailing stop is the concept that markets retrace to the ±50% level fairly often. This is often a self-fulfilling prophecy because so many people believe in it. Be very aware of where the move started. The retracement will often be from the ***inception*** of the move to the point where the correction starts, not from where you ***entered the market*** to the point where the correction starts.

If your 50% trailing stop is in the pathway of a 50% correction, it is virtually sure to be hit. Therefore, try to wait until the market has made a correction from the current leg before you begin to trail a 50% stop. The chart on the following page shows this concept.

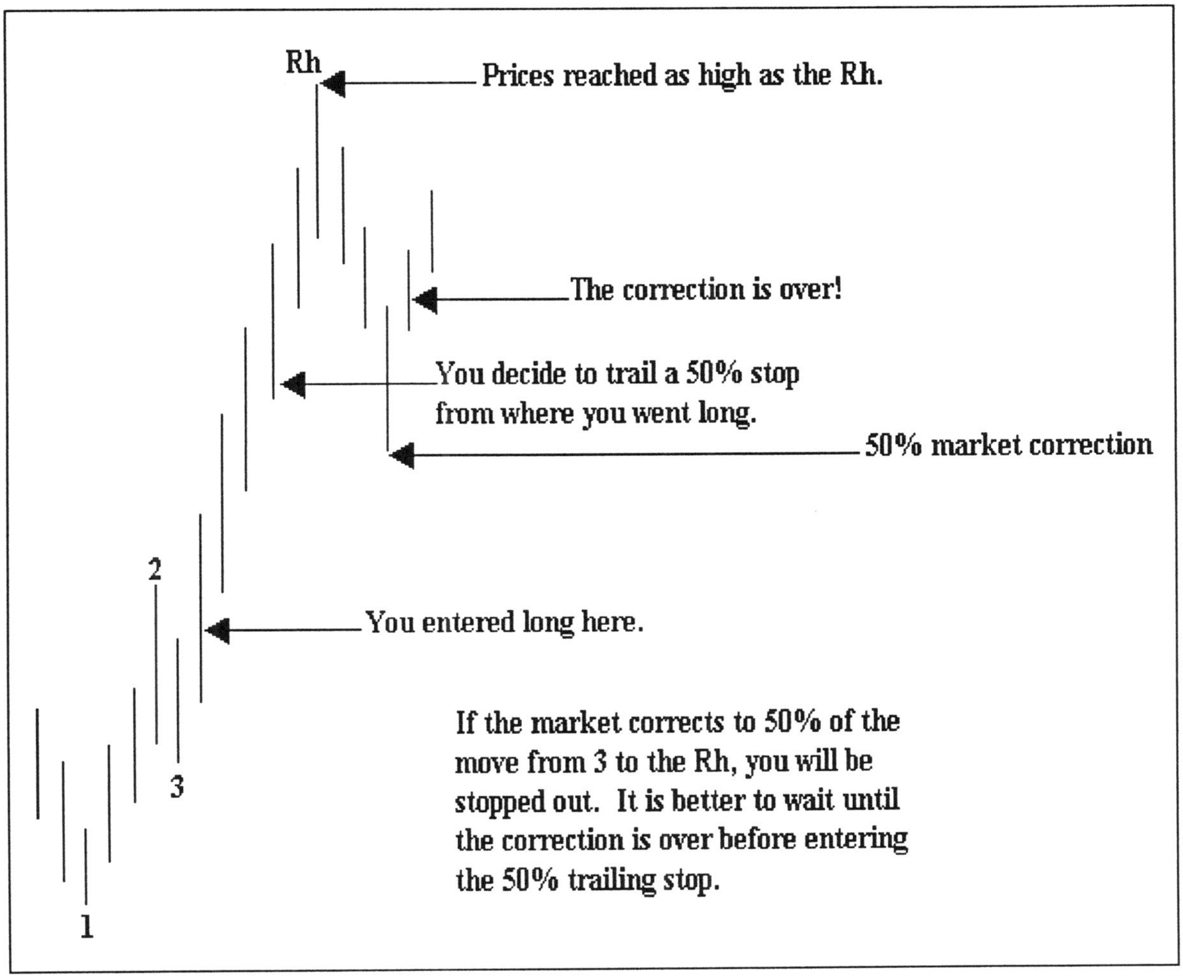

The leg of the move that began at the #3 point of the 1-2-3 formation rose to the point of the Rh. Subsequent to that the market began to correct. If you bought long on a violation of the high of the bar making the #3 point, and placed a profit protecting stop at 50% of the distance between your entry and the point of the Rh, you would have been stopped out when prices retraced 50% of the move from the #3 point to the point of the Rh. It is better to wait until prices finish correcting before entering a stop to protect 50% of your unrealized paper profits. By unrealized profits we mean the number of points available from your actual entry to the point of the Rh.

Chapter 11

FILTERING THE ROSS HOOK

There are a number of way to filter trades. Many of them have to do with the very same parameters that are taken into consideration when setting stops or exit points.

As a quick review, let's look at some of them.

1. Some types or sizes of orders eliminate some trade entries because you are never filled.

2. Too much or too little volatility can keep us out of a trade. Too much volatility may mean we have to place our stop further away than is comfortable. Too little volatility arises when prices are moving so little as to give little or no promise of movement sufficient to cover costs and make a profit.

3. Placement of stops at natural support and resistance points may keep us out of a trade. They may be too close or too far.

4. Technical studies such as the Volatility Stop may keep us from trading. They may call for our stop to be set too far away for comfort, or too close to be practical. If we are using the Volatility Stop study, too little volatility occurs when the study fails to yield a number that is not outside the range of current prices.

5. If we use it as a filter, a moving average may keep us from entering a trade by failing to confirm what other entry signals are showing.

6. Our choice of stock(s) and time-frame in which to trade. Recalling that Ross Hooks are intended to be traded in trending markets, the fact that a market is not trending in the time-frame in which we choose to trade will filter us out of the trade. Therefore, it's vital for us to be able to identify congestion. Congestion, then, is also a filter.

All of these parameters have been covered previously. They are ways to filter trades. With proper implementation, we will enter only the trades we want at a price we want. The trades we want occur in trending stocks with an affordable stop protection level. They are trades in which we have a reasonable expectation of covering costs *and* making a profit. We don't have to use all filtering methods, just the ones with which we are comfortable.

There is a lot to keep in mind when trading. It involves work and thought. We must always ask ourselves whether or not everything is right about a trade, and then take only the best trades. The filtering we've just talked about is fundamental to good trading. It means we simply cannot take every trade that comes along. It means we cannot trade too many stocks simultaneously. Trading more than four to six stocks at once is almost too much to bear. It is over trading for most traders. However we have seen traders put on as many as 23 trades at one time, you need sophisticated trading software to be able to keep track of this type of trading. Doing the work necessary for conservative filtering of trades is in itself a filter. We must select the best of the best trades.

That means sitting down each day and poring over weekly and daily charts to get market perspective. We must do that even if we are daytraders. Getting the overall picture will filter out many intraday trades, simply because perspective shows us that elsewhere there are more likely candidates for a winning trade.

A checklist that asks the kinds of questions raised is helpful. We strain each contemplated trade through the filter of our checklist. Ask:

- "Is the market trending?"

- "Can I identify congestion?"

- "If I were to place my stop 'here' how would I feel if my stop were hit? Could I stand either or both the pain or dollar loss?"

- “If prices move with the same volatility with which they've been moving, can I cover costs and make a small profit? Besides covering costs and a small profit, is there sufficient momentum that I can also expect to make even more profit?”

- “Is this stock giving better signals in another time frame? Is it perhaps more easily traded in another time frame?”

- “Where is the closest natural support or resistance? Is it too close or too far for comfort?”

CONFIRMATION FILTERS

The techniques contained in this course have proven to be consistently successful. We taught every one of them to students who are now profitably using them. However, be forewarned that in trading, one person's success with a particular technical indicator study is often another person's failure using the identical indicator. The distinction is in the deployment, discipline, management, and other ingredients that comprise the difference between the winning trader and the losing trader.

There ***are*** technical studies that can serve as confirmation filters.

- “Does the 3 x 3 DMAC show containment?”

- The 3 x 3 DMAC is often important in deciding about trade entry. The angle at which the 3 x 3 DMAC changes direction, and then begins to show containment, gives an excellent idea of the momentum behind the trade. Assuming containment of prices, when the angle formed by the 3 x 3 DMAC's change of direction is between 45 and 65 degrees, it is indicative of a strong trend in the making.

But there are confirmation filters other than the 3 x 3 DMAC. One of these is the Commodity Channel Index (CCI).

We will see together how you can use the CCI study in a way that few have seen before. We'll take it a step at a time. Pay close attention to what is being taught here. (This study is also available in most charting software packages.)

The CCI measures the mean deviation of a bar's Typical Price relative to a moving average of N bars' Typical Price. Typical Price may be computed as the high plus the low plus the close, divided by three. This gives a close-weighted Typical Price.

You need to realize that there is a potential error in the way CCI is computed. In arriving at Typical Price, gaps are ignored. In most cases this doesn't matter, but in some cases it makes the difference in whether or not to take a trade.

CCI is supposed to show overbought and oversold within a stock's range of prices. It has three lines: +100, 0, and -100. However, CCI is theoretically, if not practically, infinitely expandable. At what value is it oversold or overbought?

There is one great advantage to the scale. It is increasingly difficult for CCI to make ever greater extremes in its readings. It takes increasingly more momentum to push the CCI plot increasingly further out on its scale.

Users of CCI say you are supposed to buy when CCI crosses the +100 line from below, and you are supposed to sell when CCI crosses the -100 line from above.

Experience has shown that a 30-bar CCI works best. We tested it all the way to 50 bars, and agreed that 30 bars was best.

Any software which will allow you to insert a fictitious price bar can be used to emulate the manner in which we use the CCI. To insert a price, you need to be able to create a hypothetical price bar for what will be the next price bar. How to know what the next price bar will be will be shown just ahead. This is easily done on a daily chart with most software. On anything less than a 15 minute chart, you will really have to scramble to get the job done. The truth is, the calculation works best on an hourly, daily or weekly chart. Once you have placed the hypothetical bar on the chart, simply run the CCI study with the hypothetical bar in place, and see what the reading will be.

The hypothetical bar need have only one price for all fields. The open, high, low, and close can all be a Typical Price, but if your software will allow, you can also insert a high and a low if you want to do the extra work.

How do you know what the next bar's Typical Price might be?

We'll show you two ways to do it. Then, we'll show you how to use CCI with the Ross Hook.

Figuring the next bar's Typical Price in congestion has been done essentially this way since the inception of exchange trading. Each day many specialists and market makers come to the exchange with these figures in hand. They tend to sell at or near the typical high and buy at or near the typical low. If either the high or the low are violated by more than a few ticks, you will see them bail out and run for their lives. This shows up on a chart as an extra long intraday bar.

FIGURING THE NEXT BAR'S TYPICAL PRICE IN CONGESTION

(Open + High + Low + 2(Close)) / 5 = X

2X minus The High = Next Bar's Projected Low
2X minus The Low = Next Bar's Projected High

O H L C
Example: (24 + 25 + 23 + 2(23.5)) / 5 = 23.8

2(23.8) - 25 = 22.6 = Next Bar's Projected Low
2(23.8) - 23 = 24.6 = Next Bar's Projected High

Next Bar's Typical Price = (Next Bar's Projected Low + Next Bar's Projected High) / 2

(22.6 + 24.6) / 2 = 23.6

FIGURING THE NEXT BAR'S TYPICAL PRICE IN A TREND

TYPICAL PRICE IN AN UPTREND.

To compute the next bar's Typical Price in an uptrend, we need to find the average rate of ascent. It's important to use 4 bars for this computation.

What we want to know is, on average, how much prices are moving in the direction of the uptrend. To find out, we measure from low to high.

Here are the steps to follow:

We measure from one bar's low to the next bar's high, to see how far prices move over a two bar period. We do this for three overlapping two bar periods.

Let's take an example:

BAR	LOW	HIGH	AMOUNT MOVED
1	26.00		
2	26.50	28.00	2.00
3	27.75	30.25	3.75
4	29.25	31.00	3.25

We then add those measurements together and divide by three.

2+ 3.75+ 3.25 = 9 , 9/ 3 = 3 on average.

Adding 3 to the last known low (29.25), we obtain a number of **32.25, which is the next bar's projected high.**

Next we need to determine tomorrow's projected low.

We measure the average volatility for the last three bars. **Average volatility equals the sum of the differences between high and low, divided by three.**

BAR	LOW	HIGH
1	26.00	
2	26.50	28.00
3	27.75	30.25
4	29.25	31.00

We have:

31.00 - 29.25 = 1.75
30.25 - 27.75 = 2.50
28.00 - 26.50 = 1.50

The three differences are 1.75, 2.50, and 1.50.

Summing these and dividing by 3 = 5.75/3 = 1.92 (rounded).

Subtracting 1.92 from the projected high (32.25), **we obtain a number of 30.33 for the next bar's projected low.**

The final step is to add the projected high to the projected low and divide by two to come up with a Typical Price. In this case, (32.25 + 30.33) / 2 = 31.29.

It's important to realize that this is not an exact science, but you might be surprised how often we can come within a tick or two of being right.

We can also compute the Typical Price differently by measuring from high to high to get the projected high.

To obtain the projected low, we would then do as we've just done and subtract average volatility for three days from the projected high.

A third idea is to also measure from close to close to come up with a projected close. Then we can add the projected high + the projected low + the projected close, and then divide by three to come up with a close weighted Typical Price.

The ultimate situation would be to project an open and throw that in there as well. Then we could substitute the four prices into the formula I gave for finding Typical Price in a congestion.

It's a matter of choice, yours. With today's software in many instances being programmable by us, we can figure all the different ways and then make our choice.

Tomorrow's Typical Price in a Downtrend

To compute tomorrow's Typical Price in a downtrend, we need to find the average rate of descent. It's important to use 4 bars for this computation.

What we want to know is, on average, how much prices are moving in the direction of the downtrend. To find out, we measure from high to low.

Here are the steps to follow:

We measure from today's low to the previous day's low, to see how far prices move over a two day period. We do this for three overlapping two day periods.

BAR	HIGH	LOW	AMOUNT MOVED
1		61.25	
2	63.50	60.75	2.25
3	62.75	60.00	2.00
4	61.50	59.25	1.50

We then add those measurements together and divide by three.
2.25 + 2.00 + 1.50 = 5.75 / 3 = 1.92 (rounded) on average.

Subtracting 1.92 from the last known high (61.50), **we obtain a number 59.58 for tomorrow's projected low.**

Next we need to determine tomorrow's projected high.

We measure the average volatility for the last three bars. **Average volatility equals the sum of the differences between high and low, divided by three.**

BAR	HIGH	LOW
1		61.25
2	63.50	60.75
3	62.75	60.00
4	61.50	59.25

We have:

61.50 - 59.25 = 2.25
62.75 - 60.00 = 2.75
63.50 - 60.75 = 2.75

The three differences are, 2.25, 2.75, and 2.75.

Summing these and dividing by 3 = 7.75 / 3 = 2.58

Adding 2.58 to the projected low, we obtain a number of 62.16 for tomorrow's projected high. 59.58 + 2.58 = 62.16.

The final step is to add the projected low and the projected high and divide by two to come up with a Typical Price. In this case, (62.16 + 59.58) / 2 = 60.87 = tomorrow's Typical Price.

One last thing. For those of you who might want to know the formula for the CCI, it's as follows:

FOUR STEPS TO CALCULATE CCI

1. **COMPUTE TODAY'S "TYPICAL" PRICE, USING HIGH, LOW AND CLOSE:**

$$X_1 = 1/3\ (H + L + C)$$

2. **COMPUTE A MOVING AVERAGE OF THE N MOST RECENT TYPICAL PRICES:**

$$\overline{X} = \frac{1}{N} \sum_{i=1}^{N} X_i$$

3. **COMPUTE THE MEAN DEVIATION OF THE N MOST RECENT TYPICAL PRICES:**

$$MD = \frac{1}{N} \sum_{i=1}^{N} x_i \ \ \bar{x} \ |$$

4. **COMPUTE THE COMMODITY CHANNEL INDEX:**

$$CCI = \frac{(x_1 - \overline{x})}{1.5 * MD}$$

WHERE:

N = NUMBER OF DAYS IN THE DATA BASE

X_1 = CURRENT BAR'S TYPICAL PRICE

X_2 = PREVIOUS BAR'S TYPICAL PRICE

X_3 = BAR BEFORE PREVIOUS BAR'S TYPICAL PRICE

X_N = OLDEST TYPICAL PRICE IN THE DATA BASE

$$\sum_{i=1}^{N}$$

$$\sum_{i=1}^{N} x_i = x_1 + x_2 + x_3 \cdots + x_N$$

$|\quad|$ SIGNIFIES "ABSOLUTE VALUE"; DIFFERENCE SHOULD BE ADDED AS IF ALL WERE POSITIVE NUMBERS.

We had to take that to a mathematician to have it translated. To the best of our knowledge, CCI shows you the relationship (expressed as the mean deviation) of today's Typical Price to a moving average of Typical Prices.

Now it's time to we look at how to make money with this concept.

Rules

Here are the rules we will use to filter the Ross Hooks through the CCI: Keep in mind, that we want to enter via the Trader's Trick Entry (TTE), rather than the Hook itself.

1. THE CCI MUST EITHER HAVE PASSED THROUGH TWO OF THE "VISIBLE HORIZONTAL" (VH) LINES (+100, 0, -100) PRIOR TO TAKING THE HOOK, OR IT MUST BE PROJECTABLE THAT IT WILL PASS THROUGH TWO OF THE VISIBLE LINES. ANY TWO VISIBLE LINES WILL DO: +100, 0, -100. ONCE CCI HAS MOVED BEYOND THE ±100 LINE, WE WILL TAKE ALL TTE'S THAT OCCUR, AS MODIFIED BY RULES 3-6 WHICH FOLLOW.

2. TAKING TTE'S IMPLIES THAT WE WILL ENTER AHEAD OF THE ROSS HOOK BY PLACING ORDERS AT CORRECTION BAR EXTREMES.

3. IF THE TTE WILL NOT RESULT IN A TRADABLE READING FOR CCI, WE WILL NOT TAKE A BREAKOUT OF A CORRECTION BAR EXTREME. TRADABLE READINGS ARE AS FOLLOWS:

   CCI HAVING MOVED FROM 0 TO ±100
   CCI HAVING MOVED FROM ±100 TO ±150
   CCI HAVING MOVED FROM ±150 TO ±175, OR ANY INCREMENT OF ±25 THEREAFTER, SUCH AS FROM ±175 TO ± 200, OR ±200 TO ±225, ON TO INFINITY. WITH MOST SOFTWARE, BEYOND ±100, ALL CCI CHART LINES ARE INVISIBLE.

4. WITH CCI READING A VALUE OF ±150 OR BEYOND, IF CCI RE-CROSSES ONE INVISIBLE LINE, IT NEED ONLY CROSS THAT SAME LINE AGAIN TO BE TRADABLE.

5. WITH CCI NOT HAVING ACHIEVED A READING OF ±150, IF CCI RE-CROSSES ONE VISIBLE LINE, IT MUST CROSS TWO LINES (ONE VISIBLE AND ONE INVISIBLE) TO BE TRADABLE. NOTE: WE'VE NEVER SEEN CCI PLOTTED WHERE LINES ABOVE OR BELOW 100 WERE DISPLAYED.

6. IF CCI RE-CROSSES ANY TWO VISIBLE LINES, WE WILL CONSIDER OURSELVES BACK TO THE BEGINNING, WAITING FOR CCI TO CROSS TWO VISIBLE LINES.

Following are some illustrations to help clarify rules **1**, **5**, and **6**, followed by some charts that clarify the remaining rules.

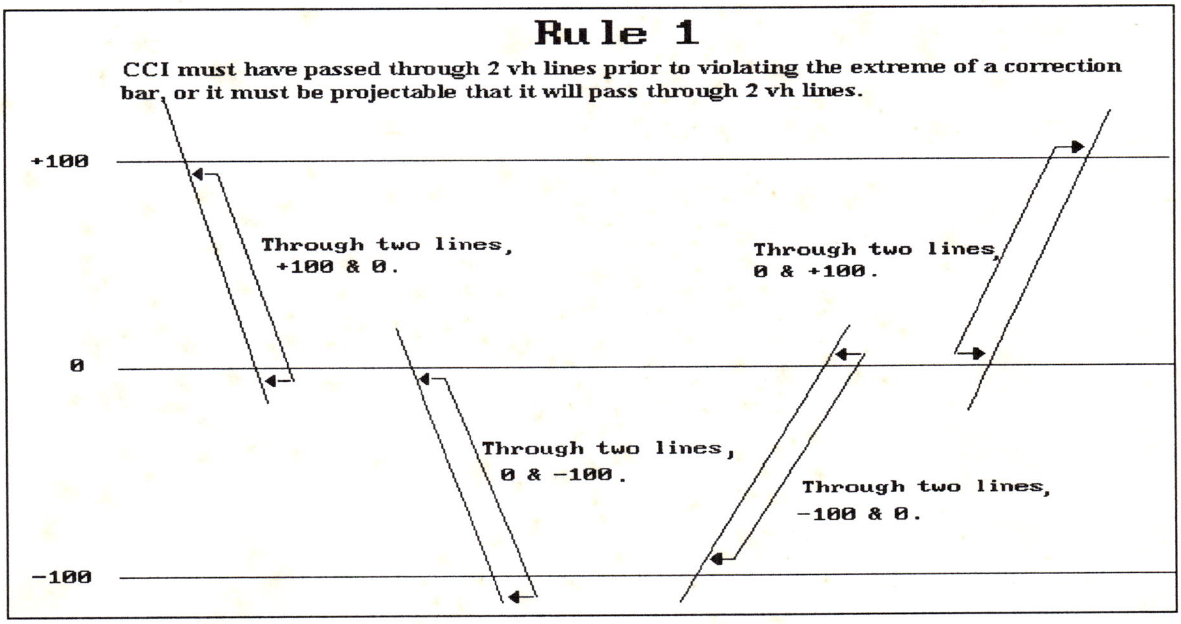

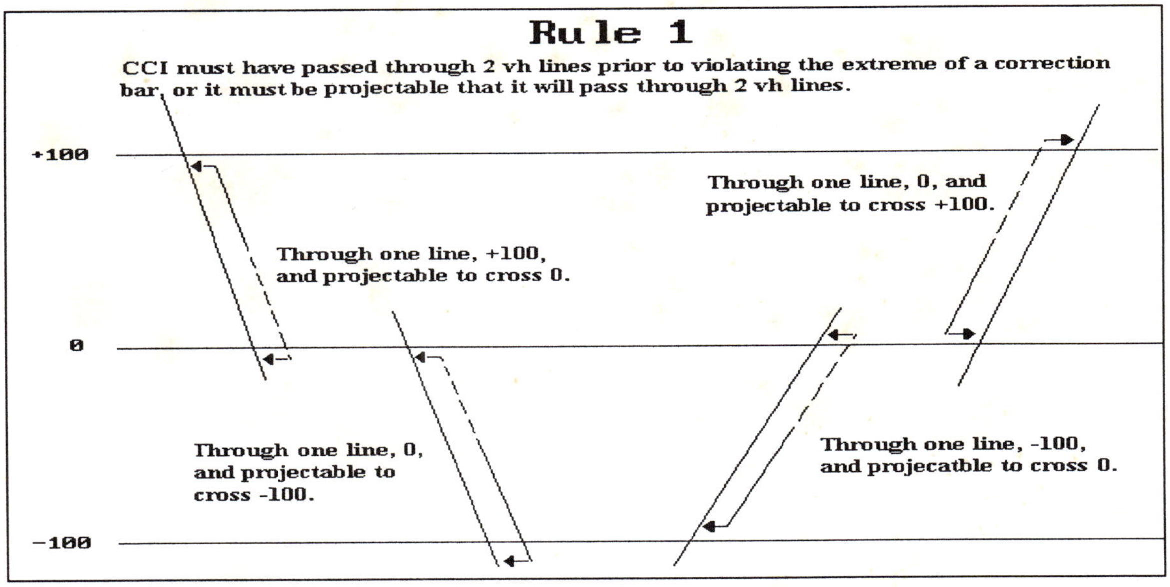

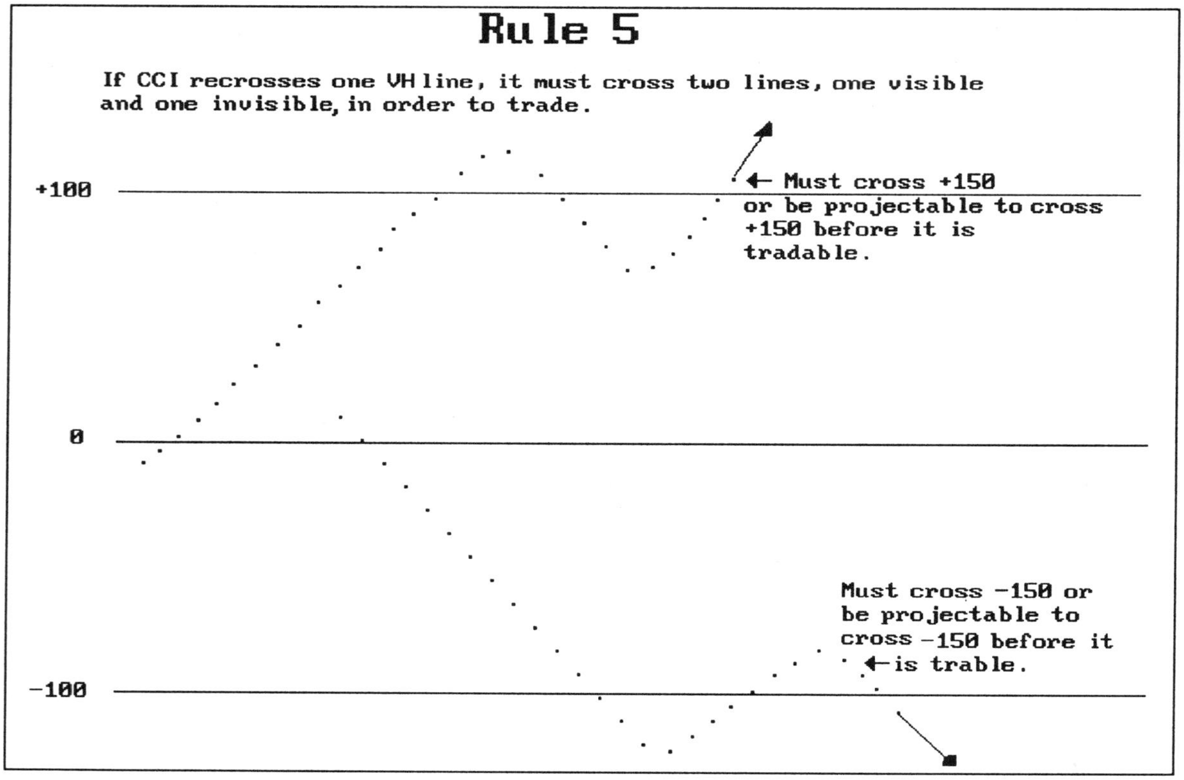

AS LONG AS CCI IS CONSISTENT WITH THE CHARTS CREATED BY YOUR OWN SOFTWARE, IT IS ACCEPTABLE TO TAKE THE SIGNALS GENERATED.

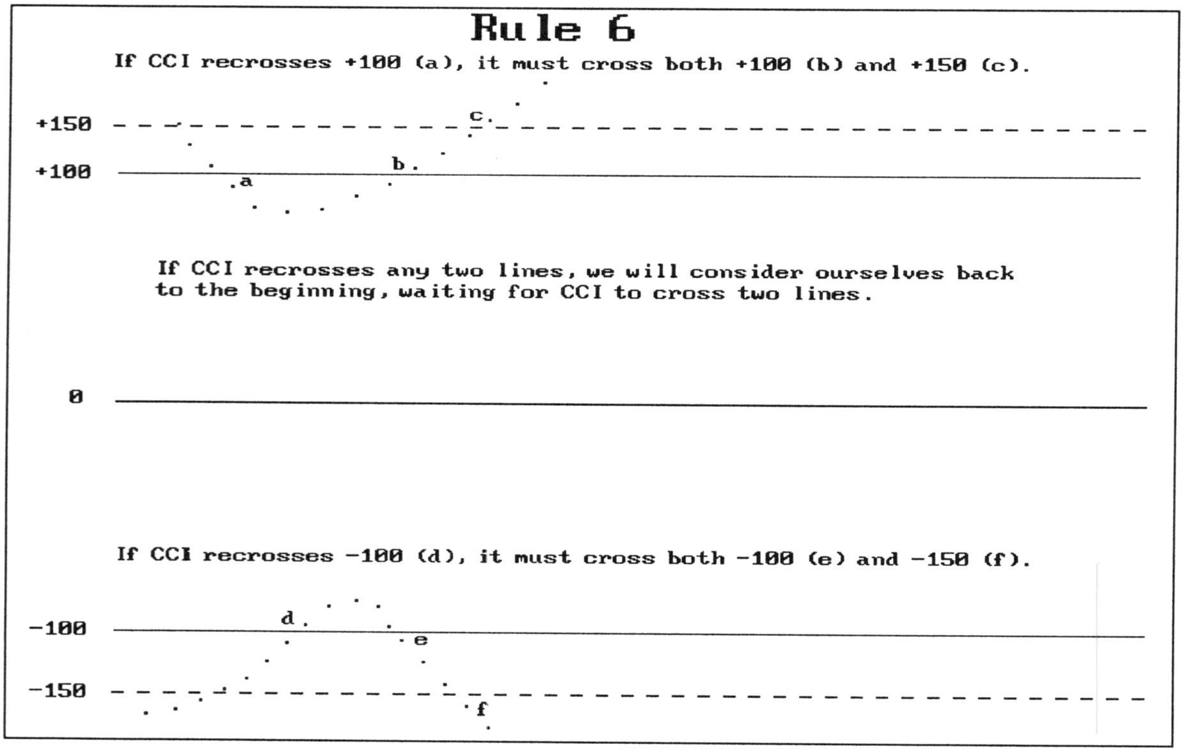

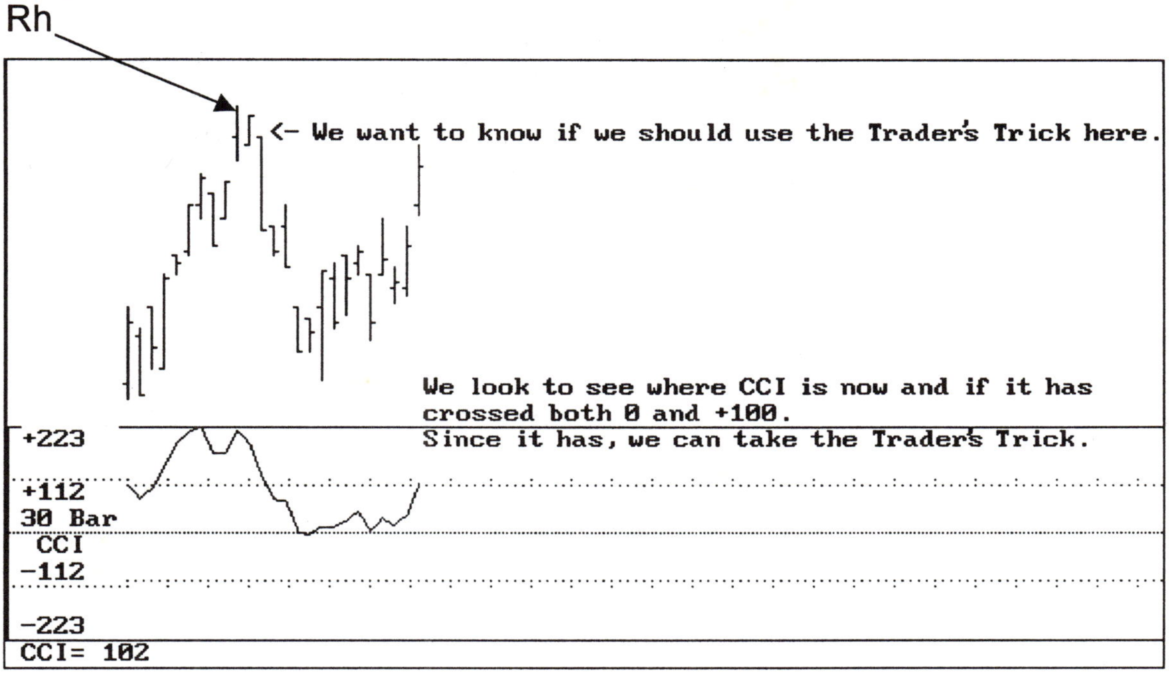

Chart above: We want to know if we may enter on a violation of the high of the 2nd bar following the point of the Rh. Since we can, we will be following Rules #1 and #2.

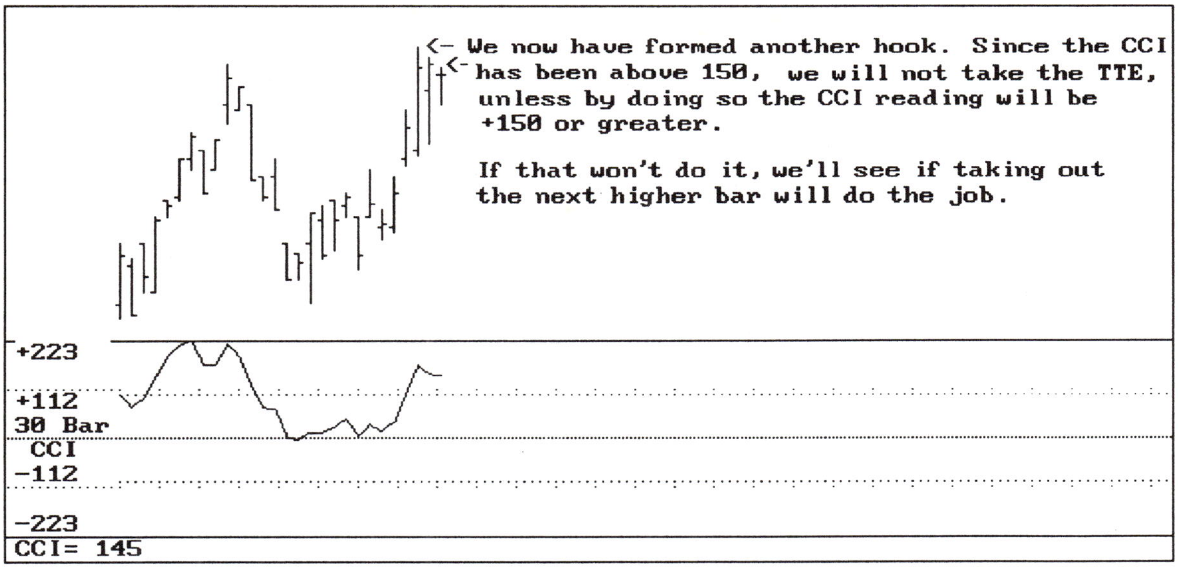

Chart above: If taking out the high of the TTE entry bar will cause CCI to read 150 or higher, we will have fulfilled Rule #4, we may enter a trade.

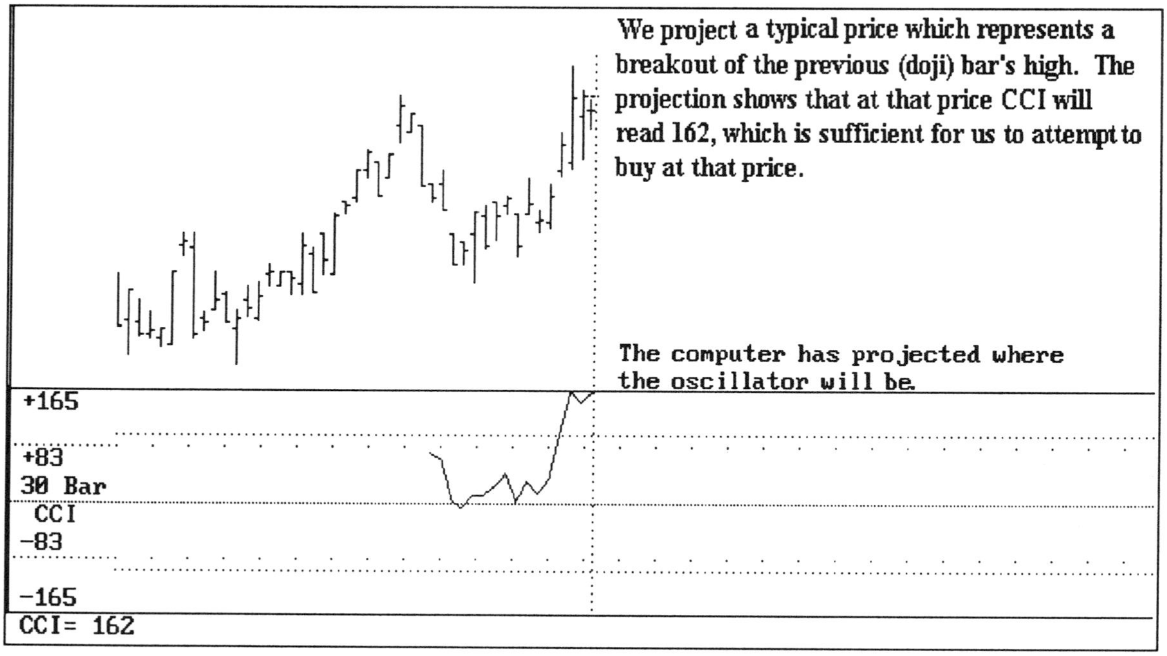

Chart above: A projected reading of 162 fulfills the requirements of Rule #4 and so we may take the TTE.

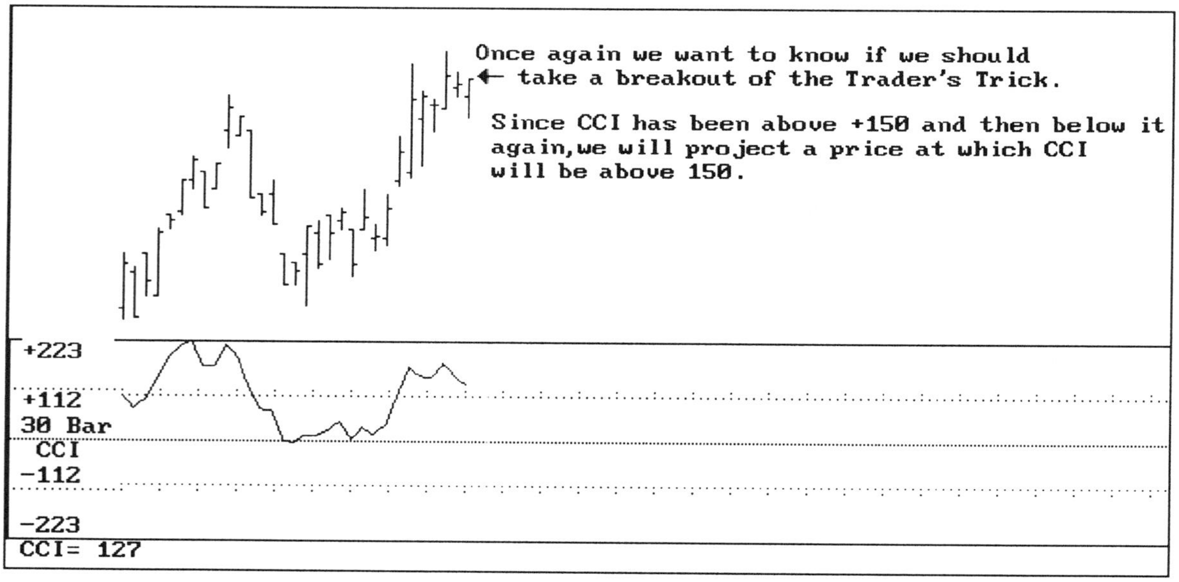

Chart above: Once again we want to project CCI according to Rule #4 to see if we may take a TTE.

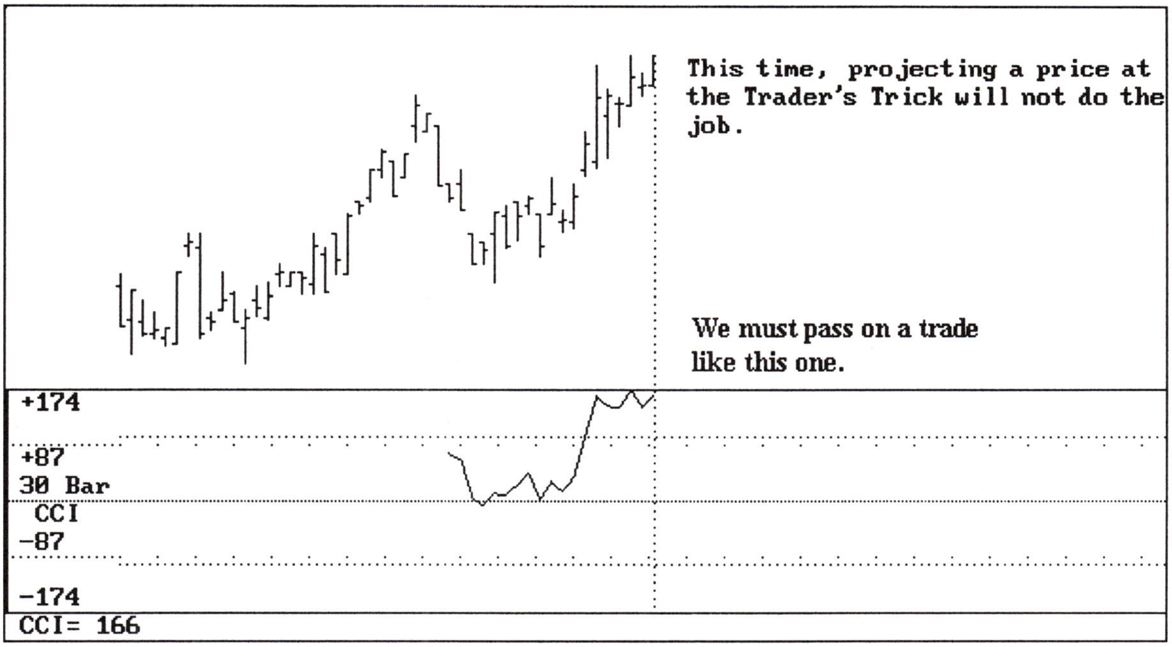

Chart above: This time the projection falls short of the requirement and so we will not take a TTE. Rule #3.

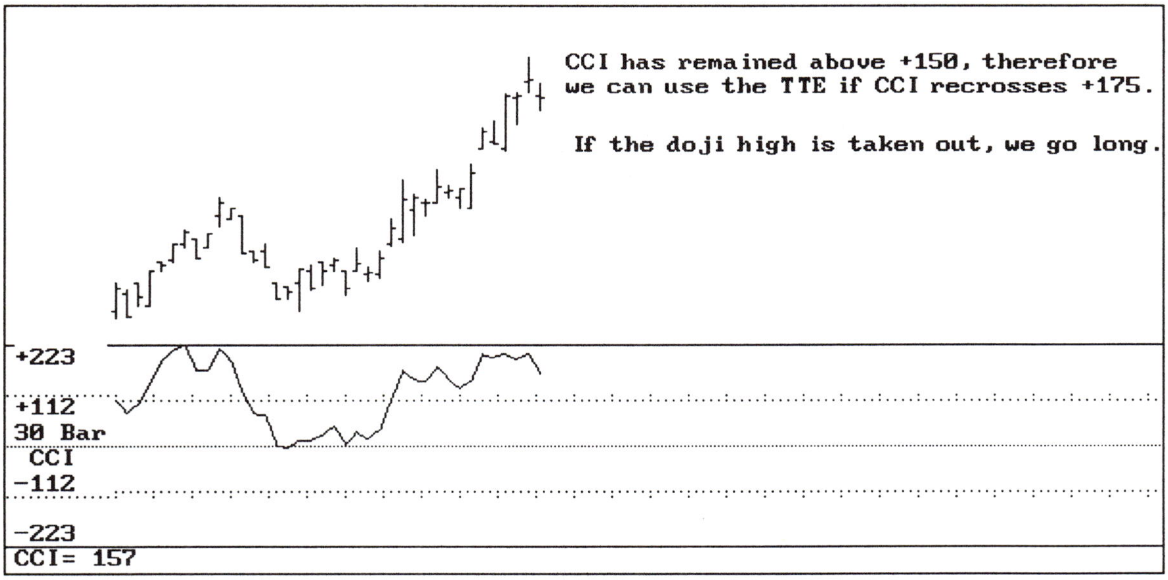

Chart above: If CCI projects to 175 or above, we may take the TTE based upon Rule #4.

However, because the indicator fell and there was no opportunity to be filled on the TTE.

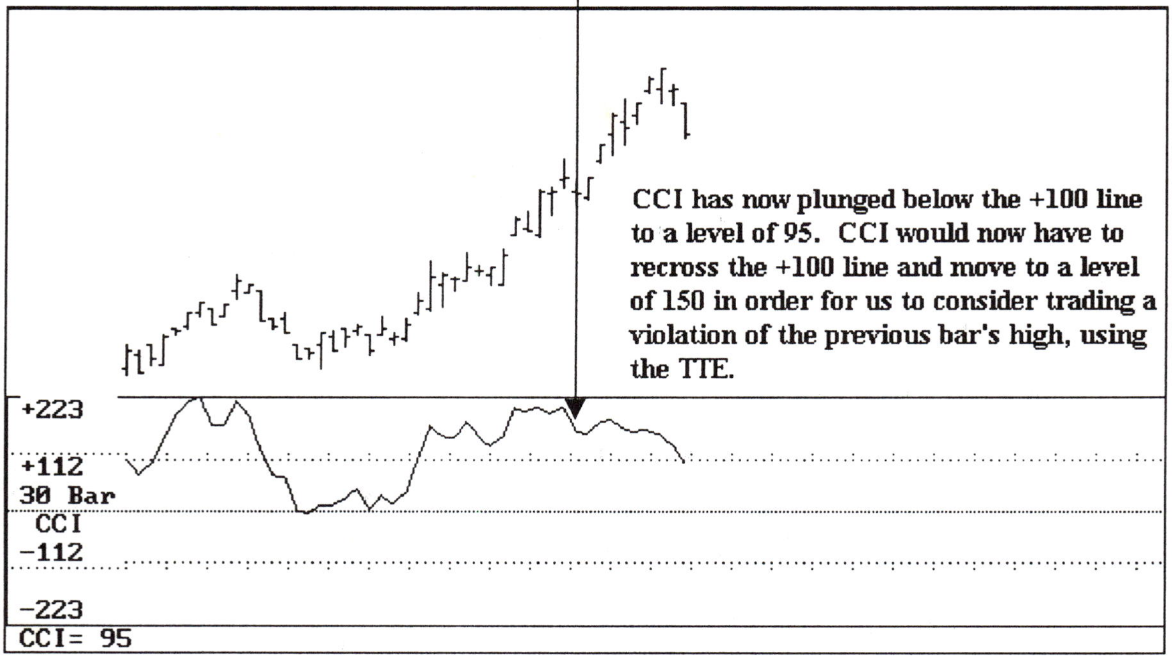

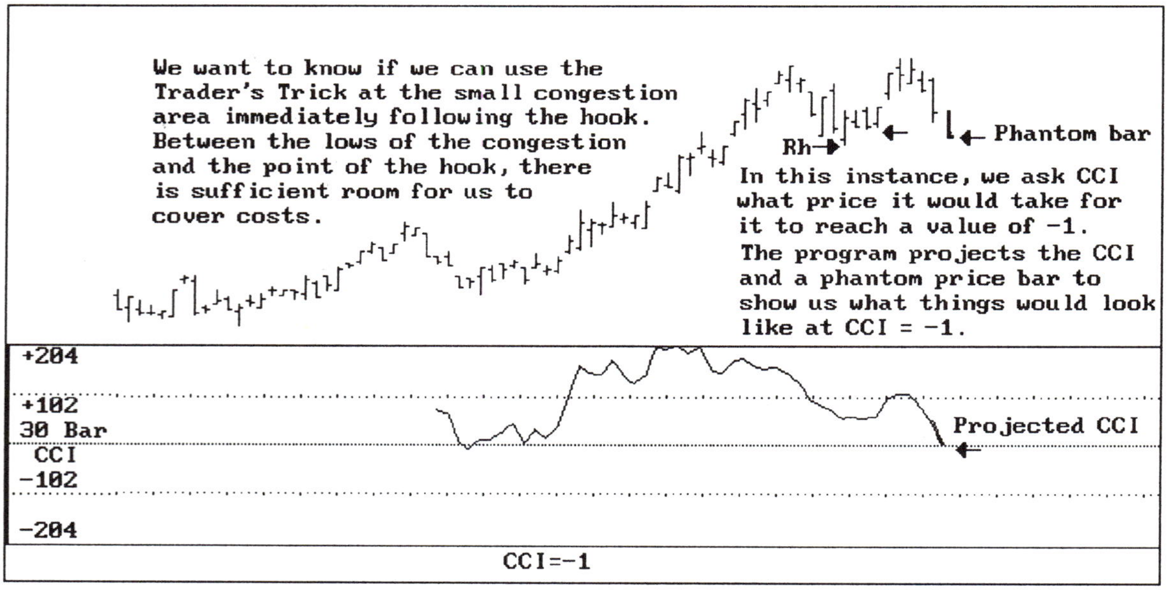

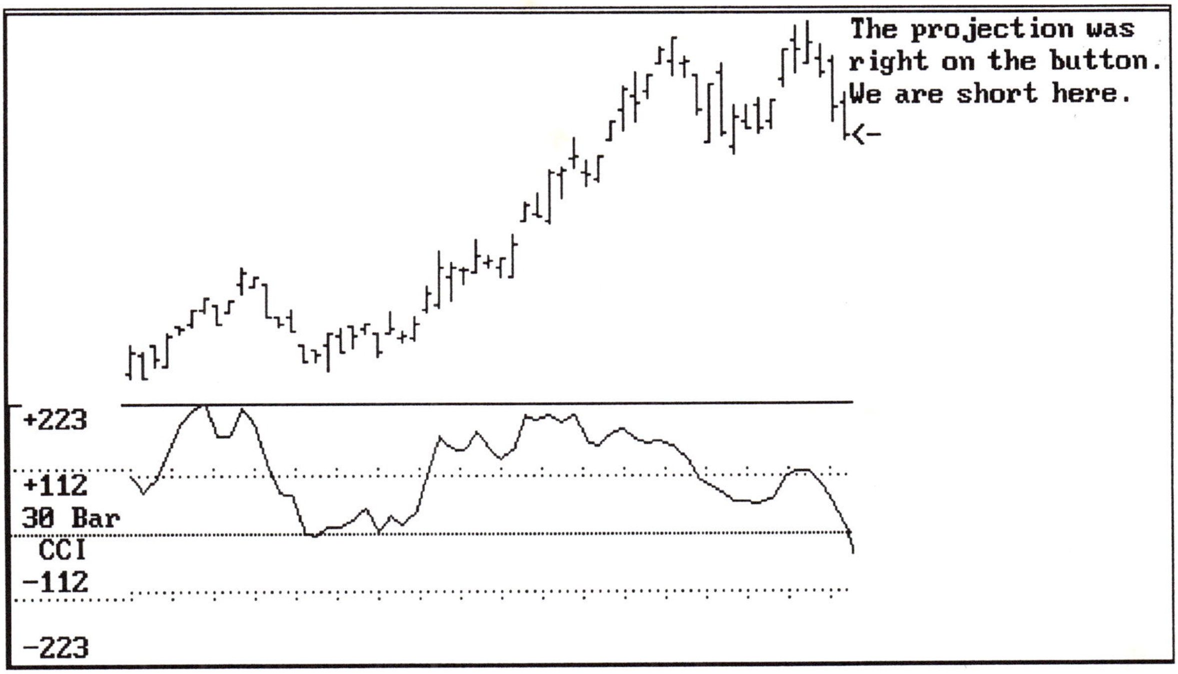

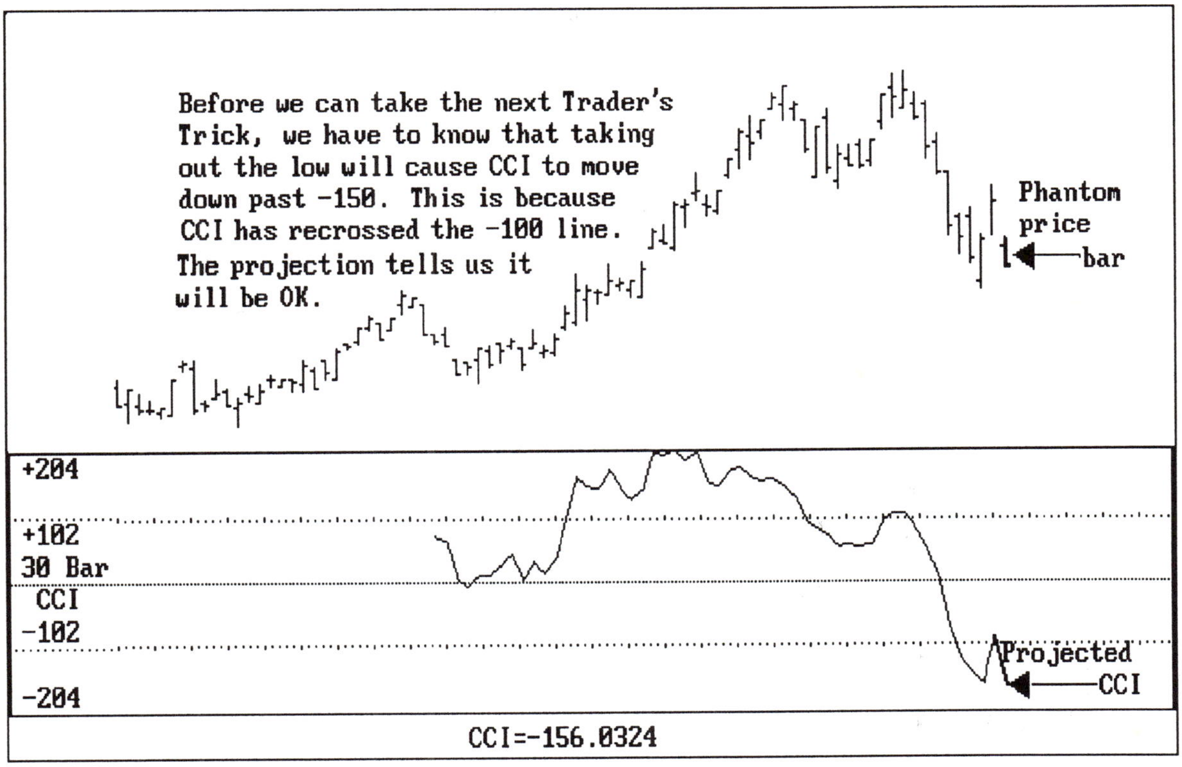

By now, you should be getting the idea of how the CCI projection is done, so let's move on.

Chapter 12

STOCHASTICS FILTERING

Although widely used for technical analysis, Stochastics has probably become the most corrupted of all technical analysis studies.

Not only is the study named incorrectly, but its original form and usage have all but been forgotten. It is sometimes referred to as "stocastics," and elsewhere as "stochastics."

A contemporary of ourshas been kind enough to fill us in on the truth. When you see how it is really done, we think you will be pleasantly surprised. We include it in this book because, when used correctly, it works quite well as a filter for the Rh's and RRh's via the Trader's Trick Entry.

First, let's make sure you know the original formula and how to compute it based on a daily chart. Here's the computational process.

Dt	Hi	Lo	Hi-5	Lo-5	Cl	R-5	U-5	D-5	K	R-3	U-3	D-3	D	D-T	D-S
1	2	3	4	5	6	7	8	9	10	11	12	13	14	15	16

Column 1 = Today's DATE
Column 2 = Today's HIGH
Column 3 = Today's LOW
Column 6 = Today's CLOSE

Take the highest figure in Column 2 for five days including today, and place it in Column 4.

Take the lowest figure in Column 3 for five days including today, and place it in Column 5.

Take the difference between Columns 4 and 5 and put it in Column 7.

Take the difference between Columns 4 and 6 and put it in Column 8.

Take the difference between Columns 7 and 8 and put it in Column 9.

Total the last three days of Column 7, including today, and put it in Column 11.

Total the last three days of Column 8, including today, and put it in Column 12.

Total the last three days of Column 9, including today, and put it in Column 13.

Divide the total in Column 7 into the total in Column 9, and put it in Column 10.

Divide the total in Column 11 into the total in Column 13, and put it in Column 14.

Total the last three days of Column 14, including today, and put it in Column 15.

Divide Column 15 by 3 and put the answer in Column 16.

Column 14 is D. Column 16 is D smoothed over a three day period.

If you have software that performs the arithmetic for you, then make sure you set it at 5,1,3, or 5,3,1. How you set it will depend on your software. Apparently different programs use the numbers differently. If you see only one plot instead of two, then switch the parameters. You need a "K" plot and a "D" plot.

To the best of our knowledge, Columns 15 and 16 were not computed in the original formula. Without a computer, here's how to calculate a later version of Stochastics.

$$100 \times \frac{\text{Close - 5 day low}}{\text{5 day high - 5 day low}} = \%K$$

(sum 3 %K) / 3 = %D

(sum 3%D / 3) = Slow %D

Enter today's high in column 1.

Enter today's low in column 2.

Enter highest high of last 5 days in column 3.

Enter lowest low of last 5 days in column 4.

Enter today's close in column 5.

Subtract 5 day low from today's close and enter it in column 6.

Subtract 5 day low from 5 day high, and enter it in column 7.

Divide the number in column 6 by the number in column 7 and multiply by 100. This is %K.

Enter %K in column 8.

Sum last 3 day's %K. Divide sum by 3. This is %D.

Place %D in column 9.

Sum last 3 day's %D. Divide sum by 3. This is Slow %D.

Place Slow %D in column 10.

1	2	3	4	5	6	7	8	9	10
H	L	H5	L5	C	C-L5	H5-L5	%K	%D	%D-S

Now if you don't mind, we will no longer call the original study "Stochastics." This is because the study that is currently called Stochastics is not the same as the original.

From now on, let's call it "Study." We can use the Study in any time frame. We simply change "daily" figures to the time interval in which we are trading.

Now let's get on with the use of the original Study.

The method is based upon an observation: As price increases, closes tend to accumulate closer to the highs of the interval range. The opposite is also true: As price decreases, interval closes tend to accumulate closer to the lows of the interval range. This observation is derived from intraday monitoring of closes.

WHEN WE USE THE STUDY WITH THE TTE, WE MUST MAKE A DISTINCTION BETWEEN CHART ANALYSIS AND TECHNICAL ANALYSIS. THEY ARE NOT THE SAME. CHART ANALYSIS LOOKS ONLY AT THE PRICE BARS THEMSELVES AND THE FORMATIONS THEY CREATE. TECHNICAL ANALYSIS IS LESS CONCERNED WITH INDIVIDUAL PRICE BARS AND NOT AT ALL CONCERNED WITH CHART FORMATIONS. THE TTE WHEN USED WITH TECHNICAL INDICATORS IS LOOKING FOR CONFIRMATION THAT ANY PRICE BARS FOLLOWING A #2 POINT OR AN RH, BUT PRIOR TO A BREAKOUT OF EITHER OF THEM, ARE VALID AS AN ENTRY SIGNAL AHEAD OF THE #2 POINT OR THE RH BEING TAKEN OUT.

There are two valid signals available when working with the Study and the TTE.

- Buy and sell signals are based on a crossing of the "D" plot by the "K" plot.

- Divergence indicates that a TTE violation should not be taken because the trend may be ready to end.

The descriptions of the signals will be repeated just ahead when we show you charts depicting plot crossings and divergence.

For example, when prices have made a new high, then react, and subsequently move to a higher high, while corresponding peaks of "D" make a high and then a lower high, *a bearish divergence has taken place*. The ascending trend may be almost over.

If prices have made a new low, then react, and subsequently move to a lower low, while corresponding troughs of "D" make a low and then a higher low, *a bullish divergence has taken place*. The descending trend may be almost over.

Here is a very important refinement: The original signal was to act upon any divergence when the "K" plot line crossed on the right hand side of the peak of the "D" plot line at a top, or on the right hand side of the trough of the "D" line at a bottom.

This concept still works and is especially true when a market is in congestion as it is when we have an opportunity with a RRh. But when we are dealing with TTE's, we are interested only in how the Study is to be understood in a trending market. When trading TTE's, all we care about is the fact that the "K" plot line has crossed the "D" plot line. It makes no difference in filtering the TTE as to which ***side*** the crossover takes place.

WE DO CARE AT WHICH *LEVEL* THE CROSSOVER TAKES PLACE. WE DON'T WANT A CROSSOVER ABOVE 75 FOR AN UP MOVE OR BELOW 25 FOR A DOWN MOVE, BUT WE MOST CERTAINLY DON'T CARE ABOUT ANY SUCH FOOLISHNESS AS "OVERBOUGHT", OR "OVERSOLD."

Let's look at the crossover concept to learn what is meant by crossover. **BUY AND SELL SIGNALS ARE BASED ON A CROSSING OF THE "D" PLOT BY THE "K" PLOT.**

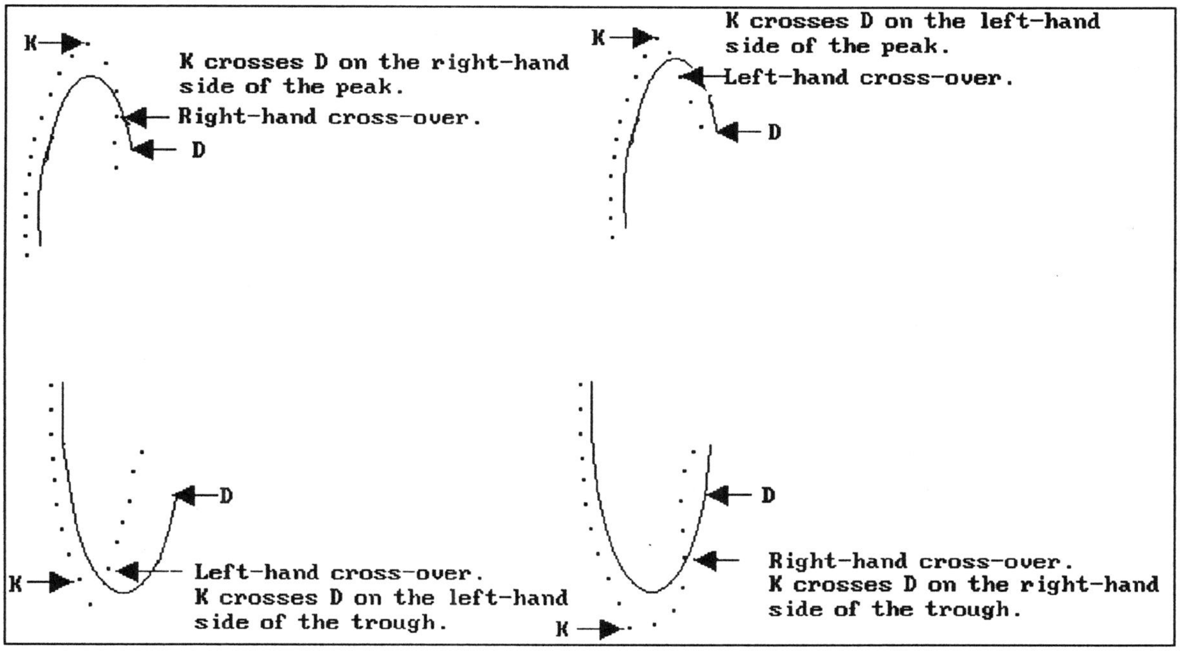

Now let's look at how this affects some Ross Hook trades in conjunction with the TTE.

On the charts that follow, the more wiggly line is the "K" plot and the less wiggly line is the "D" plot. At times the crossover may be dead center.

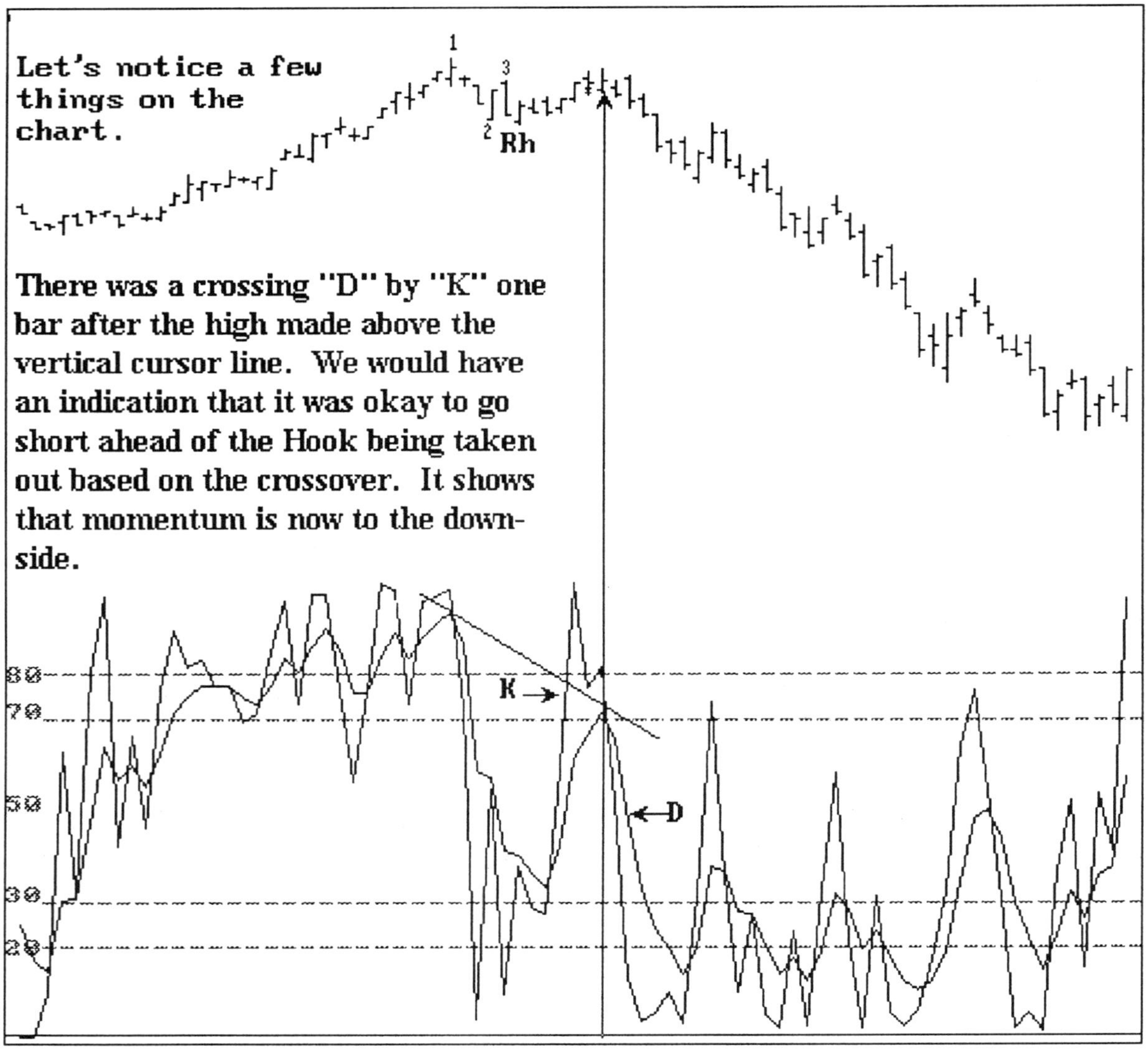

The fact of the relative divergence by the “D” plot from prices, coupled with a crossing of “D” by “K”, gave a strong indication that it would be okay to enter a trade prior to a breakout of the Ross Hook. That means it would have been appropriate to enter on a violation of the lows of the correcting bars subsequent to the Hook.

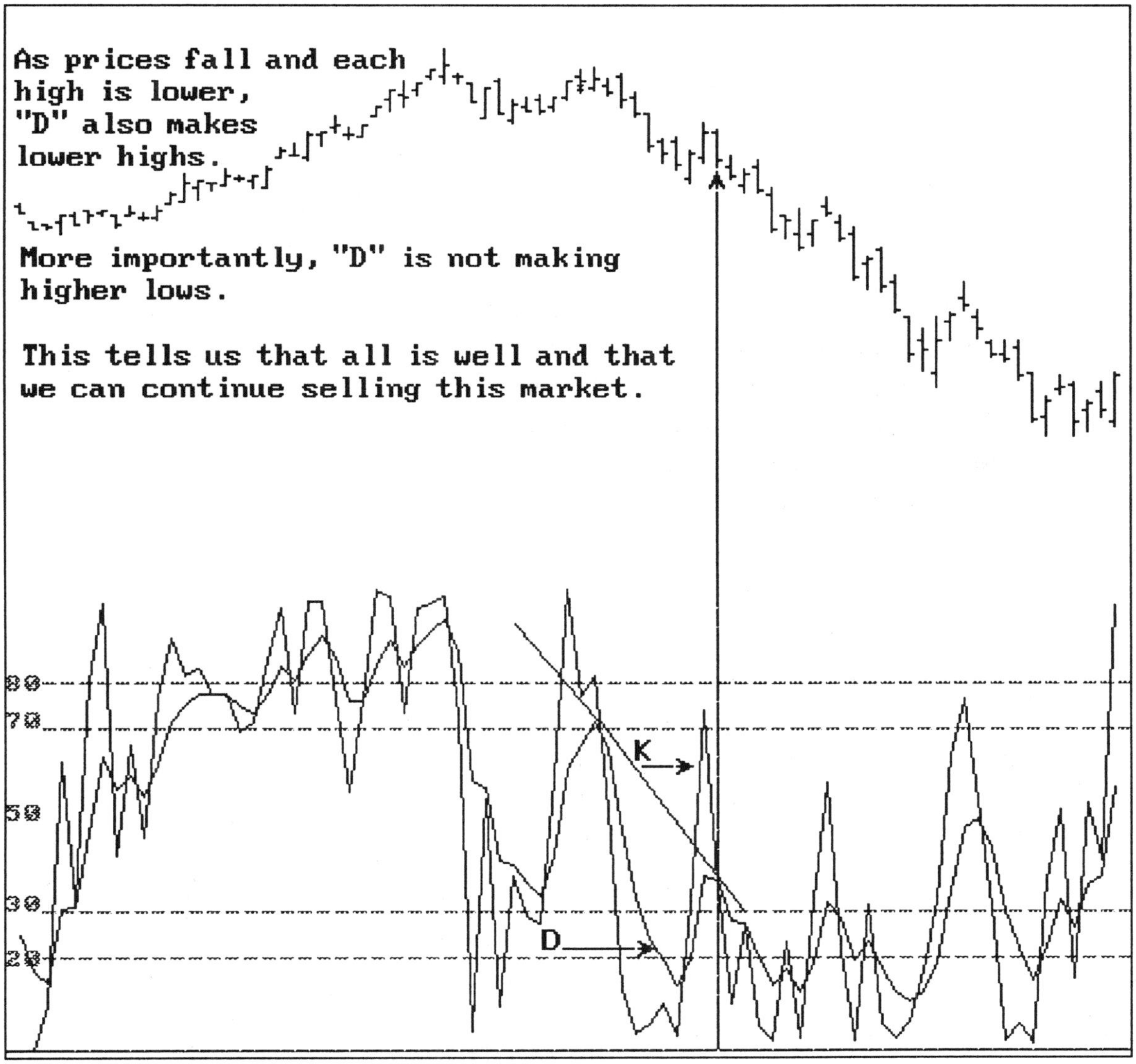

The method indicates that as long as the Study does not become divergent with prices, downside momentum is sufficiently strong to allow trading based on TTE's as each Hook is made in downtrending prices. If "D" were to cease making lower highs and lower lows, then we would no longer be willing to take TTE's ahead of Hooks. As prices move lower, if the Study did not also continue moving lower, we would have divergence. **DIVERGENCE INDICATES THAT A TTE VIOLATION SHOULD NOT BE TAKEN BECAUSE THE TREND MAY BE READY TO END.**

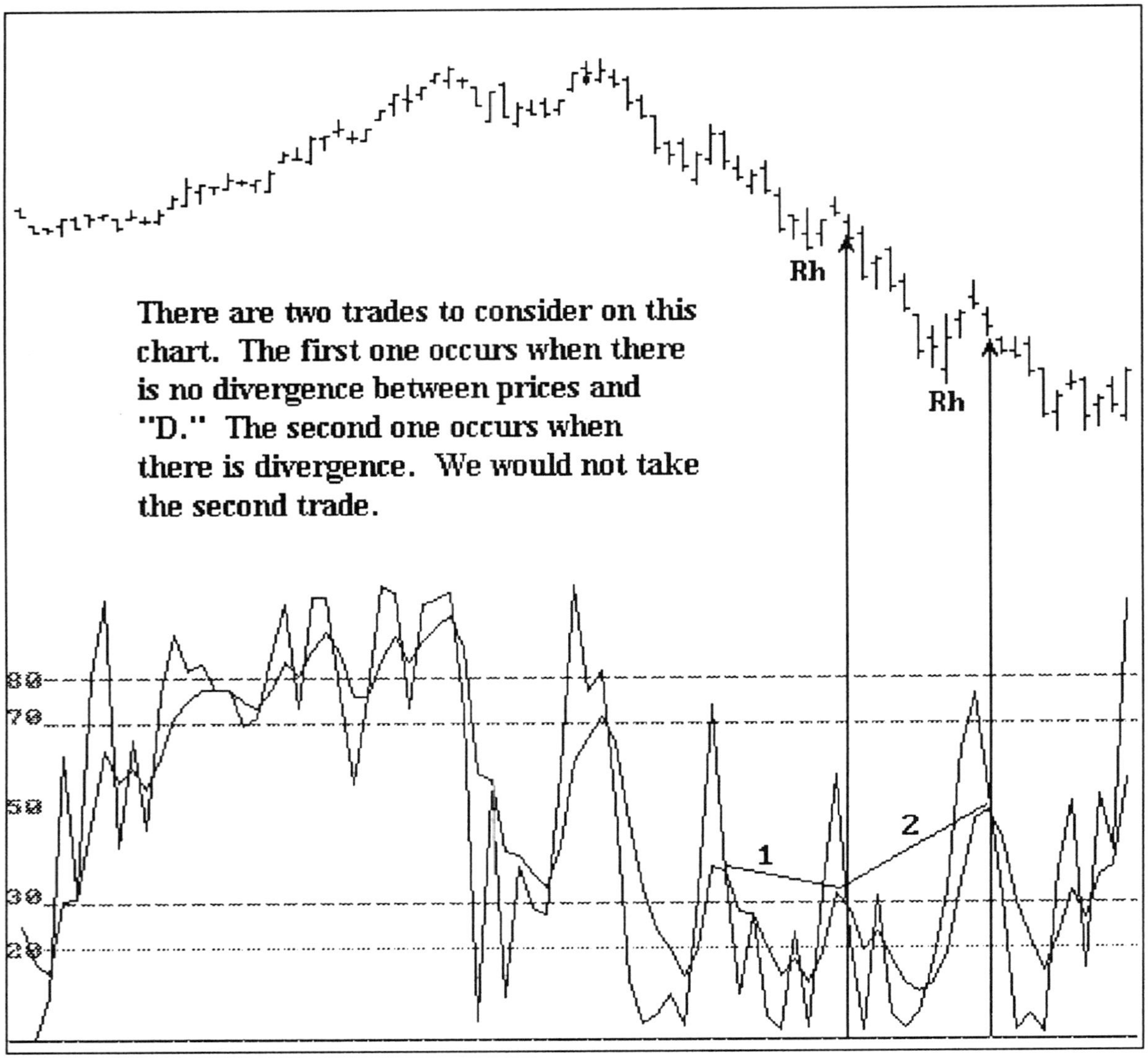

Most traders would normally look only at the lows of the "D" plot for divergence. But we teach that to trade the TTE's, we look for divergence from either the highs or the lows of the "D" plot. Any divergence is enough to keep us from taking that TTE ahead of a violation of the Hook. DIVERGENCE INDICATES THAT A TTE VIOLATION SHOULD NOT BE TAKEN BECAUSE THE TREND MAY BE READY TO END. This is the more conservative approach, but it is part of keeping losses at a minimum while attempting to maximize gains. Divergence can also indicate that it is time to make an exit from a winning trade.

Please look carefully at the following chart. There is a very important concept we need to see.

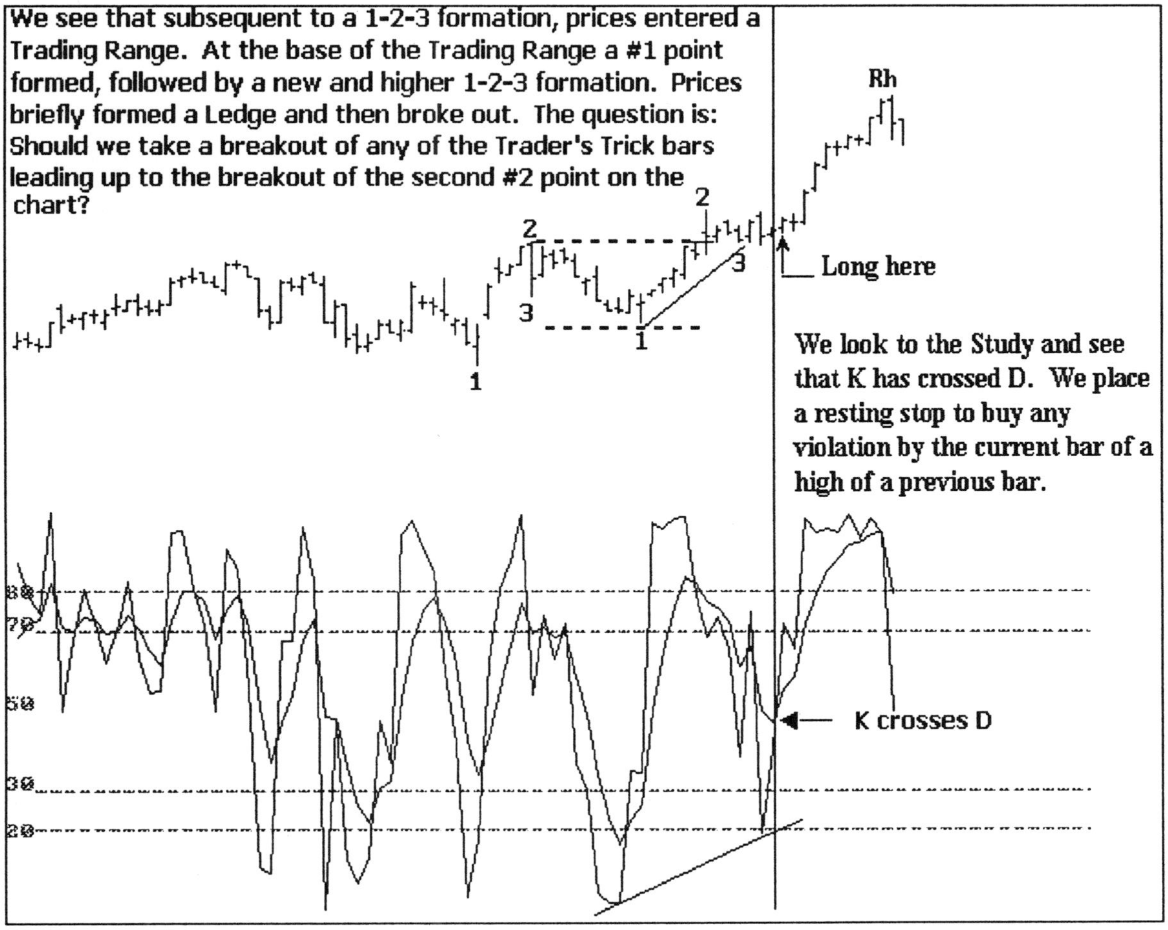

We recall that we can enter a trade on anticipated violations of #2 points and Rh's, since those are to be traded when markets are trending. A breakout of the #2 point of a 1-2-3 defines a trend. That concept would have resulted in a buy signal as shown by "Long here" on the chart.

Notice that when prices form the second 1-2-3, the Study starts to have rising bottoms. This is the tip off of what is to come.

Entering long on the bar shown actually constitutes entering ahead of the breakout of a Ledge.

With our next series of charts, let's start putting together some of what we've been learning. We'll take a price chart from the inception of a trend to as far as we have data for it.

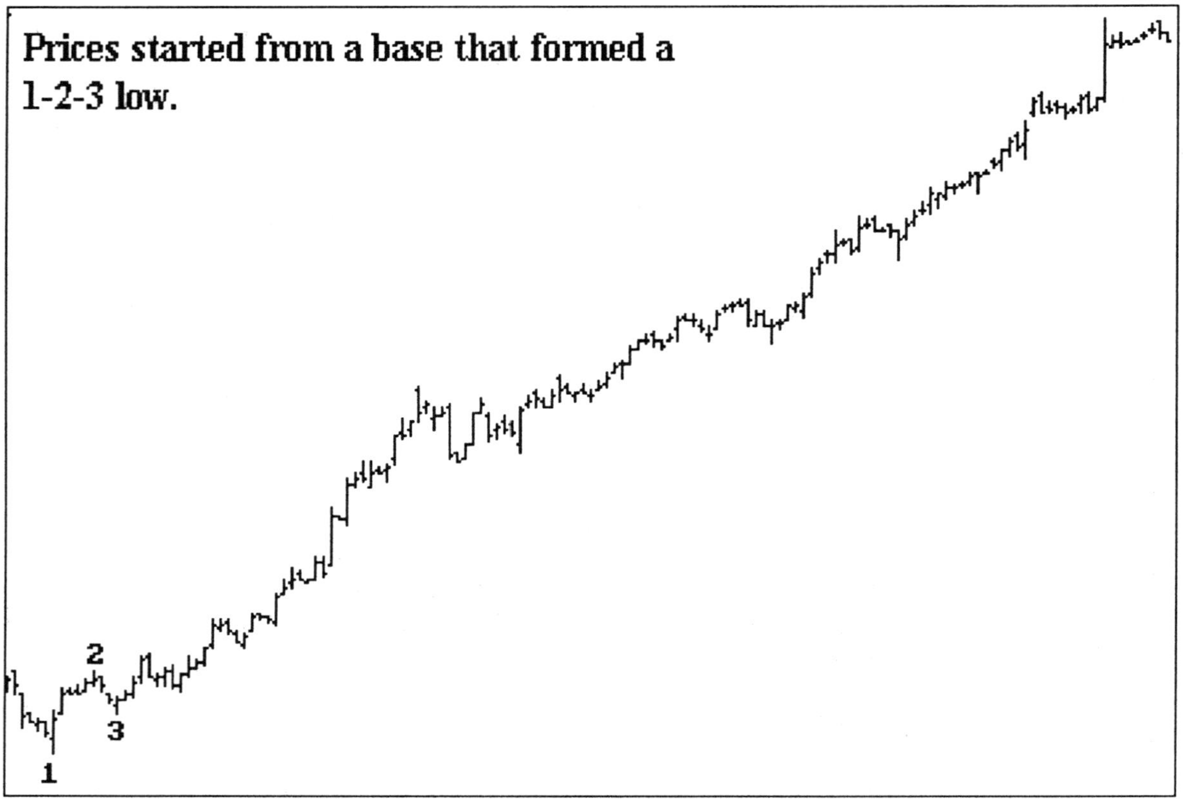
Prices started from a base that formed a
1-2-3 low.
2
3
1

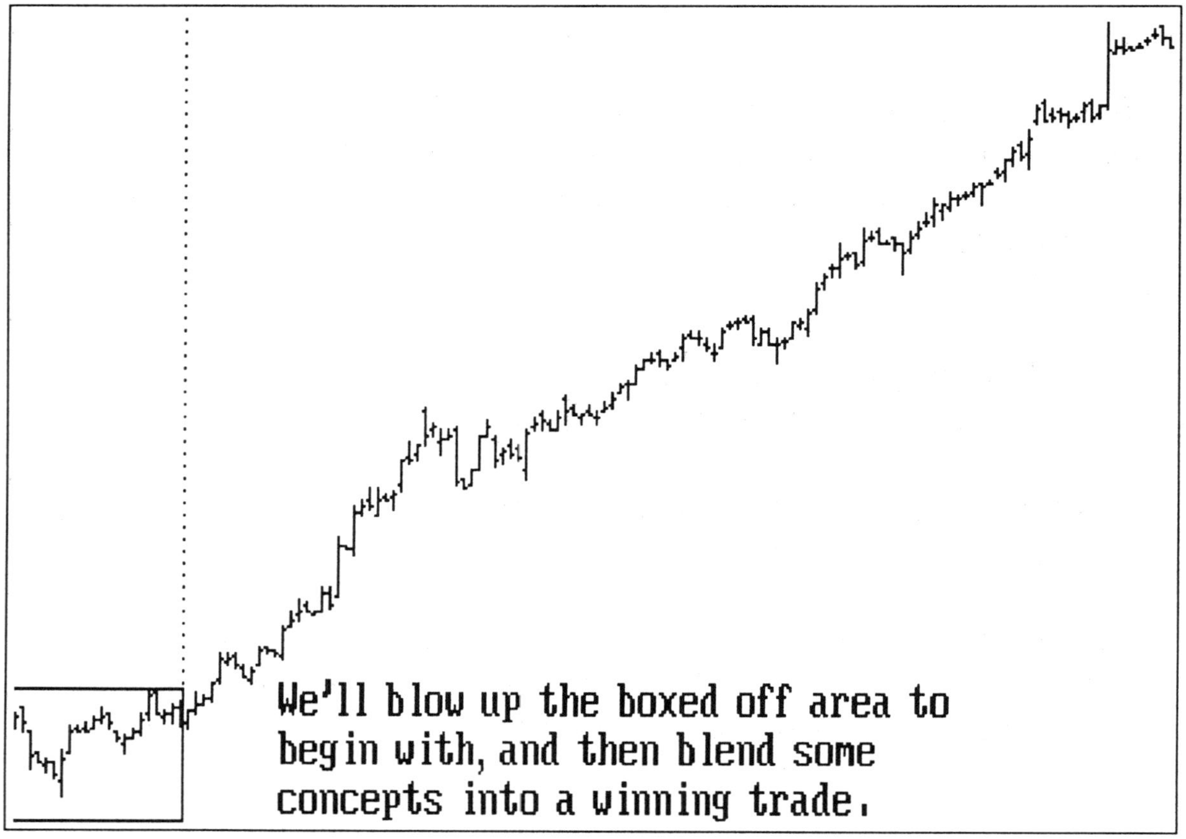
We'll blow up the boxed off area to
begin with, and then blend some
concepts into a winning trade.

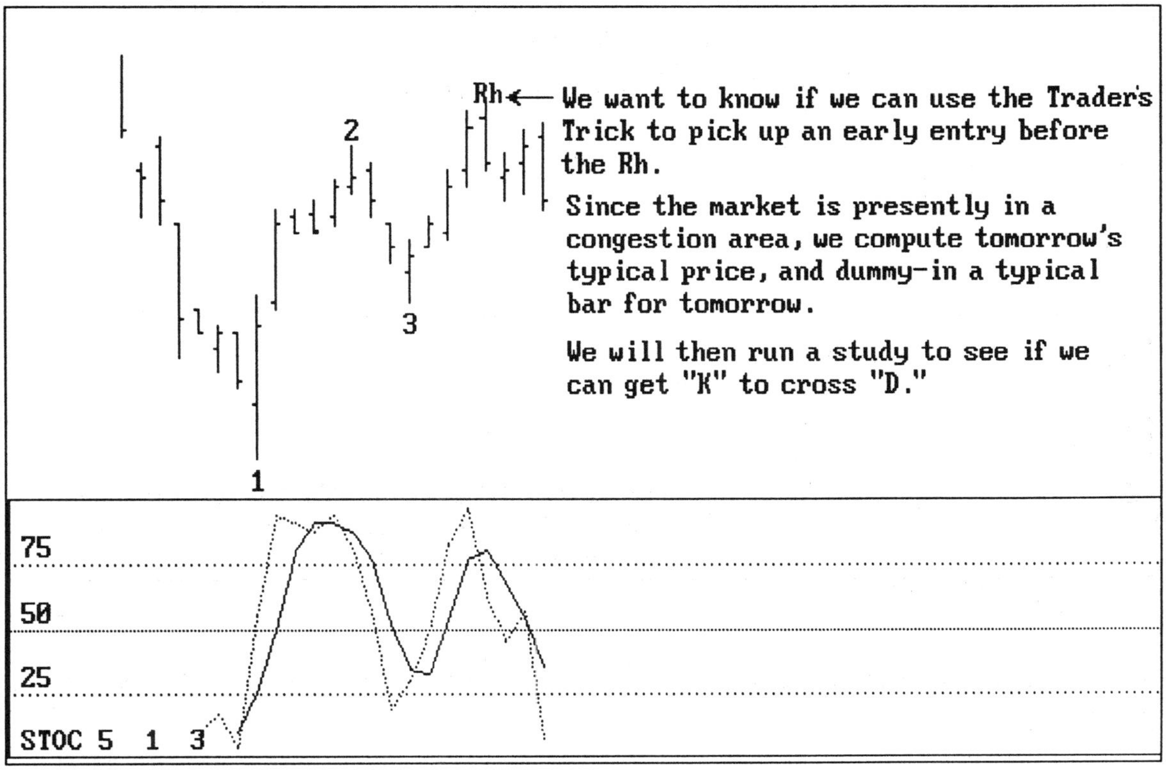

The last bar on the chart is as follows: O=86, H=88, L=85, C=87. Our formula is (O + H + L + 2(C)) / 5 = Tomorrow's Typical Price.

We have: $\frac{86 + 88 + 85 + 2(87)}{5} = 86.6$

Tomorrow's projected high = 2(86.6) - Today's low of 85 = 88.2

Tomorrow's projected low = 2(86.6) - Today's high of 88 = 85.2

We can insert 86.5 (the average of the four prices) for both tomorrow's open and close.

We then run the Study to obtain the following chart:

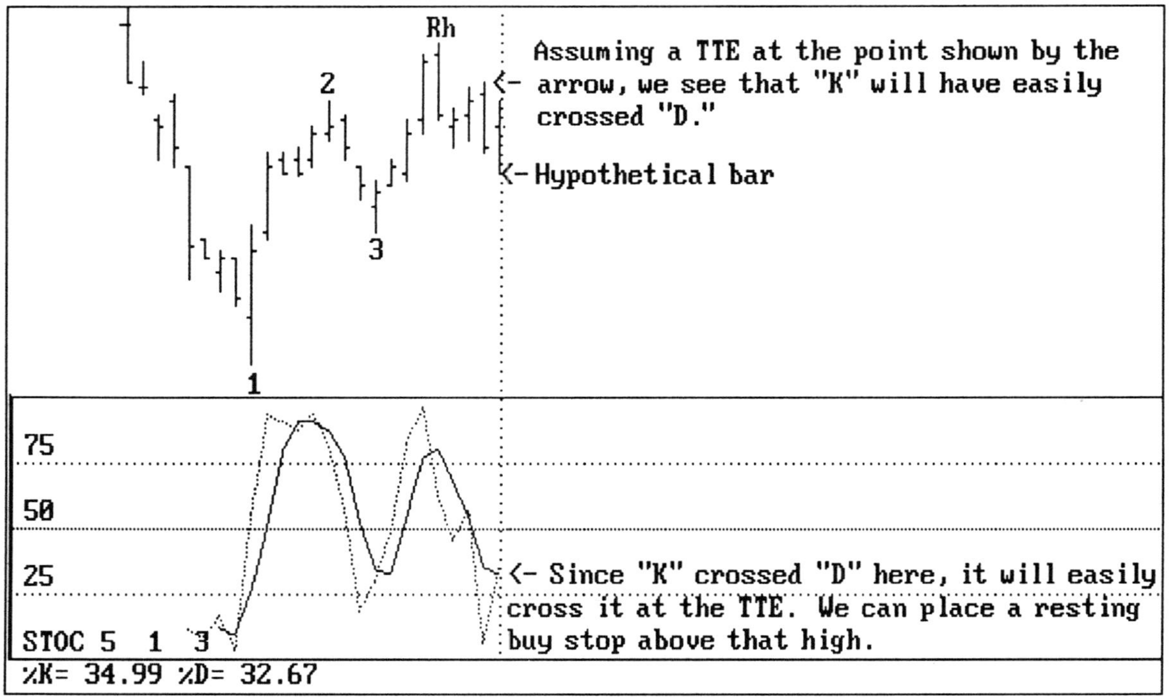

The real price bar was pretty close in both high and low to what we predicted.

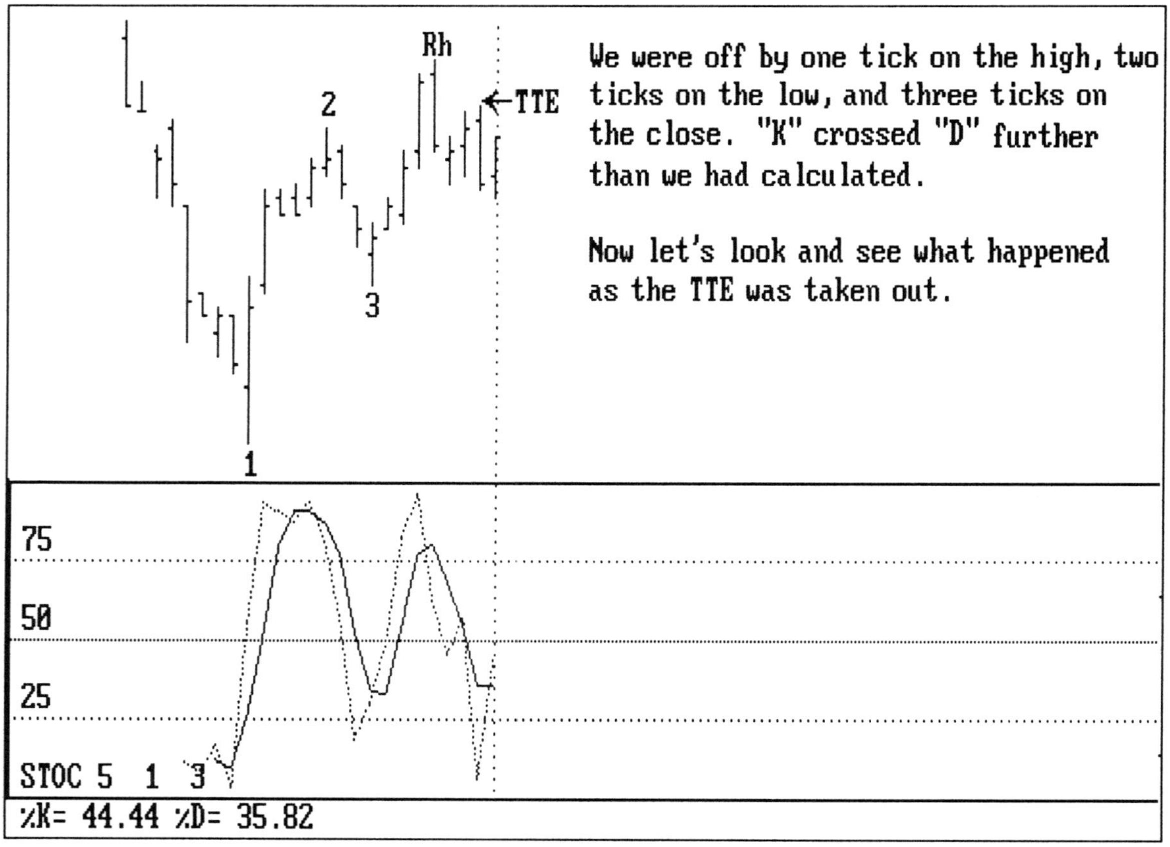

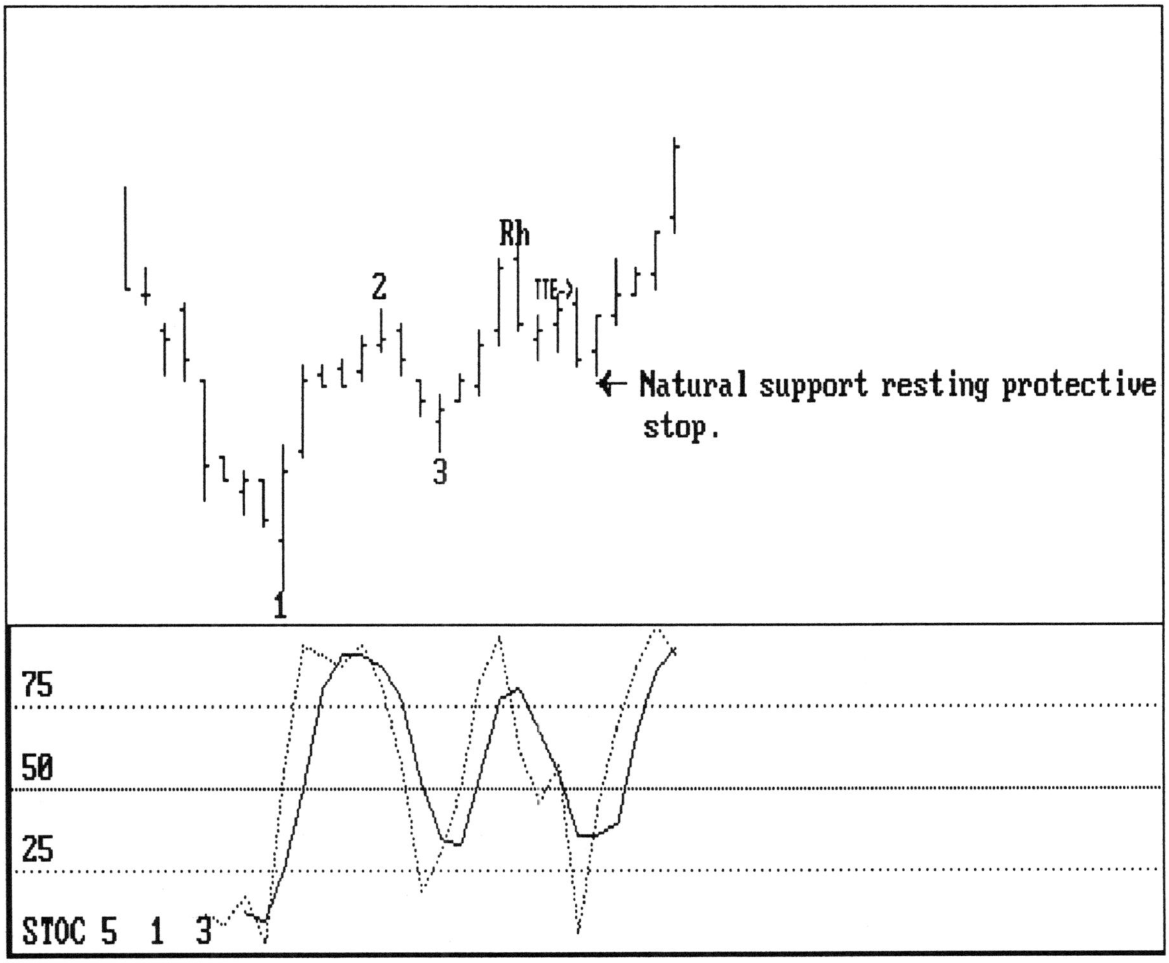

Here's the picture of how it would have all worked out for that particular trade.

The next picture shows how we can curve fit a Volatility Stop study to the new trend in the market.

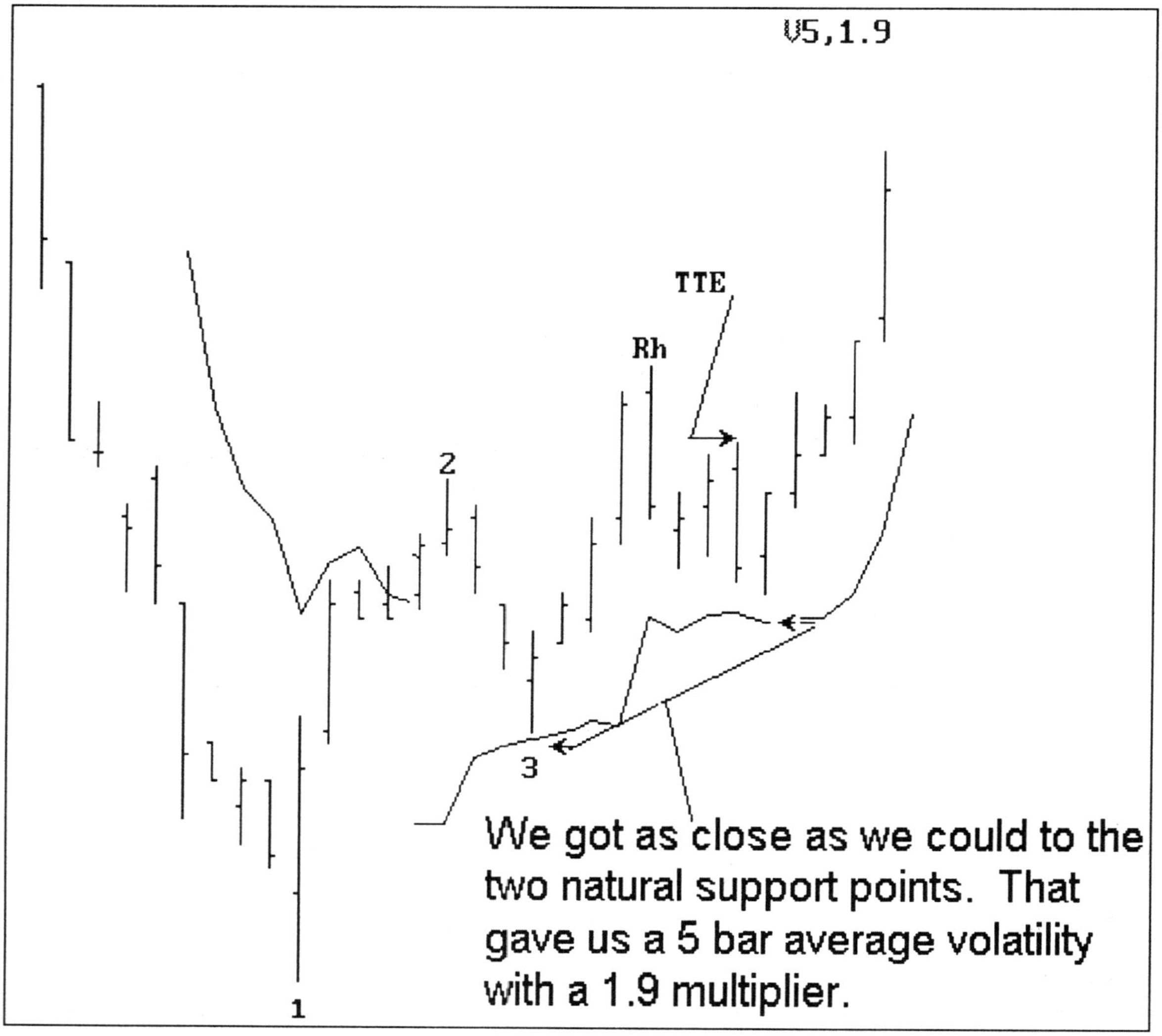

Now, let's get on with another leg of that magnificent uptrend we've been following.

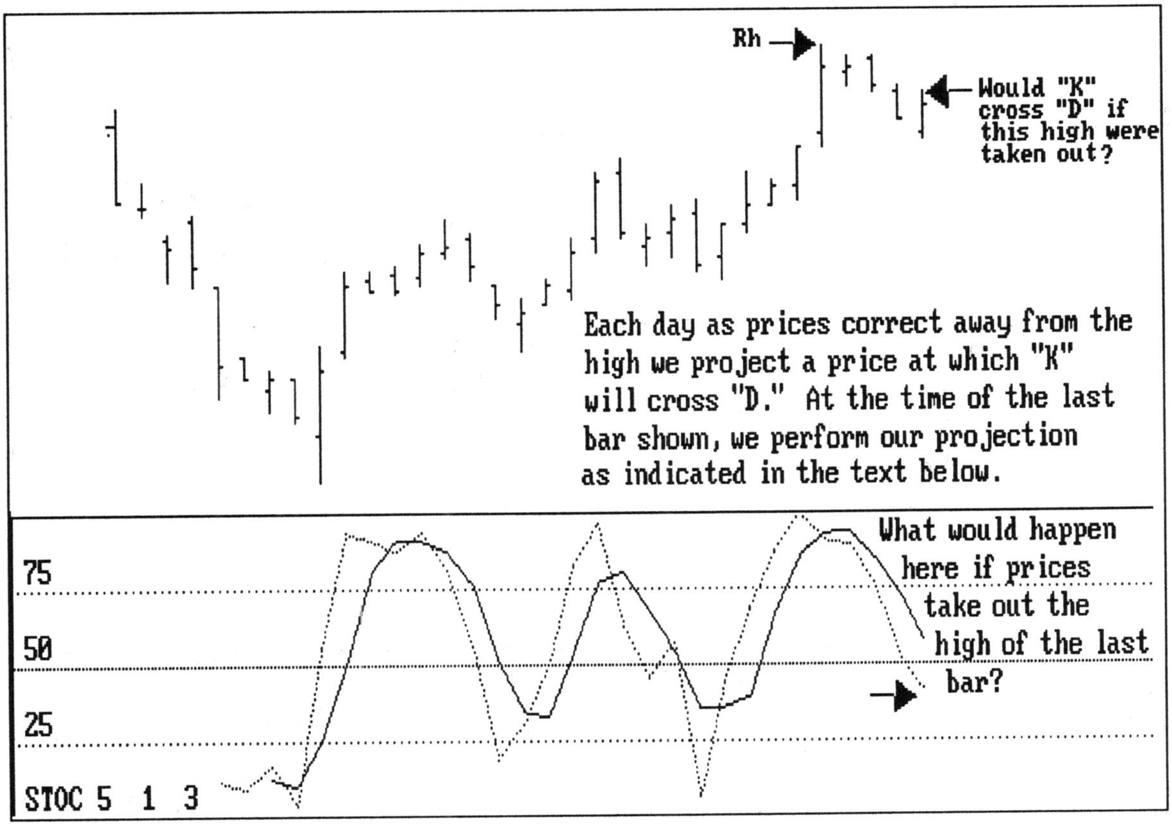

By definition, we are in a congestion during this correction. We have had four closes (and opens) all within the range of the measuring bar that made the point of the Hook. As each bar forms, we can insert a price, or ask our program if “K” will cross “D” if the current high is taken out. If there is enough room to cover costs at that price, and “K” will cross “D”, we can submit a buy order at the price that constitutes a taking out of the current high.

Using our formula for Typical Price in congestion (O+H+L+(2C))/5, we can arrive at a price, bar by bar, at which a violation of a high will occur. In the formula, a bar’s Typical Price will be our open and our close.

We can insert a bar with the computed Typical Price to get an idea of how the next price bar might look. As you can see on the next page, by doing so “K” projects a crossing of “D” with ease

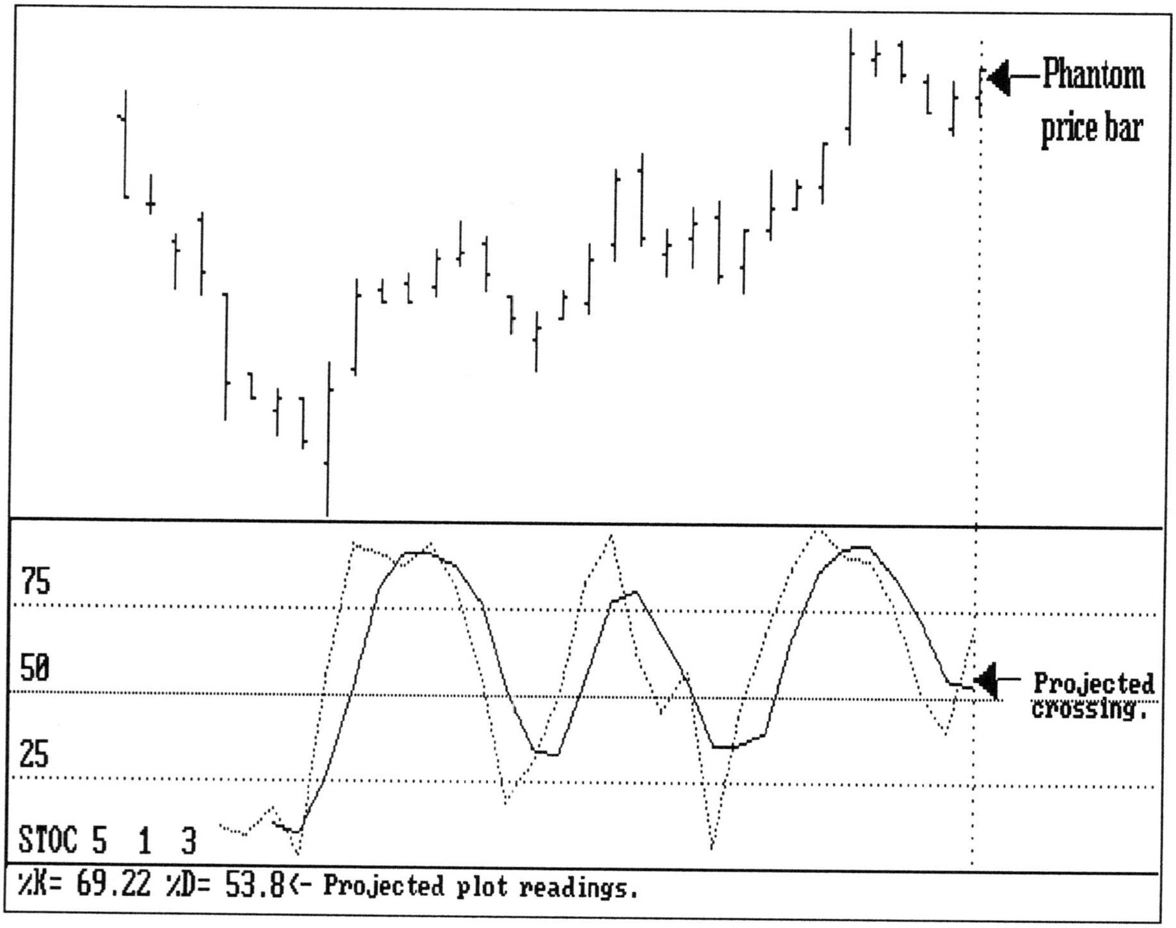

Next, let's look at what really happened.

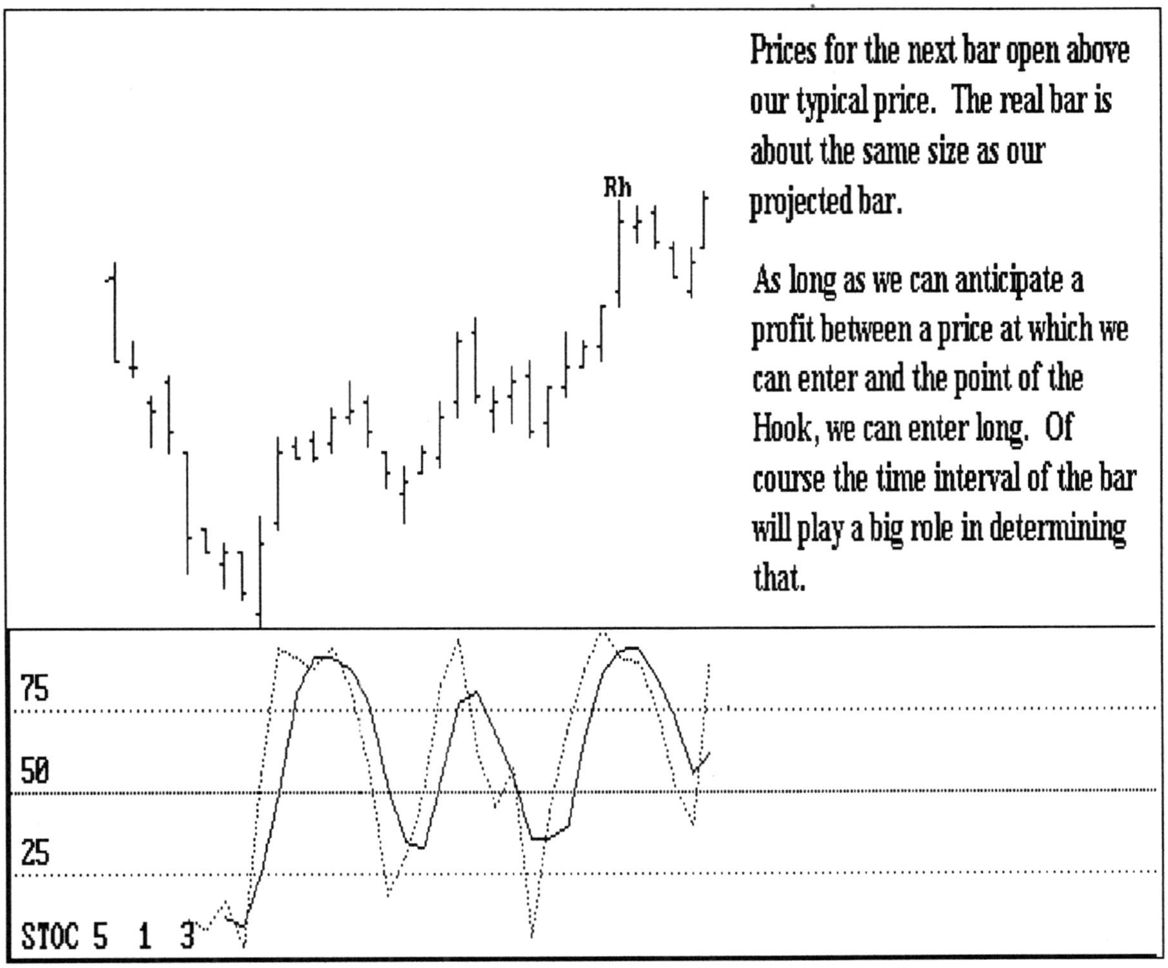

By now, you should be getting the idea of how this works, so let's move on to a new chapter.

Chapter 13

BOLLINGER BANDS FOR FILTERING HOOKS

Technical traders have long been advocates of the use of envelopes and envelope breakouts in their trading. With the advent of the computer, it has become very easy to do this type of work live, and with a variability that more correctly reflects market action.

This chapter shows two favorite ways in which to use envelopes in conjunction with the Ross Hook and the TTE.

The Bollinger Band study alone is sufficient reason for purchasing a computer if you don't already have one. If you do, and your software does not have Bollinger Bands, contact your software vendor and strongly request its inclusion in the next update version.

The methods we'll learn here are so good, we almost hate to part with them. But in keeping with our purpose of sharing what has been so good for us, get set for something special.

According to the information we have, Bollinger Bands are bands that vary in distance from a moving average as a function of the market's volatility. A simple twenty period moving average of the close is used as the center line. Moving bands are calculated concurrent with the moving average and placed two standard deviations above and below the center line. The formula as we have it is:

AV(erage) = the SUM OF THE LAST N PRICES/N

DEV(iation) = $(PRICE - AV)^2$

M(ean) D(eviation) = SUM OF DEV(iations)/N

S(tandard) D(eviation) = SQRT(MD)

BOLLINGER = AV ± 2(SD)

The way Bollinger Bands are normally used is that sharp moves tend to occur after the bands contract towards the center line.

It is said that a move outside the bands usually means continuation of the trend, not an end to it. We partially disagree with that statement because it fails to differentiate between trending and non-trending prices. Our own experience has shown that in a sideways congested market, prices will usually bounce off of the bands and begin to move the other way.

When prices are moving sideways, lows made outside the bands followed by lows made inside the bands call for upward reversals of trend. Conversely, highs made outside the bands followed by highs made inside the bands call for downward reversals of trend.

A move originating at one band tends to go all or most of the way to the other band. This tendency enables you to project a price objective for such moves.

Now, let's look at one way we can use these bands to trade the Ross Hook.

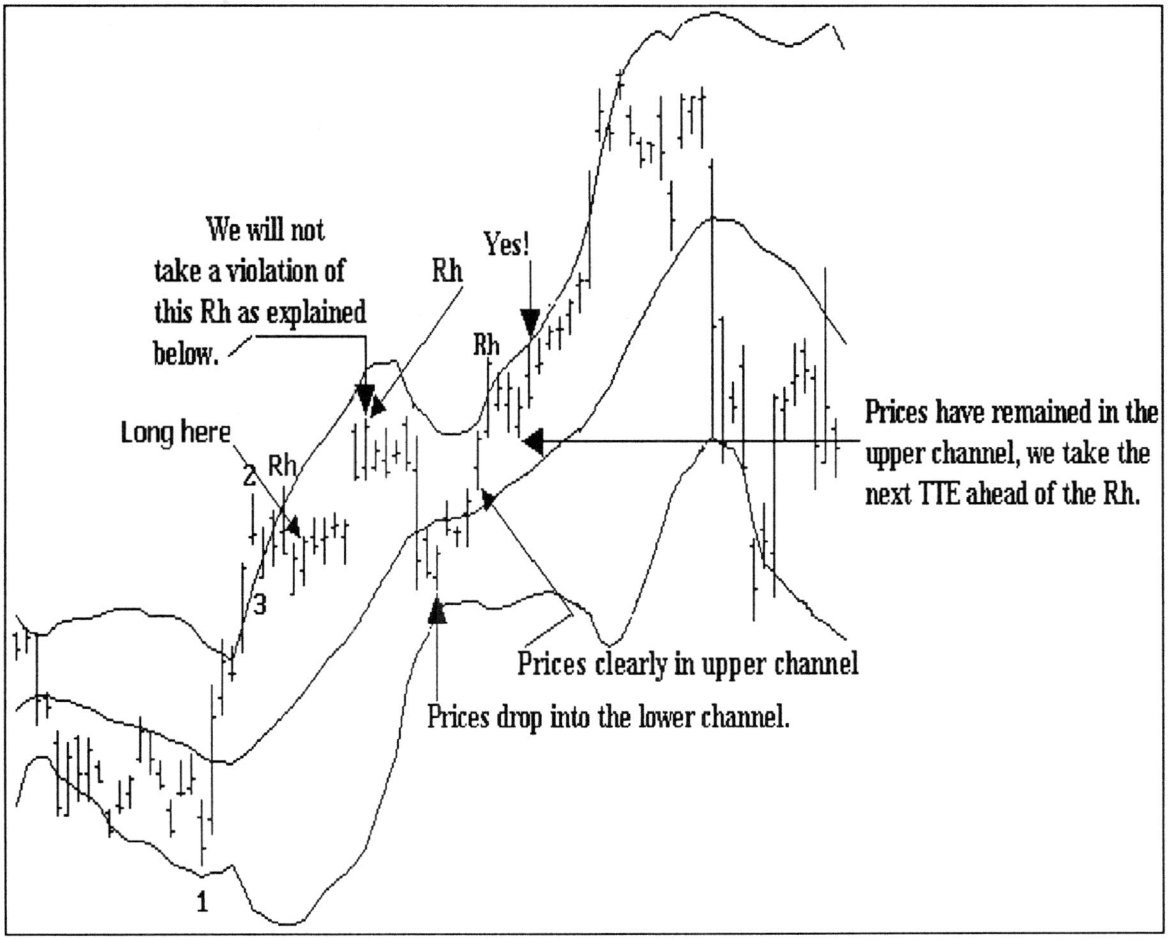

You'll need to follow along step by step, until the picture of what is being done becomes clearer. We will not consider a TTE until we get a correction that stays primarily in the upper channel. Prices will be considered to be in the upper channel as long as they have once crossed entirely into the upper channel and remain above, or in contact with, the moving average. Once prices have moved clearly into one of the channels, they are considered to be in that channel even if they subsequently come in contact with the moving average.

Beginning with the 1-2-3 formation on the left: We see that prices made a 1-2-3 low followed by an Rh. Since prices are clearly in the upper channel, we would attempt a TTE to go long.

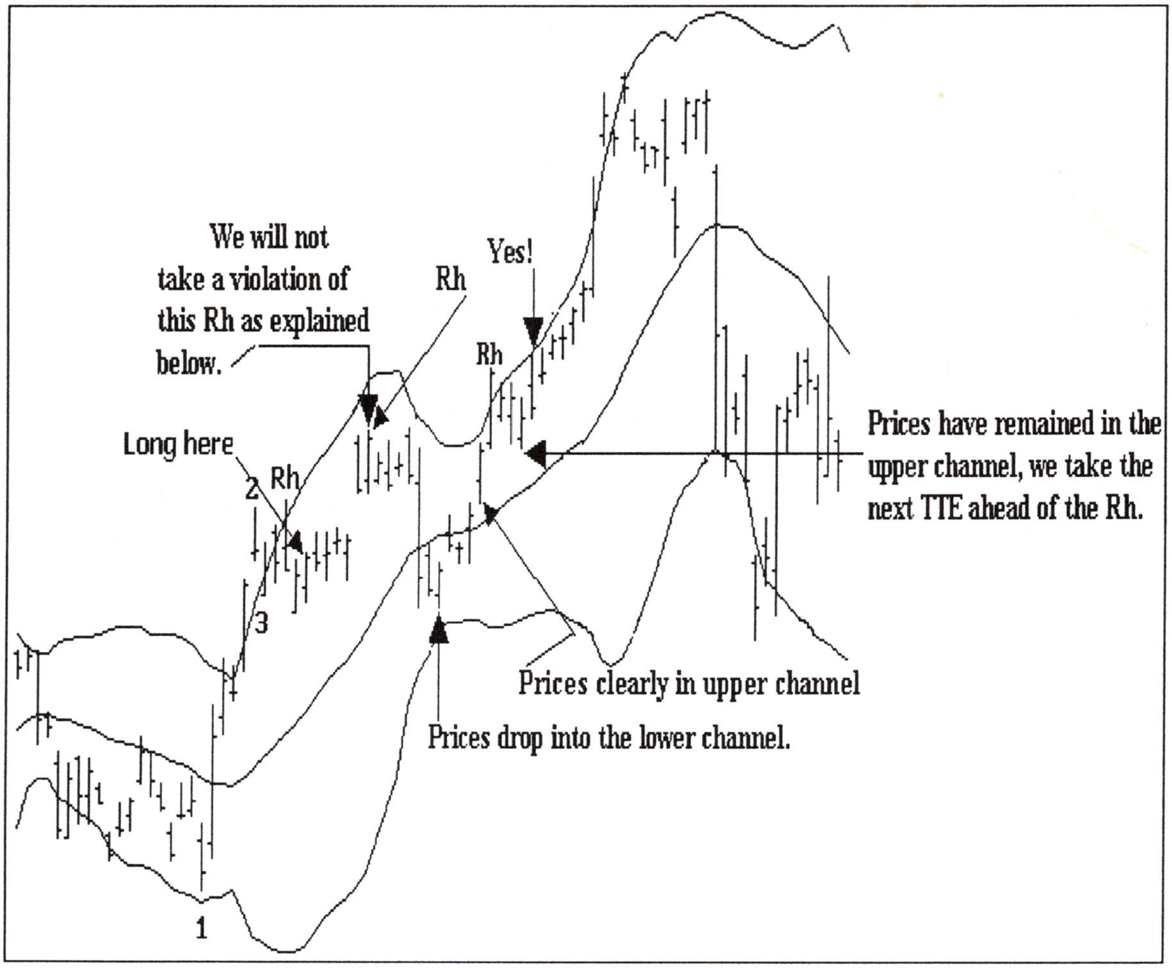

Prices then make another Rh, followed by an opportunity to go long once again. A trade at that point would have resulted in getting stopped out for a loss on the bar where prices plunged below the moving average. Two bars later, prices drop cleanly into the lower channel.

The fact that prices did drop into the lower channel means that we cannot consider any long positions until prices are once again cleanly in the upper channel. Therefore, we would not attempt to enter long via the TTE.

Prices subsequently move cleanly into the upper channel and form another Rh. Is it okay to attempt a TTE as prices retreat from the point of the Rh? Yes! Prices are clearly in the upper channel.

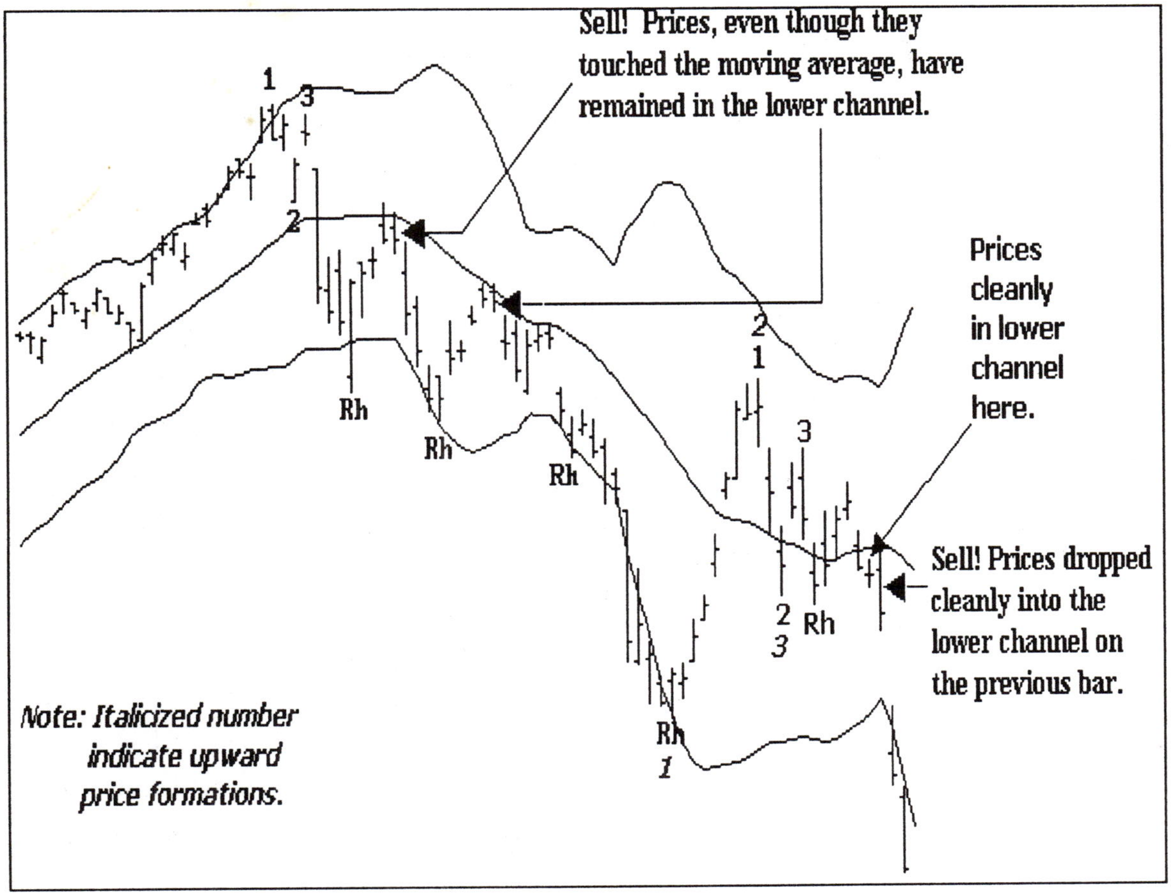

Beginning with the 1-2-3 high formation on the left, we see that the 1-2-3 was followed by a breakout of the #2 point and the subsequent formation of a Ross Hook. Should we attempt to enter on a TTE ahead of the Rh? Yes, prices have gone up to and reversed at the moving average. They have remained clearly in the lower channel. The down trend is expected to continue.

Then prices violate the point of another Ross Hook and move a bit lower to form one more Rh. Should we sell short when prices reverse at the moving average line? Yes, prices are still clearly in the lower channel. Should we sell short at the third Rh? Yes, prices continue to move lower and remain in the lower channel.

Prices eventually create a fourth Rh. Prices then move to where they are clearly in the upper channel. Should we sell short the Ledge formed ahead of the breakout to even lower lows? No! Why? Because we first need prices to once again be clearly in the lower channel.

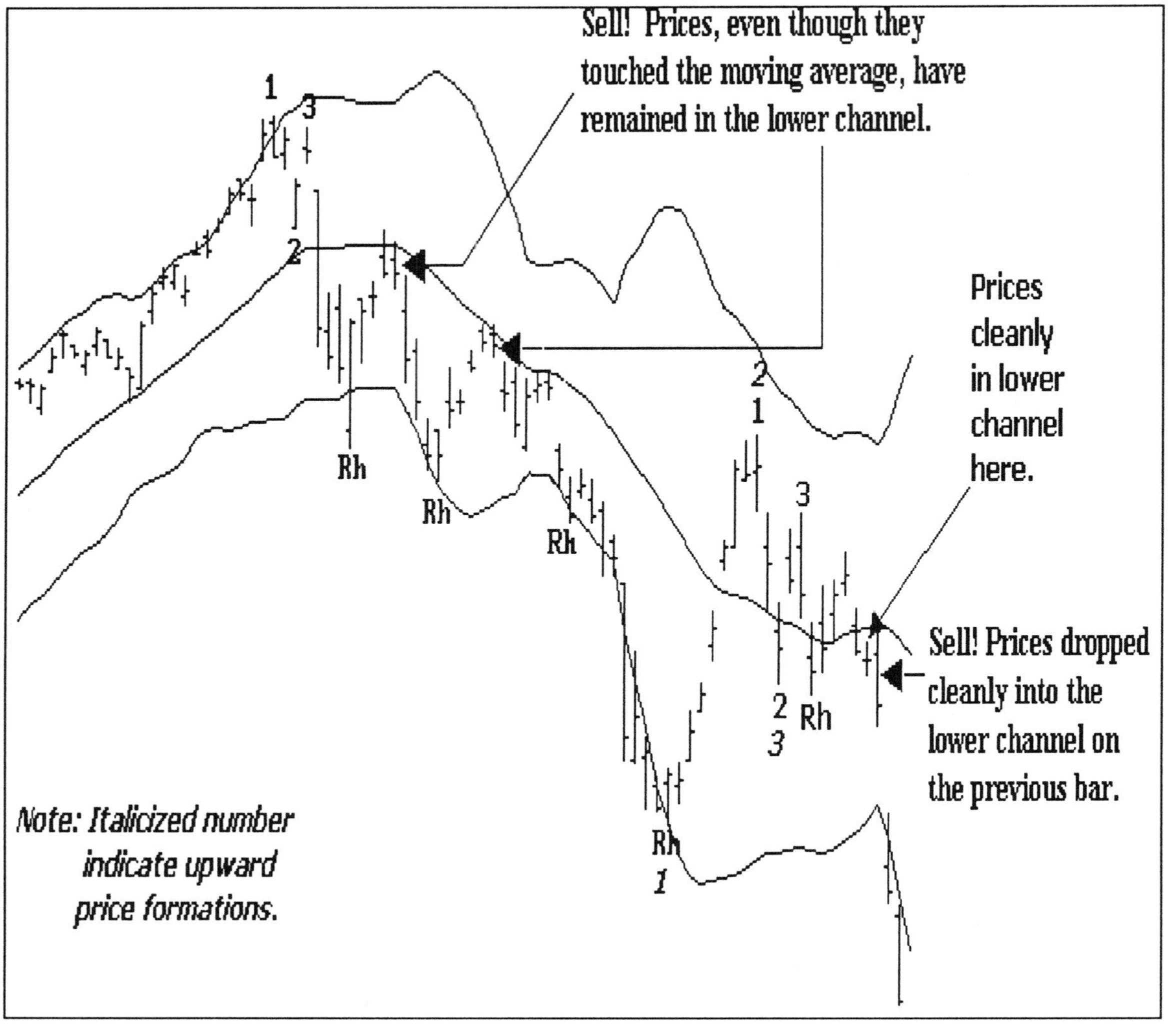

Notice that prices subsequently fall back to make another Hook, the final Rh on the right of the chart. Should we trade that breakout? Yes? Why? Because prices have dropped clearly into the lower channel.

We use the Trader's Trick on any of these corrections to get in early. Although we won't be showing it, we can also use the Study or CCI for additional confirmation if we feel we have the need.

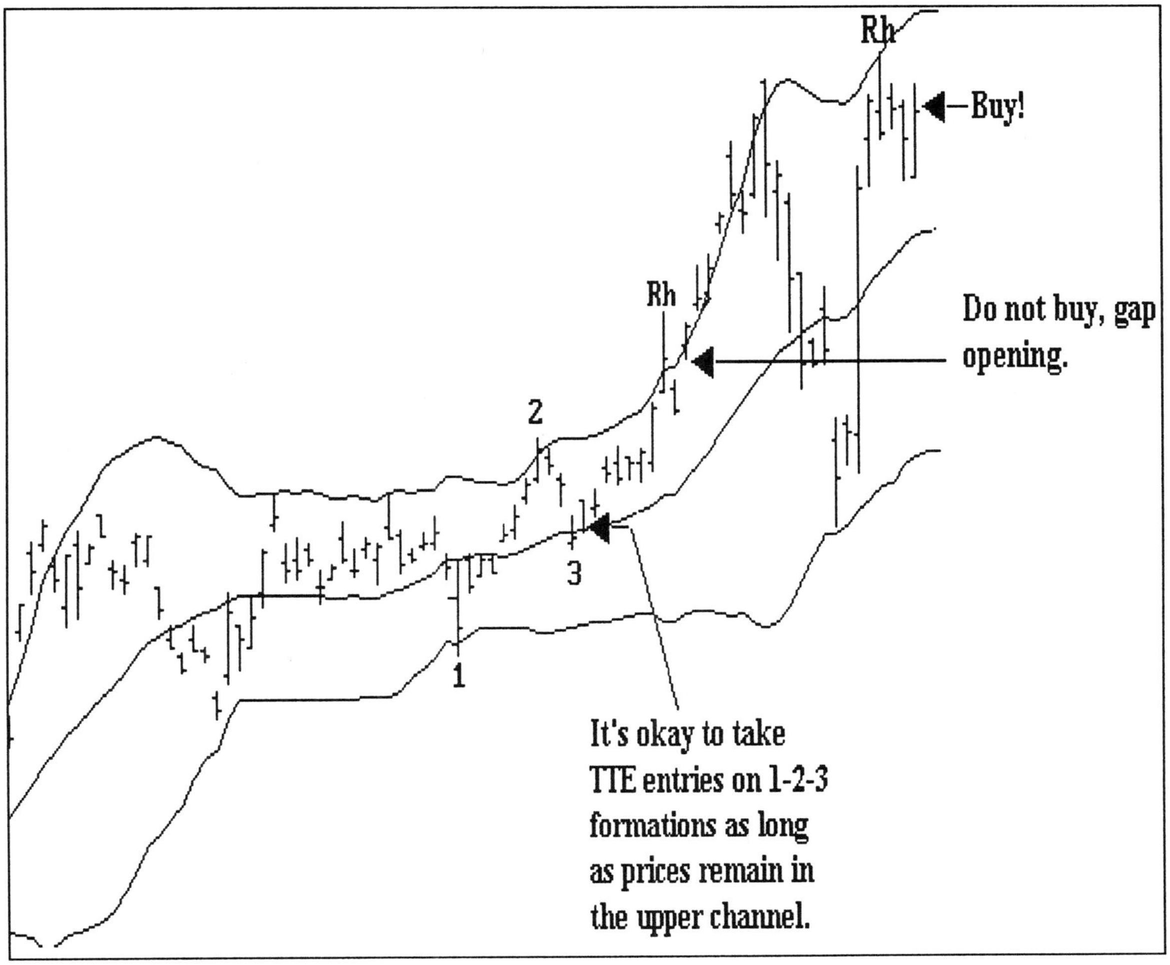

We want to take the Hooks when prices are clearly in one of the channels. We don't want prices to have totally crossed the center band to the opposite channel. When that happens, we must consider that a trend change may be taking place.

We might not been able to take a TTE on the first Rh because of the gap opening. But if you are willing to accept the risk of a gap opening, you might consider it a valid entry. We feel it is better to wait for a non-gap opening trade, but experience has shown that some of you will be trying to somehow change the method in order to not miss a trade like the one we bypassed on the above chart.

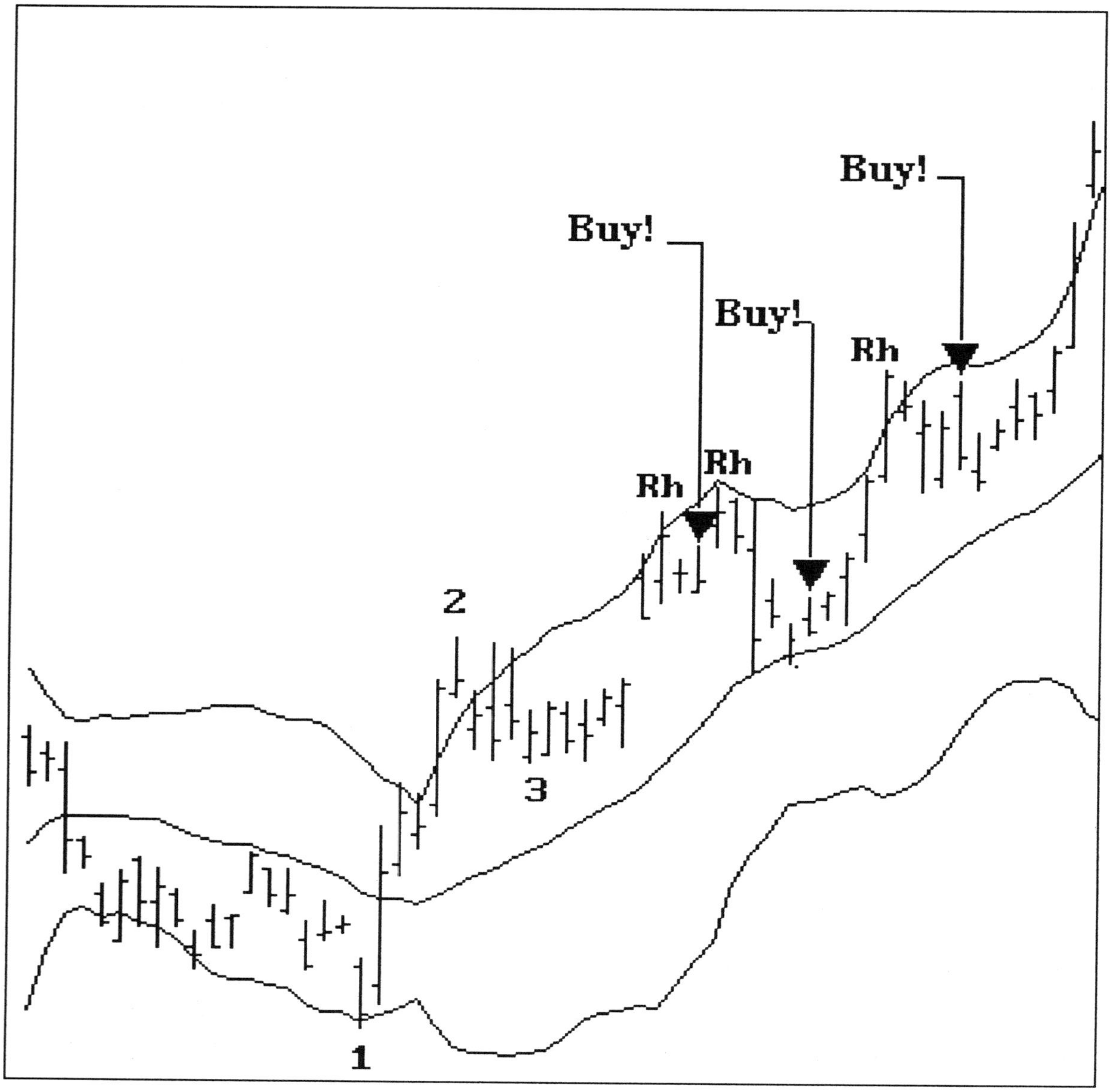

It's okay to use the TTE ahead of the #2 point. Just make sure prices are in the upper channel.

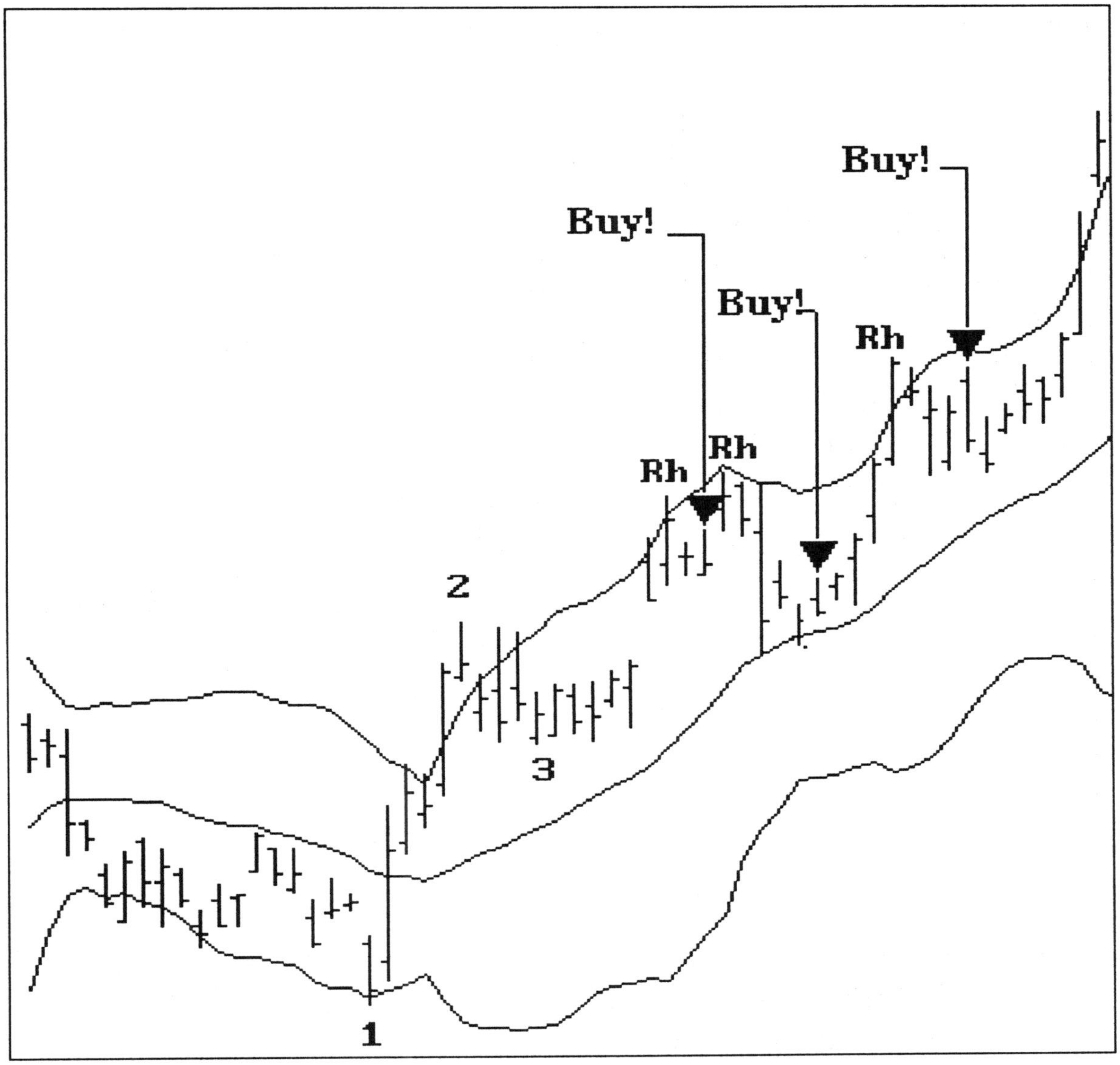

Sometimes we have to view 1-2-3's in the context of their overall pattern. This one wasn't very clear.

Depending upon where our exit points are and whether or not we entered that last Rh after the gap and prices retraced to close the gap, we are hurt only a little if we exit on the fact that a bar made a lower low than the previous bar. Of course, that does not prevent us from getting right back in as price move higher.

When you're trading, you never win them all, but using these methods requires that we try more than once if we want to take advantage of the momentum in the price action.

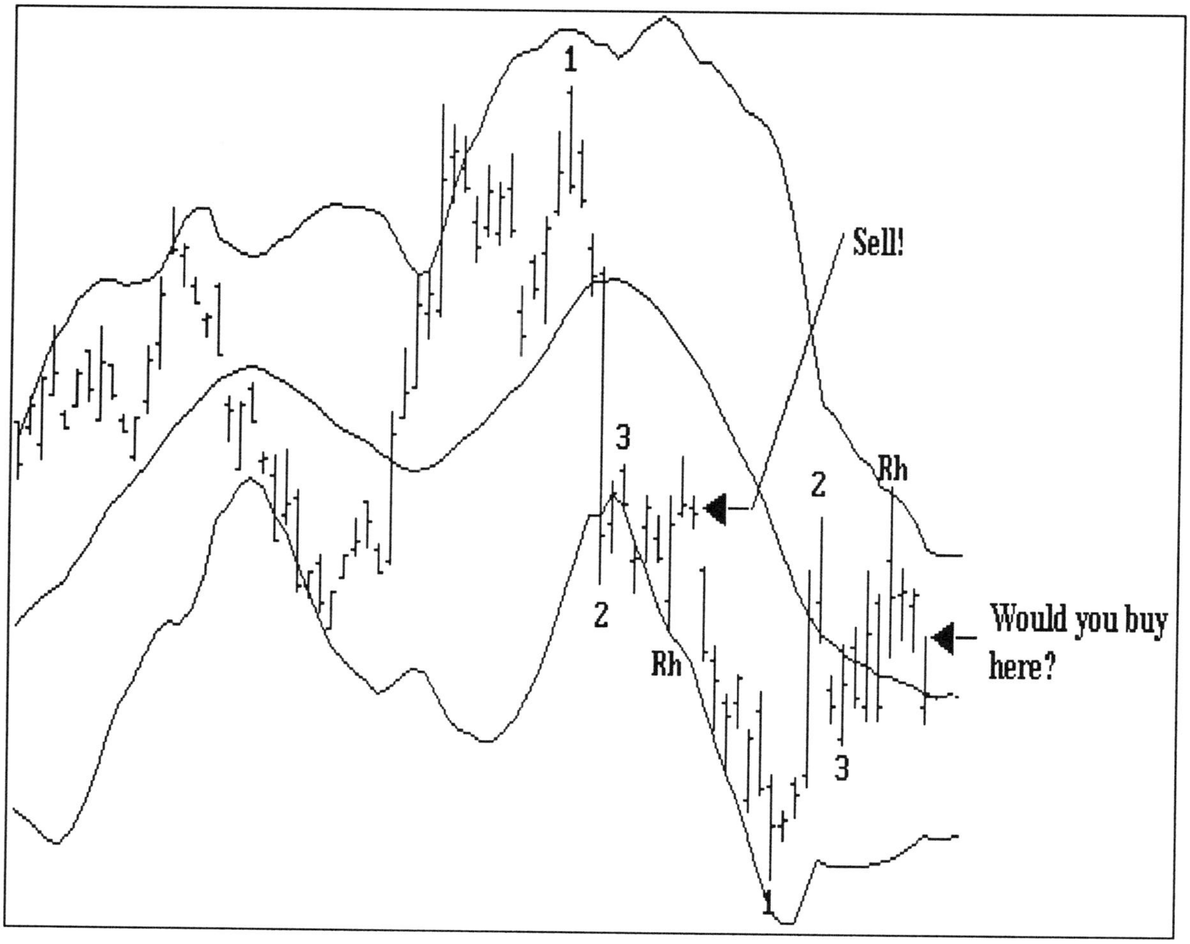

This chart is a test situation! Would you buy at the last arrow shown? If so why? If not, why not! This is not a trick question, it is a chance to see if you are understanding what is happening.

Make your decision strictly on what you see on the chart. Do not bring any other filtering devices into this situation. Do you take this trade or not, if prices violate the high of the last bar?

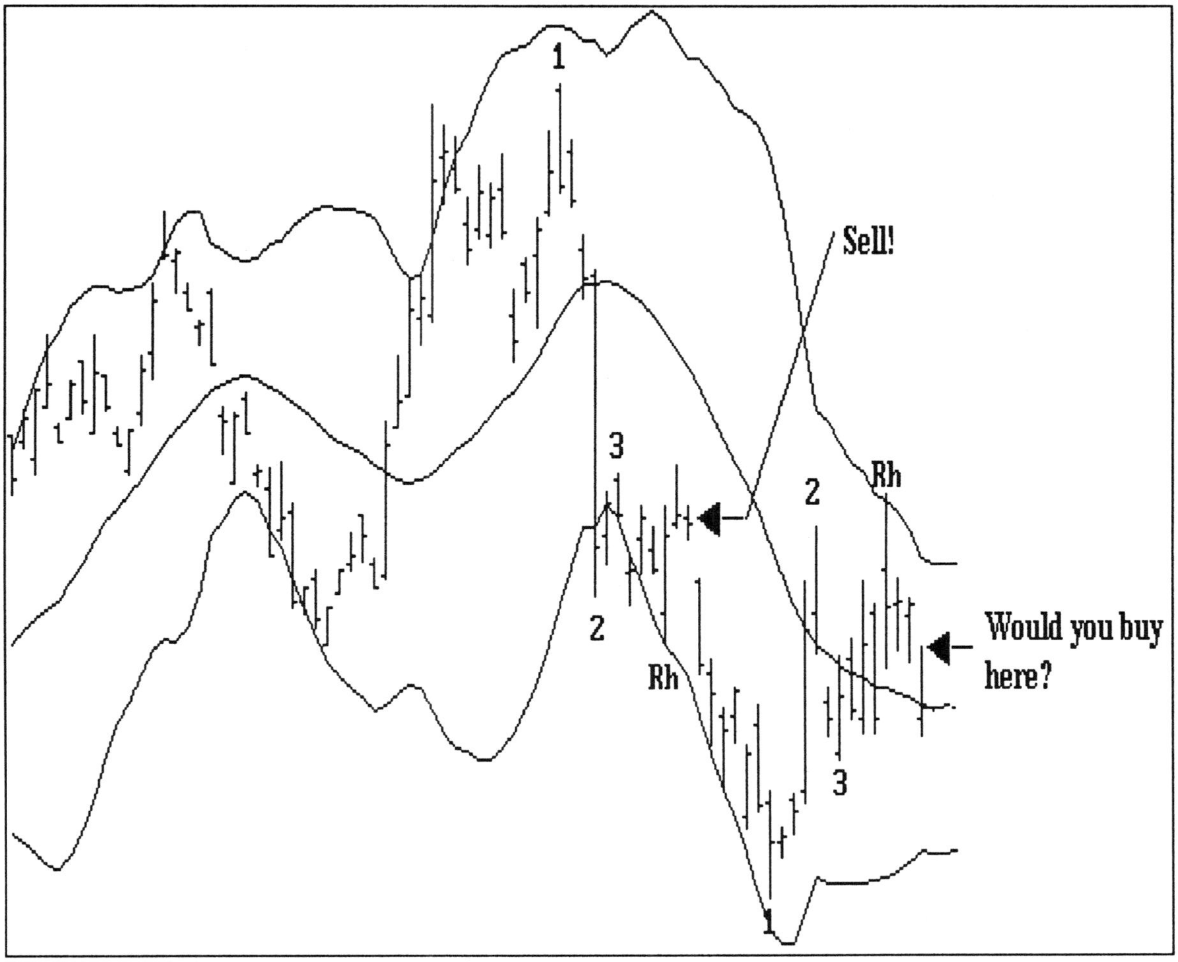

The preferred answer is YES! Buy a violation of the high of the last bar. Why? Because it constitutes a TTE. Prices clearly broke into the upper channel 3 bars previous to the last bar.

NOTE: ONCE PRICES ARE IN ONE OF THE CHANNELS, AS LONG AS ANY PART OF A PRICE BAR REMAINS IN CONTACT WITH THE MOVING AVERAGE PRICES ARE CONSIDERED TO HAVE REMAINED IN THE CHANNEL. EXAMPLE: PRICES ARE IN THE UPPER CHANNEL. A PRICE BAR OPENS AND CLOSES IN THE LOWER CHANNEL BUT THE HIGH OF THAT BAR REMAINS IN CONTACT WITH THE MOVING AVERAGE. PRICES ARE CONSIDERED TO BE IN THE UPPER CHANNEL. IF PRICES WERE IN THE LOWER CHANNEL AND PRICES OPENED AND CLOSED IN THE UPPER CHANNEL, AS LONG AS ANY PART OF THAT BAR REMAINS IN CONTACT WITH THE MOVING AVERAGE, PRICES ARE CONSIDERED TO BE IN THE LOWER CHANNEL.

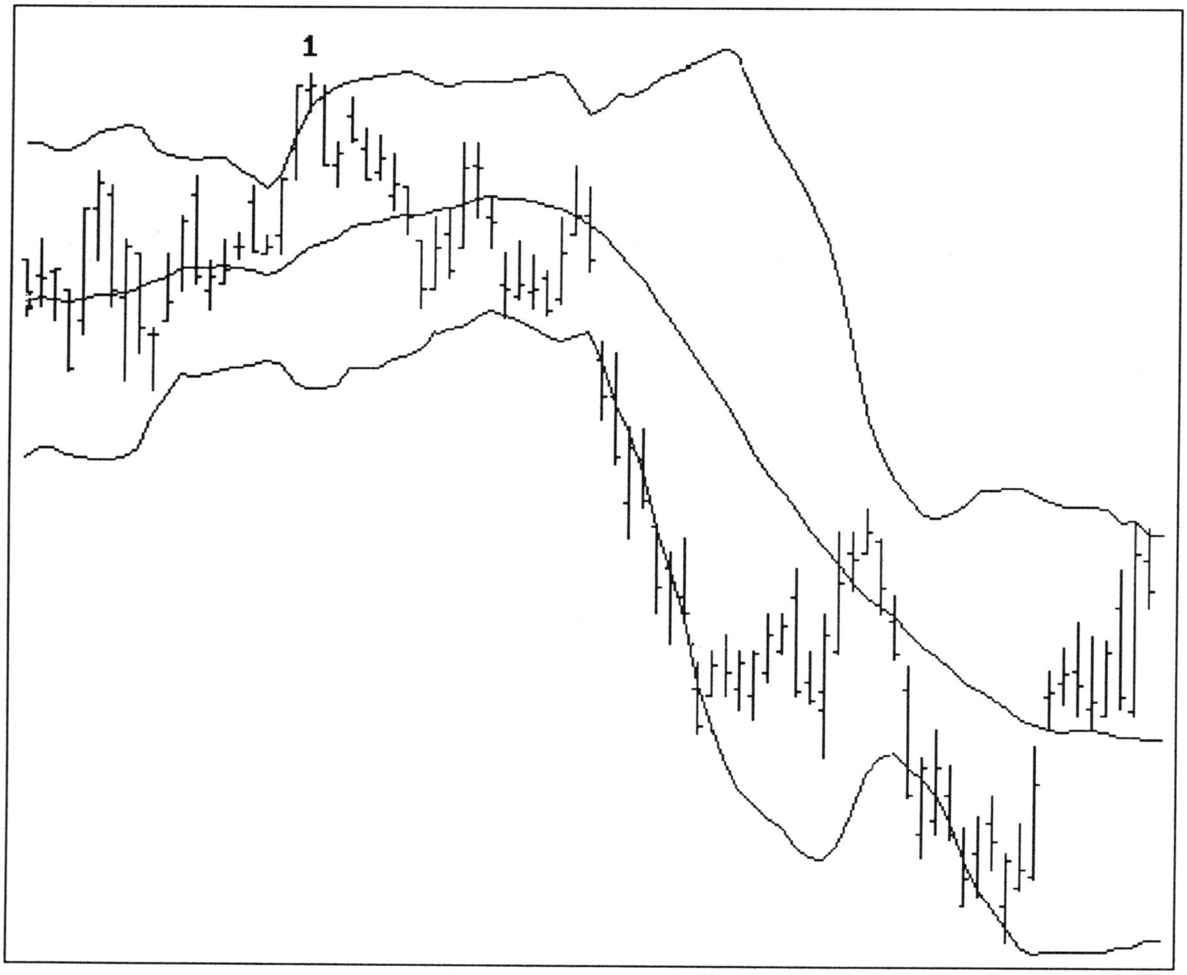

On the above chart, beginning with 1, label the chart showing 1-2-3's and Rh's, and show which trades you would have taken, and why you would have taken them. Also indicate where you would have placed an exit order using natural support or resistance, or exit by the method taught in <u>ELECTRONIC TRADING 'TNT' I — GORILLA TRADING STUFF</u> — two reversal bars in a series or the violation of a previous bar's low when prices are moving up, or the violation of a previous bar's high when prices are moving down.

Comment: DON'T GET UPSET IF A TRADE TURNS OUT TO HAVE A LOSS. THAT'S LIFE AS A TRADER. YOU WON'T WIN THEM ALL!

Answers are on the following pages.

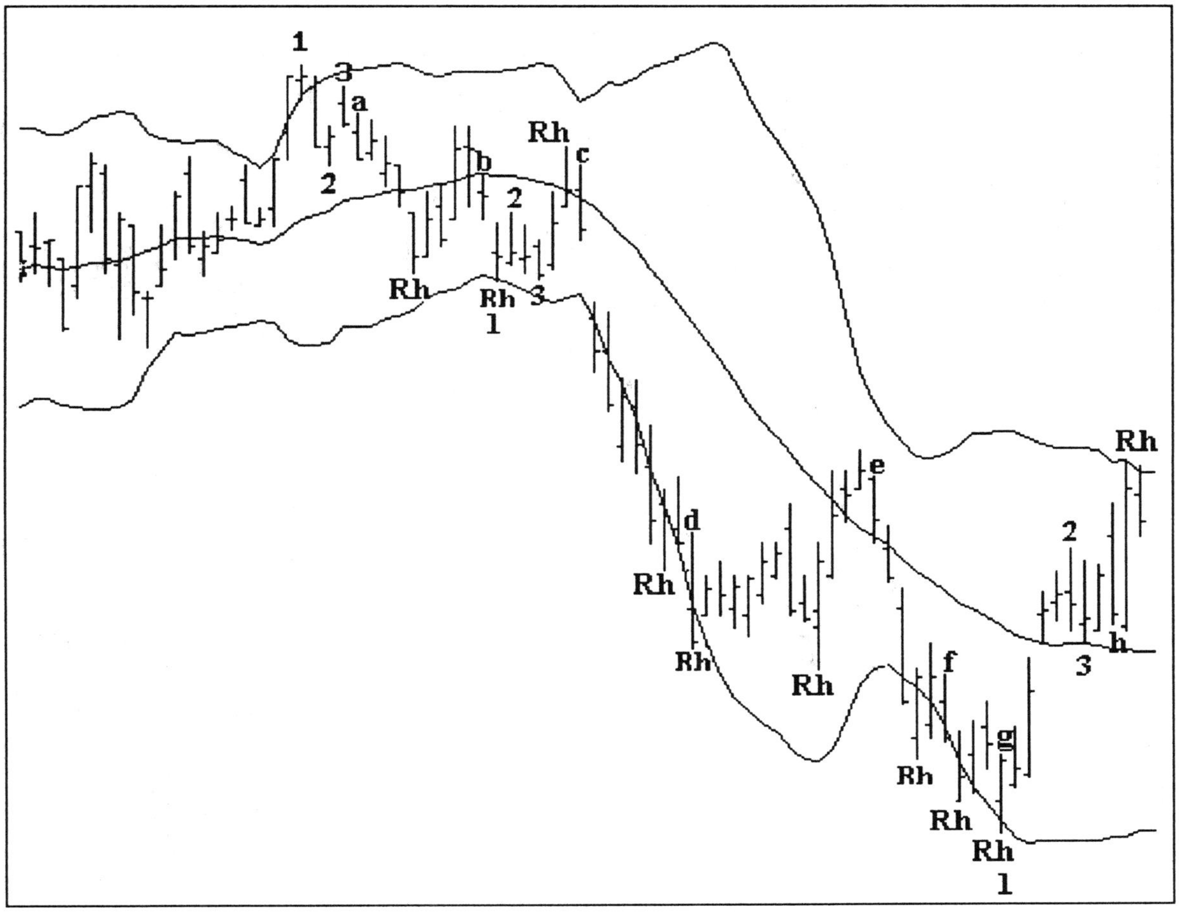

a) Although this is a TTE for a 1-2-3 it cannot be taken short because prices are in the upper channel.

b) Prices have dropped cleanly into the lower channel. This is a TTE to go short ahead of a violation of the Hook. If the exit is to be above natural resistance, the trade does not have to be exited and an exit point can be trailed behind natural resistance all the way to the high that violated d. If the exit is to be two reversals or a higher high, then the trade is exited as soon as possible in light of the violation by the bar labeled 2. Note that prices make a 1-2-3 low while prices are essentially in congestion, just before they begin to drop sharply.

c) Is a TTE to the short side. If taken, the exit does not come until a higher high is made just prior to bar d. When the bar before bar d takes place, natural resistance exit points can be moved to just above its high when bar d is completed.

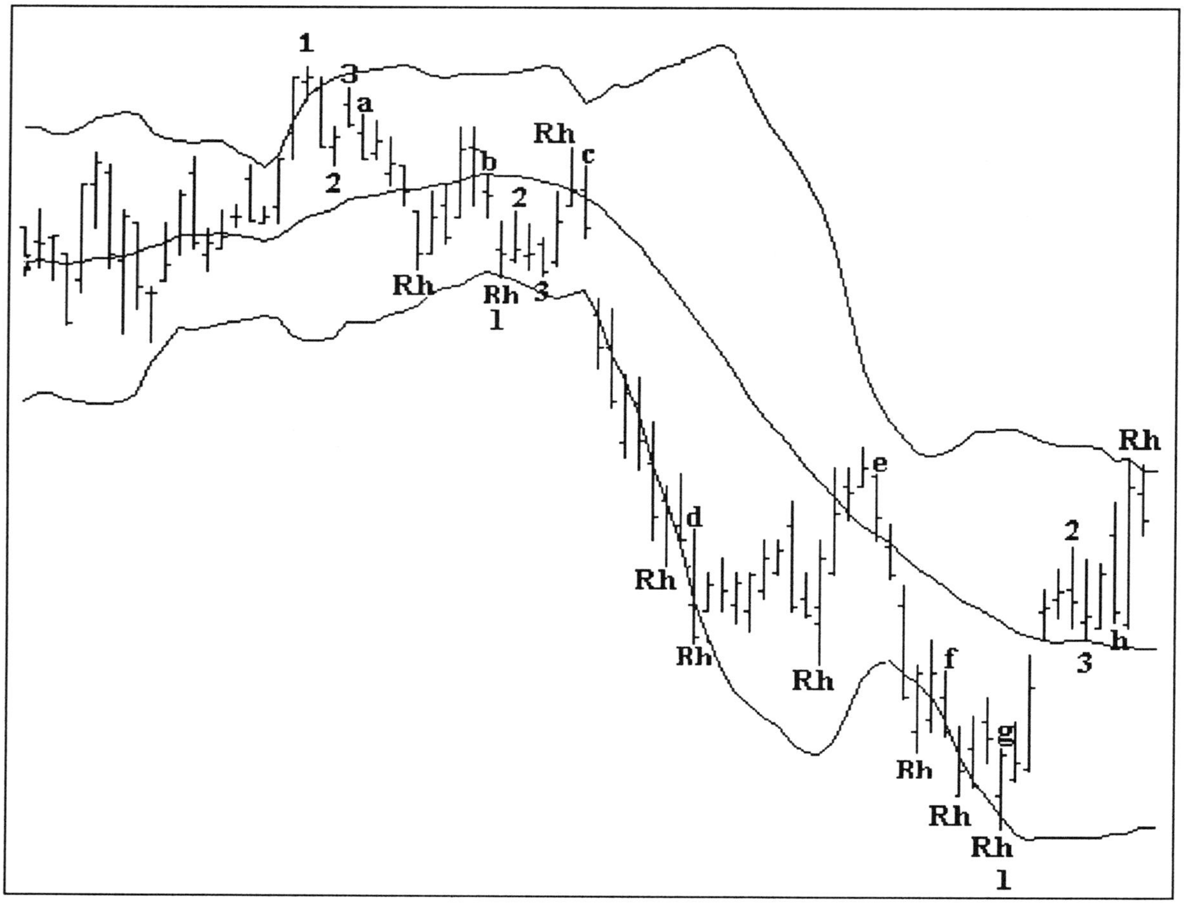

d) Is a TTE to the short side only if you are willing to trade a severe gap open, or wait until prices rally and then trade through the low of the bar preceding bar d.

e) Is not a TTE. Why? On the bar before e, prices were clearly in the upper channel with no connection to the moving average. You would not go short there.

f) Is a TTE. The natural resistance exit point is the bar before e. The violation exit point comes on the second bar after f. That bar violates the high of the bar that preceded it.

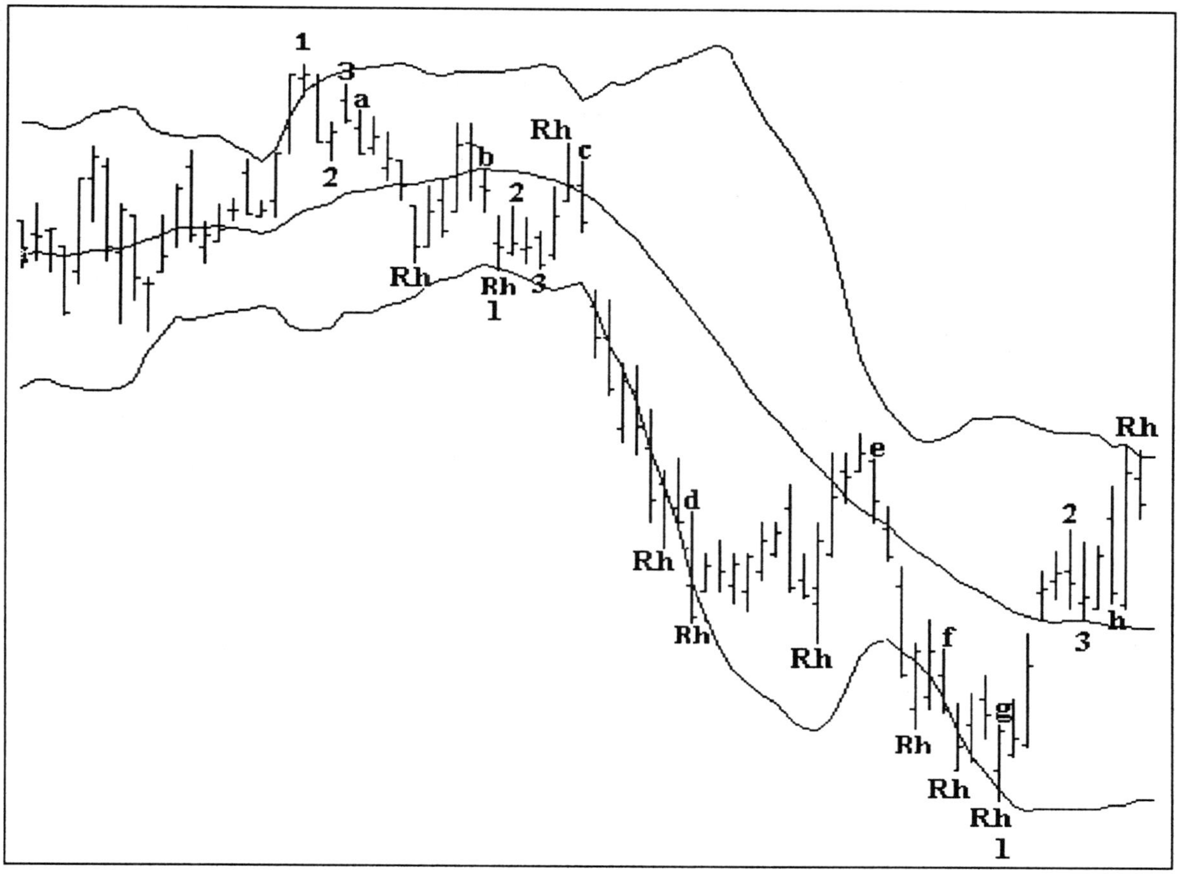

g) Is a TTE only if you are willing to enter on a gap opening or a trade through the low of the bar preceding g. It is likely that such a situation was possible. By any exit method this trade, if entered, would have been a loser. Natural resistance was above the high of the bar preceding g. A violation exit was via the bar that followed g.

h) Is a TTE for the 1-2-3. Prices are clearly in the upper channel ahead of the 2 point being made. If you took the gap entry on bar h, or waited for a trade-through fill of the high of the 2 bar (likely), you got long. If you use a violation exit, you are out with a loss via the open of the following bar. If you used natural support your exit point is below 3.

PLEASE NOTE THAT EVERY RH IS A POTENTIAL #1 POINT. HOWEVER NOT EVERY #1 POINT IS AN RH. SOMETIMES #2 POINTS ARE RRH'S. IN A STEEPLY TRENDING MARKET, IT MAY BE BETTER TO USE NATURAL SUPPORT AND RESISTANCE AS EXIT POINTS, IF THEY ARE AFFORDABLE.

However, this is not true in less steeply delineated trends. We did manage to keep losses very small compared with the size of wins regardless of the exit method used. Finally, it turns out that entering on gap trades is not a good idea. As a rule, you will have more losers than winners.

NOTE: WHEN ROSS HOOKS APPEAR VERY CLOSE TOGETHER, IT IS A WARNING THAT, AT LEAST TEMPORARILY, THE TREND IS NEAR ITS END.

The method that follows is a bit different from Method #1. Did you notice that in Method #1, we never actually used the "bands??" Actually, all we used were prices relative to the moving average. The bands were there only as a visual aid to enable us to see the channel. In Method #2, we will use the bands in the same way, to delineate the extremities of the channel, but we will also use them to help us to stay out of a whipsawing market, and also to tighten our exit points.

BOLLINGER BANDS — METHOD #2

This method generally results in fewer trades than does Method #1. However, the trades are less risky.

YOU WILL FIND SOME SIMILARITIES BETWEEN METHODS #1 AND #2, BUT PAY CLOSE ATTENTION TO THE DIFFERENCES.

In Method #2, we set the moving average for the Bollinger Bands to a value of 9 bars (In Method #1 we used 20). This means the bands will tend to be tighter. The standard deviation set at two remains the same.

We use the same technique of determining in which channel prices exist. Once prices are clearly in the upper channel, they remain there until prices drop cleanly below the moving average. Conversely, once prices are clearly in the lower channel, they remain there until prices rise cleanly above the moving average. It requires only one price bar to move entirely into the opposite channel in order for us to make the switch in our thinking about in which channel prices exist.

Our trade management will be different as well. We will tighten up our exit points considerably once prices touch one of the bands, and make sure we take profits if we get a reversal bar at the bands. Anything else that we need to know will be shown in the context of the charts that follow.

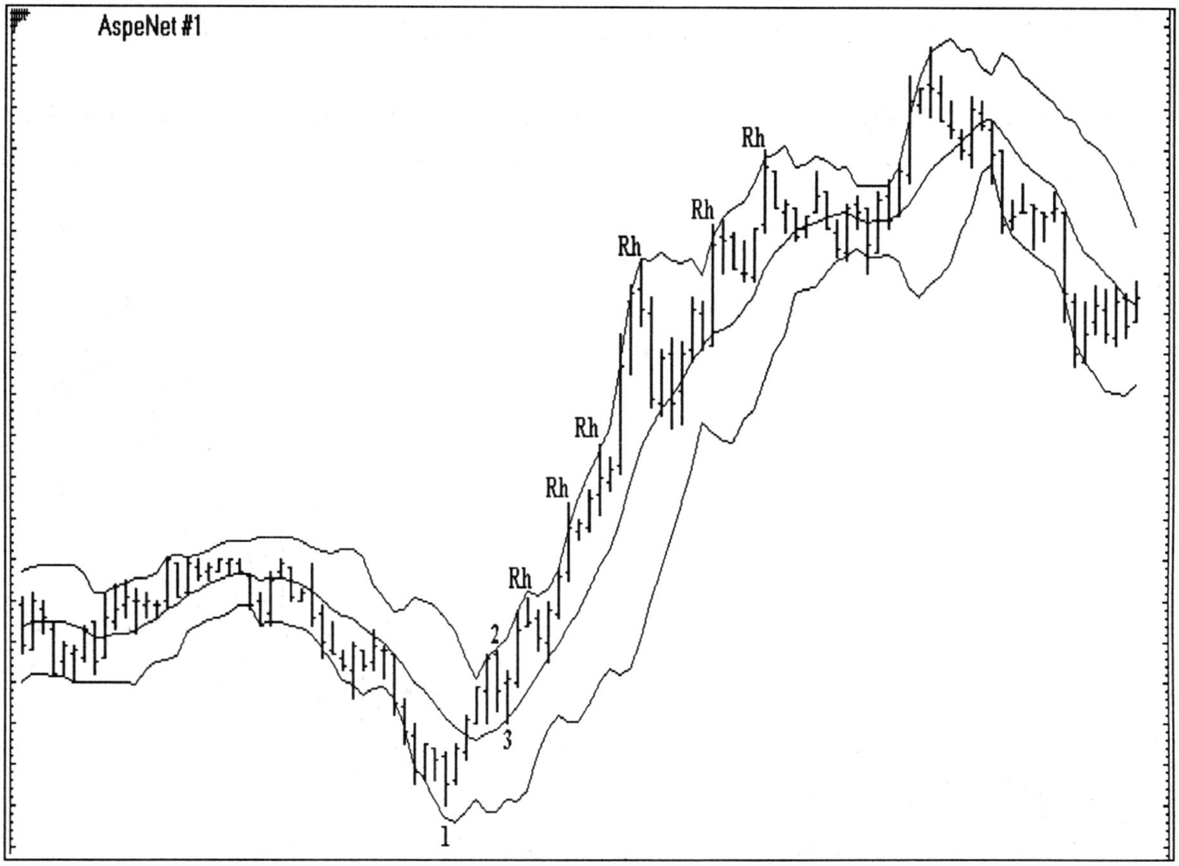

Let's begin by looking at the trending portion of this chart, from 1 to the final Rh shown.

Here are the rules for trading:

- **PRICES MUST BE CLEARLY IN ONE OR THE OTHER OF THE CHANNELS.**

- **WE CAN ENTER A TRADE AHEAD OF A #2 POINT VIOLATION OR A RH ONLY IF PRICES FIRST CORRECT BACK TO THE MOVING AVERAGE LINE. PRICES MUST TOUCH OR EXCEED THE MOVING AVERAGE, BUT THEY CANNOT MOVE CLEANLY INTO THE OPPOSITE CHANNEL.**

- ONCE PRICES HAVE TOUCHED THE MOVING AVERAGE, WE ENTER ON A VIOLATION OF THE EXTREME OF THE BAR THAT TOUCHED THE MOVING AVERAGE.

- WE REMAIN IN THE TRADE UNTIL PRICES VIOLATE THE EXTREME OF THE PREVIOUS BAR BY MOVING AGAINST THE DIRECTION OF THE TREND, OR WE TAKE PROFITS ON REVERSAL BARS AT THE BANDS.

The rules are truly simple. Let's look at that chart and see the trades.

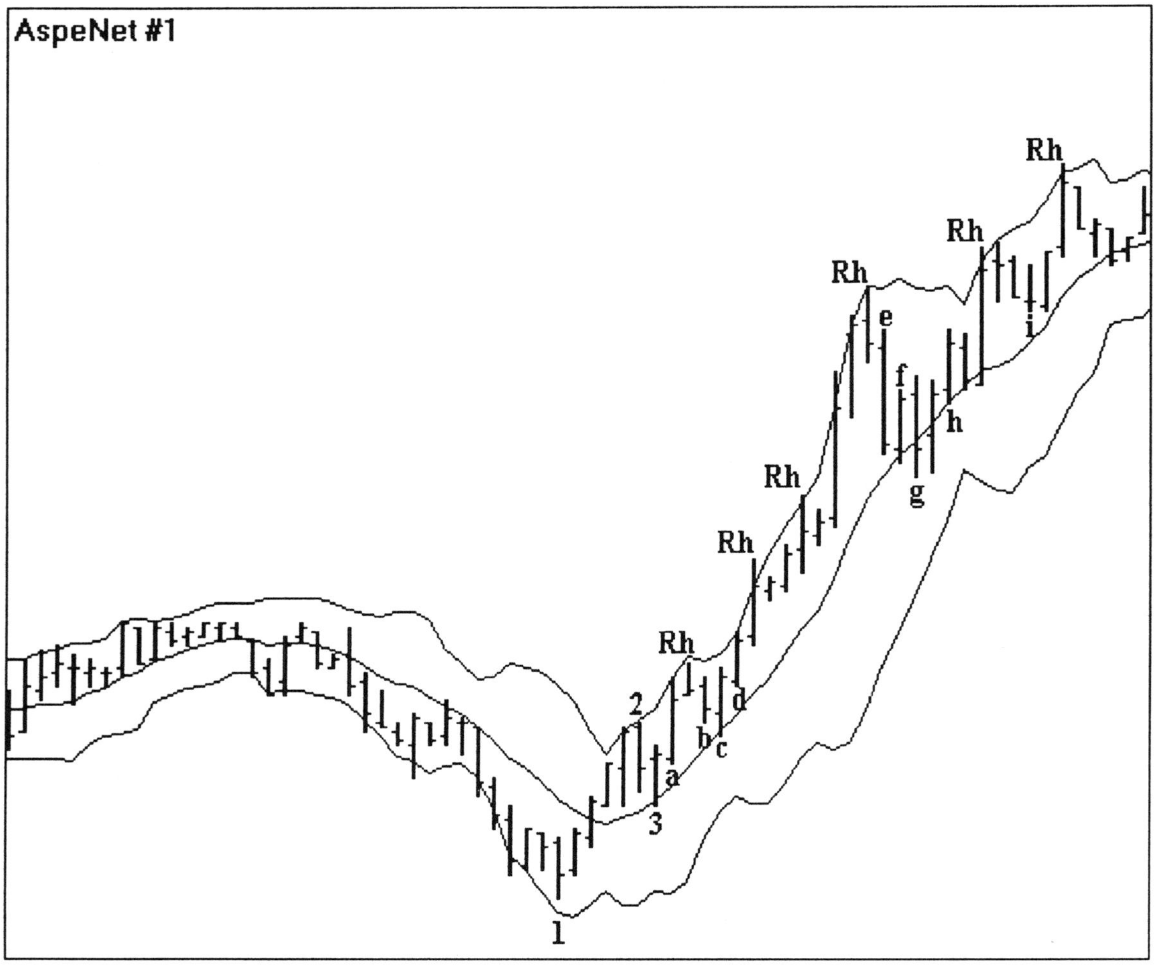

a) Point 3 touches the moving average, we go long on a violation of the high of bar 3.

b) We exit as soon as possible on a violation by b of the low of the bar that made the point of the Hook.

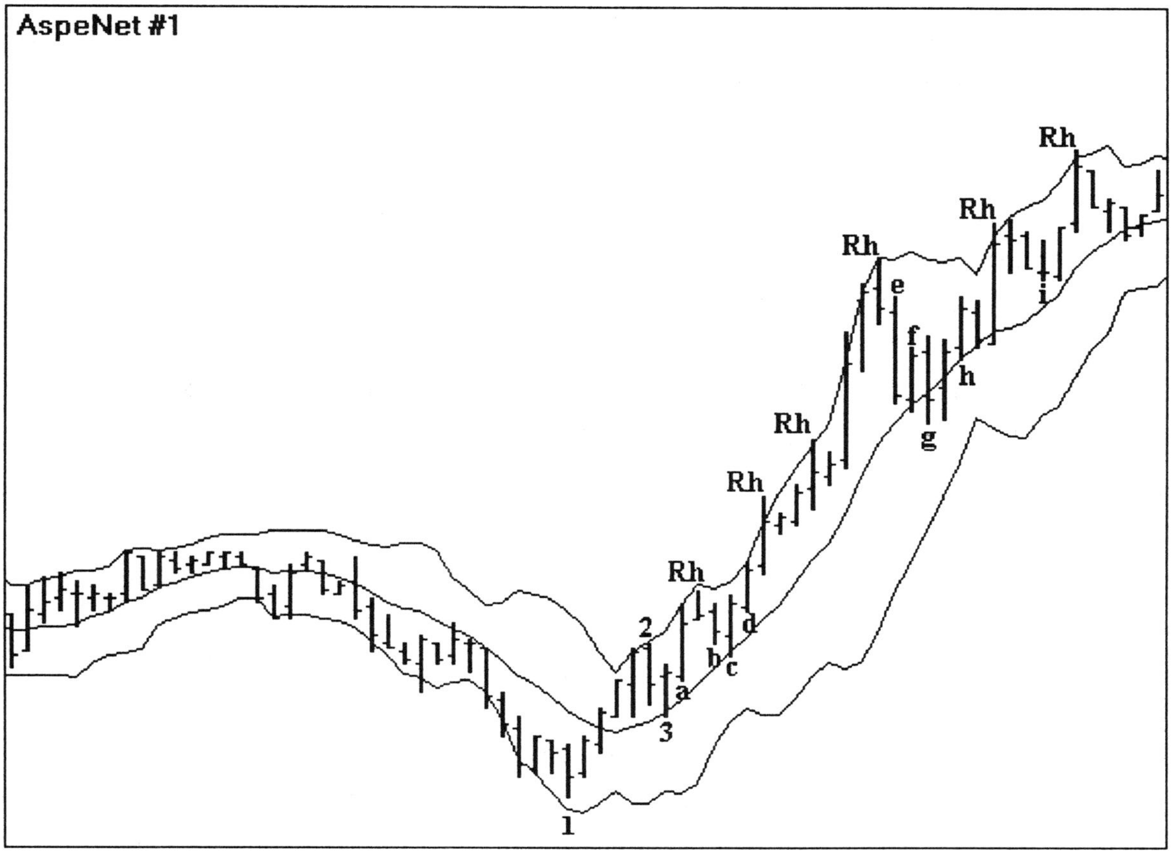

c) Bar c touches the moving average.

d) We go long on bar d as it trades through the high of bar c. We are long until bar e.

e) Bar e violates the low of the bar that made the point of the Hook. We must exit as soon as possible after the violation.

f) Prices touch the moving average.

g) We enter as bar g takes out the high of bar f. We must exit with a loss as bar g violates the low of bar f.

h) We go long as bar h trades through the high of the previous bar. We remain in the trade until bar i.

i) Bar i violates the low of the bar previous to it. We must exit.

That was easy, wasn't it? We could wish that all trading was so simple. If it were, we would have a world full of billionaires.

However, it isn't always so simple. The problem of course comes when prices are moving sideways. Fortunately, the tighter bands created by the 9 bar moving average provides a solution of sorts, and so do the bands themselves.

Let's take a look at how the moving average and the bands can help. We'll begin with the moving average.

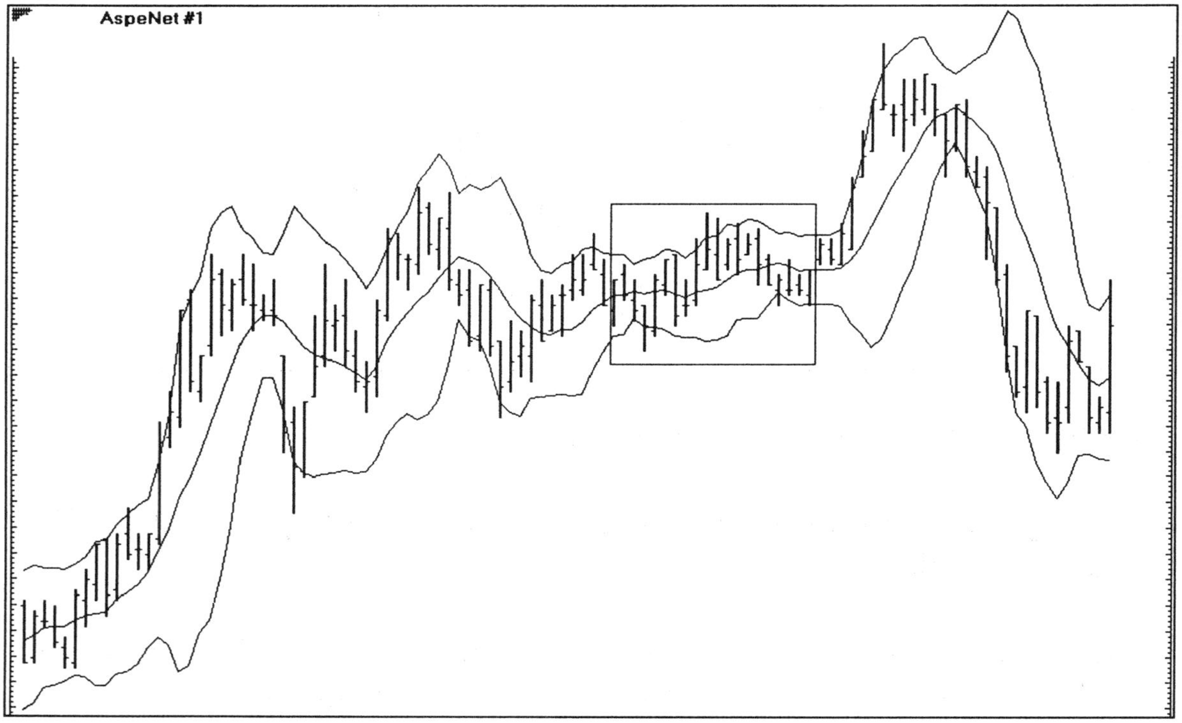

Notice the boxed off area above. The moving average has gotten fairly flat. While that is not a perfect filter, it is helpful to be aware of the condition of the moving average.

Notice also that prices are straddling the moving average. Few price bars are able to break clearly into one channel or the other.

Next, let's look at the bands. Notice how narrow they have become. They are quite a bit closer together than they were when the market was trending. The bands are also less pronounced in their fluctuations.

Another thing to notice is that prior to prices becoming congested, the bands begin to move towards each other. This is a clue to avoid using the bands for taking trades. Of course, as we learned in <u>ELECTRONIC TRADING 'TNT' I — GORILLA TRADING STUFF</u>, prices are in congestion. We can use any of the methods for identifying congestion that were presented there or earlier in this manual to help us to avoid trading until prices are truly trending.

Here's another test! Your assignment, should you choose to accept it, is to trade Microsoft on a 5 minute chart. Begin at the arrow. Use everything possible from this volume of the course as well as <u>ELECTRONIC TRADING 'TNT' I — GORILLA TRADING STUFF</u> and <u>ELECTRONIC TRADING 'TNT' II — HOW-TO-WIN TRADING STUFF</u> to trade this chart. Think about and write down why or why not you are taking each trade. Our answers are on the following pages. Hint, there are no right answers, just do your best. Good luck.

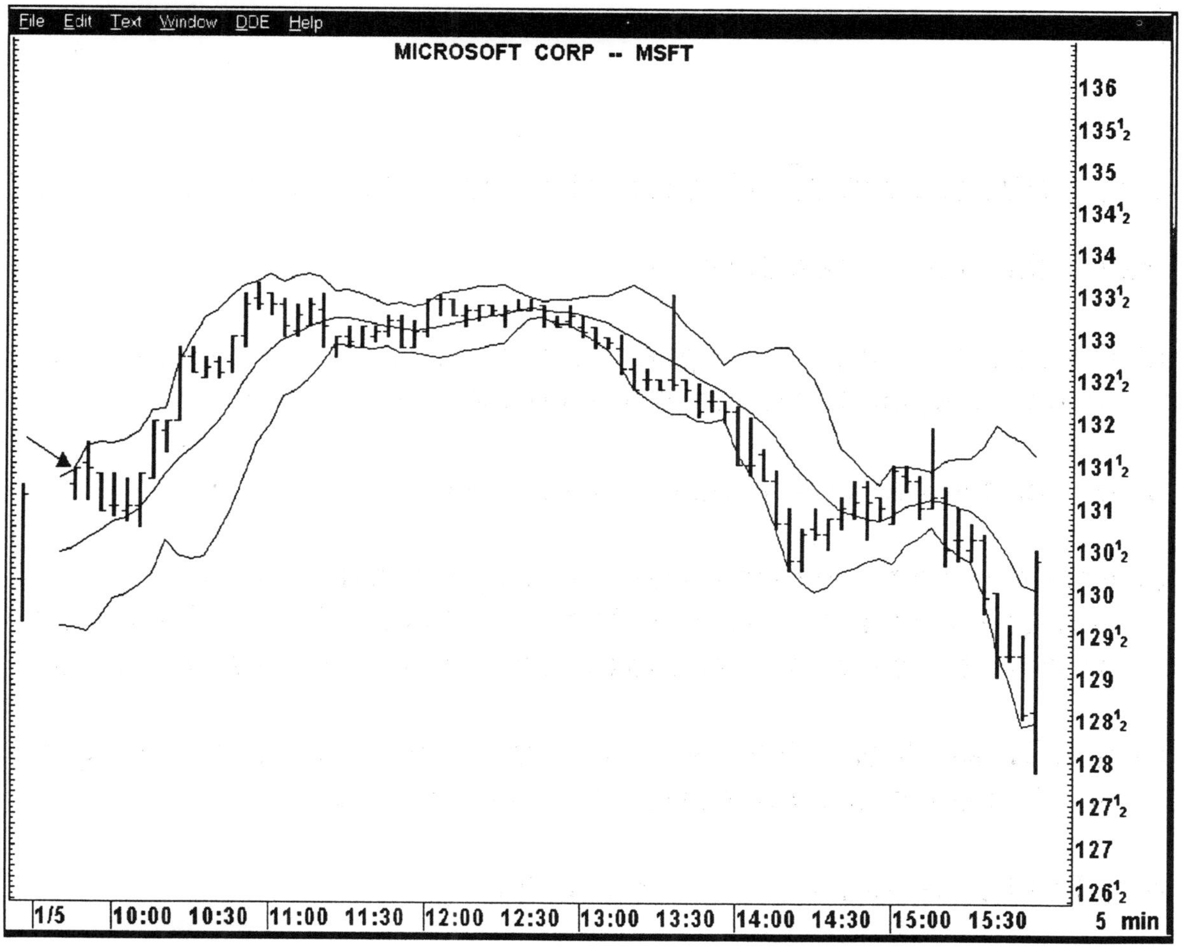

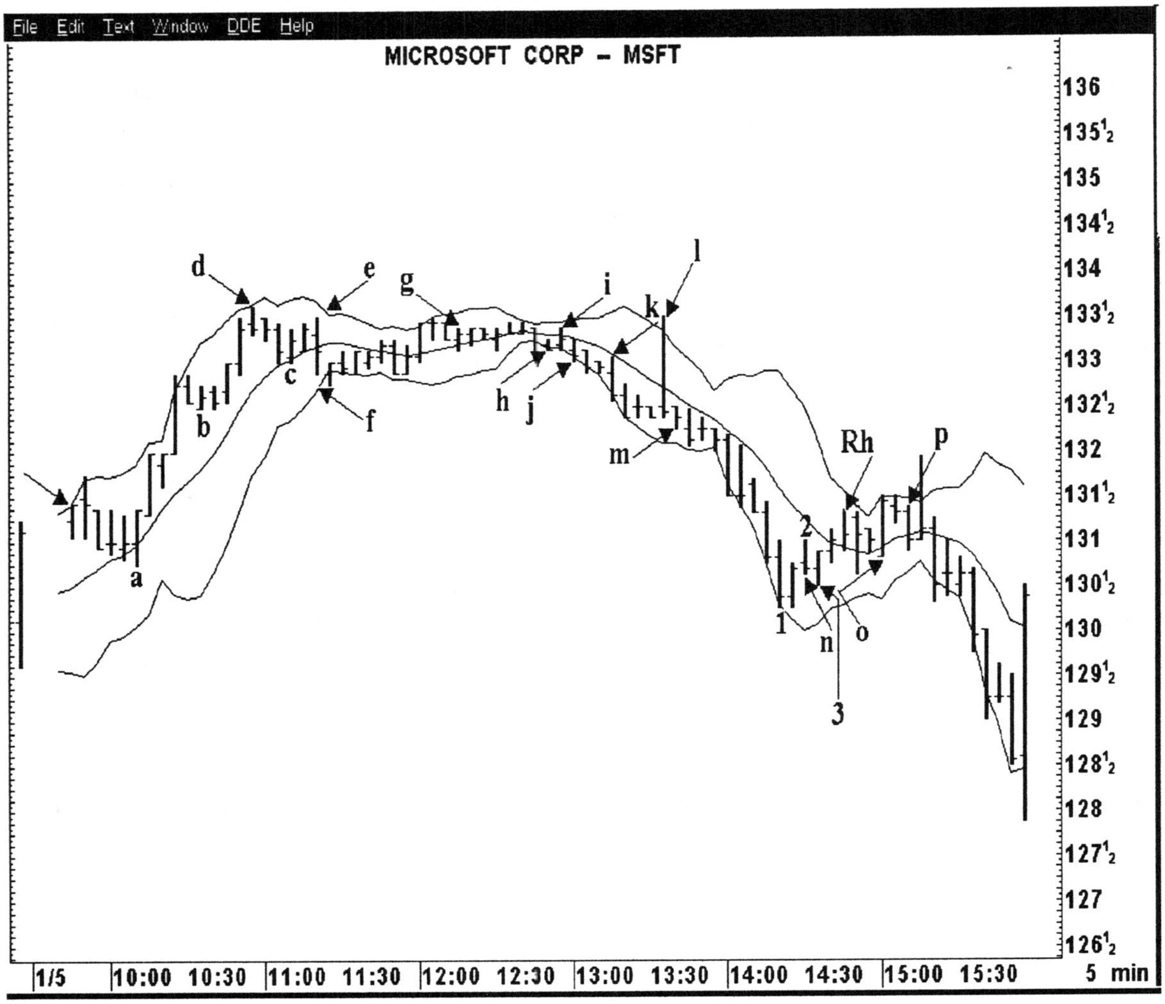

Here's the way we see the chart.

a) Prices are clearly in the upper channel. Buy a breakout of the high of the price bar that touched the moving average line.

b) Exit on the violation of the low of the previous bar.

c) Prices touch the moving average. Buy a breakout of the high of c and exit with a partial loss two bars later. It may have been possible to cover costs and take some profit before having to exit.

d) Is a Ross Hook. Interestingly, it is a reversal bar at the upper band. Take profits on reversal bars at the bands.

e, f) The bands turn in towards each other.

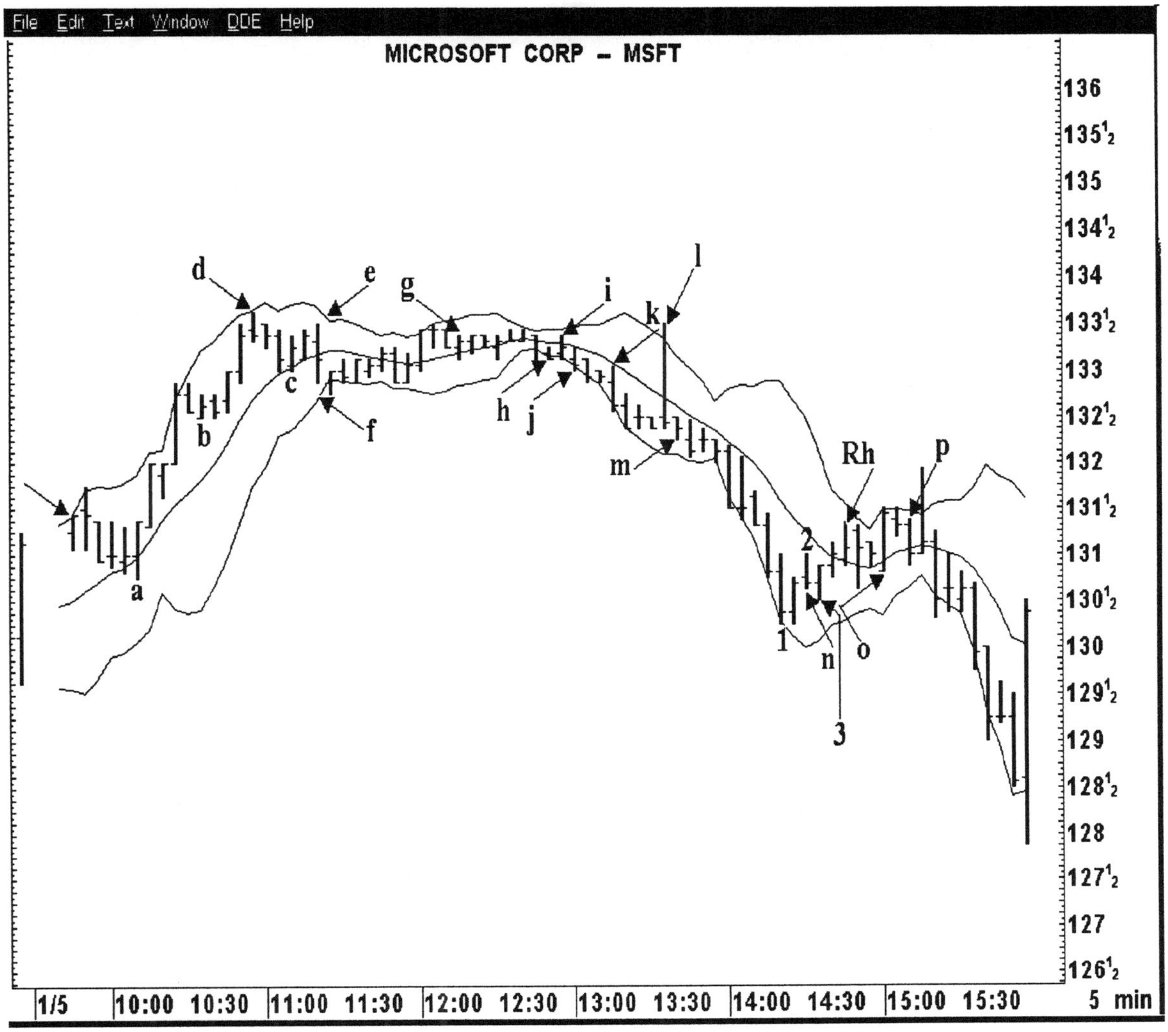

g) Prices are whipsawing across the moving average. The moving average is essentially flat.

h) Prices break cleanly into the lower channel. Note that the bands are beginning to move apart.

i) Prices touch the moving average.

j) Sell a violation of the low of bar i. You are now short.

k) Exit the short position on a violation of the high of the previous bar. Prices touch the moving average. Sell a breakout of the low of the bar preceding k. (The moving average is now clearly trending down. Prices remain in the lower channel. The bands have widened considerably from where they were in congestion.)

l) Exit short position based on a violation of the previous bar's high. Prices are still in the lower channel because bar l never lost contact with the moving average.

m) Sell a breakout of the low of bar l. Stay short until the bar that makes the 2 point of a 1-2-3 low violates the high of the previous bar.

n) Exit short position. 2 and n are the same bar, and n violates the high of the previous bar.

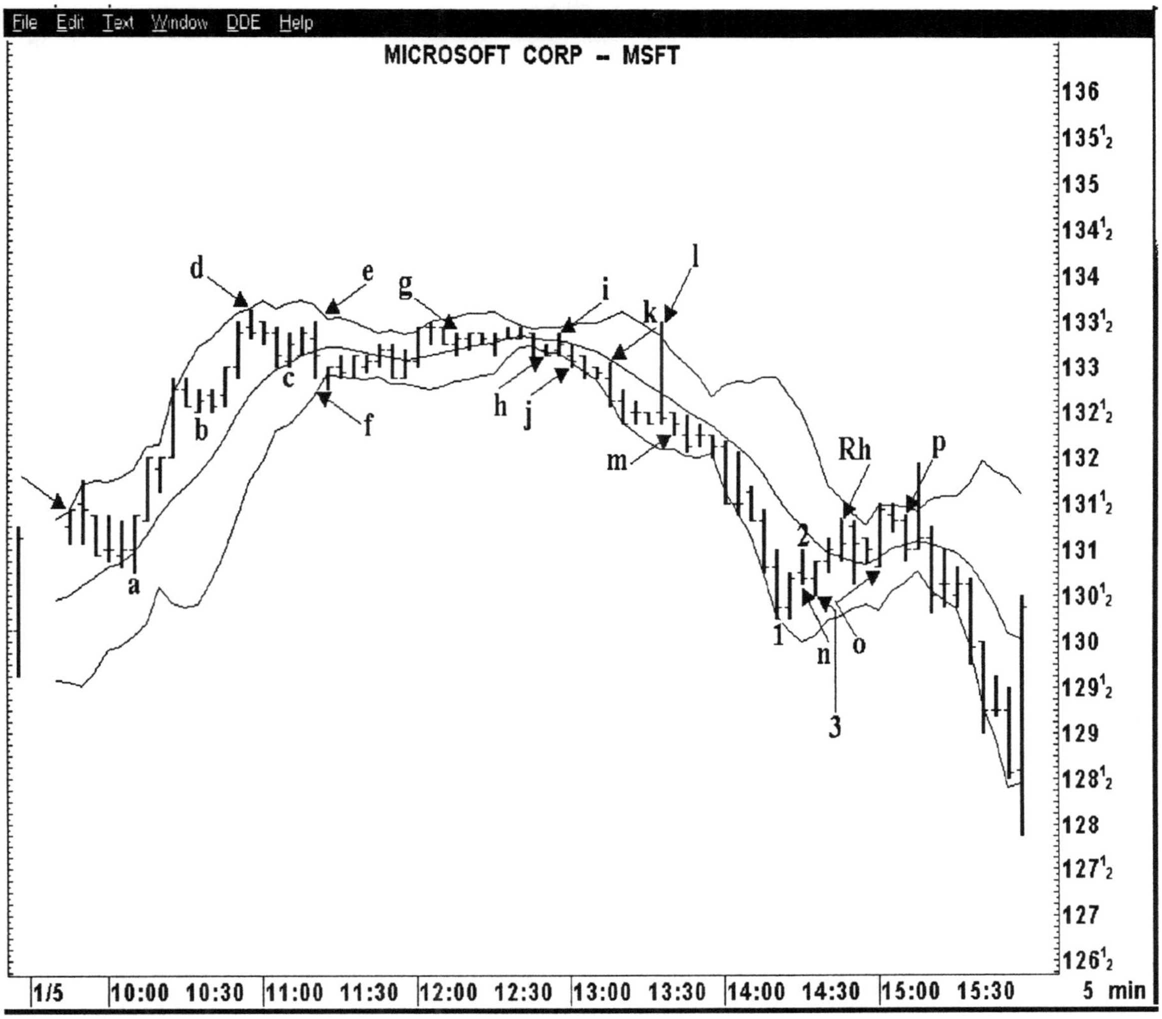

o) Violates a TTE ahead of an Rh, but prices are not clearly in the upper channel. Do not go long.

p) Buy a breakout of the high of p. Two bars previous prices move cleanly into the upper channel.

Subsequent to being long at p, profits were available on the long bar move up. That long bar is a reversal bar requiring that you take profits the moment it completes. If the remainder of the position is not moved to breakeven, then it experiences a loss when the low of p is violated.

Prices then move into the lower channel but never again touch the moving average. Besides, who wants to trade into the last fifteen minutes the market is open?

Chapter 14

VANILLA HOOKS

We've spent a good deal of time and space showing you how to use and trade the Ross Hook along with some of the more popular indicators being employed by some of our students.

In this chapter, we're going to trade the Ross Hook in combination with the Trader's Trick, with no indicators or oscillators of any kind.

We trade this way much of the time, but it is entirely respectable to choose to trade with indicators, oscillators, or other visual ways if you do it correctly and profitably. You do what works for you. We must choose the way to trade that best fits our personality and comfort zone.

Trading without any extra baggage is our favorite way to trade. It brings great results, and nothing more is needed than a simple chart. As a matter of fact, unless you are daytrading, all that's really needed is a newspaper! The chart is there for visual confirmation of the truth that is confirmed by the price action.

We're going to prove conclusively that this method works. It has been working for a very long time. It's possible to take data going back over one hundred years and prove that plain vanilla trading has worked consistently for that length of time.

Companies come and go. Traders come and go, and yet this method that has consistently made money is still here. It has not failed.

The trading community has gone from a few thousand traders worldwide, to many thousands, perhaps millions of traders worldwide. This has changed the nature of the markets, but not changed the way we can trade them using vanilla hooks.

We have seen the introduction of computerized trading utilizing models, programmed trading, intraday trading by computer from one's home, Internet trading, trading from a terminal in a trading office, and the concept of intraday charts down to the tick level. Still none of these have caused us to change one iota from trading the truth that exists within the concept of the Ross Hook.

When we presented the simplicity of the Ross Hook to one of the great Fibonacci luminaries of our time, he snickered. He patronizingly told us about the magic of Fibonacci retracements.

When we explained what we do to another famous hustler (trader?) of a "magic" triple-dipple trading system, he laughed, and wondered aloud how such nonsense could ever work in today's sophisticated markets.

We do not all have the same orientation. We do not all see the markets in the same way.

We have shown you many successful ways to trade and use the Rh. However, we have students who use only the "plain vanilla" trading methods, and might we add, with very great success.

What we do with the Ross Hook works. It has always worked under the conditions we have established for its use. It has withstood the test of time. It works in every time-frame for which we've tried it. However, it does not work in every time-frame for every stock in the market. This is because, in the lesser intraday time intervals, a chart may not form properly to enable the visualization needed for trading the Hooks.

An example of this would be a five minute chart of an illiquid stock. These rarely make formations other than "boxy," flat charts, in which the same prices are hit repeatedly. Our solution to this is to simply trade a greater time-frame, one great enough to enable us to clearly identify the Law of Charts. But if a stock has good liquidity, these formations work fine with a five minute chart.

We want to trade a stock when prices are trending. Since, by definition, a Hook cannot be formed when a market is not trending, we are essentially attempting to trade only when we believe that prices are trending.

The Ross Hook cannot be identified until and unless a market is trending, is about to trend, or has broken out of congestion. The breakout may take the form of an explosion or of a collapse. The violation of the Ross Hook itself is synonymous with the identification of an established trend. Let's look closely.

We must first identify a 1-2-3 high or low. On intraday, weekly, or monthly charts the 1-2-3 formation may consist of only three bars. On daily charts, it's better to have at least four bars comprising all three points. We must next form a Ross Hook.

No matter what happens with prices, we cannot consider that we have a trend reversal unless and until we form a 1-2-3 high or low in the direction opposite to the recent trend as explained in **ELECTRONIC TRADING 'TNT' I — GORILLA TRADING STUFF**.

We also consider that a market may have begun trending when we see the breakout from a Ledge or from a Trading Range.

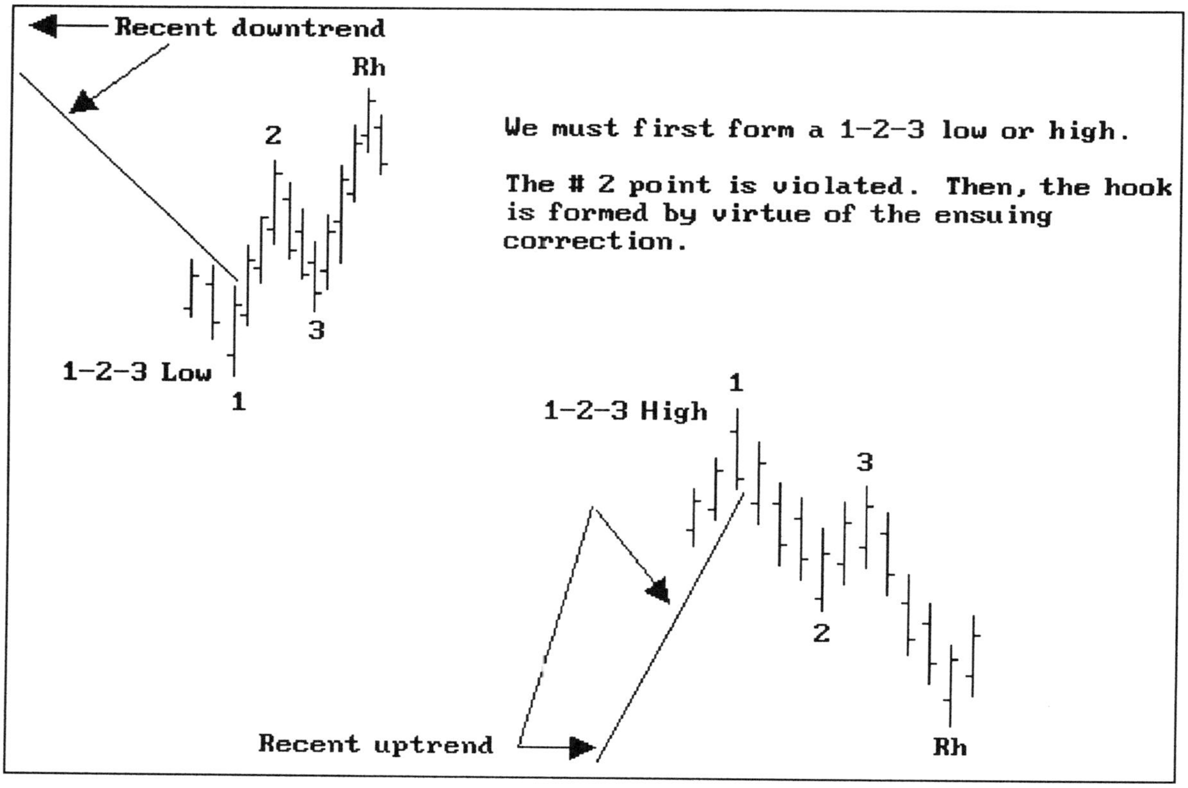

Once we have had a trend reversal, we can trade the Ross Hook that establishes that reversal as a new trend, and of course, any subsequent Hooks. We'll now answer some common questions about what we have discussed to this point.

1. Where do we place the exit point?

When trading without indicators, we use natural support and resistance points or the violation technique. The next series of charts will show varying time intervals from monthly to five minute, but not necessarily in any order.

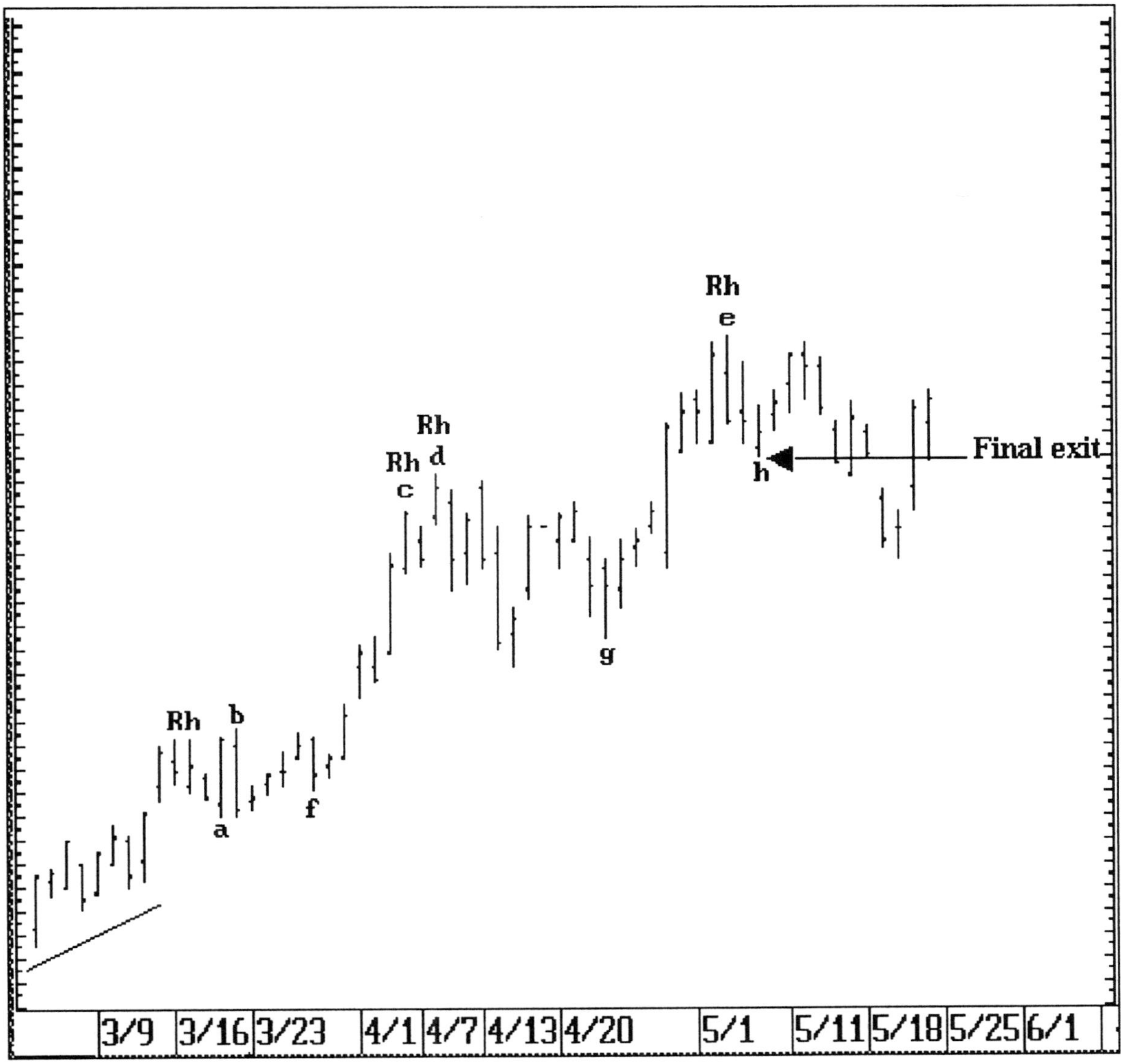

As soon as possible after entry, we may sell as many as one-third of our shares to cover our costs and give us a profit. It is important to start out every trade on the right foot.

Let's look at a sequence of events. When the bar labeled 'a' takes out the high of the previous bar, we have entered long via a Trader's Trick Entry (TTE). We plan on exiting one tick beneath 'a' if it becomes necessary. Since 'a' made a new low, and then bounced, it is now support. We attempt to take additional profits when 'b' takes out the high of 'a'.

At this point, we want you to concentrate on the ***where*** of natural support and resistance.

"f," "g," and "h" are natural support points.

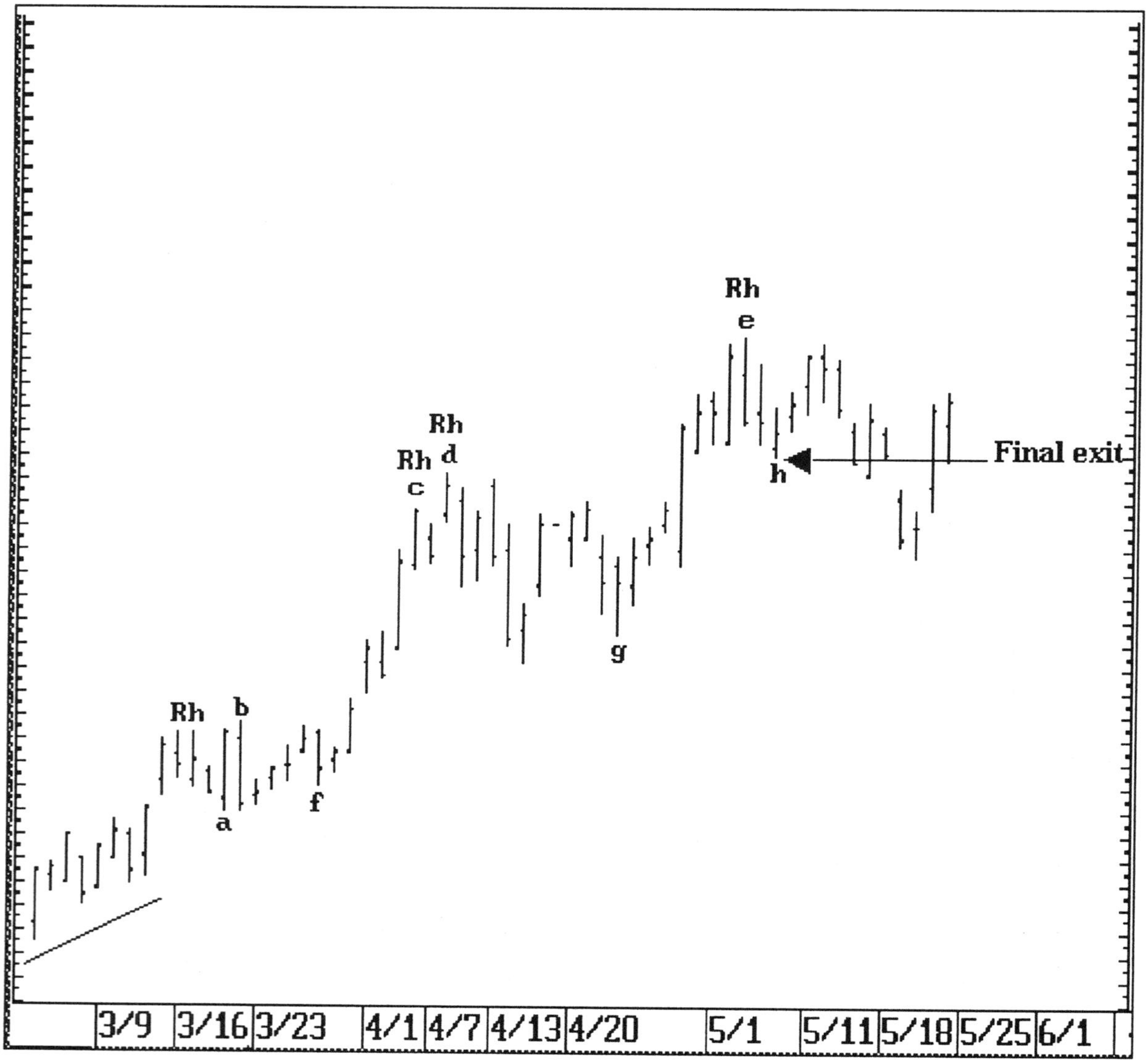

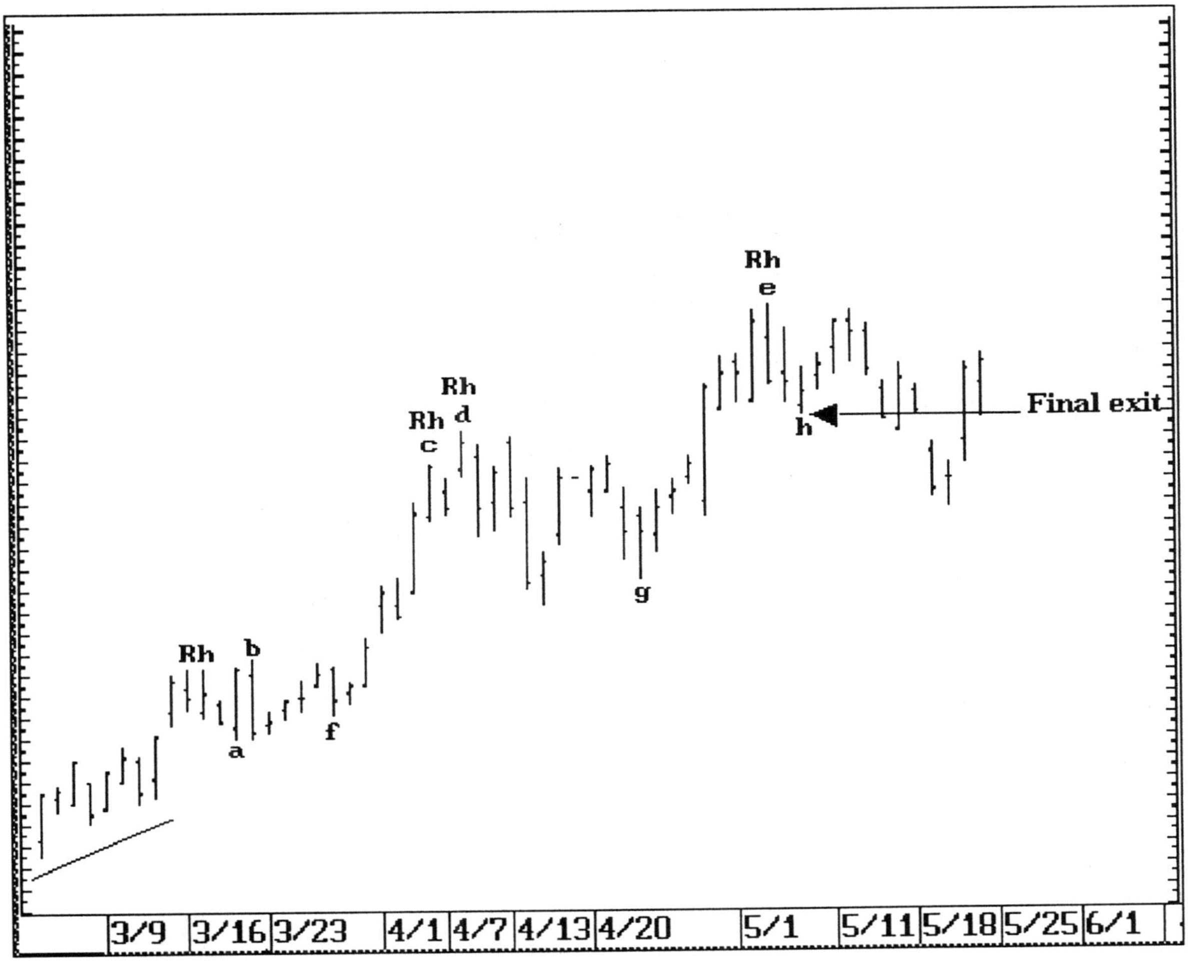

Bar "b" did two things: it took out the Rh, and became double support because it has the same low as "a". It is also a reversal bar, indicating that "b" moved where it did solely to grab the orders resting above the Rh.

However, since we're concentrating on natural support, we will keep the final third of our shares.

When the point of the next Rh, 'c' is violated, we will move the stop to one tick below 'f'.

When the point of the next Rh, 'd' is violated, we will move the stop to one tick below 'g'.

When the point of the next Rh, 'e' is violated, we will move the stop to one tick below 'h,' where we will exit on a violation of the low of 'h.'

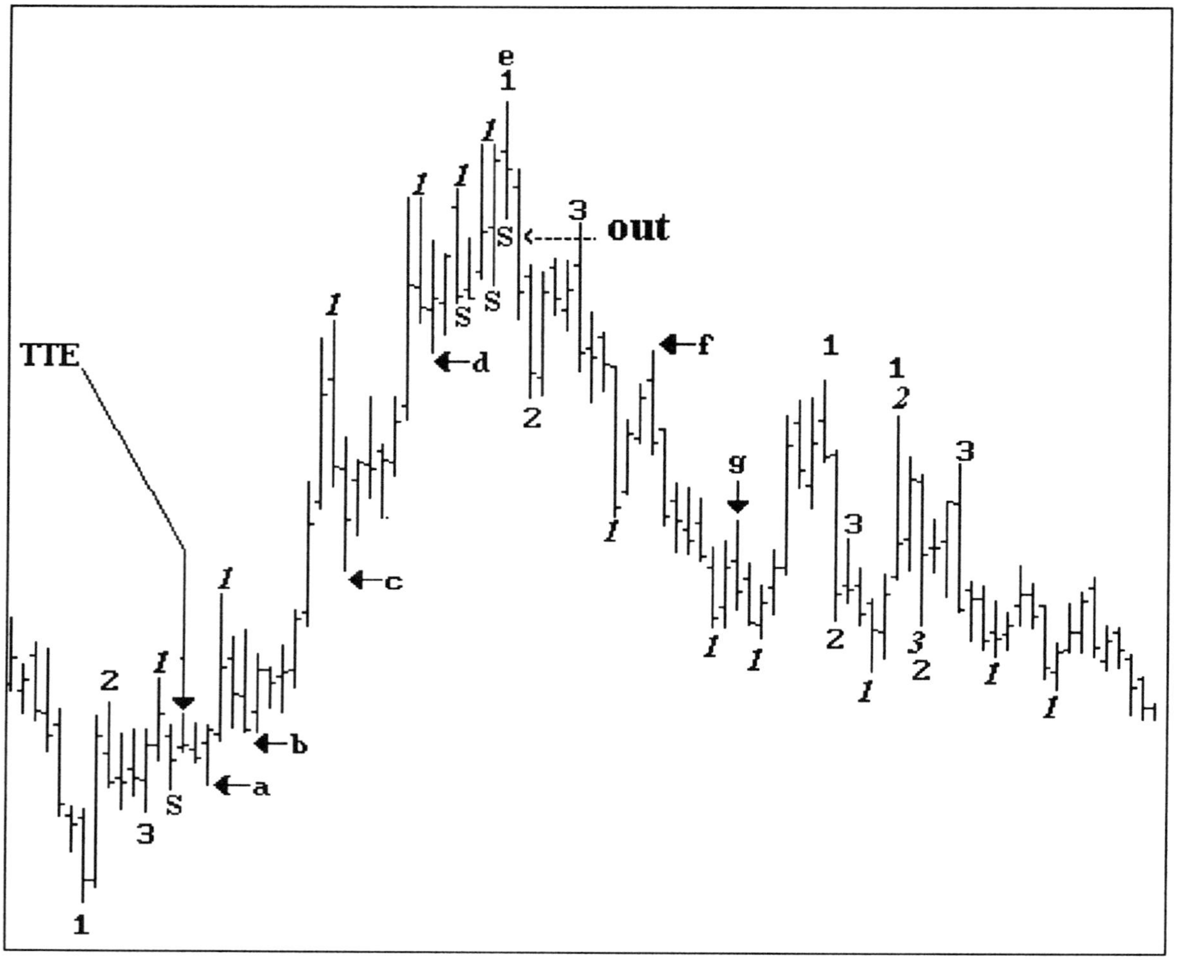

Let's go through the above chart in great detail. All Ross Hooks on this chart are marked with a ***1*** in *italics.* This is to remind you that every Rh is a potential #1 point. We'll start with a 1-2-3 low. Notice the first point marked '3.' Originally it was two bars to the left, but price movement causes us to move the '3' point.

We enter on a TTE and place our initial exit point under the closest natural support which is marked 's.' The bar labeled 's' creates an Rh. When the Hook itself is taken out, we mark our exit point at 'a' which is the most recent natural support point consisting of two equal lows.

Next, prices make another Ross Hook. When it is taken out, we mark our exit point at 'b.' This process is repeated at both 'c' and 'd'.

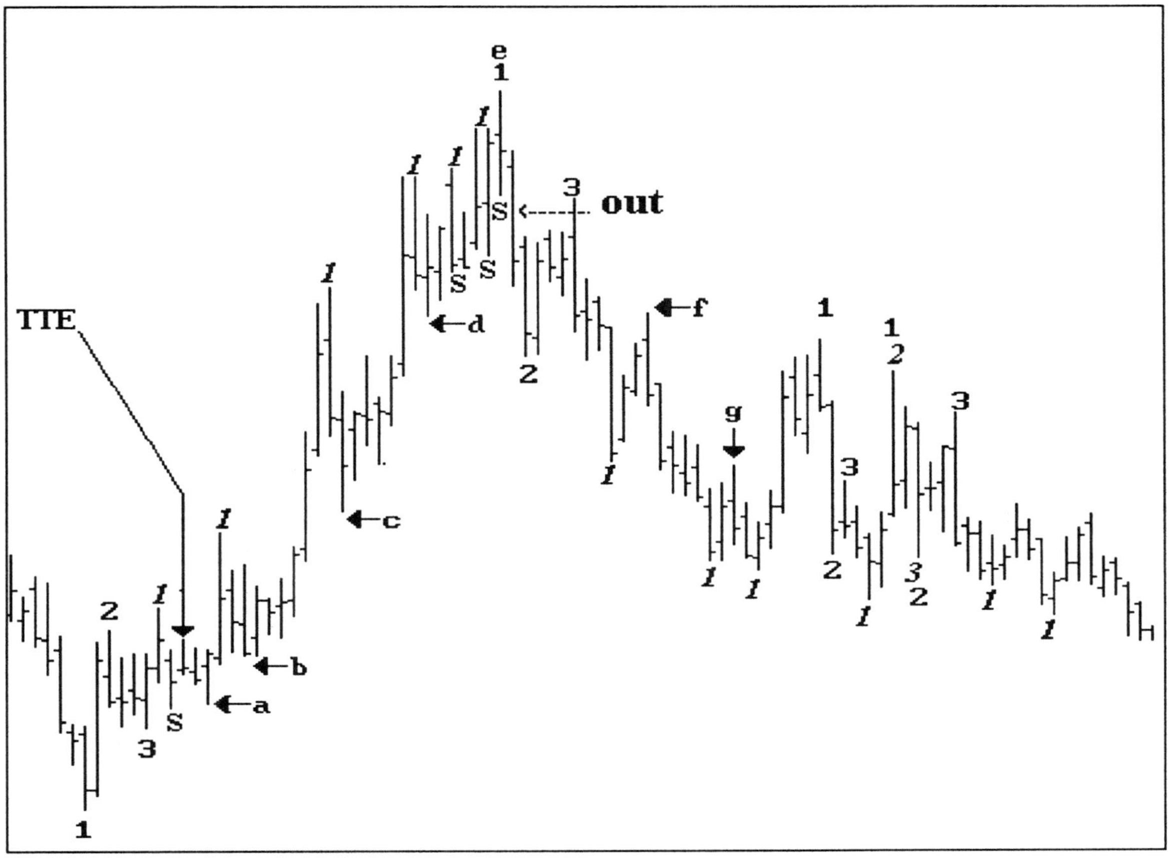

Notice that subsequent to bar 'd' the Hooks are forming at a much greater frequency. The market makes its last move up. The trend is about to end due to exhaustion. The market is running out of buyers. Consequently, we begin to move the stops, '*s*', up tight. We trail them just below the low of each bar until we are stopped out on the bar following the top 'e.'

Eventually prices make a 1-2-3 high followed by a Ross Hook (***1***). We trail our stop at natural resistance points, 'f' through 'g'.

After 'g' the trend is broken. We begin to get 1-2-3's (*1-2-3's)* in both directions. Whenever you have a 1-2-3 high and a 1-2-3 low mixed together, you automatically are in congestion because depending upon the order in which they occur, you have either /\/\ or \/\/. Prices have entered a major congestion. When Hooks begin coming close together, one right after another, and the angle of descent/ascent flattens out, we are seeing price action typical of bottoming/topping, i.e., congestion. In the chart above, first we ran out of buyers. When prices plunged and flattened out, we ran out of sellers.

Now, with reference to natural support and resistance, some will ask:

2. *"But doesn't it matter what time interval each bar represents?"*

What if we told you that the chart we've been using was a 15 minute chart? Would that be any different, insofar as the action taken, than if we told you that the chart was a weekly chart? A chart is a chart is a chart. The only difference the time interval makes is one of magnitude of move, and of course, magnitude of risk. The actions taken relative to each are the same.

Some of our readers and certainly some of our students can afford to trade monthly charts. They have become seasoned, patient traders, and add monthly chart trading to their regular trading activity — yes even some of our students who daytrade on five minute charts can find time to pick up beautiful monthly trends!

In the material for this course, we will not penalize the trader with deep pockets in favor of the trader with a small account.

The opportunities with Ross Hooks are numerous.

For those who daytrade, please notice that with the exception of the amount of money involved, the price action on the monthly chart of a less well-known and less liquid equity is not at all unlike a five minute chart of a highly popular, extremely liquid stock.

We're going to give you a real life example from a trade taken in the S&P 500. Even though this trade took place in the S&P 500, there are numerous examples of traders doing similar trades in stocks. This trade is a classic example of the proper long term use of natural support. The futures trade was entered by one of our students seven years ago. As of the time we are writing this course he is still long.

This student began with a $600,000 trading account derived from a business he had sold.

First he went long the S&P 500 based on a TTE entry ahead of a Ross hook. That was in early 1991. He then trailed an exit point behind natural support until he realized that he could move his exit point below natural support on the weekly chart. Prices continued to move up overall, and eventually he was able to move his exit point below natural support on the monthly chart. The last time we spoke with him, his exit point was located below two natural supports back of current price action.

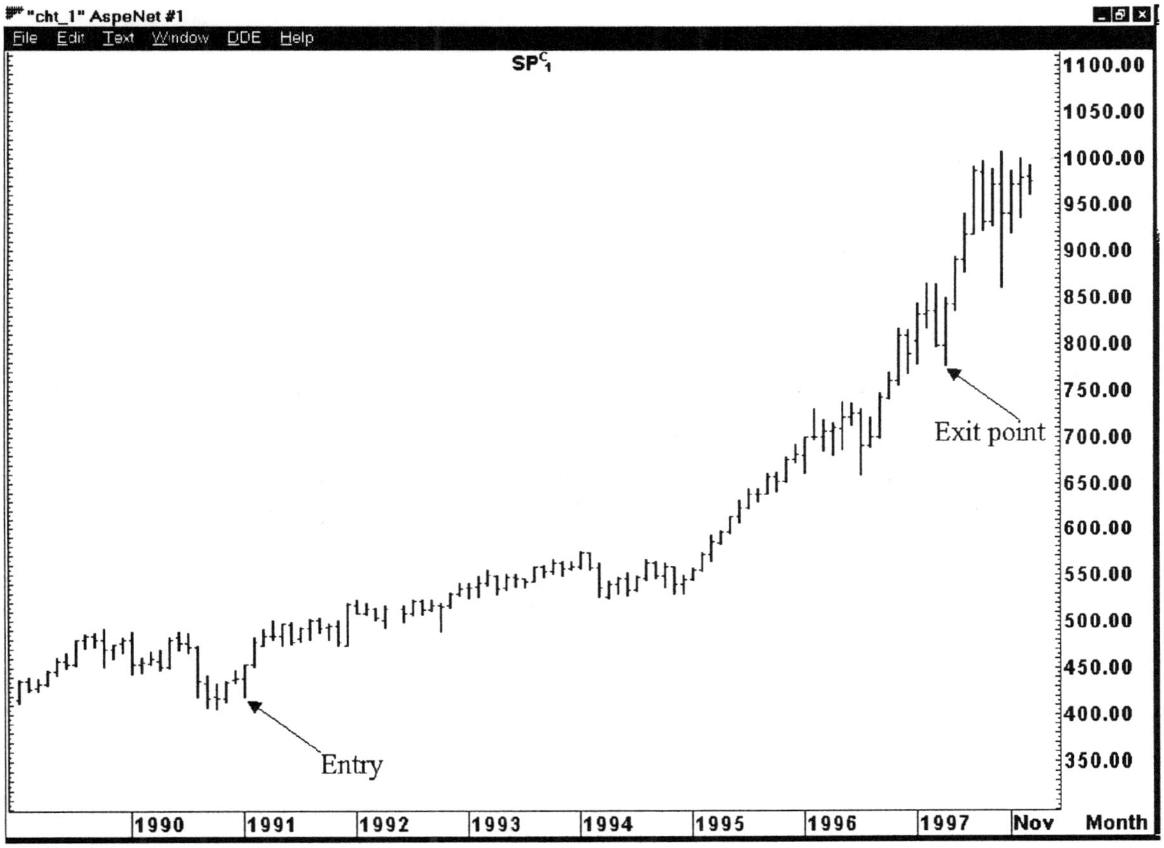

The chart above is a monthly continuous chart of the S&P 500 futures. It's not for me to reveal how many contracts this man is holding, but if he entered the market at 425.00 and exits at 775.00 each contract he holds will be worth $175,000 on an average margin of $10,625 per contract. So now let me answer the next question.

3. "How can you afford to keep the stop so far away?"

By patiently building an account to a size suitable for trading monthly charts.

4. "How can you afford to keep stops at natural support or resistance?"

By reducing the time frame in which you trade to an affordable level. This means that if you have a very small account, you may have to trade a five or ten minute chart in highly liquid stocks.

5. "Are there problems with trading as little as a one minute chart?"

Problems with one minute charts arise only when you simply cannot get the job done quickly enough.

6. "Are some Hooks better than others, and if so, which are the best?"

Some Hooks are better than others, but we have never been able to determine ahead of time which they will be. Sometimes a shallow retracing Hook does best, but all too often deeply retracing Hooks do best. We try to limit our trade entries to TTE's resulting from clear and well defined Hooks.

Chapter 15

FINE POINTS

There is a lot more to trading Ross Hooks than you might initially think. We feel they are the single best trading formation we've seen in the markets when preceded by a 1-2-3 formation.

Ross Hook trading can last from several minutes on an intraday chart to several months on a daily chart. They can even be traded on weekly or monthly charts for long term trading.

We're going to make some statements with regards to the following charts. What we say will help you fine tune your trading of Ross Hooks. The things we point out will be true for trading in all time frames.

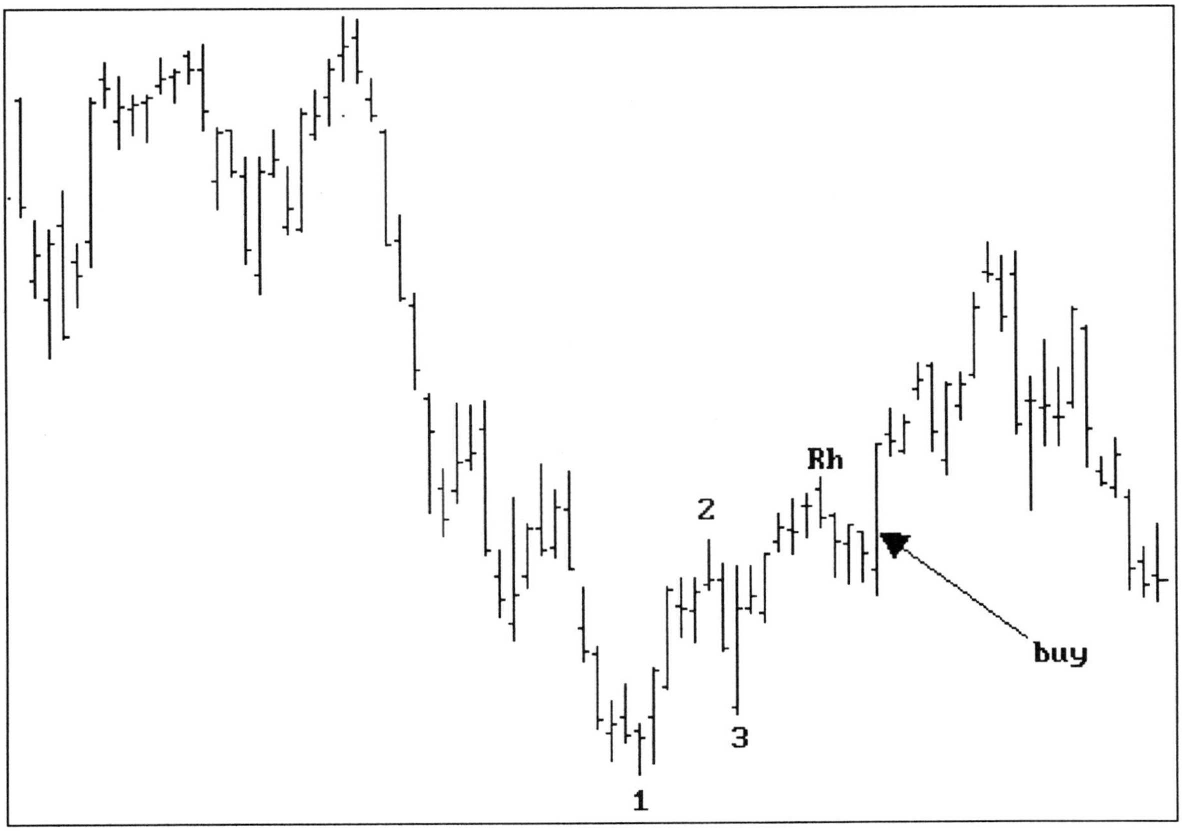

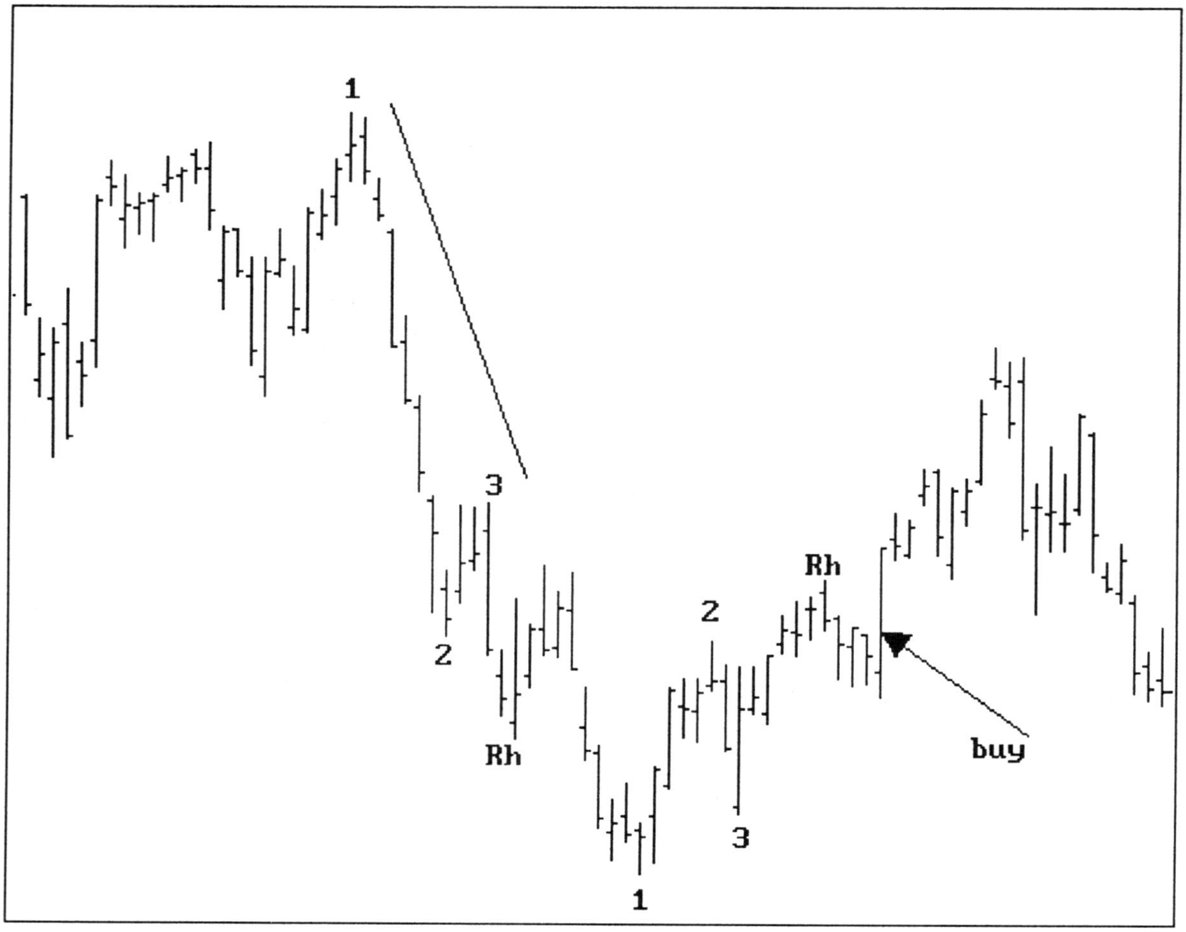

Be patient to trade from well formed charts. You want a well formed, clearly seen 1-2-3 to precede the Hook.

Trade only in a time frame in which you can afford to place exit points according to the Volatility Stop study, or better yet, a time frame in which you can afford to place the stops at natural support and resistance points. Otherwise, exit when you see two reversal bars or a bar making a higher high in a downtrend or a bar making a lower low in an uptrend (Violation Method).

For some, that will mean trading a five minute chart. Yet we know that some of our more affluent readers and some of our large traders and commercial students can afford the natural support and resistance stops on charts as great as weekly and monthly.

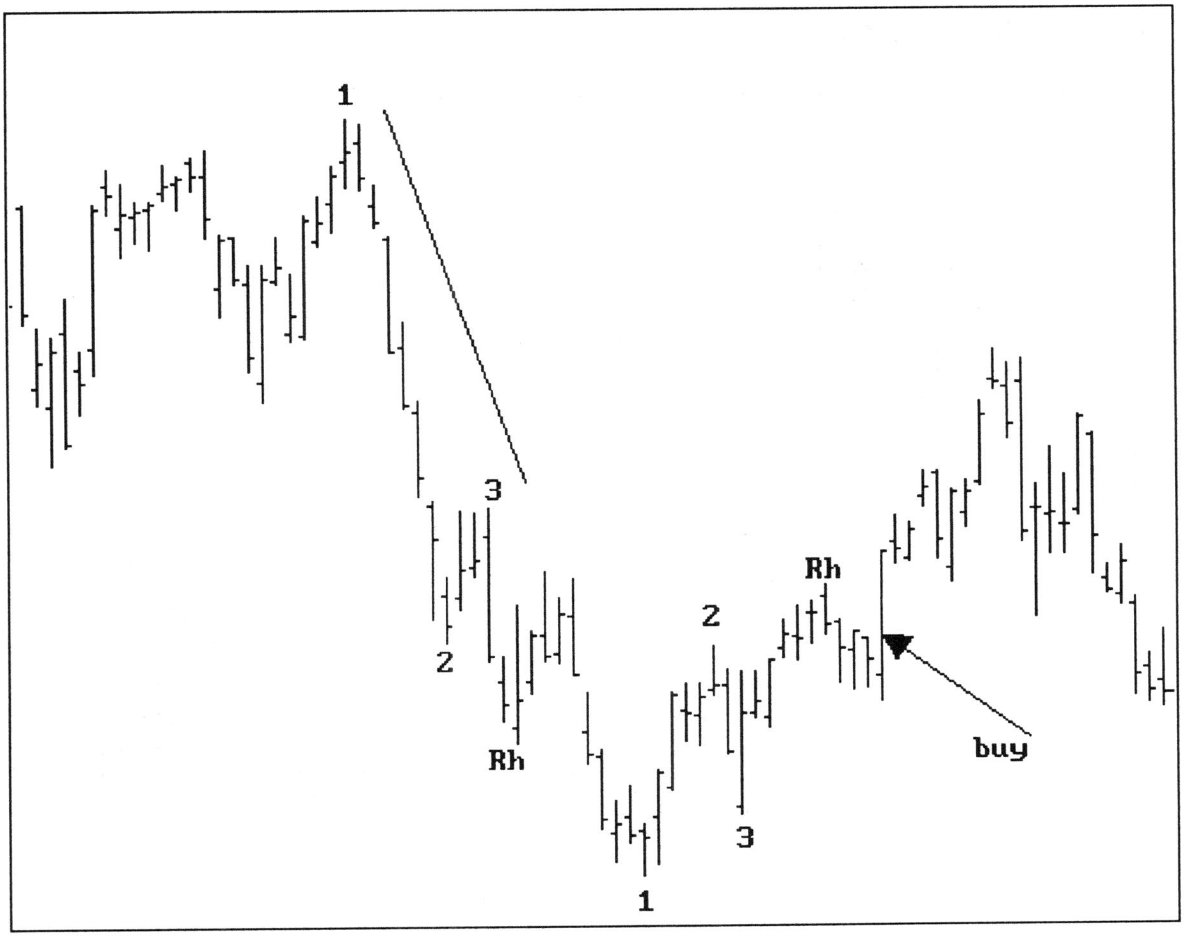

Avoid Hooks that are made subsequent to a very long 1-2-3 formation.

The #2 point of the 1-2-3 high in the chart above is much too far from the #1 point. This causes the #3 point to be very short in relation to the move from #1 to #2. The best 1-2-3's are more proportionate, with the #3 point being anywhere from less than 1/3 to a 2/3 retracement from the #1 point to the #2 point. In other words, on the chart above, the 1-2-3 high preceding the Hook is not well formed. However, the 1-2-3 low on the chart is reasonably well formed.

1-2-3 formations should be well formed and "tight." One way to tell this is to make sure the #2 point is contained within, or is formed just outside the most recent congestion. When they are, the chances are excellent that prices will move to test the boundary of the congestion. The TTE at the arrow gave a good entry.

Here is another chart.

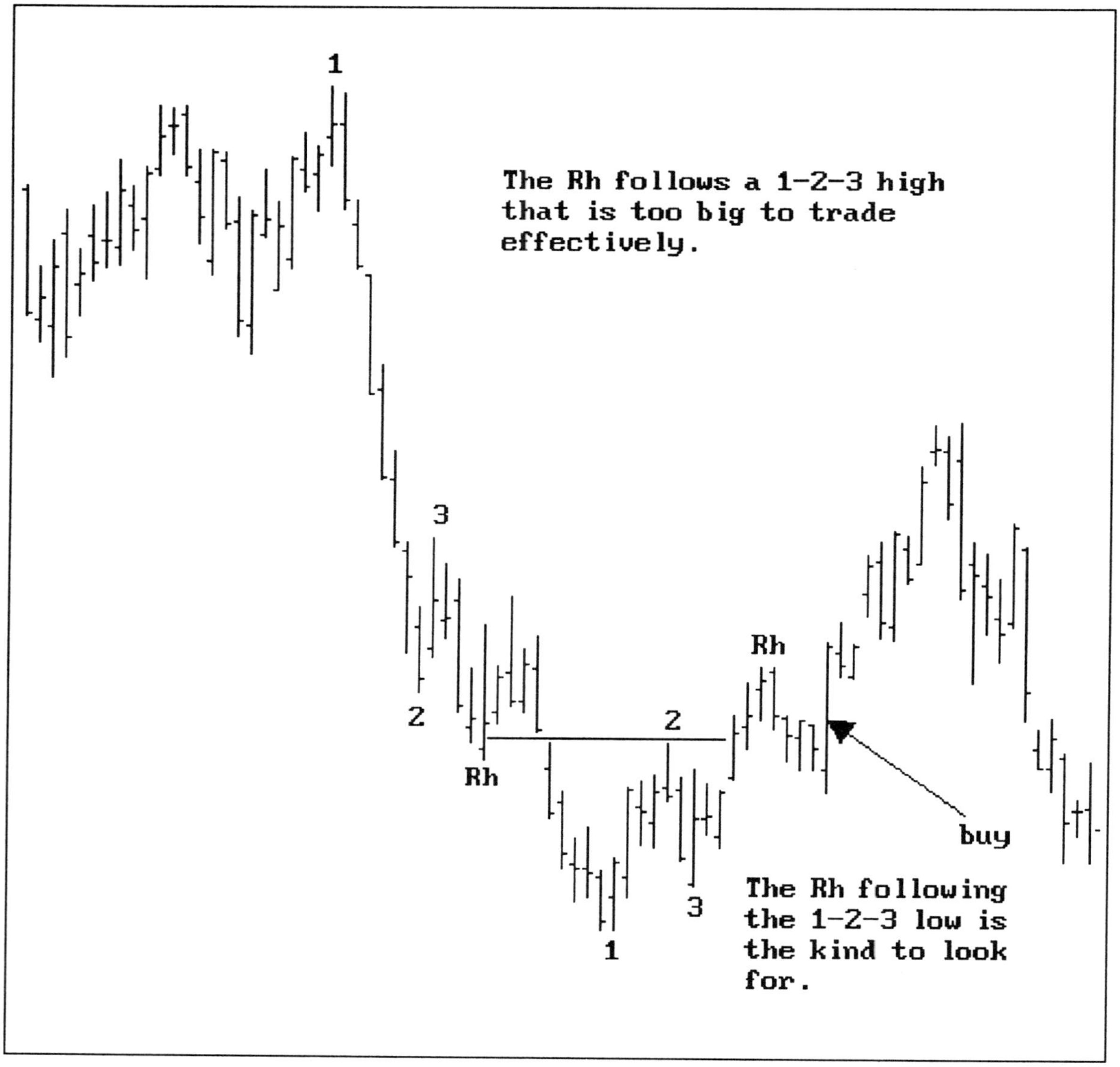

This chart is similar to the previous one because it shows prices for another entity in the same market. That brings up a point. If a trade is missed on a stock in one sector, quite often you can enter a trade in a similar company in the same sector.

Looks like test time again.

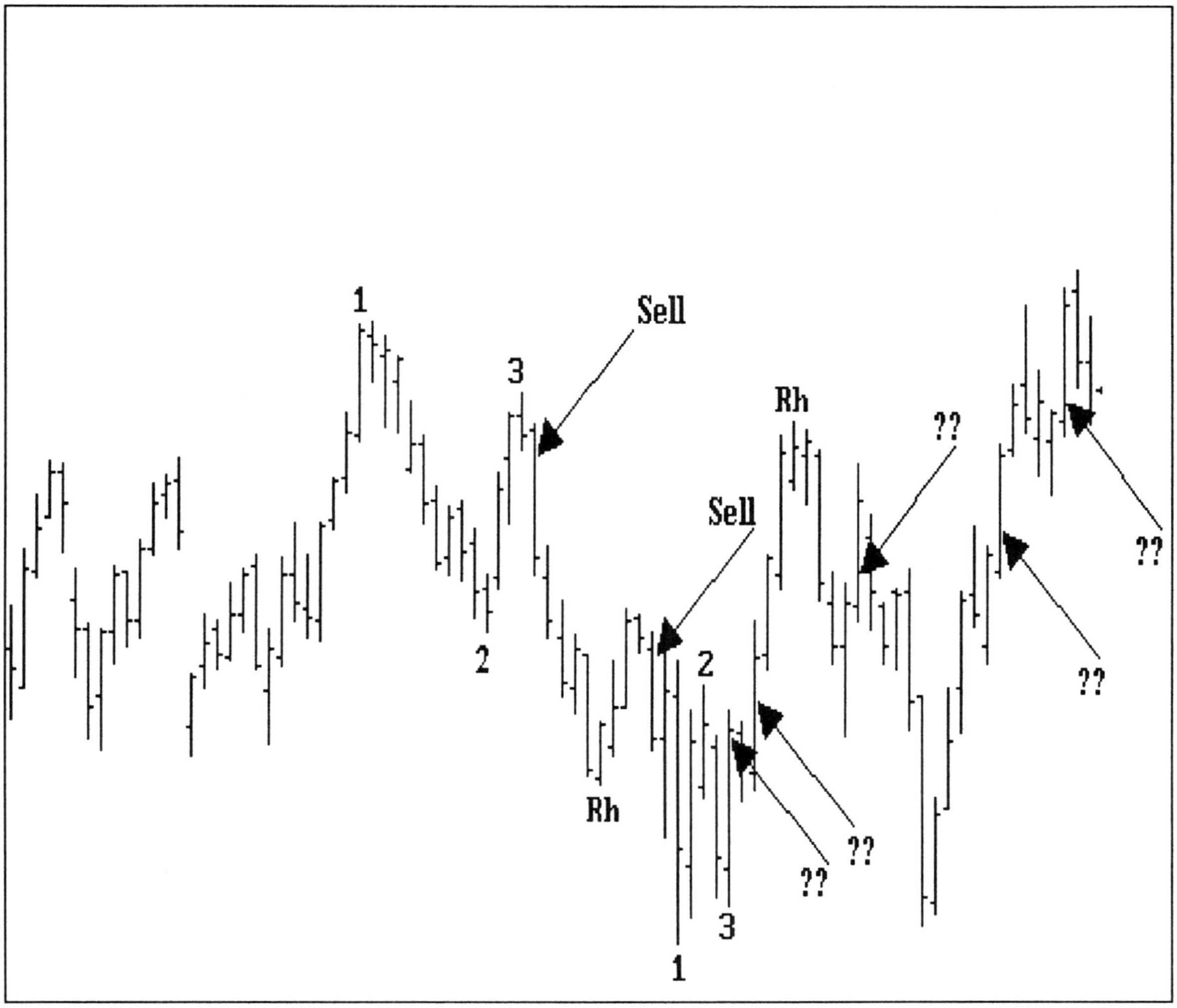

Please label the rest of this chart and decide at the question marks what you would do. Are there any more 1-2-3s? Are there any other Ross Hooks?

Which are the clean 1-2-3s or Rh's? Which trades would you take or not take? Why??

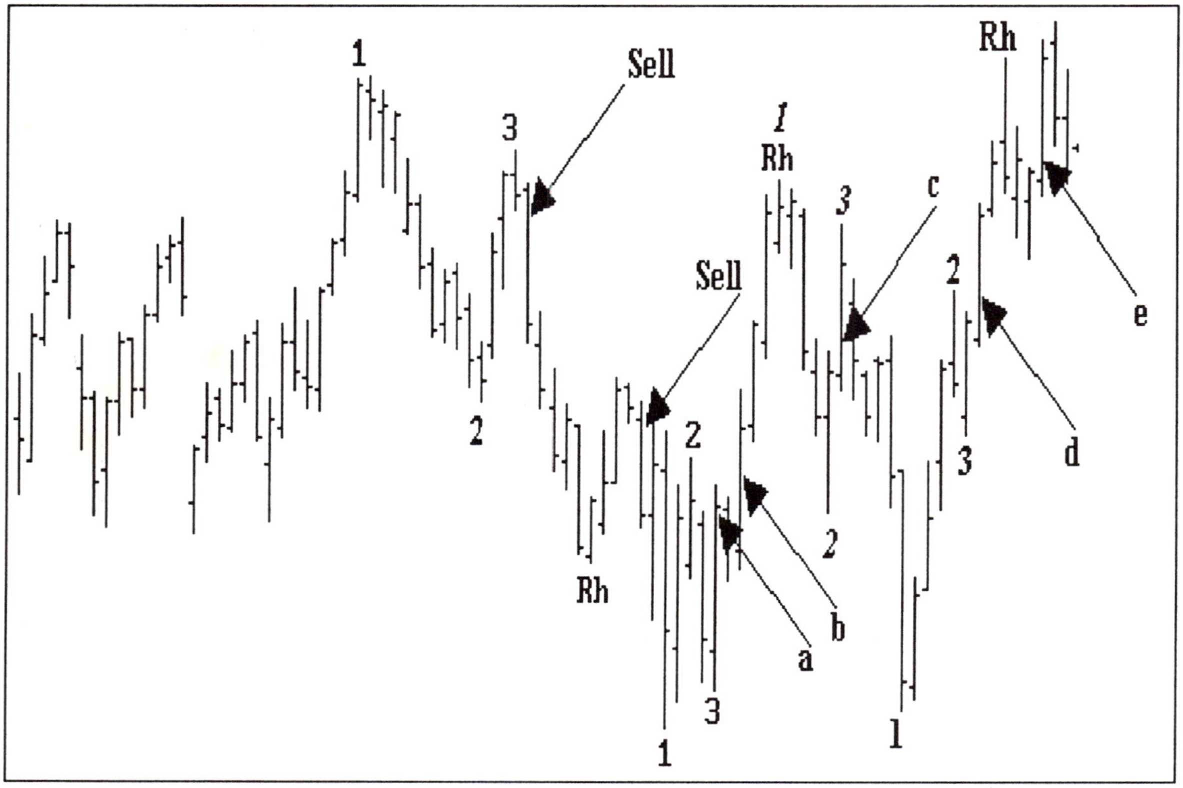

On the above chart, the #2 point of the first 1-2-3 high is formed well but not below the recent congestion. A decision must be made to enter the trade on a TTE if there is room for a profitable trade between the TTE and the bottom of the congestion area. In this case there is and an excellent trade can be made.

The first 1-2-3 low is poorly formed and to take a TTE there would be to trade straight back up into resistance. We would not take a trade at 'a'. 'b' has the same problem, it is a Ross Hook straight into the middle of a major congestion area. We would not take a TTE at 'b.'

Notice that the second Rh on the chart is also the number ***1*** point for a 1-2-3 high. When that 1-2-3 high is completed, we have 1-2-3s going in both directions. That means we are in congestion. Hooks cannot occur in congestion, only in trending markets. We would not take the trade at 'c.'

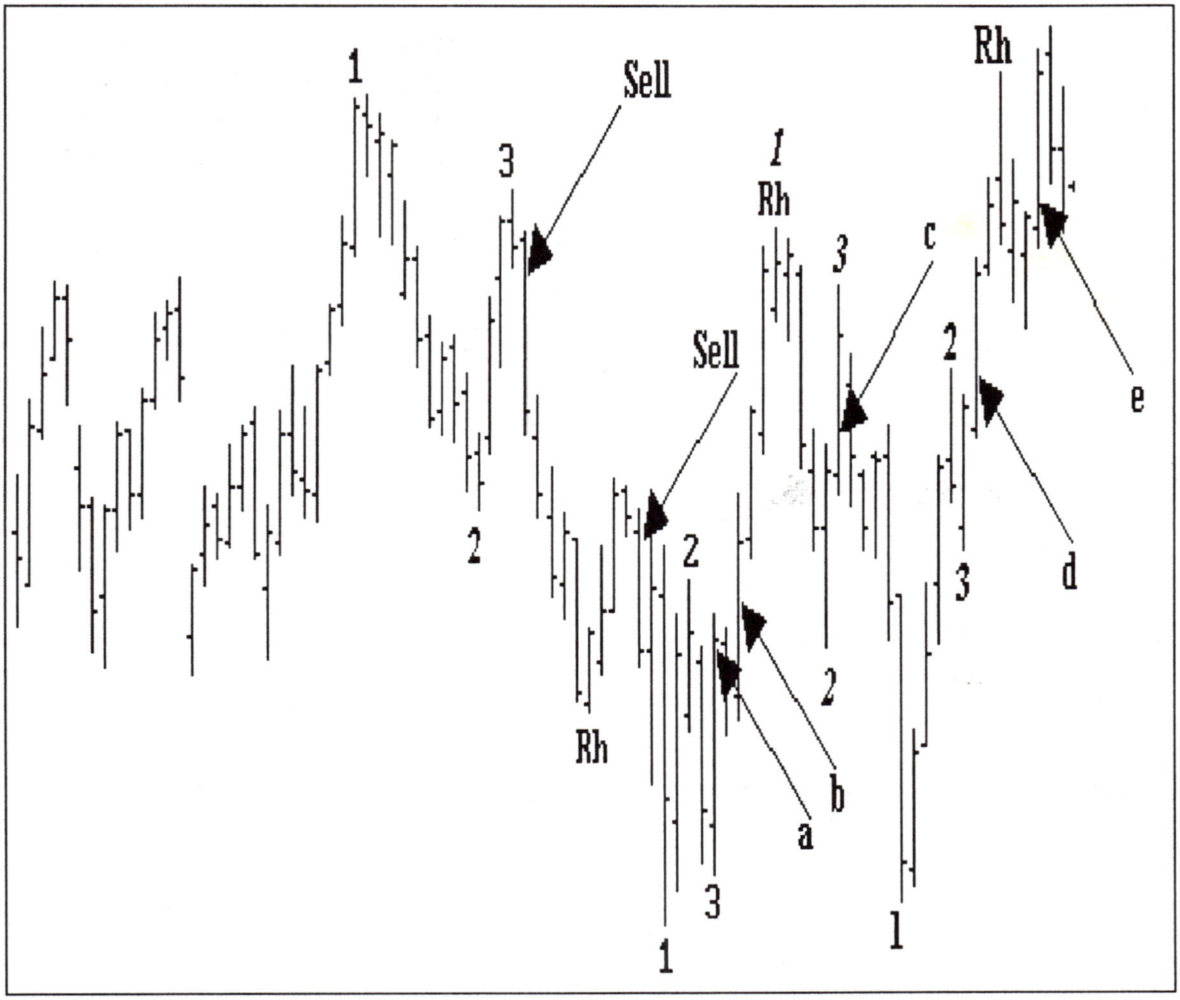

'd' comes as a TTE from a somewhat elongated but well formed 1-2-3 low, with prices still in congestion. If you think that 'd' could result in a test of the highs of the congestion area, then the TTE is appropriate for an entry. 'd' is a trade we would take.

'e' is a trade we definitely would have taken because it is a Rh set to blast out of the congestion. Notice that by the time 'e' occurs, prices have been in congestion for a great number of price bars.

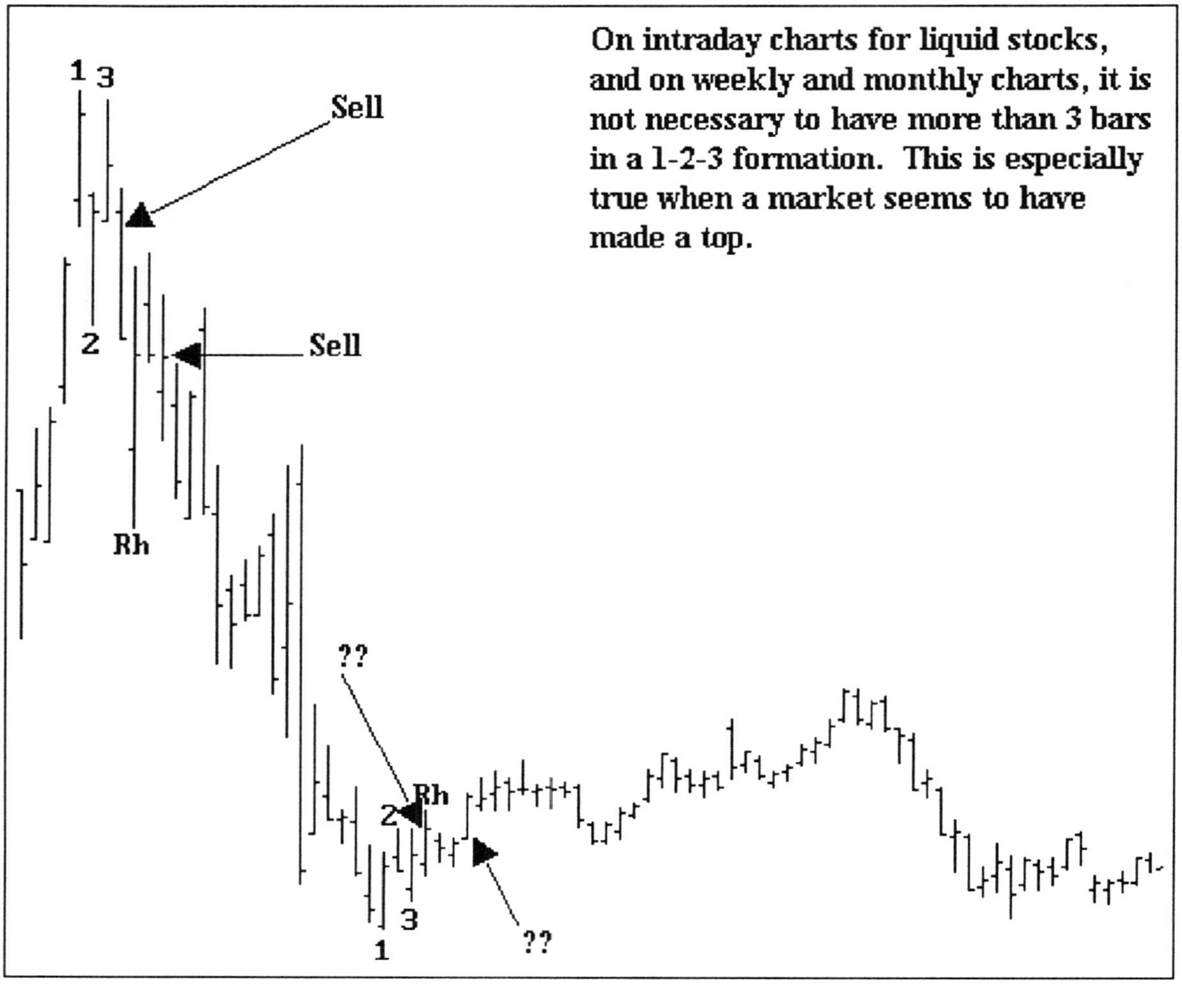

Should you buy at either of the arrows with question marks??

If yes, why? If no, why?

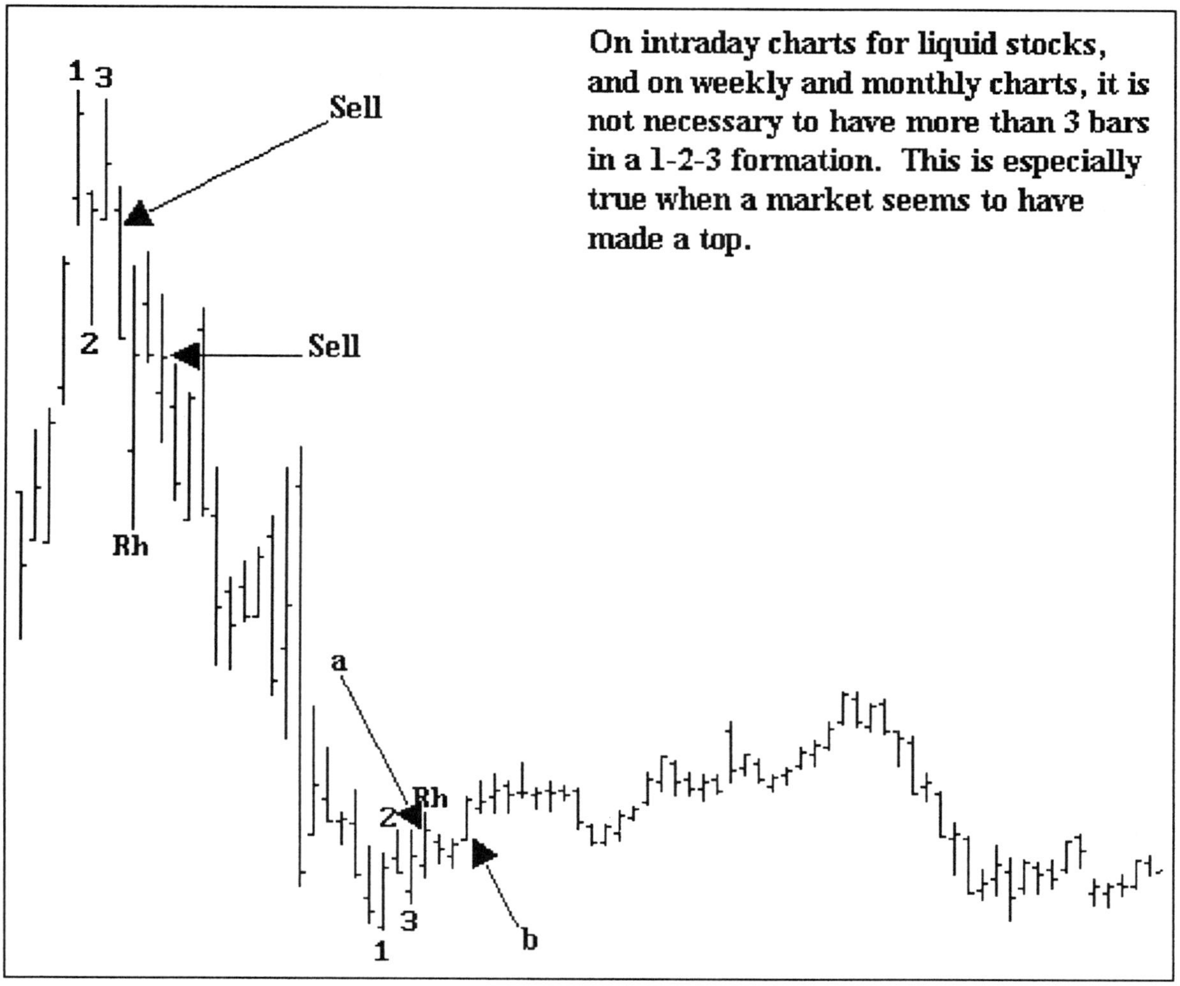

Usually, at the end of a major collapse or explosion in prices, or at the end of a very long trend, there will be a sizable congestion. We would definitely not attempt to buy at 'a' for two reasons: 1) There is no TTE on the bar that made the '3' point. 2) It is a 3 bar 1-2-3 at the end of a long plunge down. Prices would normally go into congestion after such a plunge.

The TTE at prior to bar 'b' is fine and if you said you wanted to trade this that's fine, too. However, because it comes so soon after the low, we wouldn't expect prices to move very far. The correct anticipation is for congestion, and a Trading Range.

Chapter 16

DON'T TAKE THAT HOOK

Are there conditions under which you do not want to take a Trader's Trick Entry (TTE) ahead of a Ross Hook?

Yes, there are. They are not all absolute, and certainly you would want to proceed with great caution. We will explain each after this brief summary.

Be careful with the TTE approach to a Hook...

> When prices suddenly become volatile.
>
> When Hooks come too close together.
>
> When volume dries up.
>
> When a Hook is too far away.
>
> When prices have not firmly started to move back towards the Hook after three bars of correction

We will examine each of these concepts more fully.

PRICES BECOME TOO VOLATILE

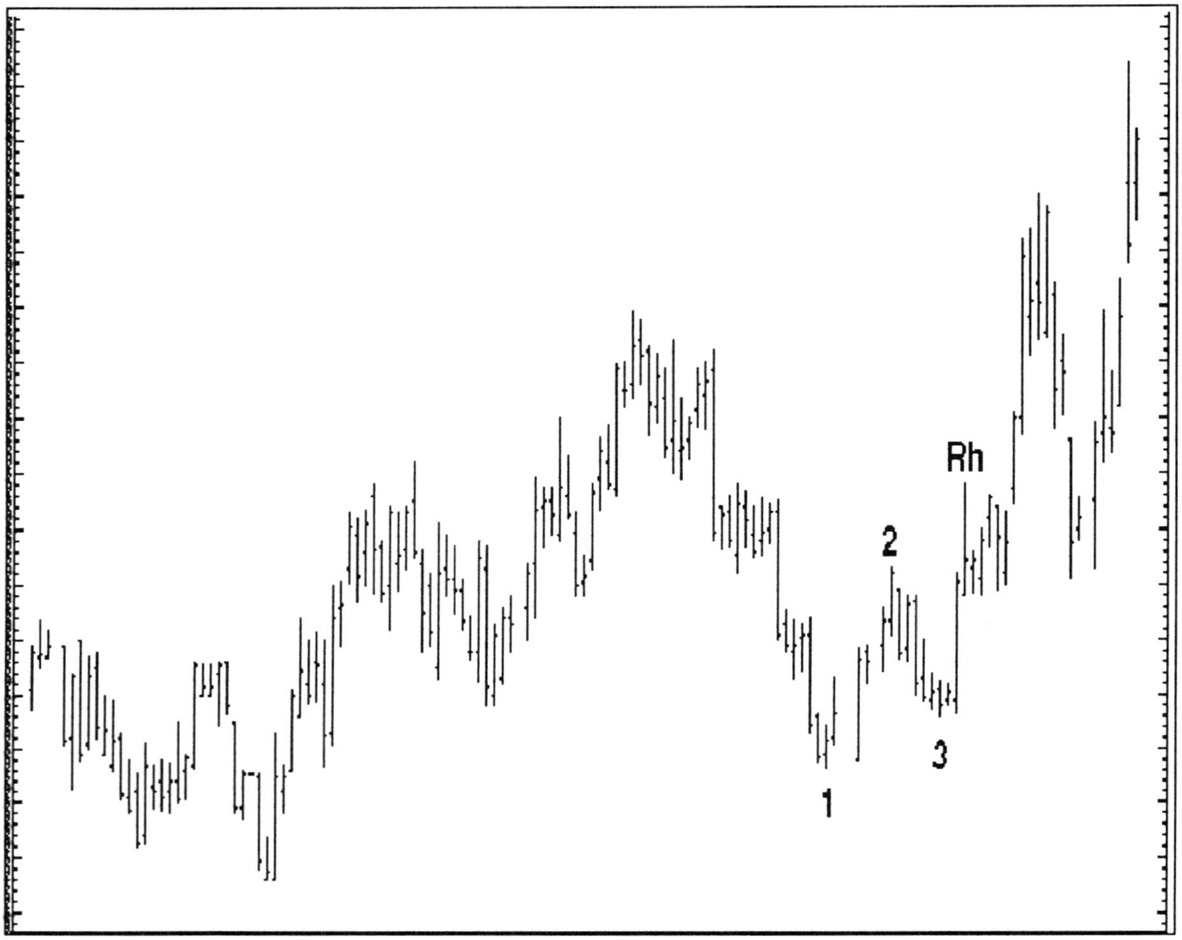

The problem with sudden volatility as seen on the chart is that the market moves too fast. It does not trend up, it explodes up. A correction is inevitable. The correction, if it results in a congestion area as above, gives market makers a perfect place to run the orders just above the point of the Hook.

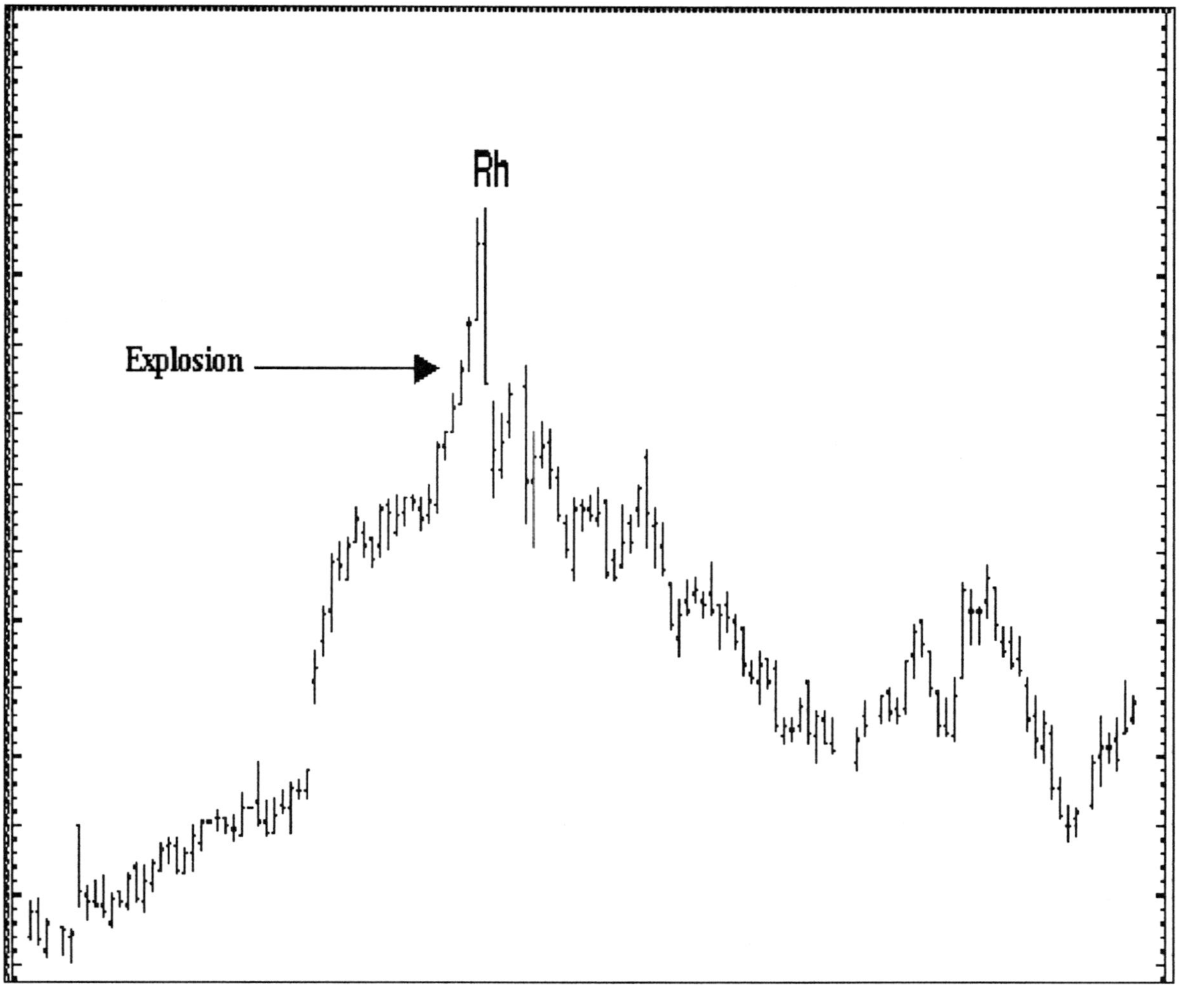

Just prior to the Ross Hook, prices suddenly become very volatile. Subsequently they retreat sharply. If prices rise up to challenge the Hook marked on the chart, we would not attempt entry by any available means. Such events take place in conjunction with rumors or other major news scares.

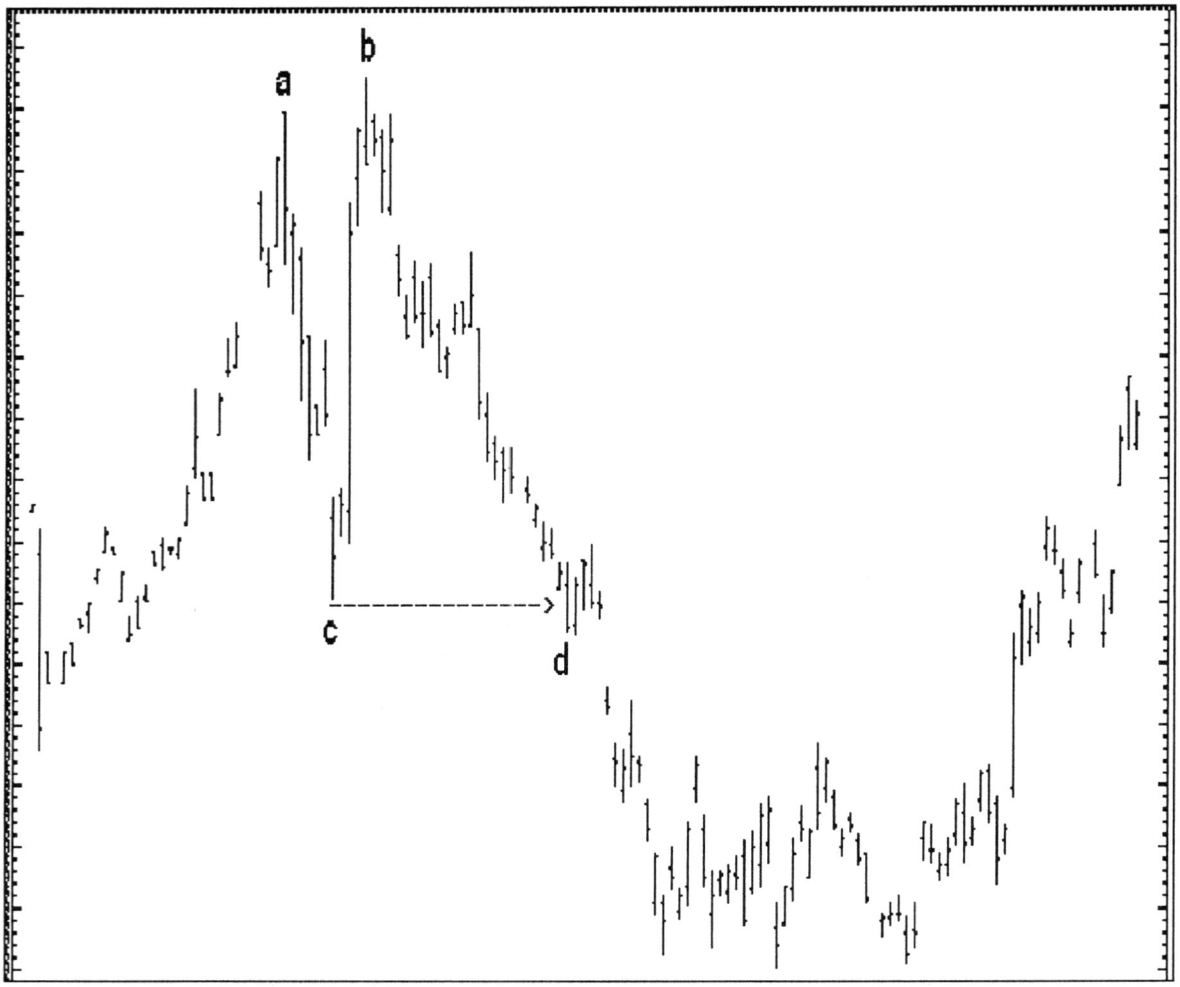

At points a and b, the market is much too volatile to attempt to take upside Hooks had they been challenged. At d, we see the market is much more orderly when it takes out the point of the Hook at c.

A couple of thoughts must be kept in mind. Volatility, as seen by long bars and gaps, is not as meaningful in a downtrend as in an uptrend. Prices as a rule drop much faster than they rise.

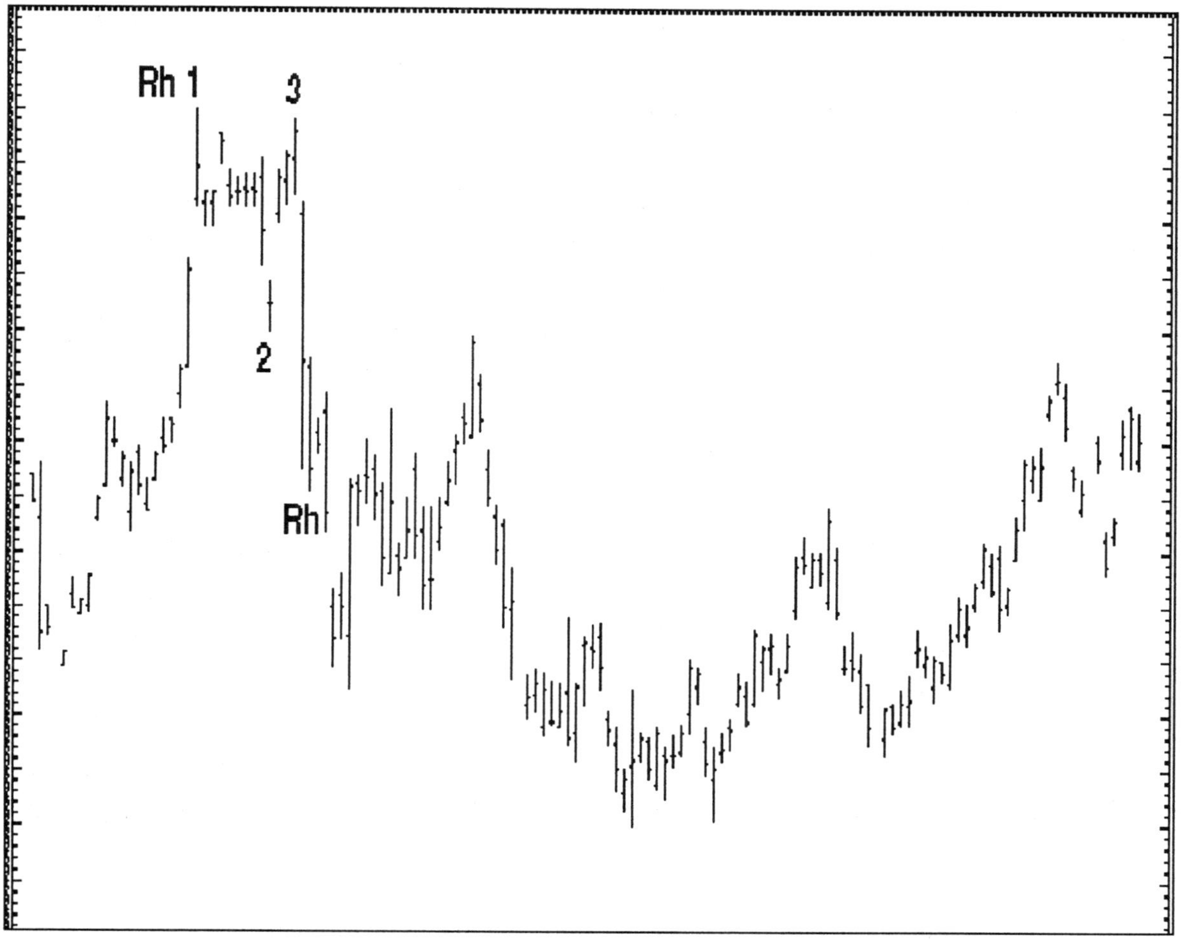

We would not take TTE's at either of the Ross Hooks shown on the chart. The market is too volatile. Even though we could make a nice profit on the downside Hook, we must be willing to bypass such moves in favor of more orderly price movement. All too often, when a Hook comes at the end of a series of gaps or long bar moves, the move is all but over. Experience has shown that most of the time these do not work well.

WHEN HOOKS COME TOO CLOSE TOGETHER

Normally, when a market is trending and making Ross Hooks, each Hook will have from one to three bars of correction and then the market will resume its movement in the direction of the trend. Each move in the direction of the trend will consist of three to five bars. A move in the direction of the trend may consist of only one or two bars if they occur as long bar moves or gaps.

However, if the market begins to have only one or two bars in the direction of the trend, without the benefit of long bars or gaps, and then after one or two bars it corrects, Ross Hooks will be very close together. When this happens it is a warning that the move, at least temporarily, probably is over.

WHEN VOLUME DRIES UP

When prices have trended for awhile, sometimes a long while, they will reach a point of exhaustion. They cannot continue to make new highs or to make new lows. Normally, exhaustion is reflected in a market coincident with a drying up of volume. New highs are made on low volume, or new lows are made on low volume. The market simply can no longer sustain new extremes without many participants. The market is either running out of sellers or running out of buyers.

When we see a large move on low volume, typically after a large bar move or a gap, we must suspect that for the time being the move is over. We suspect that a Hook will occur, and most of the time it does. But a severe reduction in volume may occur on either side of what turns out to be a selling or buying climax.

When we see the point of a Hook made on low volume, we should refrain from attempting to get in ahead of a violation of that Hook.

This is true no matter what the time frame. On the daily chart, we look at the volume for the stock we are trading. Use actual trading volume as reported for the day of what becomes the point of the Hook. There will usually be time to obtain it as the market corrects.

WHEN A HOOK IS TOO MANY BARS AWAY

A Hook is too far away under two conditions:

- When the 1-2-3 which preceded it is very long from the number 1 point to the number 2 point.
- When the point of the Hook is far from the number 2 point.

When either of these occur, there is usually very little room for prices to move subsequent to the Hook being taken out.

This situation occurs more often in down markets than in up markets. However, it can occur in any market in any time frame, regardless of the direction of the move.

The chart below is an example of the #2 point being too far away from the #1 point. There was little downside potential getting in ahead of a takeout of the point of the Hook.

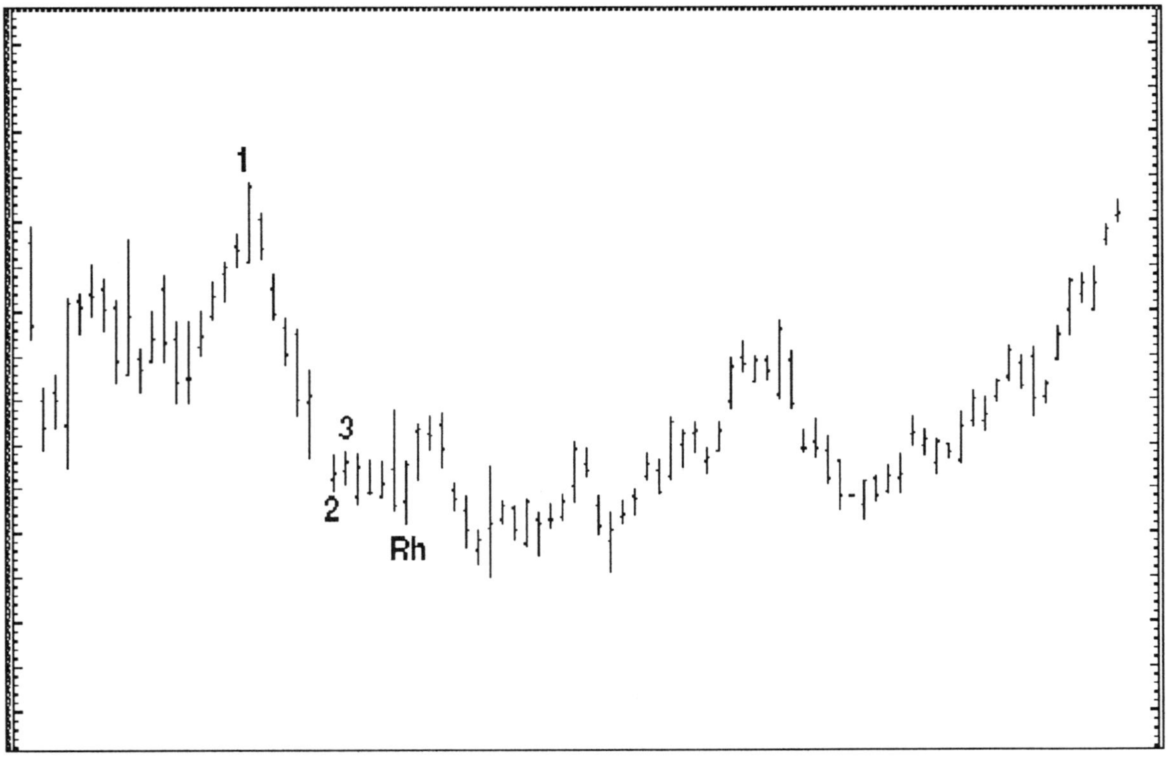

Chapter 17

SECOND TIME THROUGH IN CONGESTION

This is a very important consideration regarding Hooks. It is this situation under which most traders will make mistakes.

It is a virtual certainty that the last Hook in a series will come and develop into some form of congestion. The only time this doesn't happen is when prices make an abrupt Vee top or bottom. True V tops or bottoms are rare, and not worth the risk involved in trading them. There is certainly no way to predict them ahead of time.

What starts out to be /\ tops usually end up becoming some sort of /\/\ tops. What start out as V bottoms usually end up as VV bottoms. These are actually forms of congestion and therein lies the danger of the Ross Hook that forms just prior to congestion.

Please note the following:

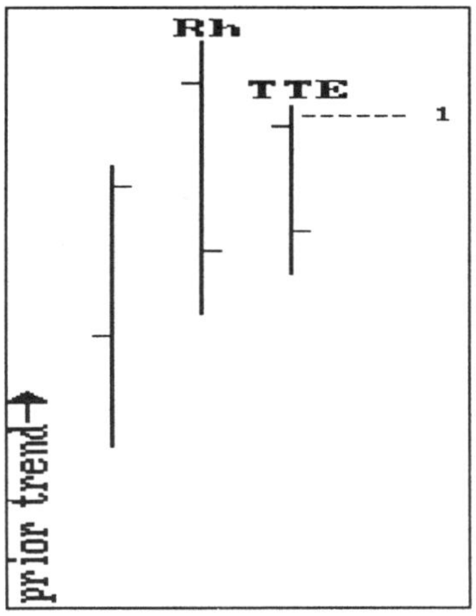

As long as volume has not fallen off and there is room to profit between the TTE and the Rh, take a breakout of the first correcting bar.

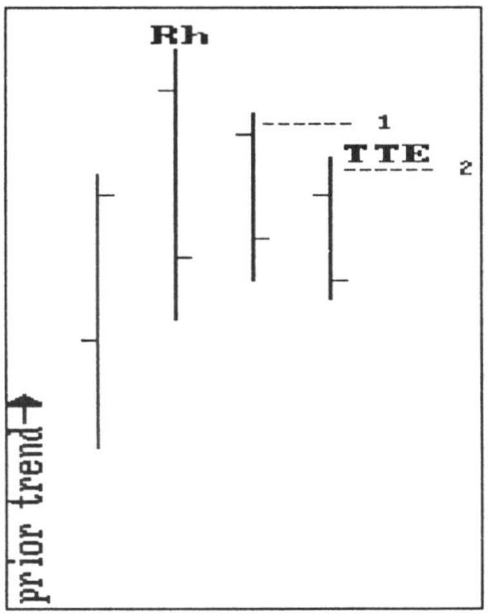

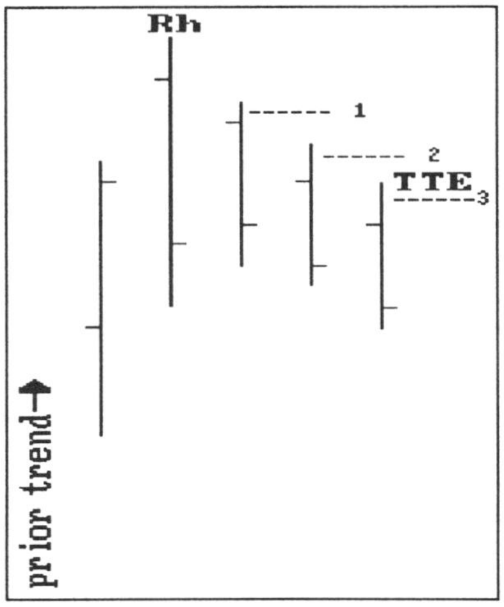

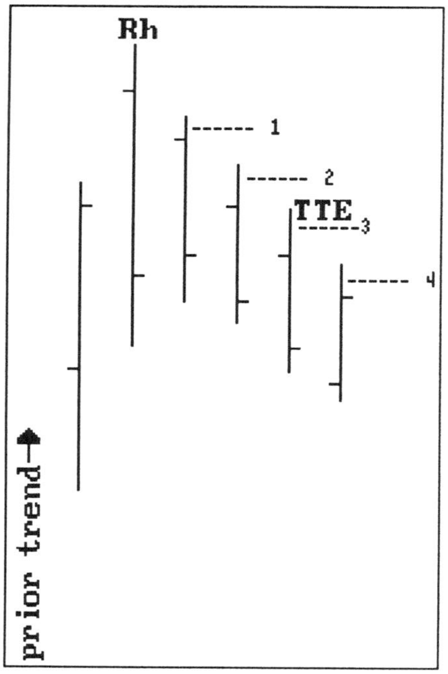

There is an extremely important concept to grasp here.

WHEN A TREND HAS A CORRECTION CONTAINING MORE THAN THREE BARS AWAY FROM THE POINT OF THE HOOK, THE ORIGINAL TREND IS BROKEN, AND WE HAVE NOW DEFINED A MINOR TREND IN THE OPPOSITE DIRECTION THAT MAY PROVE TO BE A TREND REVERSAL OR A CONGESTION. THIS MINOR TREND IS EXPLAINED IN VOLUME I OF THIS COURSE.

We want to repeat something we said earlier:

WE MUST MAKE A DISTINCTION BETWEEN CHART ANALYSIS AND TECHNICAL ANALYSIS. THEY ARE NOT THE SAME. CHART ANALYSIS LOOKS ONLY AT THE PRICE BARS THEMSELVES AND THE FORMATIONS THEY CREATE. TECHNICAL ANALYSIS IS LESS CONCERNED WITH INDIVIDUAL PRICE BARS AND NOT AT ALL CONCERNED WITH CHART FORMATIONS. THE TTE WHEN USED WITH TECHNICAL INDICATORS IS LOOKING FOR CONFIRMATION THAT ANY PRICE BARS FOLLOWING A **#2** POINT OR AN RH, BUT PRIOR TO A BREAKOUT OF EITHER OF THEM, ARE VALID AS AN ENTRY SIGNAL AHEAD OF THE **#2** POINT OR THE RH BEING TAKEN OUT.

However, when trading plain vanilla charts, we are concerned with only the first three bars of correction. Once we have more than three bars of correction we cease in our attempts to enter a trade based on the TTE.

The Ross Hook is still there, but in order to trade it on a plain vanilla basis, the point of the Hook itself must be taken out not once but twice. In plain vanilla trading It is as prices make a second time through actual breakout of the Rh that we may attempt an entry. The buy point is one tick beyond the point of the Rh.

Let's illustrate this.

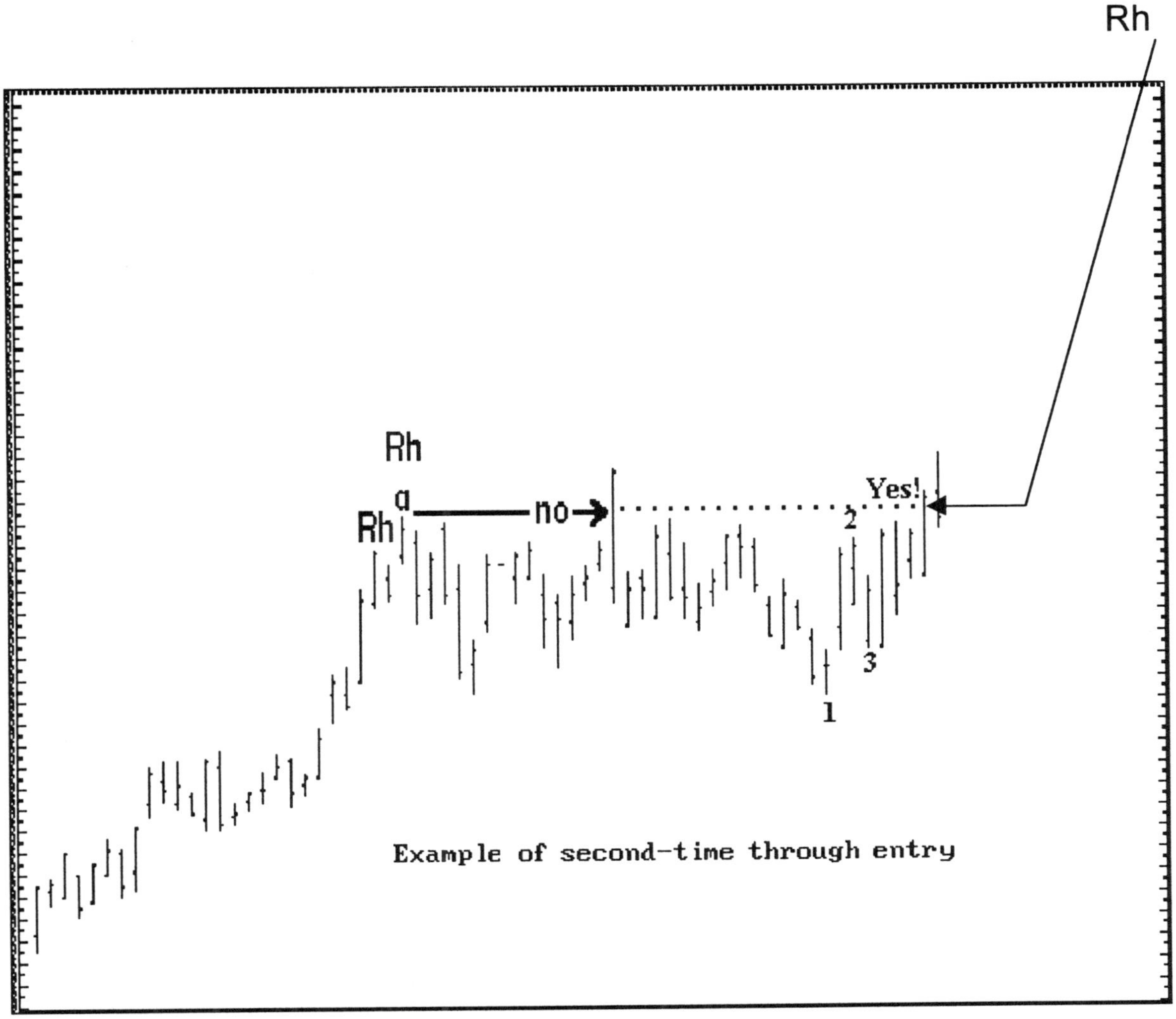

The Rh at 'a' gets taken out after congestion has formed. We do not take that first breakout. In fact, some excellent traders actually scalp the first breakout from congestion that violates a Ross Hook by fading the breakout — they trade it back into congestion. Why? Because it is just beyond those Hooks that the insiders will run the order accumulations. They can see those orders. You, too, must train yourself to see them. Once the resting orders are run, it's okay to trade a violation of the original Rh made prior to the false breakout.

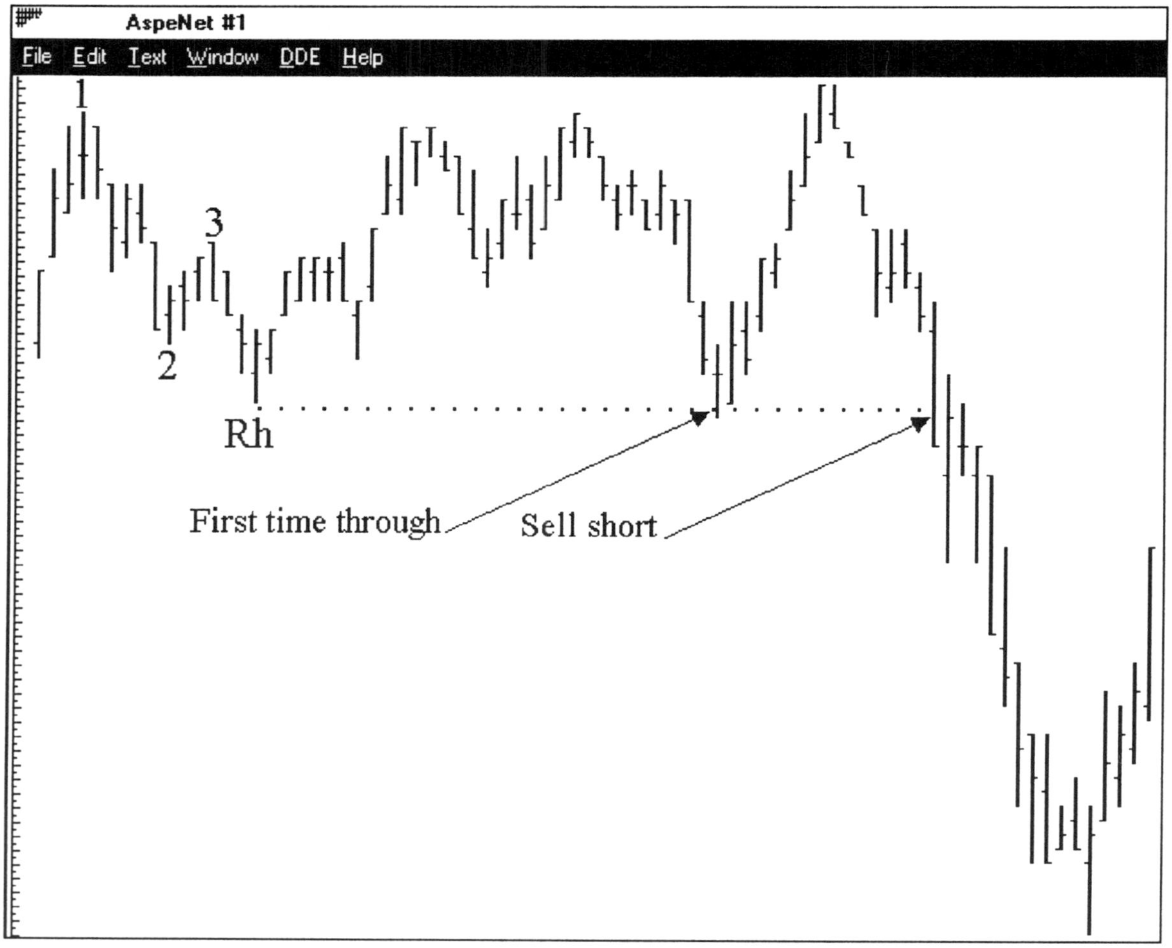

As prices pass through the point of the Rh the first time, we do not trade because prices are truly in congestion. We wait for the second time through the Rh and then enter one tick below the point of the original Rh. We do this no matter how long it takes for the violation to take place.

IN THIS TYPE OF TRADING IT DOES NOT MATTER HOW FAR DISTANT THE ORIGINAL RH IS FROM THE SECOND ENTRY POINT.

Here is yet another example:

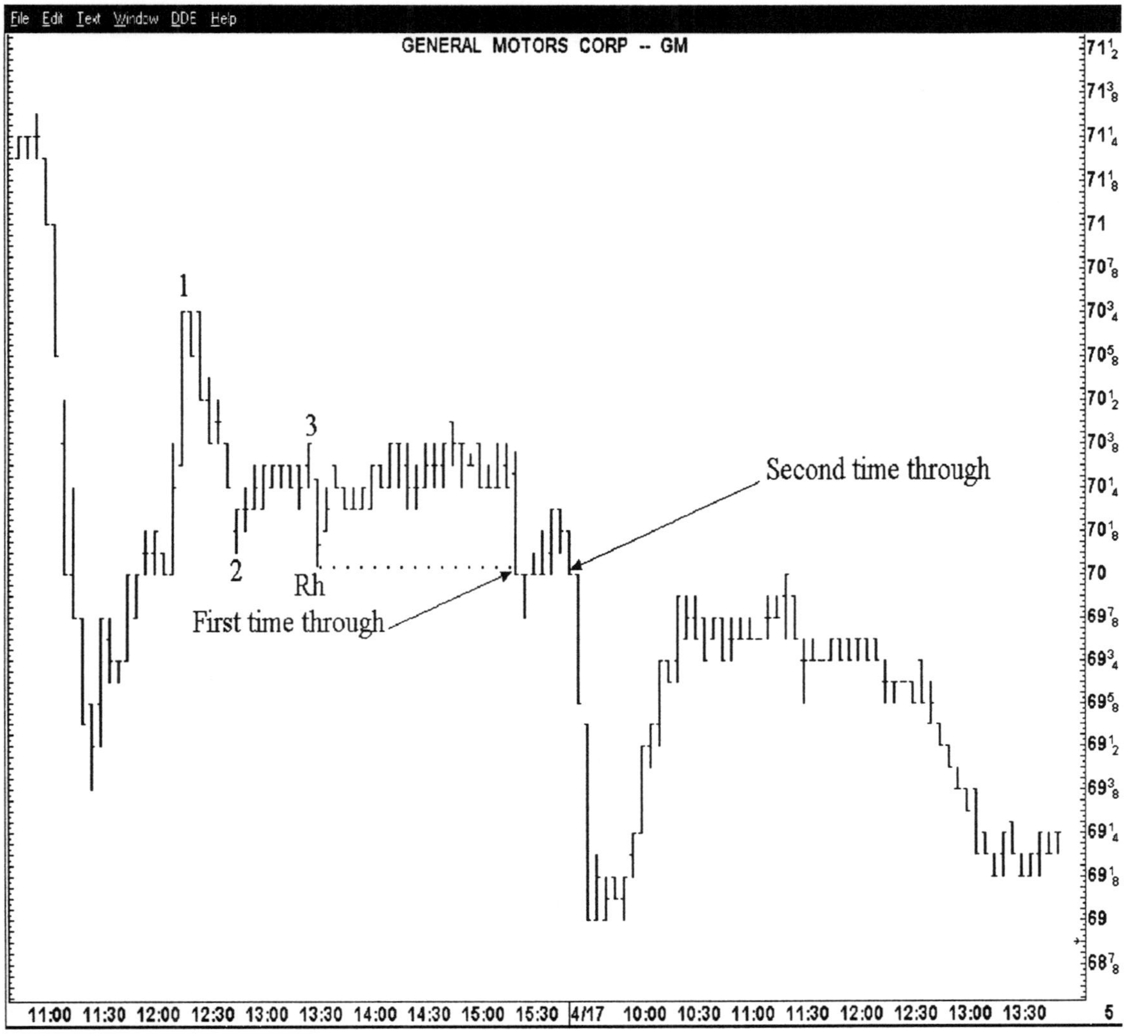

Chapter 18

VANILLA ENTRY PATTERNS

From time to time, a student will ask, "Which entry signals should I take?"

While there is no such thing as a magic entry signal, there are certain chart patterns that seem to be profitable for our own trading.

The trick is in having the patience to wait for them to occur.

We have found that all too often a trader will become so involved in trading a particular stock that s/he will attempt to take everything and anything that appears to be an entry opportunity. The result is that they over-trade. Over-trading is one of the greatest evils with which each trader has to wrestle. It is so common a problem that many traders do not even realize when they are over-trading.

The highest percentage of winning trades will come from taking the most conservative patterns. We cannot tell you exactly which ones to trade, or which ones will work for you. In part your selection will come as a result of your comfort level, the depth of your financial resources, and your desire for action.

As you go through these patterns, a congestion means any overall sideways movement of the market, but is best defined in accordance with the methods we have presented earlier in this course.

What we are looking for are patterns that tend to precede strong moves in the market.

Although these charts were taken from intraday patterns, they also appear on daily and weekly charts, so look for them there as well.

The patterns:

First breakout of the
1st congestion

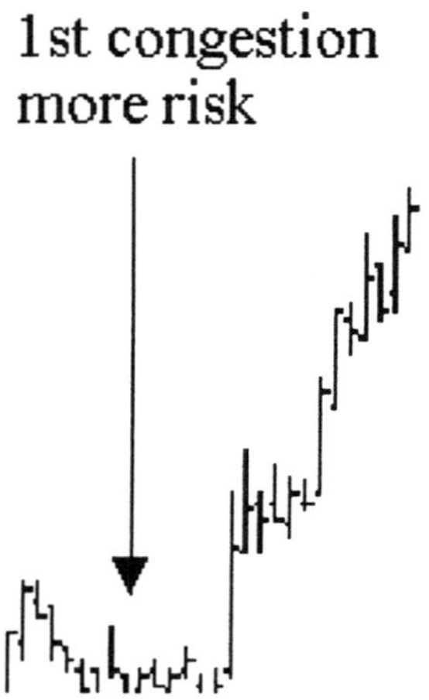

Second breakout of
the first congestion

Less risk

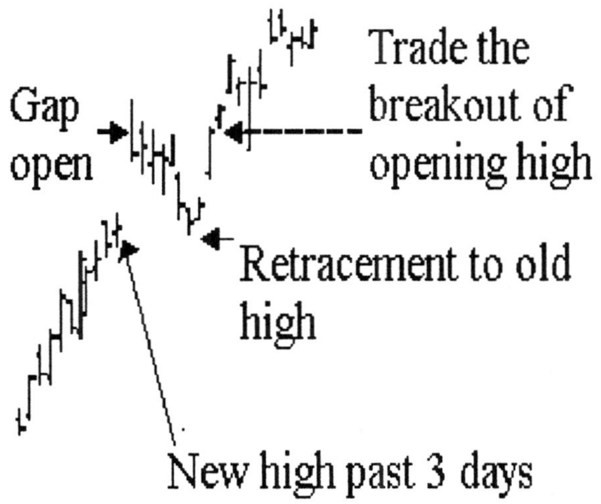

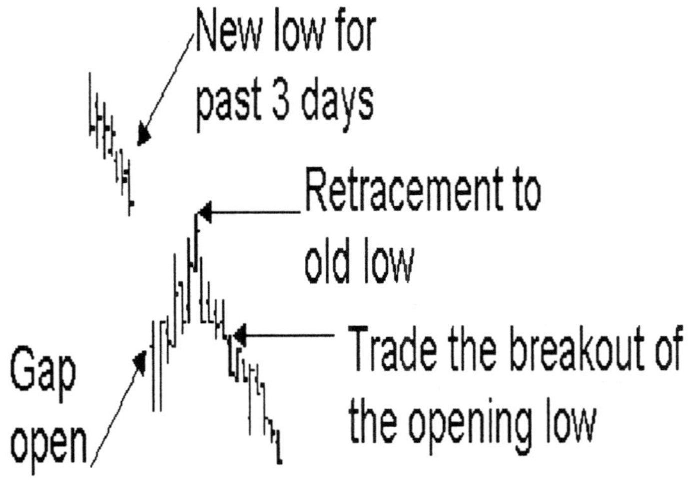

Entry Patterns

If you do trade the first break-out of the congestion, it's best if it dips, makes an attempt to breakout, dips again, and then breaks.

The opposite is true for a downside breakout. It's best if you get a congestion followed by a hump, and then trade the breakout of the congestion.

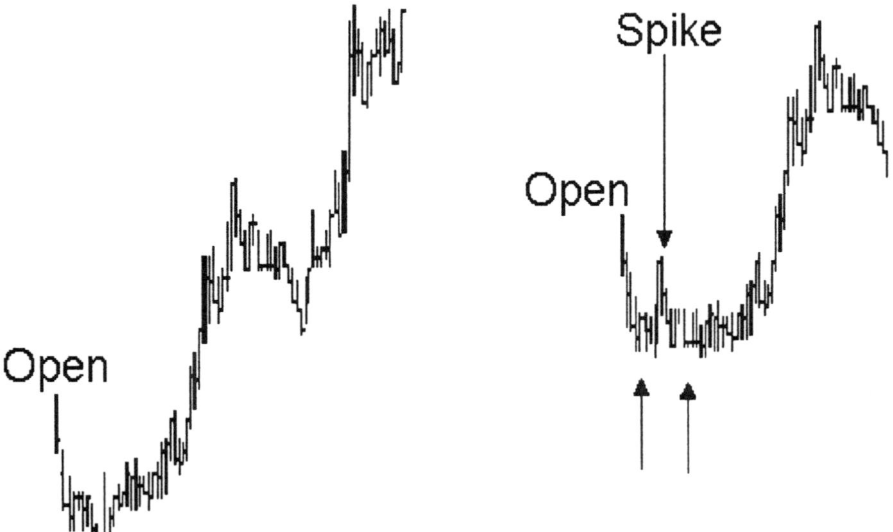

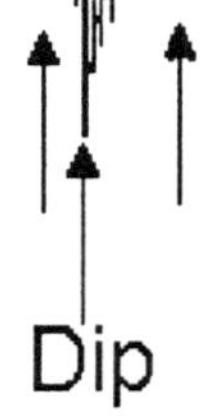

Congestion followed by a dip, then back into congestion. Trade a breakout of the higher congestion. Instead of a dip there could have been a spike. You would still trade a breakout of the congestion

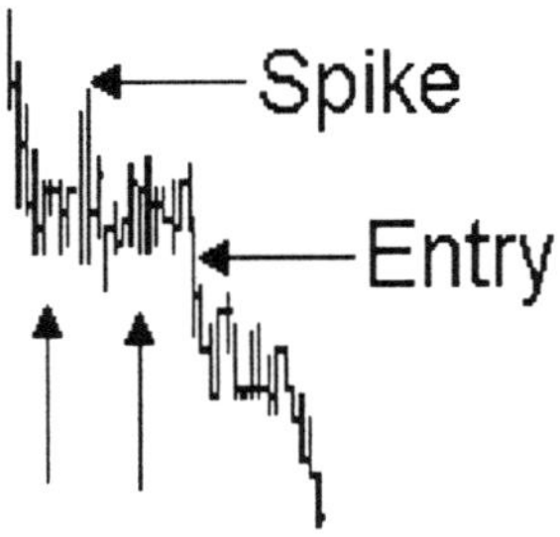

Congestion followed by a dip, then back into congestion. Trade a breakout of the lower congestion. Instead of a dip there could have been a spike.

Entry Patterns

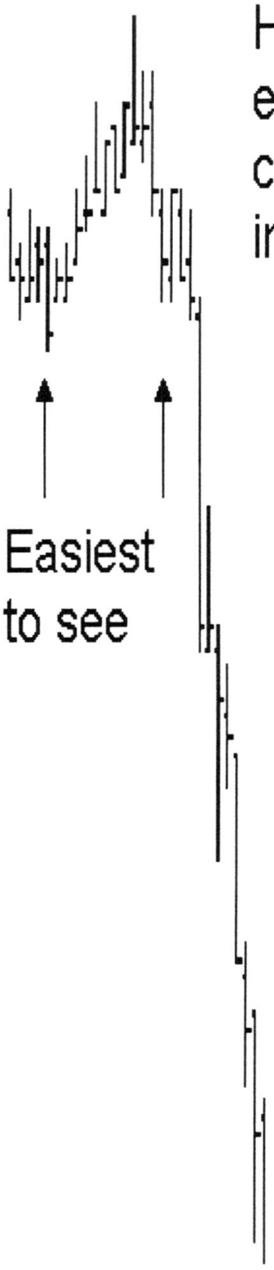

Here is a classical example of matching congestions with a hump in the middle.

Gap down opening followed by matching congestion prior to a spike down low. Sell short a breakout of the lowest congestion. Be sure there is sufficient room between the breakout and the low to take a profit.

We've shown two ways you could have traded a breakout of an old extreme; above is a breakout of a low, and below is a breakout of a high.

You could trade a breakout of the high of the congestion prior to the previous high.

Medium risk.

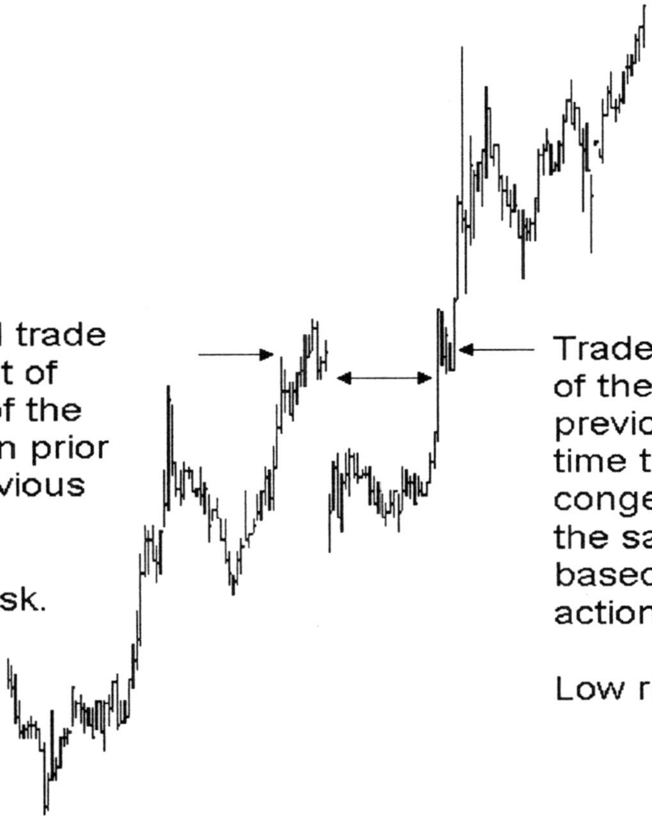

Trade a breakout of the high of the congestion prior to a previous high the second time through after the congestion based briefly at the same price level. By based we mean basing action.

Low risk.

Entry Patterns

Here is a more spread out view of the matching congestion pattern. Since the congestion on the left is so sloppy, trade a breakout of its midpoint. You can see the midpoint by looking at the clustered closes and highs that all occurred at the same price level. We've shown it with a dotted line.

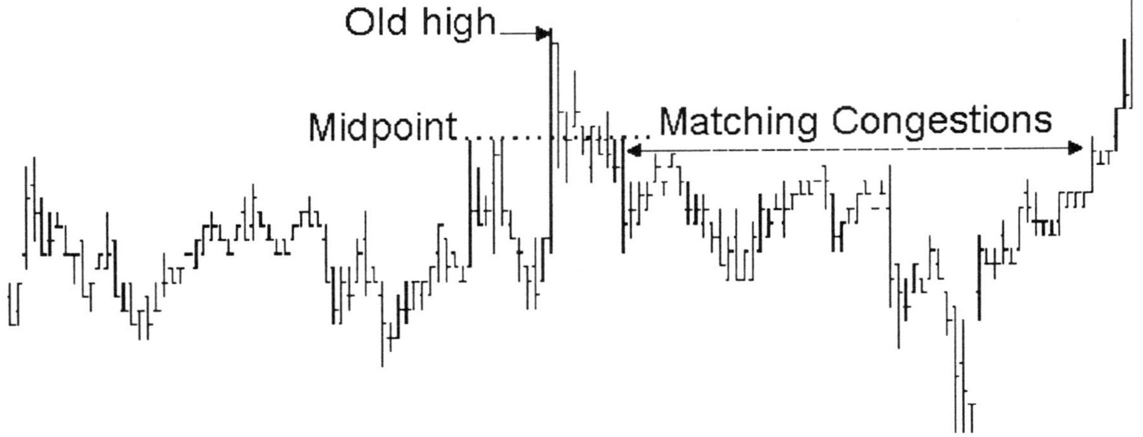

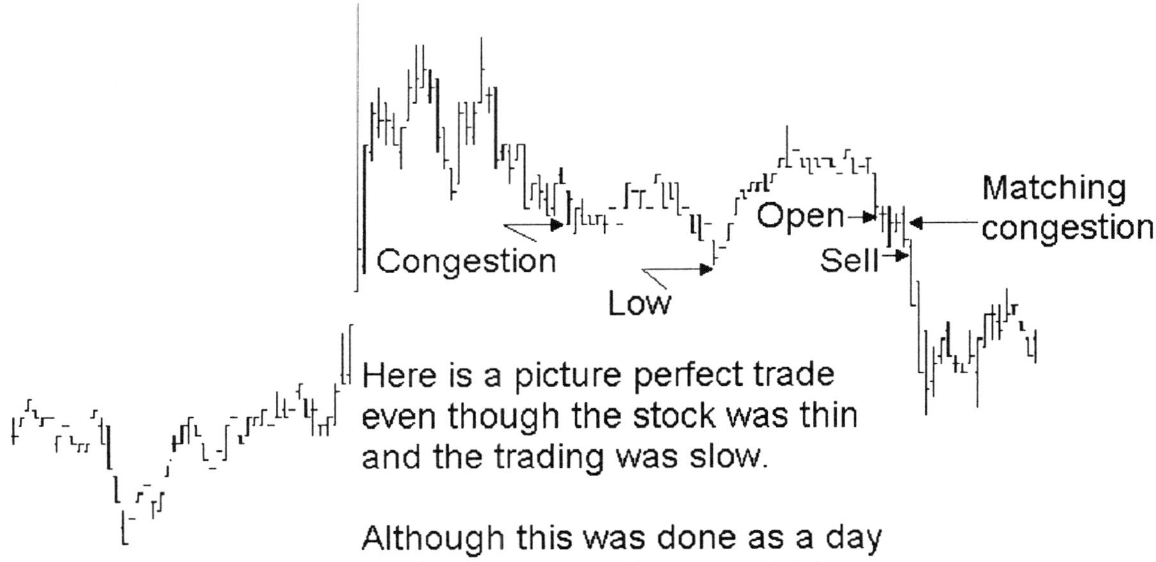

Here is a picture perfect trade even though the stock was thin and the trading was slow.

Although this was done as a day trade, the same thing could have been done in any time frame.

Notice that the matching congestions here have nothing to do with heads and shoulders.

Entry Patterns

Chapter 19

ANTICIPATING HOOKS

When can we anticipate a Ross Hook?

Since Ross Hooks are caused by profit taking during and at the end of a trend, there should be times when we can anticipate their formation.

- We can anticipate a Hook any time from a very long bar.
- We can anticipate a Hook any time prices form consecutive long bars in an established trend.
- We can anticipate a Hook any time prices form a gap or a series of gaps.
- We can anticipate a Hook to form any time prices explode or collapse out of a congestion area.

By anticipating when Ross Hooks may occur in the market, we have a basis for planning our trades. Simply the act of anticipating helps in obtaining market perspective. We have something concrete to look for.

By examining the chart and looking for potential Hook situations, we become more familiar with price behavior as depicted on a bar chart. This exercise in itself will help us to become more astute observers of market action.

Chapter 20

ANOTHER KIND OF FILTER

At times traders, either because of limited funds, or because of unwillingness to commit sufficient money resources, find themselves undercapitalized for the trading of some markets.

Naturally, if market volatility is sufficiently great in any market, the risk may prove to be more than can be comfortably traded for the size of the trading account.

In that event, sufficient thought and consideration should be given to daytrading the markets in order to take advantage of the lower volatility available in the shorter time frames.

This, of course, will hold true only for those who have sufficient time to devote to daytrading. We also have a number of students who have been able to arrange their full-time work hours to accommodate daytrading on a part-time basis.

If this cannot be done, and the account is to be small, the only way to logically trade and not gamble is to be extremely patient and wait to take only those trades that offer opportunities well within the liquidity and size of the account.

This can mean waiting for days, weeks, or months to take a trade that exactly fits the account size. There are not many new traders willing to exert this kind of discipline and patience. Typically, traders are eager to place a trade in the market. If only they would patiently wait for the right situation, there would be a great many more traders who would succeed rather than fail in the markets.

The volatility on a five or ten minute chart will fit well with many small accounts. The wins will be proportionately small, but with careful trading, an account can be built to sufficient size to move up to a larger time-frame.

On a lesser time interval chart, exit points can be placed at natural support and resistance levels without the greater risk that occurs on the daily charts.

This will afford additional trading opportunities more quickly.

The concept we're setting forth here is the use of time-frame as a filter for trading. Use a time-frame in which sufficient trading opportunities arise that are consistent with your temperament and the size of your margin account.

Trading Ross Hooks with the proper filters helps you to get into trades early. Trading Ross Hooks virtually forces you to trade with the trend.

We have consistently and persistently taken a simple approach to our own trading of the markets. Most people who want to trade make trading far too complicated. It's as though a simple method is not worthy of the markets.

Perhaps some feel guilty about making money easily. They feel unless something is sophisticated, intellectual, scientific, or mathematical, that it can't possibly be any good. That attitude and mindset seem to be a result of the technical society in which we live. Too bad, because so many have lost so much attempting to trade in a complicated manner.

Exit point determination when trading is a matter of individual choice. The sooner you realize that, the better off you will be. Run far and fast from anyone who tries to tell you otherwise.

The most important statistic in your trading must be money won versus money lost. Once you have a sound method for trading, such as the Ross Hook, the amount of money you win or lose becomes a function of managing the trade, your money, the amount of risk, and yourself.

To properly engage in good management, you must learn to discipline yourself. Unless you have vast amounts of capital, you cannot change the market, nor can you become a part of the solution in solving the problems the markets present to you when trading.

You must come to realize that the only thing you can change is yourself, and the way you react to market stimuli. Your self-discipline, or lack of it, will determine in large part the way you manage your money, trades, risk, and self.

You must trade with the realization of what trading is all about. To do that you need to study.

You must learn how both the insiders and the markets operate.

You need to know at which point scalpers will bail out of the market and abandon it, and why. You should learn to recognize that condition when you see it on a chart. Why? Because when they abandon a market, that is exactly when you want to be in the market.

You must come to realize that trading is a high risk business. Even when you are right about a trade, you can lose money.

There are plenty of vultures out there who can turn wonderful winners into sudden losers. Risk lies at every level of trading. If you trade without realizing this fact, you will soon be parted from your money.

As if that were not bad enough, large funds, other large traders, and market makers can all run the markets in such a way as to cheat you of your potential profits. Markets are engineered by these interests, and you can be sure they do not have your interest in mind.

They can make markets go sharply up and turn around and make them go sharply down — all within a single day.

Any intraday chart will show you the way markets are engineered by those on the floor. Whenever trading becomes too tight, the market makers will run prices, first one way, and then the other. They do this to create "trading room" for themselves.

That doesn't mean you can't make money trading. It does mean you have to use all the tactics and methods you have available. You must be nimble and quick. You must learn to take profits when they exist. You must learn to use strategy when you trade.

Chapter 21

A WORD TO THE WISE

The following paragraphs are presented in the hope that we can convince you to be realistic about your trading.

Far too many traders are undercapitalized. We have had them come to our seminars, recently out of work, with $5,000 or less trading capital, hoping for a miracle. If this fits you, you will not be trading, you will be gambling. No matter how determined you are to do well, it will take a small miracle for you to be successful. The odds are heavily against you.

All too often traders tell us they can't afford to place stops at natural support or resistance on the daily charts. They also cannot afford, or are unable to have intraday live data. This happens when the trader is undercapitalized, or must work full time at a job, business, or profession. Some overseas traders are unable to obtain live data.

Whatever the case, you have only three choices:

1. Build your account.

2. Patiently wait for Hooks that have acceptable risk.

3. Delay your trading until you have sufficient capital with which to begin trading.

If you could arrange your schedule so that you would be able to use live data to at least enter the trade, then it will be cost effective to obtain a live data connection of some kind and the appropriate computer hardware and software. You can build an account much faster by taking the lower risk associated with intraday natural support and resistance. In many cases, a few successful trades will more than pay for the additional costs that may be associated with live data. However, realize that you can find a provider who will let you trade from a live terminal, simply for the cost to you of commissions.

Software to read and chart live data does not have to be purchased. It can be leased on a month to month basis. If it doesn't work out for you, you can stop using the software.

If you should choose to trade intraday, please do not attempt to trade from a delayed data feed. That is tantamount to committing financial suicide.

Remember, intraday you are up against traders who are marvelously equipped with live data, sophisticated software, and who are in many cases much better connected to the exchanges.

Top notch trading software does not have to cost the most. You can obtain some of the best for far less than some of the worst.

If, after examining all avenues, you realize that trading is an expensive proposition, then by all means do not feel badly if you choose not to trade at all.

If you are bound and determined to trade without proper preparation and facilities, please realize that trading is a very expensive hobby. Surprisingly, there are many for whom that is what trading really is. If you can afford it, and don't mind losing the money, then go for it. We will be very happy to spend our share of what you lose in the markets. It will be a win-win situation. You will have fun, and we will add to our trading accounts.

Chapter 22

REVISITING THE SEGMENT COUNT

In ELECTRONIC TRADING 'TNT' I — GORILLA TRADING STUFF, WE introduced segment counting as a method of finding the trend.

We will explain here what was touched on there, but we will also show how the segment count may be daytraded.

SEGMENT COUNTING

Here's a technique that has stood the test of time It involves connecting corrections and double bars.

This technique is a bit more difficult to perceive, but over the years it has proved to be one of the best ways to spot a move before most people even suspect it is going to happen. As we view this technique, we want to realize a ***very*** important concept which is applicable not only to segment counting but to the simple count method, and the sagging tops/rising bottoms method:

WHEN ANY TWO OF THESE METHODS ARE OCCURRING SIMULTANEOUSLY, THE SIGNAL BECOMES CONSIDERABLY STRONGER THAN WHEN ANY ONE OF THEM OCCURS ALONE. WHEN ANY ONE OF THE METHODS IS COMBINED WITH OR CLOSELY PRECEDES A SIGNAL FROM THE LAW OF CHARTS (TLOC), WE HAVE A TREMENDOUSLY STRONG INDICATION THAT A SIZABLE MOVE IS JUST AHEAD.

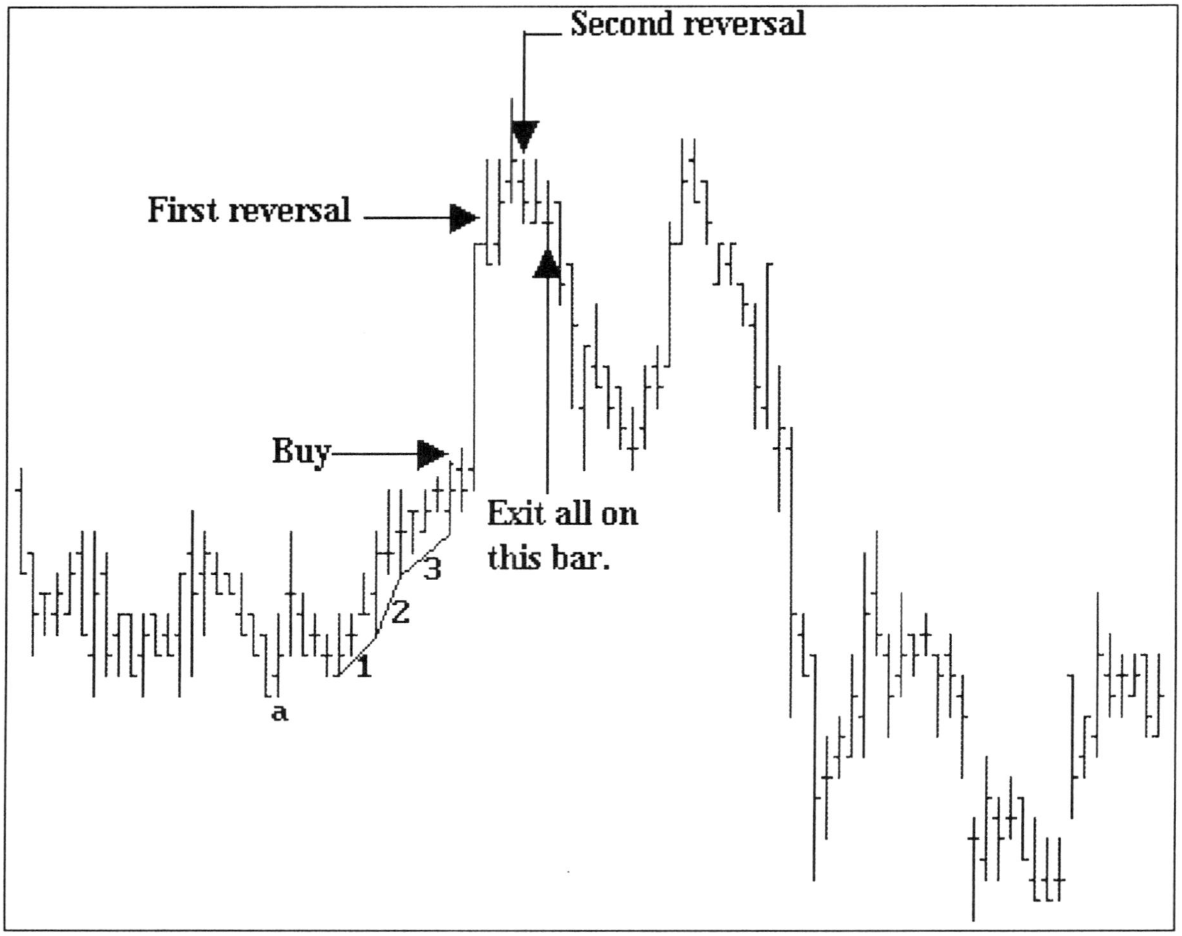

Take a close look at how we've connected the lows on the chart. The numbered segments positioned between the lows.

We've connected a low to a second low. We've connected the second low to a correction low, and the correction low to a double low.

We will buy a breakout of the high of the bar whose low made the third segment.

This technique will work in any market, in any time frame, so long as you are seeing something that has well formed patterns.

We've had a brief look at numbering segments. Each time prices made a lower low than any previous bar since we began counting segments, we connect our last segment to the bar making the new low. If a bar ever goes lower than the original low, we can no longer count segments in the same direction. Later, we'll see this concept in greater detail.

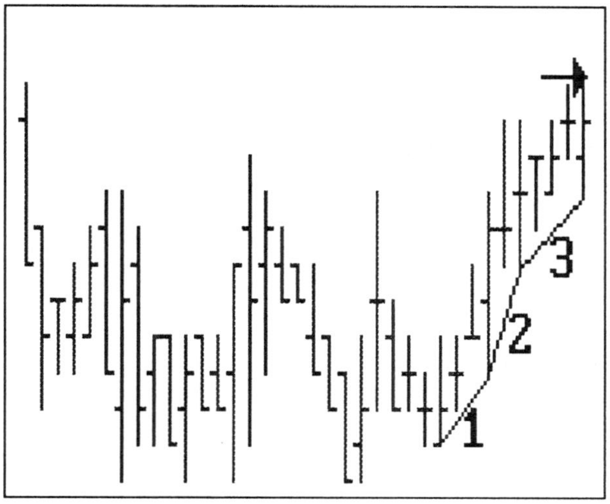

We want to get long based upon a breakout of the high of the price bar whose low completed the third segment drawn on the chart.

Notice that this segment is occurring in conjunction with the breakout of an intraday Trading Range. Prices have already violated a minor triple high, and if they were to take out the high of the bar making the third segment, it would constitute a take out of the double high of the last two bars. If prices were to do that, the move might be explosive.

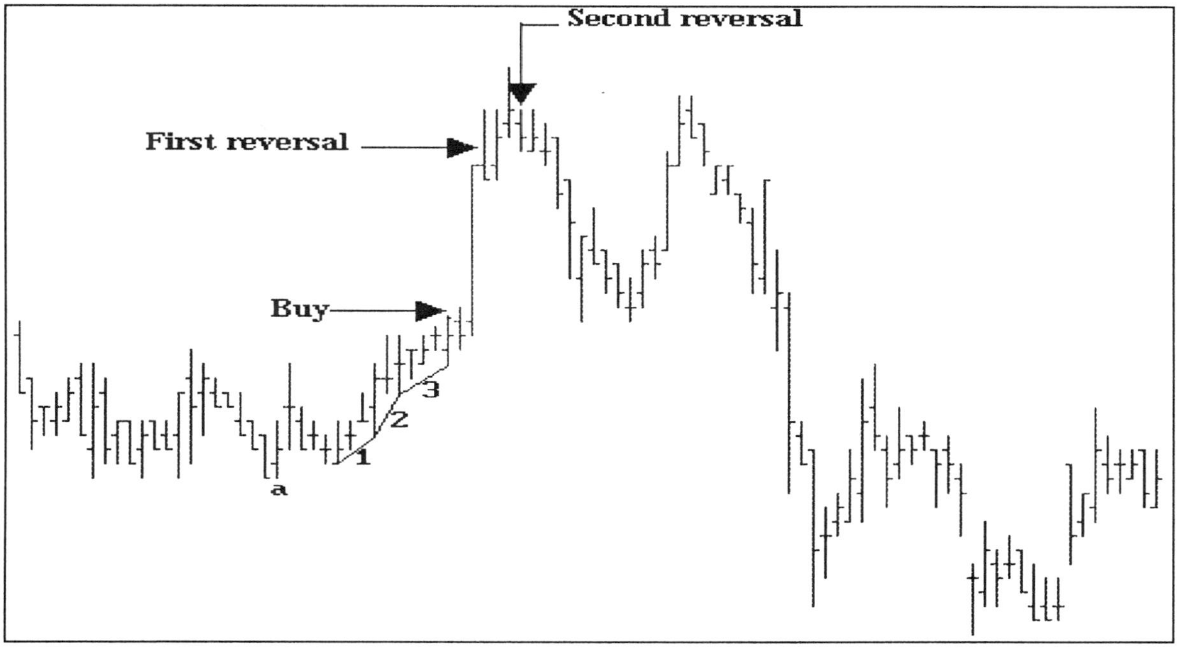

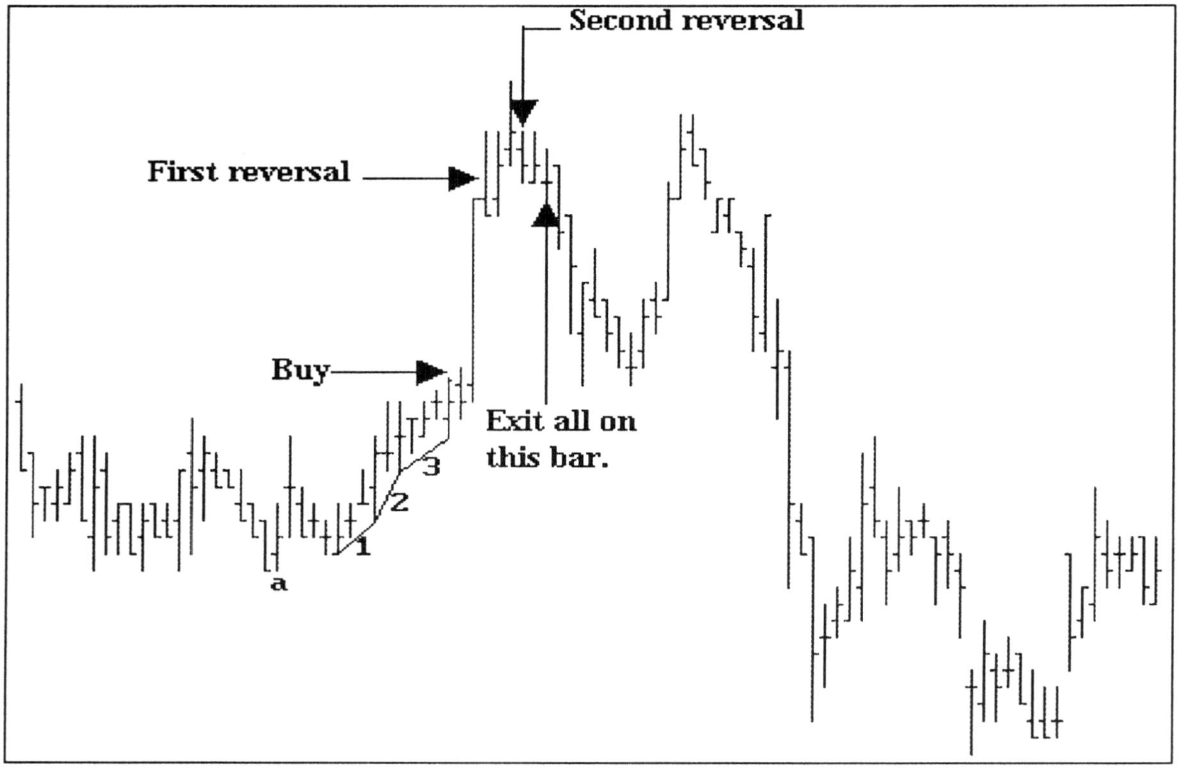

There are two ways to handle exiting this trade. One would be to cover costs and take some profits at the first reversal. Begin taking additional profits as soon as the second reversal is in place. Begin liquidation of all remaining shares the moment any price bar makes a lower low than the bar preceding it. This is the "***continuation***" method discussed In Volume I of this course. The other is when you exit all shares upon two reversals or the making of a new low in a rising market or the making of a new high in a falling market. This was shown in volume I as the "***violation***" method.

Why didn't we enter a trade earlier on a breakout of the doji 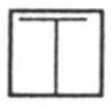 bar that opened and closed at the high of the bar? The answer is that we could have. However, we felt it was better to wait until prices cleared the congestion. At the time the low of the doji bar occurred, the segment was connected to that bar as shown by the following chart.

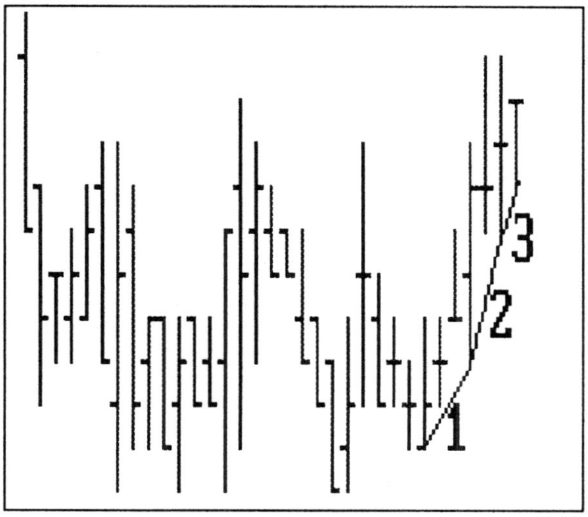

The last bar shown is the doji bar referred to on the previous page. A breakout of the high of the doji would have been a valid entry signal.

Let's understand. The segment line is drawn from bar to bar until we get a bar that makes a lower low than the previous bar. At that point, the segment line is moved from the previous bar that made a lower low to the current bar making a lower low. In the case of the chart we've been examining, the progression would have been as shown on the next three charts.

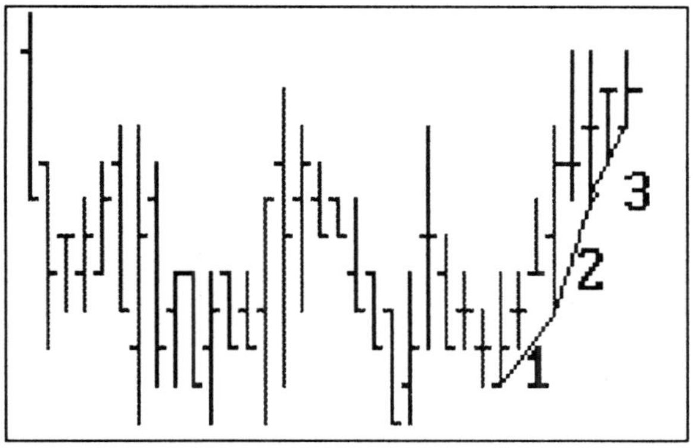

Notice that the segment line is moving along at the lows. We will not move away from hugging those lows with the segment line until we see a bar that makes a lower low than the previous bar. A breakout of the high of this last bar, or the high of the next bar, would also have been a valid entry signal.

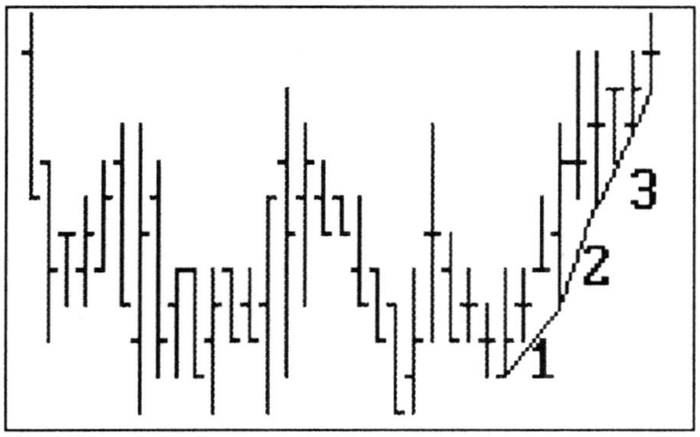

On the left was the last part of the segment prior to a bar making a lower low. The next chart shows how the segment line for segment 3 finally ended.

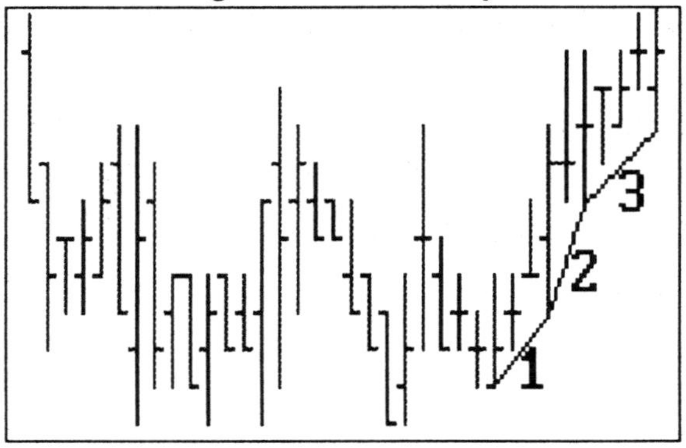

As prices retreat from the 30 minute bar that made the high and also the close of the previous day, we begin to count and connect the diminishing highs.

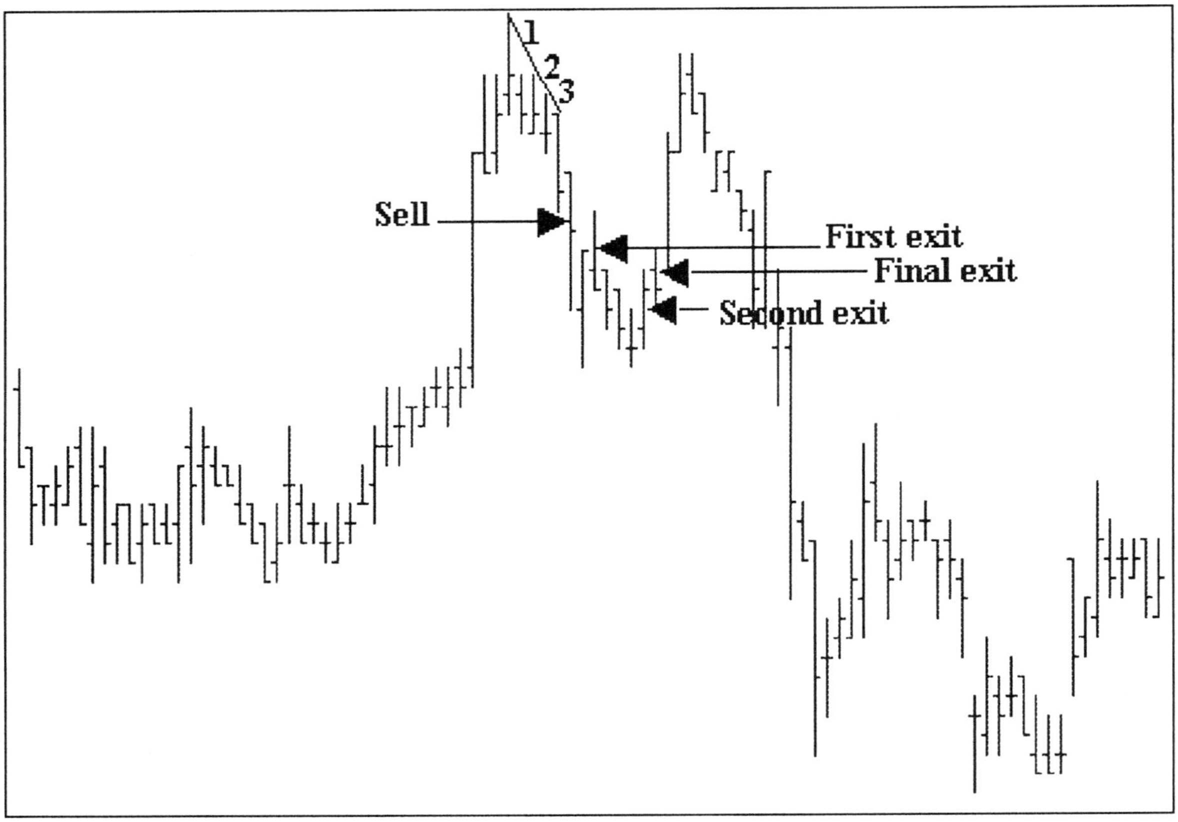

Depending upon the entry and exit prices, something, but not much, would have been made on the first portion of the position, a bit more on the second portion, and a profit on any remaining shares. Of course, we could choose to exit the entire position.

What we are seeing is the reality of intraday trading. The most important thing for us is to not lose money, and to be there as often as we are able when prices run.

Continuing with the 30 minute chart, we see that the final exit for the day was made within the last half hour of trading. The next day, prices shoot up in the first 30 minutes of trading. Let's look at that now.

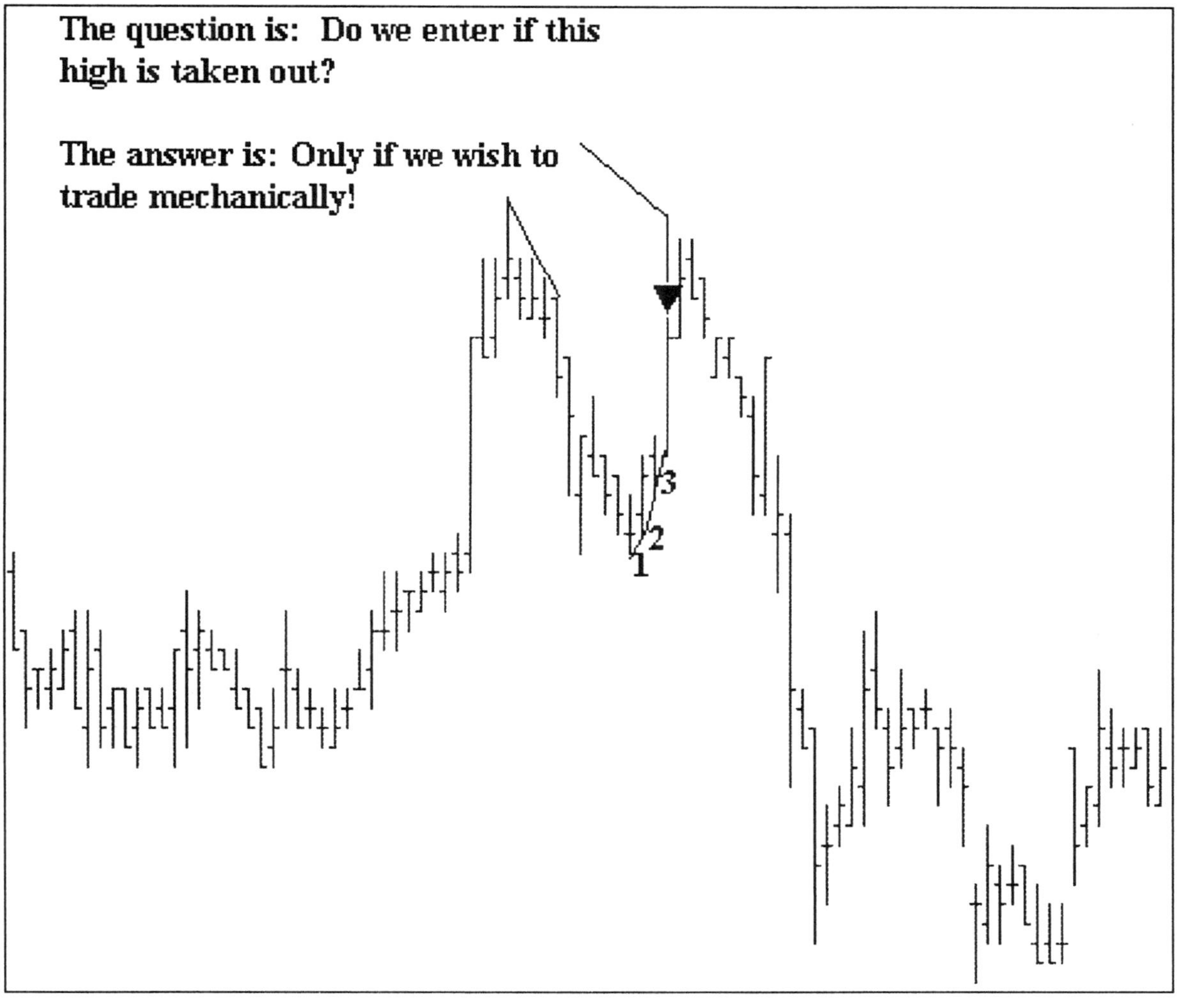

If we are determined to trade a mechanical system, then the trade must be entered. Note that our exit signal will keep us from disaster. We exit a portion of our shares as soon as we see a bar making a lower low than the previous bar, a portion when two reversal bars are in effect, and the rest on the second bar to make a lower low.

Taking it from the double top, after the arrow on the chart above, the first bar after the double top makes a new low: liquidate one part of the shares. That same bar ends up being a reversal bar: exit a second part of the shares. The next bar gaps down: exit all shares.

But should the trade have been entered at all? That's a tough decision and one that we each have to make on our own. There were no coordinating signals from any of the formations we've studied. But then, neither were there any on the previous trade.

There was a coordinating signal based on rising bottoms and another on simple counting. Our opinion is that the trade was worth the attempt. We don't win on every trade. But we were able to keep any losses very small. Let's continue with the next trade. It comes during the fourth hour of trading.

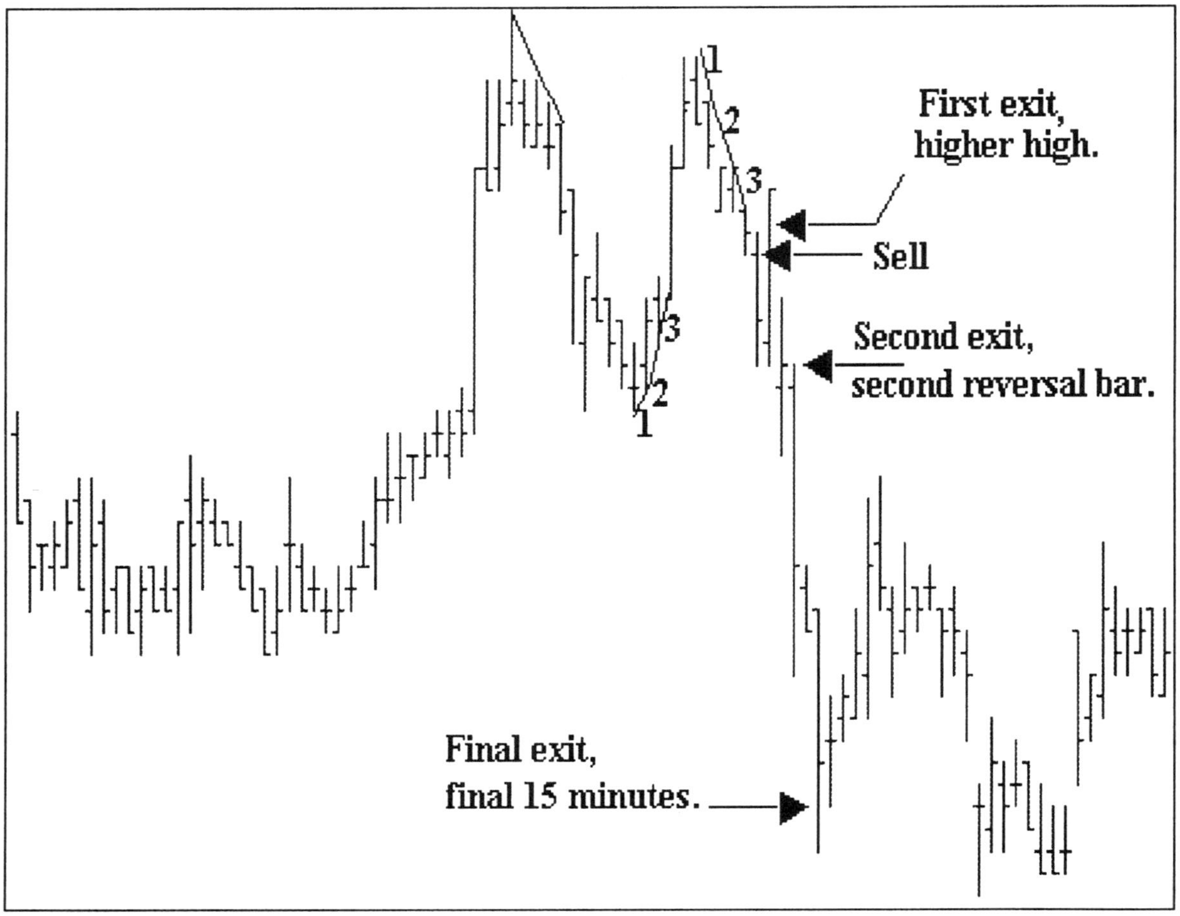

By now, you should be getting the idea of the segment count. So why don't you try the next one. The day begins with the bar following the final exit bar. We'll reproduce the chart on the next page and give the answer on the page following that.

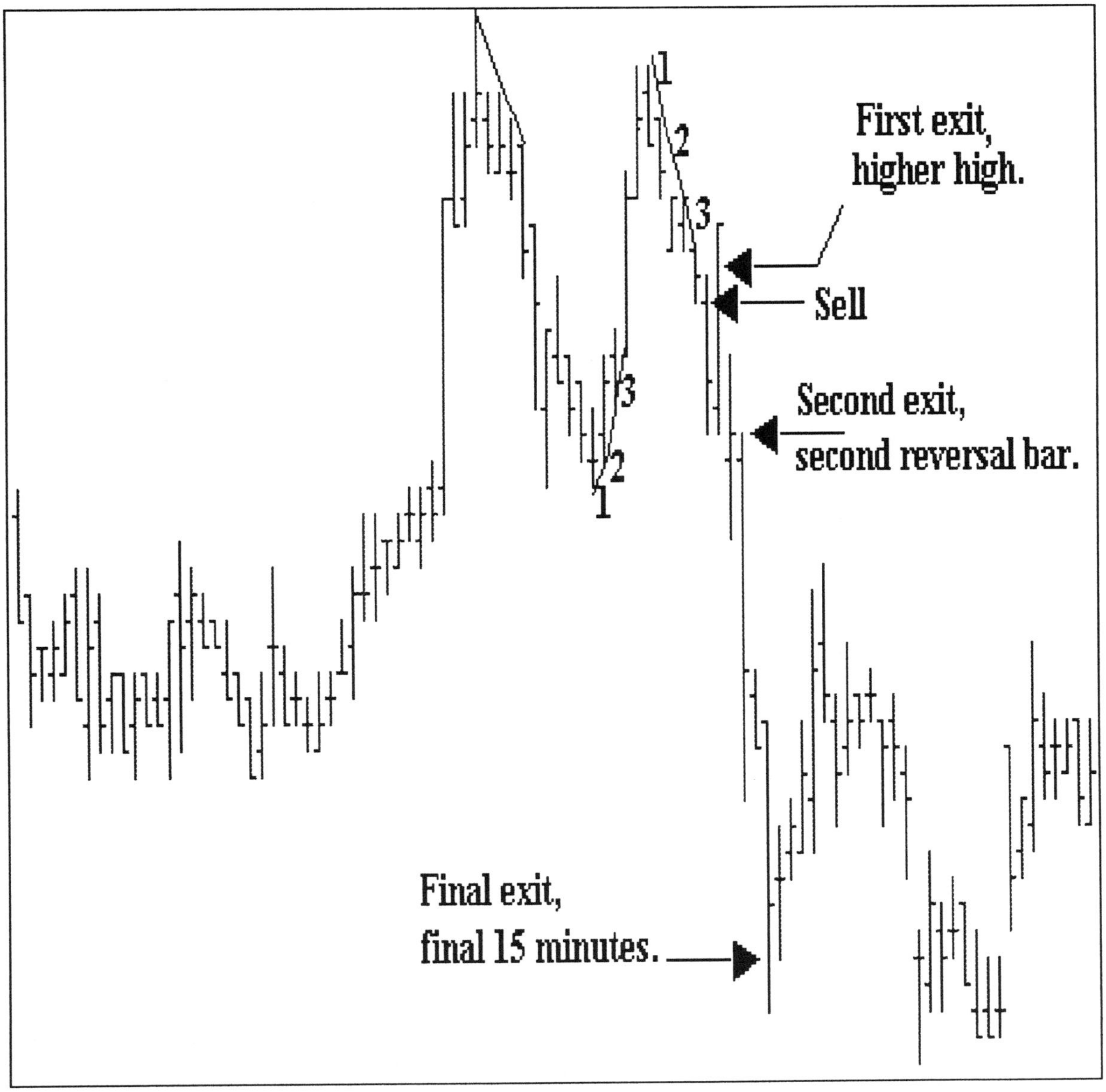

Your turn! Count the segments, and figure out the entry point and the three exits. Probably one-quarter of all the trades you make will have results similar to this one.

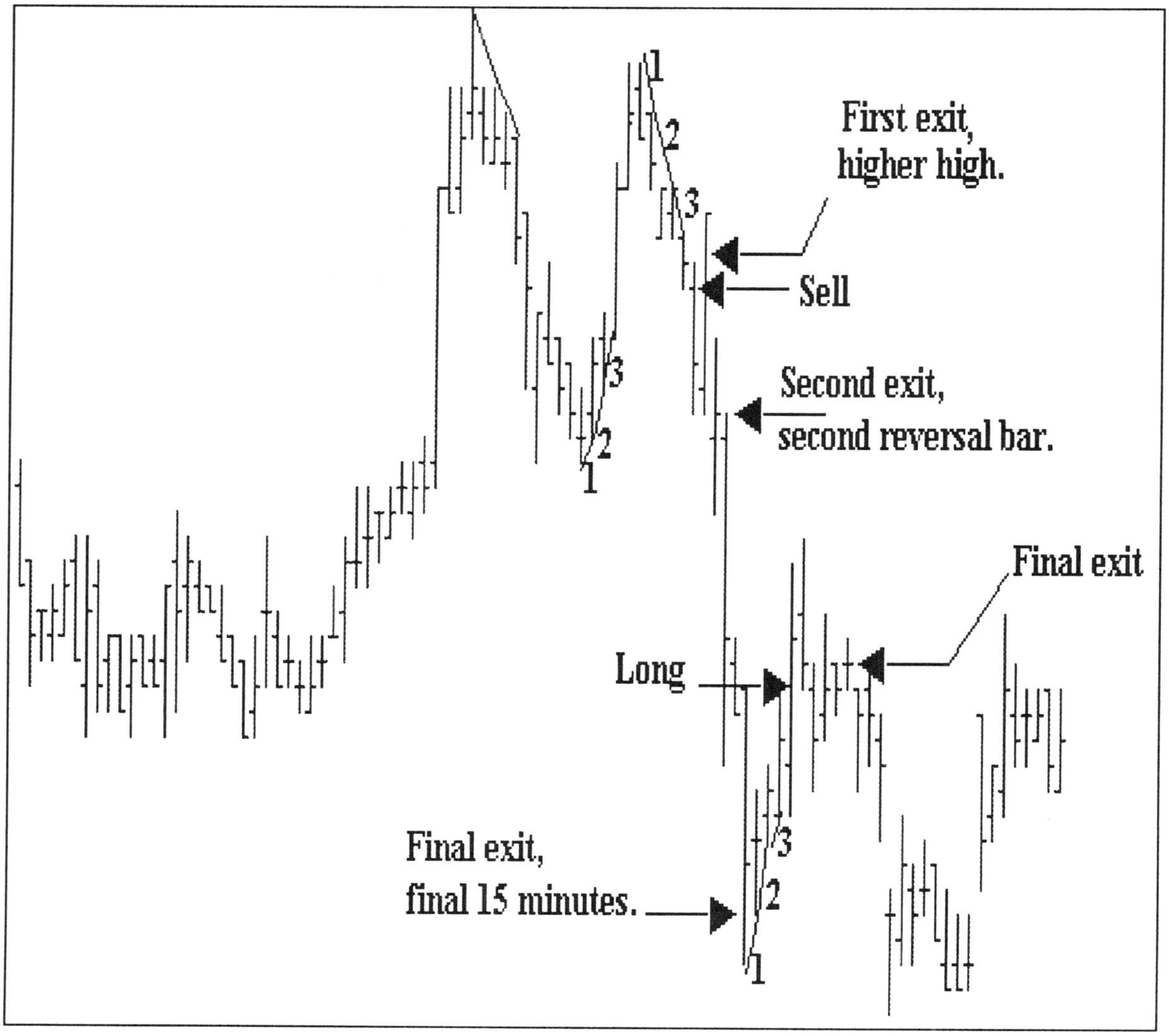

Well, how did you do? Our entry was on a violation of the high of the bar that gave us the third segment. Prices moved up to the local high. Our first exit is almost exactly where our entry was, and we couldn't fit another arrow in there, but it came as a result of the bar following the local high, making a new low. We are using the continuation method for our exits. Our second exit was right at the open of the second bar following the local high, because the bar preceding it was a second reversal bar. Our final exit might have tricked you. We went out on the open of the doji bar, because the bar preceding it was a third reversal bar. This was an early exit because we didn't like what we were seeing. If you picked the bar following the doji bar as your final exit, you made a good choice because it made a lower low that the preceding (doji) bar.

It would be very easy to load you up with nothing but examples of winning trades, but that is not the way actual trading really happens. All too many traders fool themselves when they study charts, they sit for hours looking for some magic way to trade that never shows a loss. In this course, we take the good with the bad — exactly the way it happens in real life.

DAYTRADING THE SEGMENT COUNT

There is probably nothing more difficult to trade than a stock when it's in a trading range. It has to be one of the most treacherous of times. Here's a 60 minute chart. It will trade the same way as any other chart. The difficult part is that as we view it, prices are only 16 bars into a Trading Range. For us, that is sort of a no man's land — too many bars to be considered a Ledge, and not enough for a full blown Trading Range.

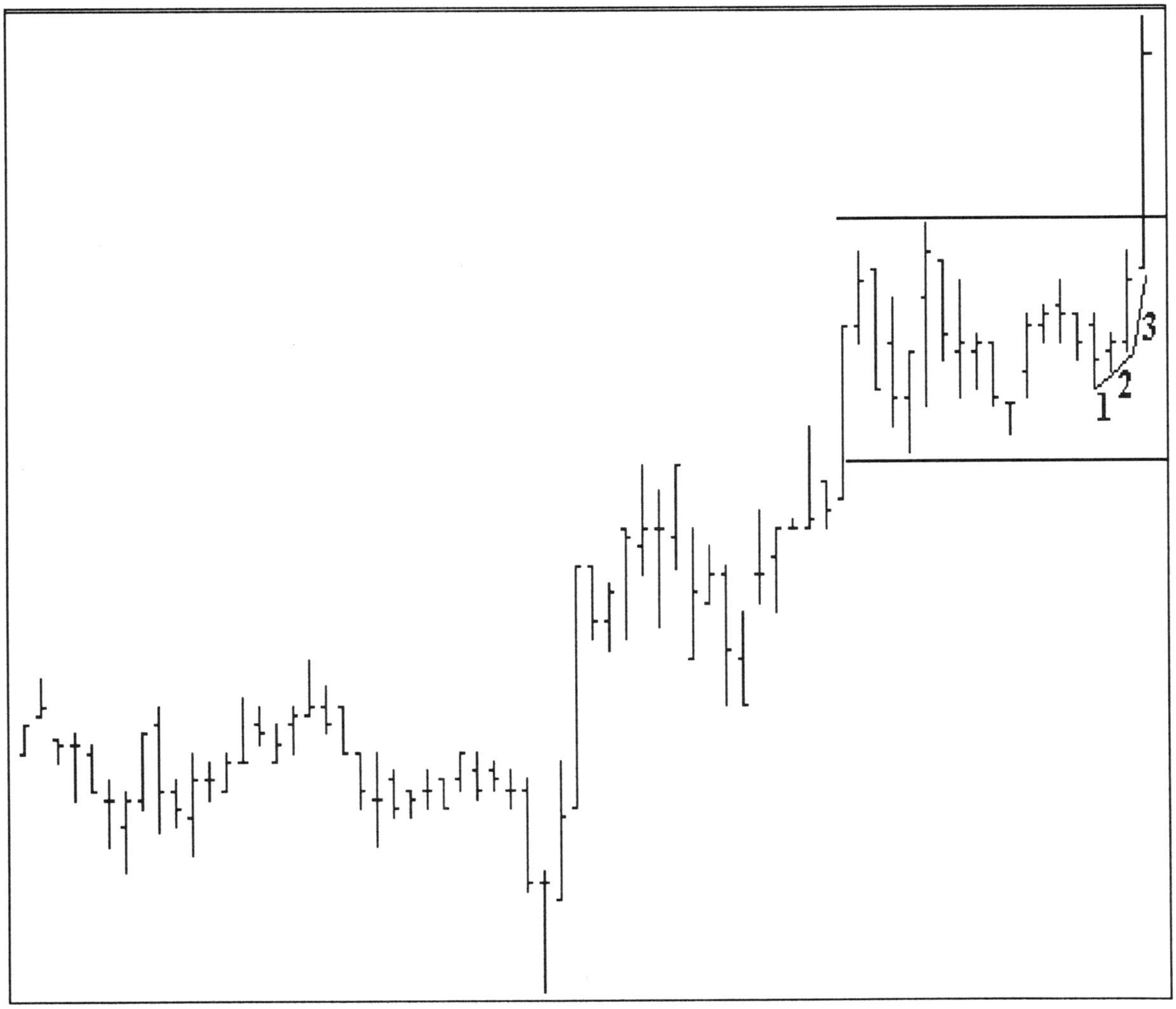

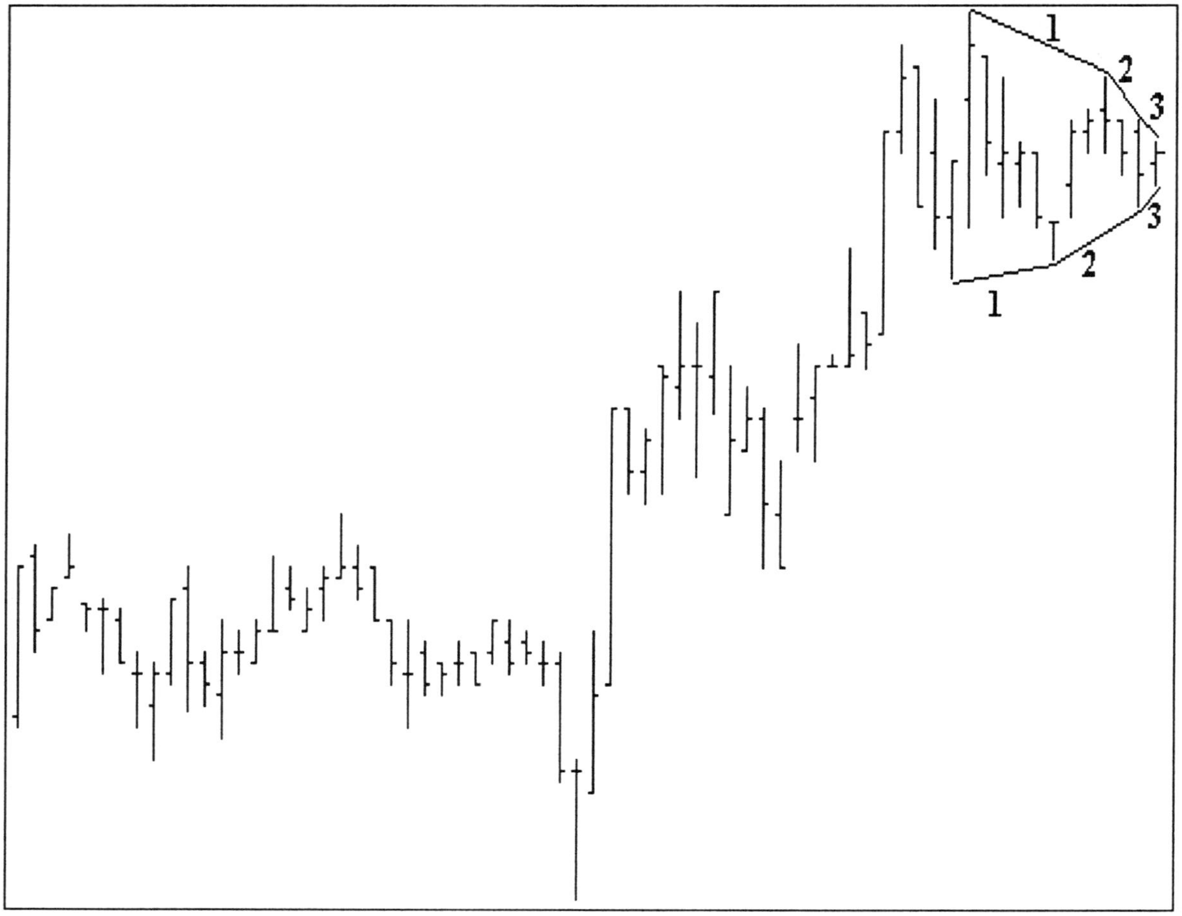

We'll begin by introducing the way we should be marking off the segments. We connect the segments going in each direction. The segments are the space between connecting lows or highs. Connecting segments is a very important part of the way we trade. As we go along, we will see more details being explained. Hopefully, by the time this manual is done, we will have a complete picture of segment counting as a way to find a trend at its inception. The first thing to notice is that there are intervening highs and lows between the bars that were connected. There may be more than one intervening bar between the highs or lows connected. Notice also that we connected the highest highs and the lowest lows going back from the current prices until we could number three segments. We never have more than three segments. As new ones are created in each direction, we always drop the oldest ones.

We want to buy on a violation of the high of the bar making the third segment to the upside, and sell on a violation of the low of the bar making the third segment to the downside.

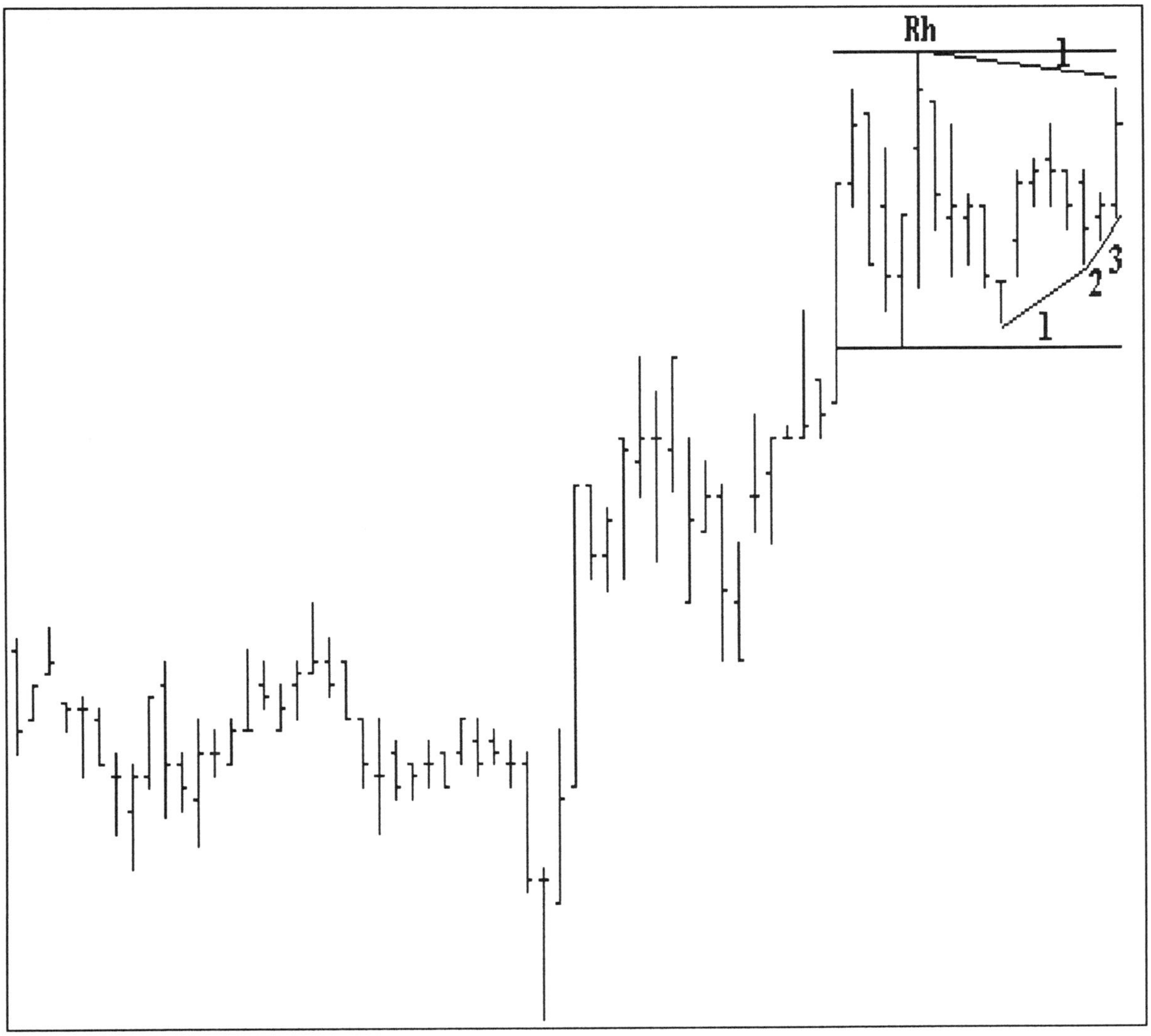

We buy as prices take out the high of the upside third segment. This is the last hour of trading. Prices are approaching the Ross Hook that was defined at the end of a prior 60 minute trend. The Ross Hook was the high of two days ago, and was also the highest high of the past three days.

If we choose to exit as a day trade, we will have a essentially breakeven trade for the day. We must place a buy order at a price that will mean a violation of the high of the current third segment bar has occurred. For our purposes, one tick above the high will suffice. At the end of the final hour, we have only one downside segment marked on the chart, and three upside segments. Of course, we could have chosen to hold overnight.

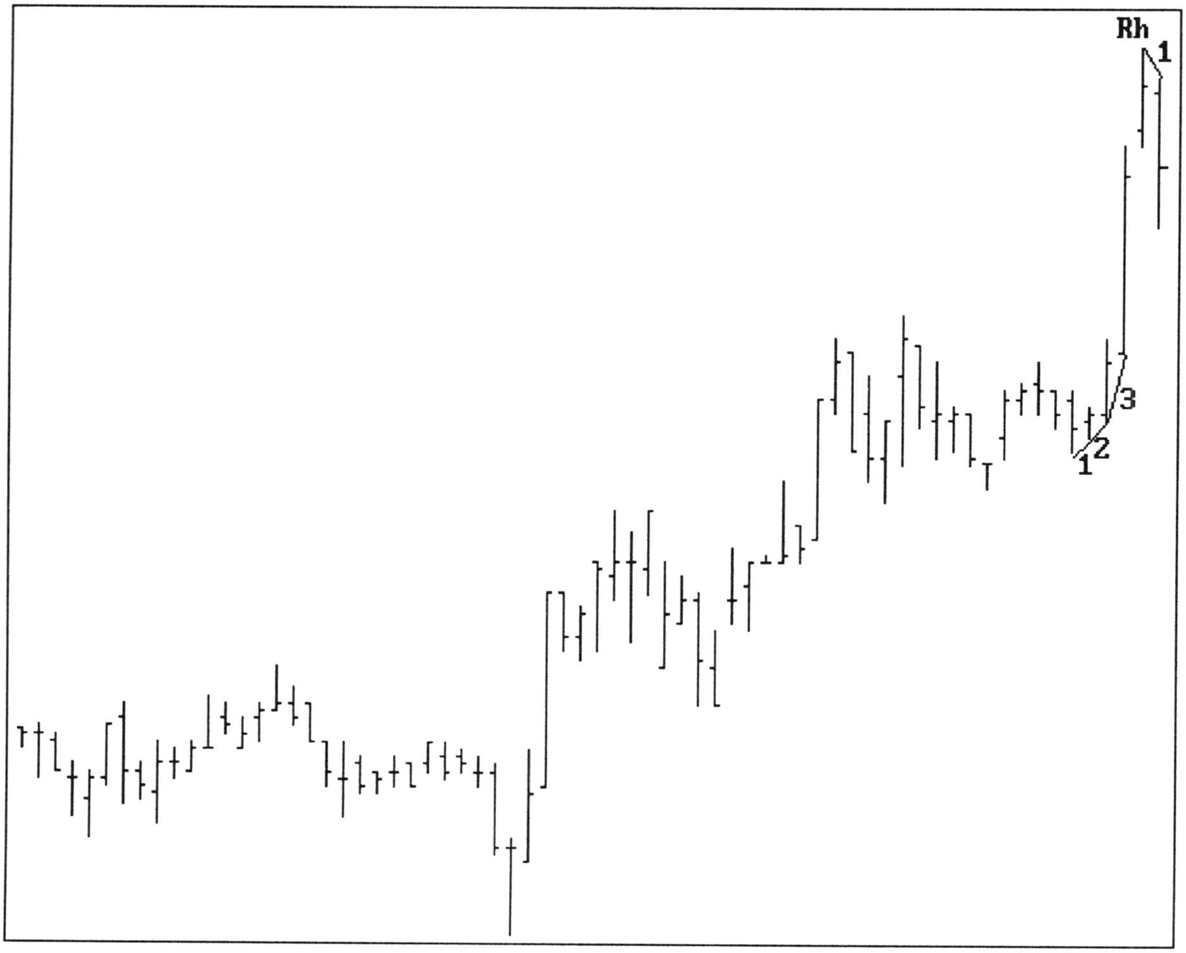

Prices violate both the third segment and the Ross Hook with great thrust during the opening 60 minute bar of the next day.

From there they move even higher in the second hour of trading (Not shown). On a move this big, profits can easily be taken at the end of the first hour of trading and protected on remaining portions of the position in such a way as to guarantee that no part of the position fails to end up profitable. In addition, with such a strong move, we should anticipate that some sort of correction will occur shortly. Prices rarely go straight up for very long.

The third hour of trading brings a correction as shown on the following page.

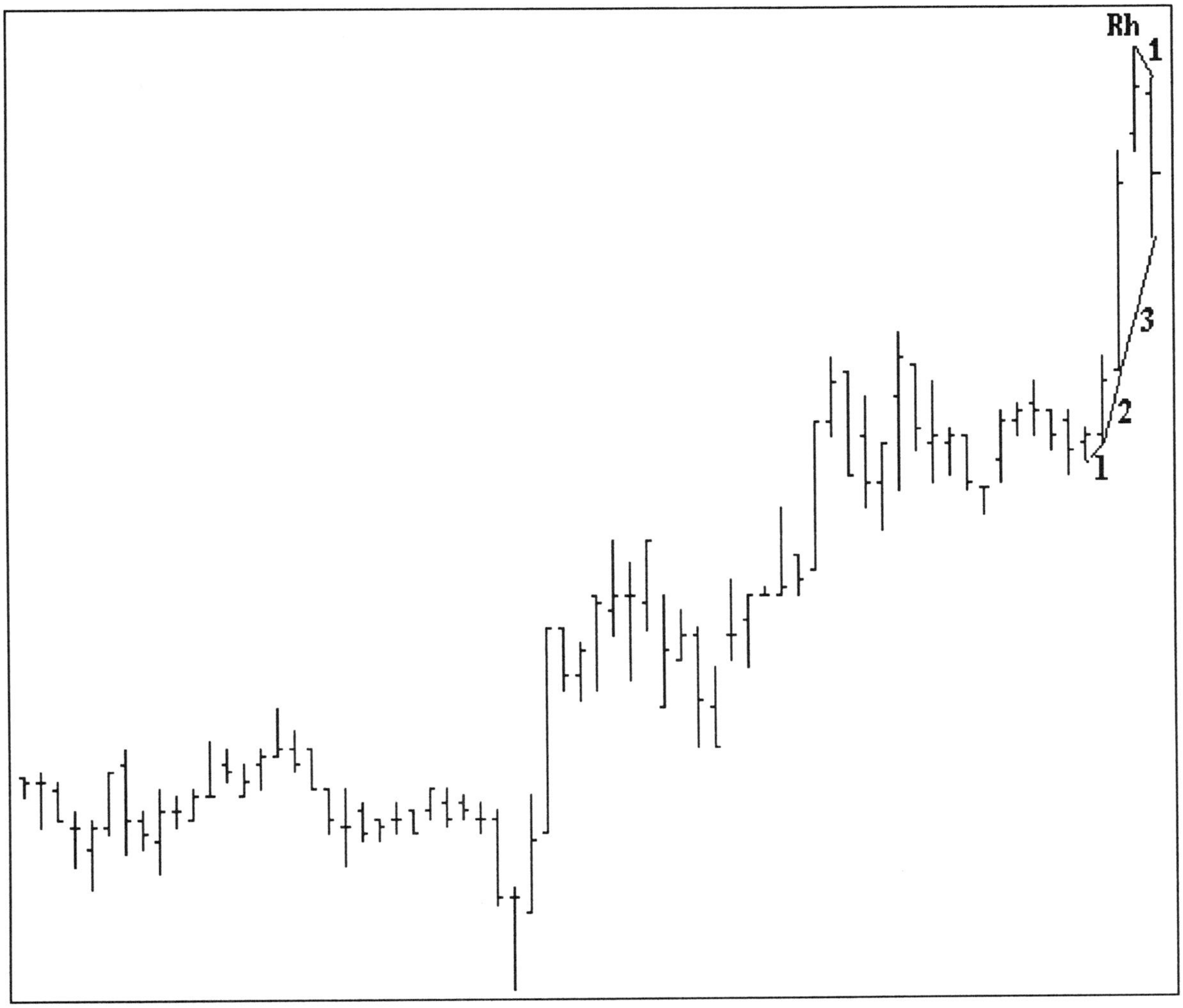

The breakout bar resulted in a new third segment up, but with the correction the last segment is moved to the low of the correction bar. We are shifting the segment count one bar to the right. Segments are always counted from the latest 3 to have occurred.

Notice that by entering on the basis of a violation of the high of the previous hour's segment, we were able to enter the market before a taking out of the Ross Hook. That is really what we want to accomplish, to get in before everyone else.

The correction bar makes a lower low than the bar that preceded it. The correction is severe. Since all shares were in a profit protecting position, it is appropriate to exit all of them on a correction as severe as this one. After exiting, we mark the latest Ross Hook, and resume numbering and counting segments.

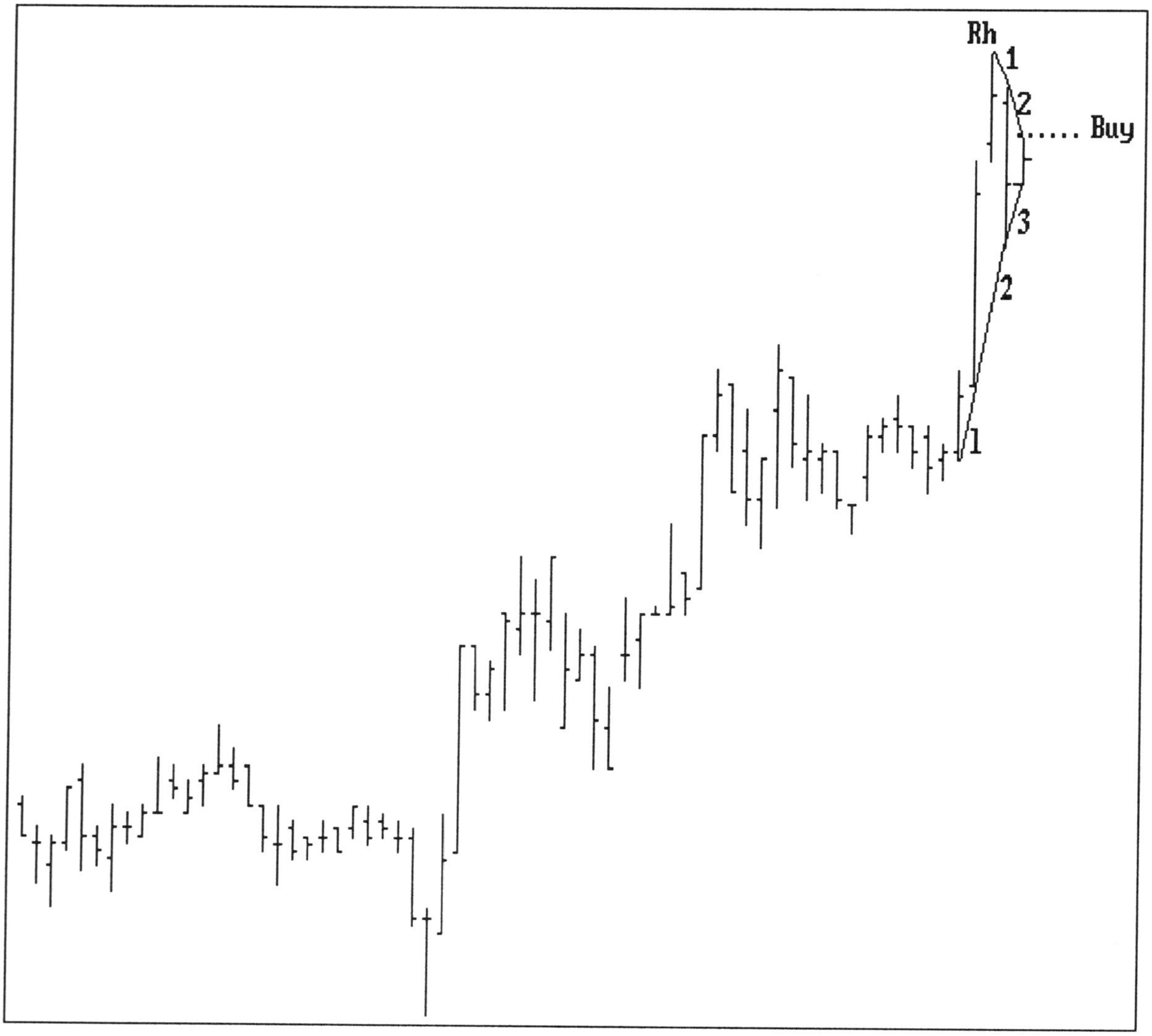

Although this second bar of correction doesn't amount to much, yet it is important because it makes the picture change. When the market talks, it is up to us to listen. Every price bar is important for chart reading.

We now have two segments going down. The market is still correcting. We will allow for three bars of correction and no more. Probabilities dictate that when a correction has a duration of more than three bars, we will usually see the formation of a congestion or an actual change of trend. The point here is that strong moves that lead to trends seldom display more than three bars of correction.

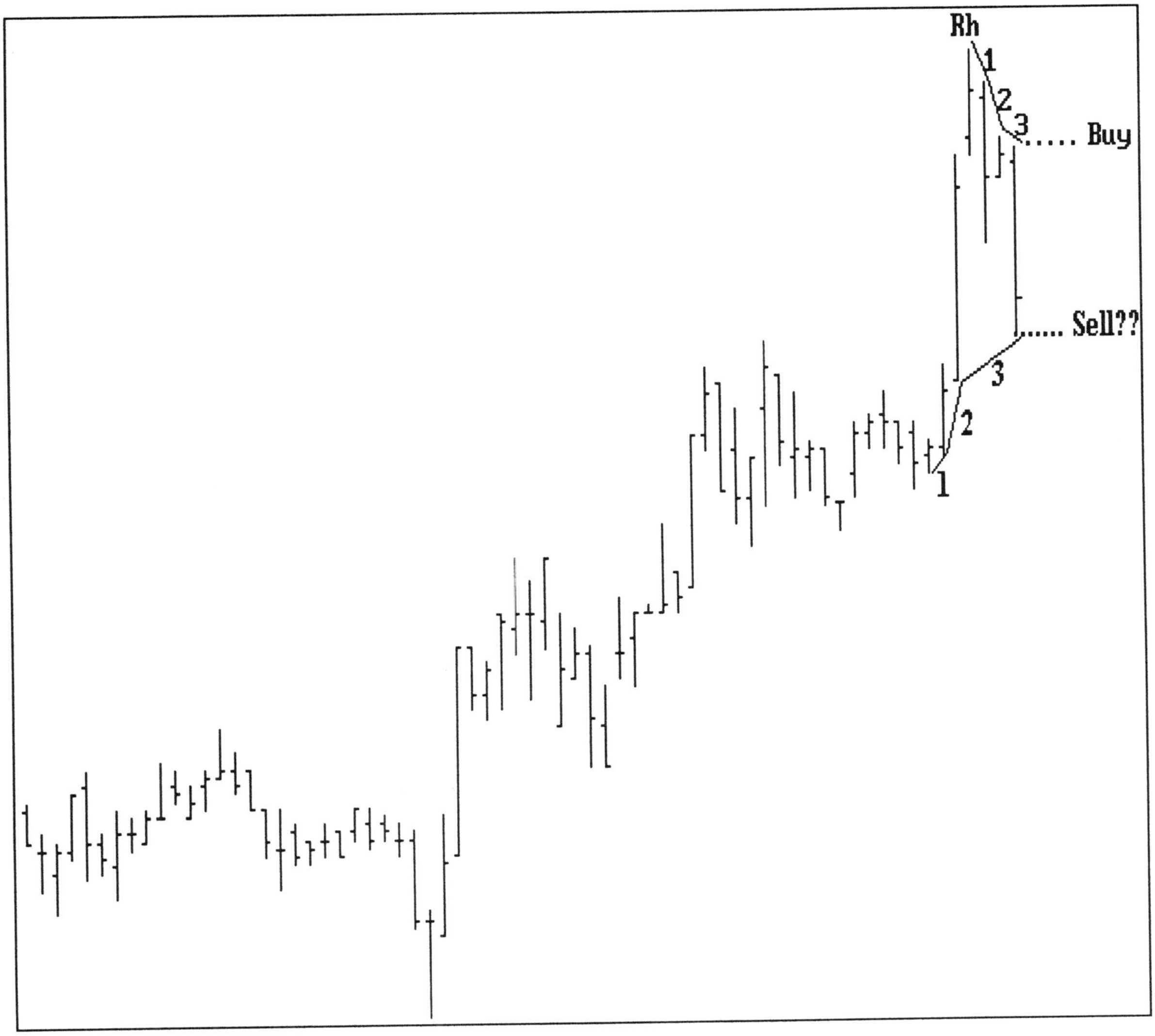

We now have three bars of correction in place. We shift segment 3 to the new low. We place a buy order to buy above the high of the third bar of correction because buying there fulfills a breakout of a third upside segment.

Why don't we also enter a sell order below the third downside segment? Although technically we could, if we were to be filled we would be trading directly into support at the previous congestion.

Our entry is during the last hour of trading. Getting in ahead of everyone else is our purpose. Had we entered on a violation of the Ross Hook, we would be looking at a loss by the time the market closed

If we are daytrading, we must exit before the close of trading and wait to see what the following day brings. Position traders may choose to hold overnight.

We still have three upside segments, but now we have no downside segments. We will want to buy if the high of the last bar is taken out.

The opening bar of the next day brings small additional profits to those who held overnight. Daytraders must wait for an entry signal. There is now one down segment on the chart. A breakout of the high of the last bar is an entry signal for daytraders.

Let's see what happened in the next hour.

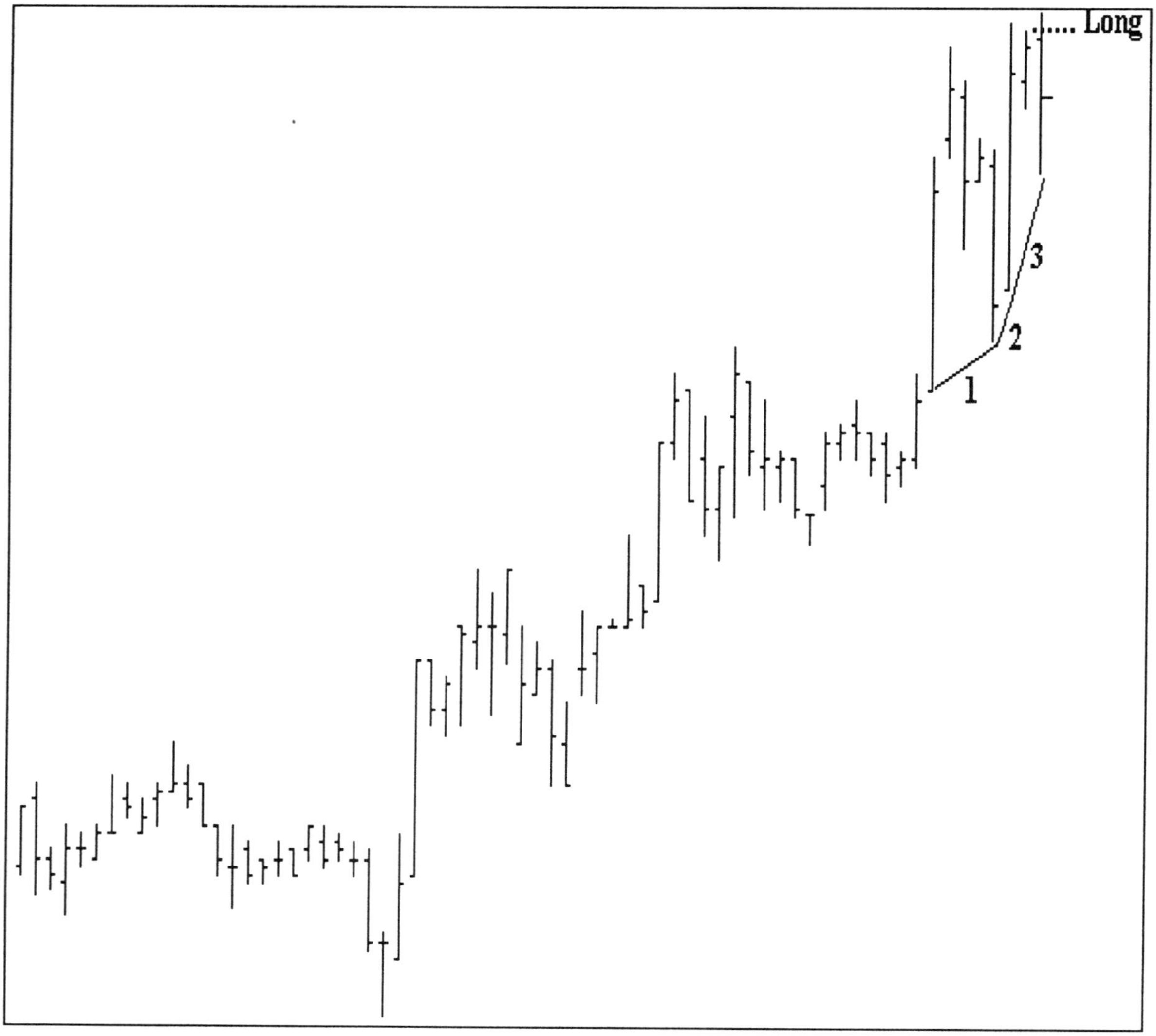

We're long in the second hour of trading. Our technique got us in ahead of the crowd who might have been buying the breakout of the Ross Hook which had occurred two bars previously. We are now definitely in a trending market. The trend became established at the time prices took out the previous Ross Hook.

The way the latest bar finished as a reversal bar making a lower low would have caused us to have to liquidate what was left of our position.

We have three segments up, so we place a buy stop above the high of this latest bar.

Once again, we are long. We are now in the third hour of trading. We should have been able to take some profits on this last move and be protecting profits on the remainder of our shares.

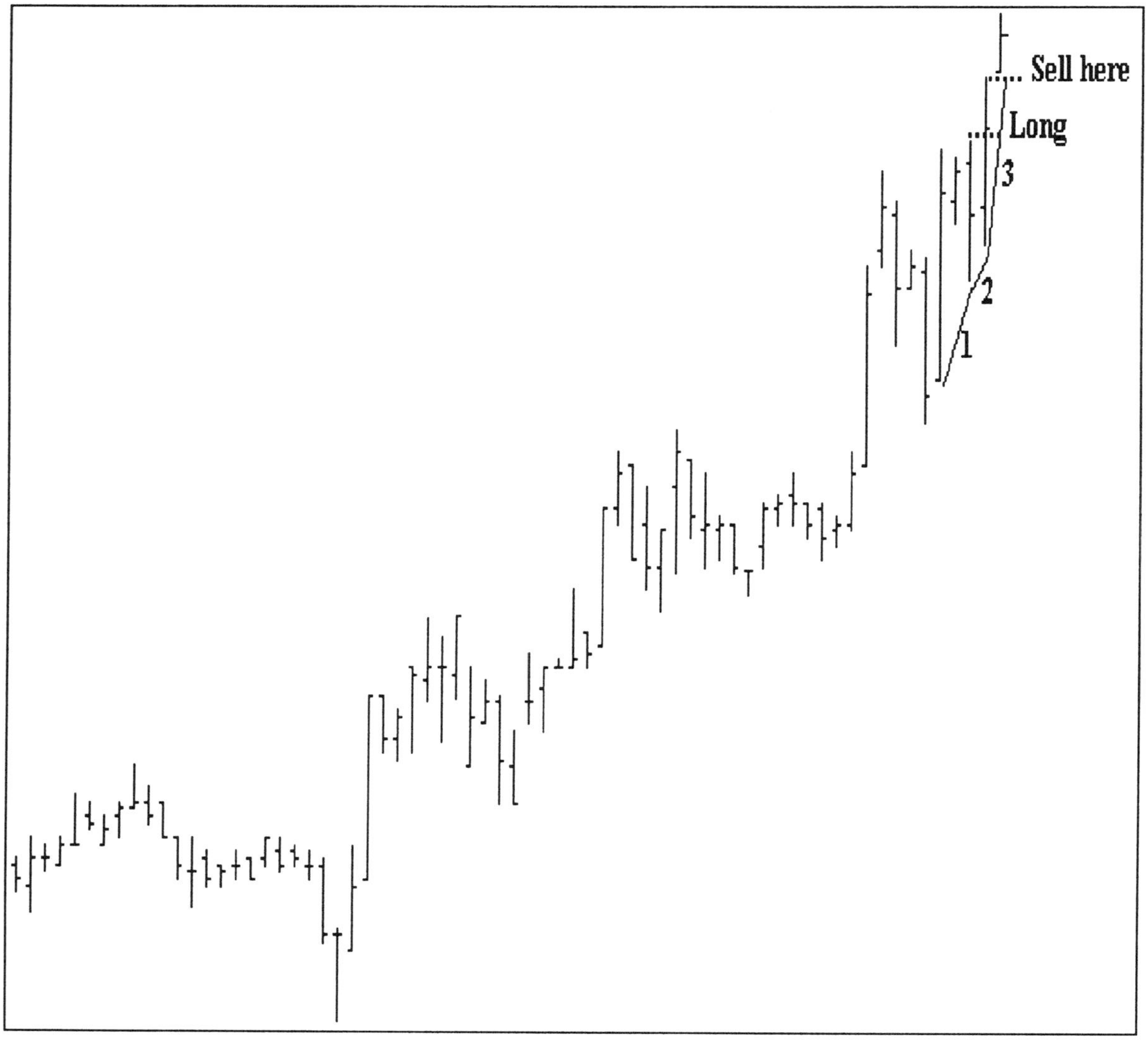

By this time, the fourth hour of trading, we have adequate profits on all shares retained. We will have taken profits the previous hour to cover costs and keep a reasonable amount for our efforts. This hour should have seen us take even more profits. They are ours to keep if we are not greedy and take them. We protect our final profits by planning to sell the moment a new low is made. The place where we would place our sell order is indicated on the chart above.

How the day ended is shown on the next chart.

The price action took back some of the profits we made by taking out the place at which the sell order would have gone into effect. Overall, this was quite a good trade, and typical of many that we can make by following the segment counting method.

With experience, more and more information about the price action becomes clear.

For example, look at how the next to last bar failed to make a higher low. That was a warning in itself to take profits before allowing so much to be given back to the market. It is because chart reading is somewhat interpretive that eventually you won't want to blindly follow a method, but early in our career as traders, we need to survive. The segment counting method enables us to do that.

Chapter 23

TRADE WHAT YOU SEE

We are firm believers in trading what you see, and not what you think. The two must be divorced. We also want to introduce another concept to you in this chapter. It is that of selecting trades in a time frame that is five times greater than the one in which you actually execute the trade. This means that if you are going to trade a five minute chart, you make your trade selection from a 25 minute chart. If you are going to trade the daily chart, you make your trade selection from the weekly chart.

Trading what you see can be applied to every aspect of trading, even classical technical chart analysis.

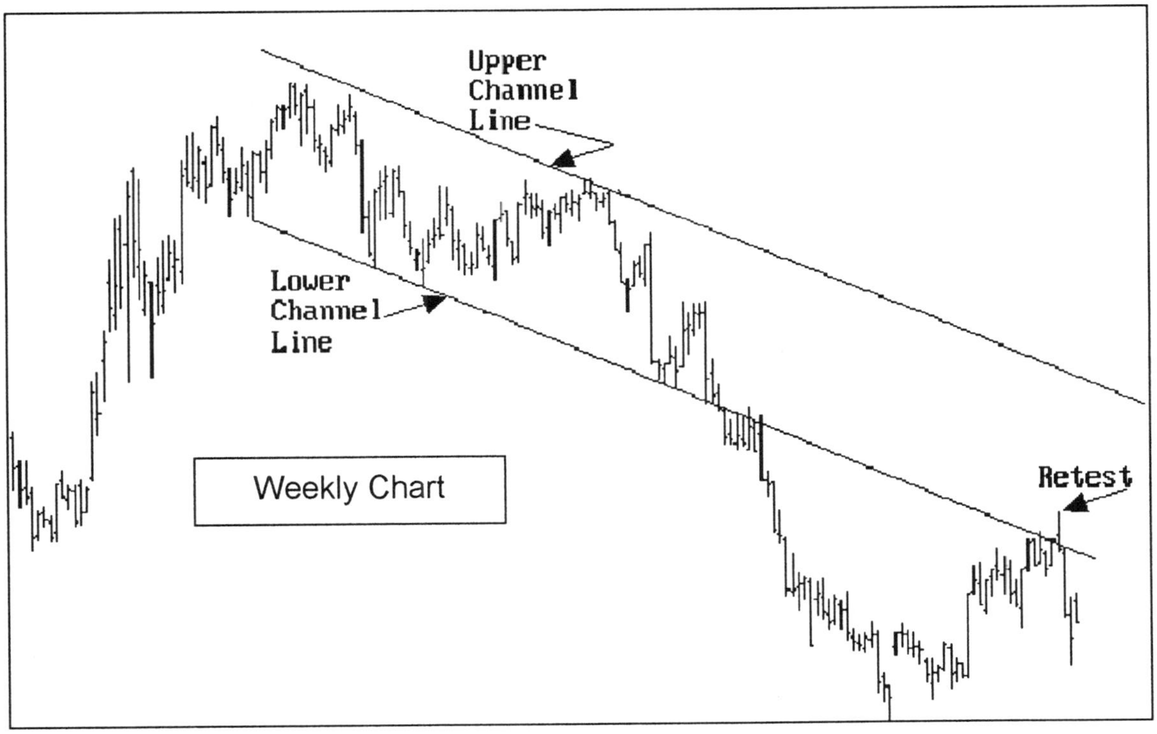

Notice the chart above. Prices had been in a long term downtrend, when they formed a pattern that can be considered a beautiful case for classical analysis.

The fine job of performing the analysis was ruined because the technician who performed it deviated from what he saw to what he thought. His thoughts caused himself and his followers a great deal of money.

It involved what has come to be known as a "Head-and-Shoulders" formation along with a second formation known as a "Megaphone Top," (see the following chart (A-B, C-D).

The combination of these two technical chart patterns suggested that prices would see a significant downside erosion before bottoming out.

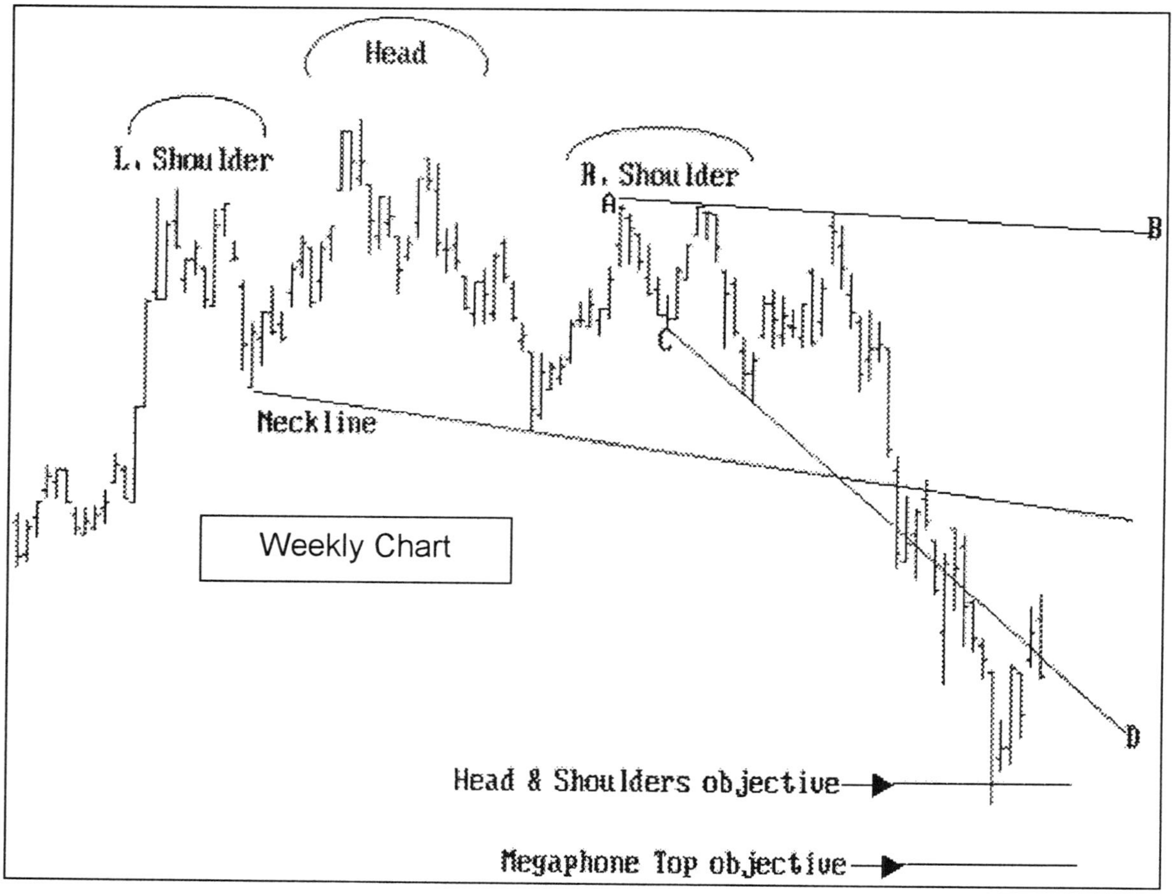

THE HEADS-AND-SHOULDERS TOP

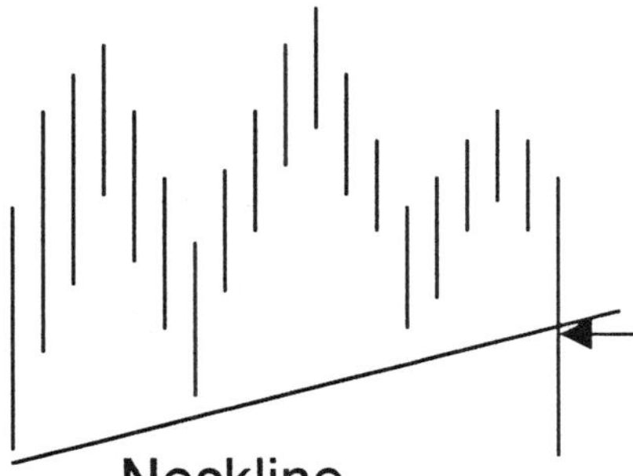

The head-and-shoulders reversal formation is perhaps the most well-known of all technical patterns. Though usually found at the end of major up or down trends, it also can occur at the end of medium-term trends.

A head-and-shoulders bottom is a graphic representation of accumulation by investors, while a head-and-shoulders top is a graphic representation of distribution by investors. Since we will be discussing the head-and-shoulders top on the previous chart, we will limit our remarks to the mechanics of the head-and-shoulders top.

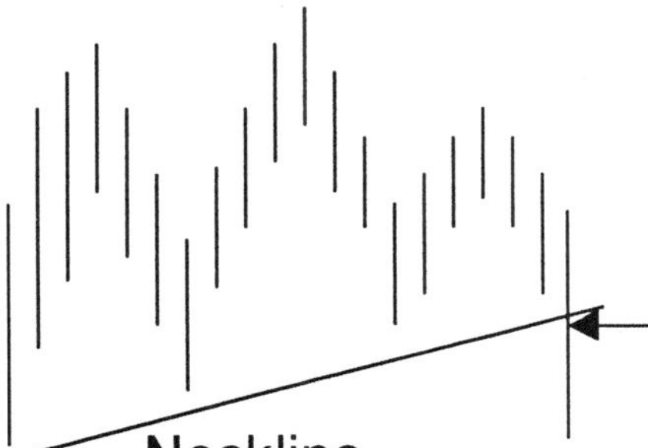

First, an extensive rally ends on heavy volume as investors take profits in what they consider to be an overvalued situation. The decline is halted at the low of what will be the end of the left shoulder, prior to rising to the top. At this point, volume drops off and buyers enter to take advantage of the perceived bargain opportunity.

Next, demand is sufficient to take prices to new highs at the top of the head of the head-and-shoulders formation. However, typically this advance will take place on less volume than the advance that created the top of the left shoulder.

Looking at price alone, you would see no indication that the trend is over, but the alert trader will have noticed the decline in volume on the rally to the top of the head.

Then, profit takers sell into the strength of the rally to the top of the head, pushing prices back down to what is to become the base for the rise to the top of the right shoulder. Prices may even descend to break the support line from the rise to the previous high.

Then, the remaining bulls step in again to push up to the top of the right shoulder. Usually volume is thin compared with the previous rallies.

Finally, one last sell-off follows on very heavy volume, pushing price down through the *neckline*. The neckline is a trend line drawn to connect the low at the end of the left shoulder to the low at the beginning of the right shoulder.

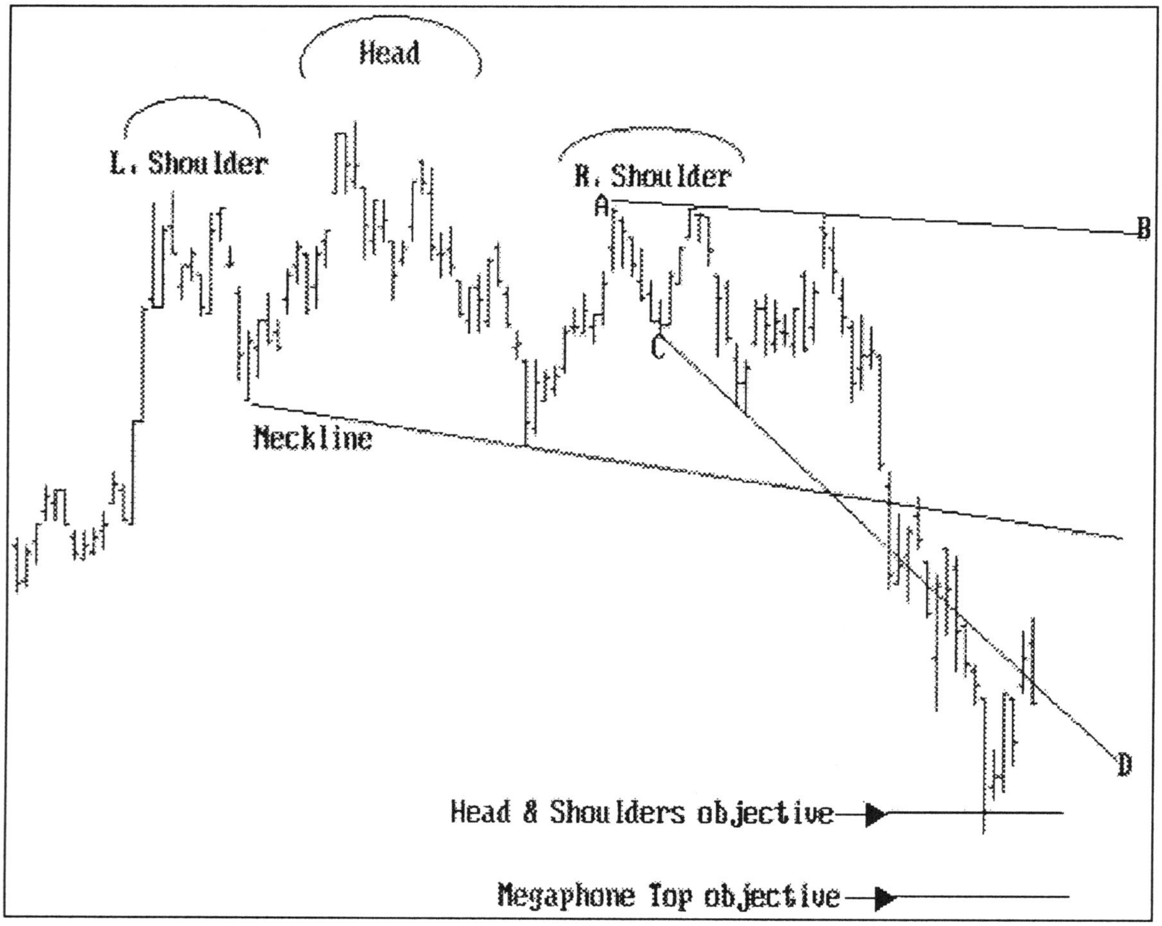

ESTIMATING THE FALL

The question becomes, “How far will prices fall?”

The traditional way to do this from the head-and-shoulders formation is to measure the distance from the top of the head straight down to the neckline. This distance is the amount that prices are supposed to move downward from the point at which prices penetrate the neckline to the downside. We’ve shown this objective on the chart. Note that time is not a factor here. It is not known how long prices will take to make their plunge.

MEGAPHONE TOPS

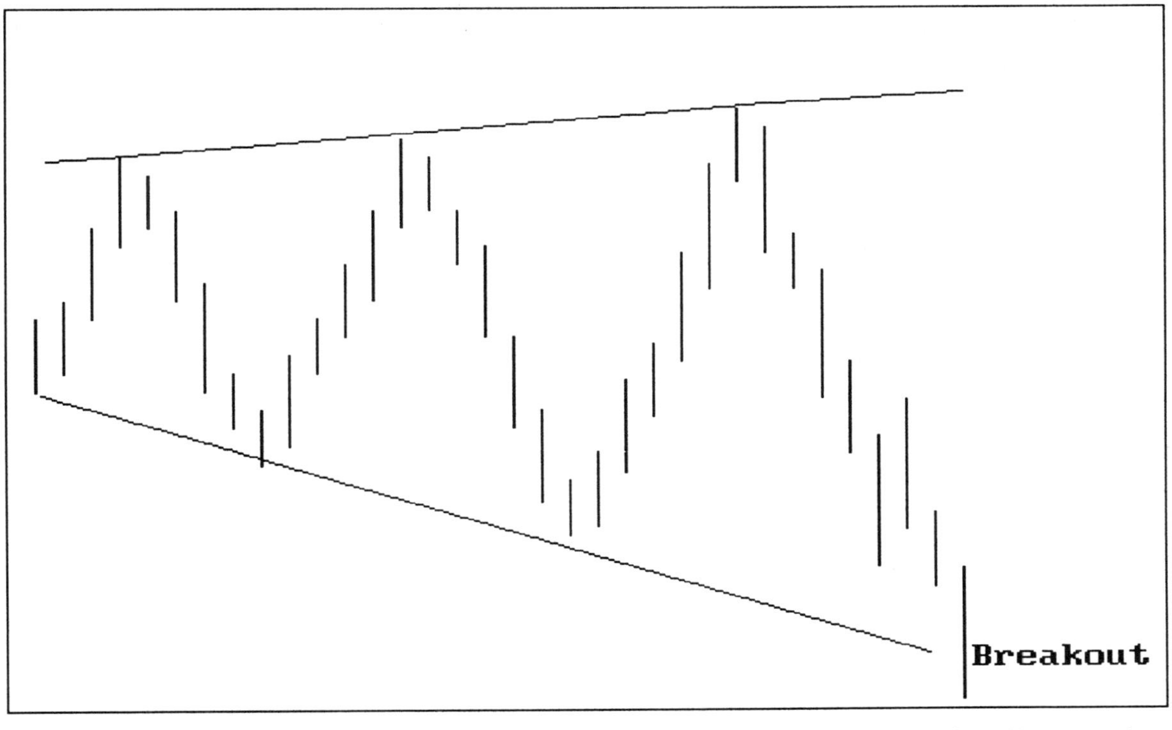

A megaphone top is also known as a broadening top. Similar to the head-and-shoulders, it consists of five stages. The broadening top in prices occurred as part of the right shoulder. It, too, is found at the end of a major advance.

Trader’s perceptions of value continually fluctuate in response to rumors and unexpected news releases.

This uncertainty causes prices to move from a low to new highs.

Shortly, prices move back to new lows, only to be followed by new highs. The final push to new highs warns the trader to prepare for a strong sell-off, which will take prices to new lows and complete the megaphone top.

With the price chart we've been viewing, the highs tended to be rather flat, but the lows were continually lower.

We've labeled the top of the megaphone A-B, and the bottom as C-D, on the Chart.

Once the trader has seen the five stages take place, i.e. the swings from low to high and back again, he determines the objective of the megaphone top by measuring the distance from the highest high of the megaphone, straight down to the point at which prices break through the lower line of the megaphone. This distance is then marked downward from the point of the breakthrough. We've shown this as the Megaphone Top Objective.

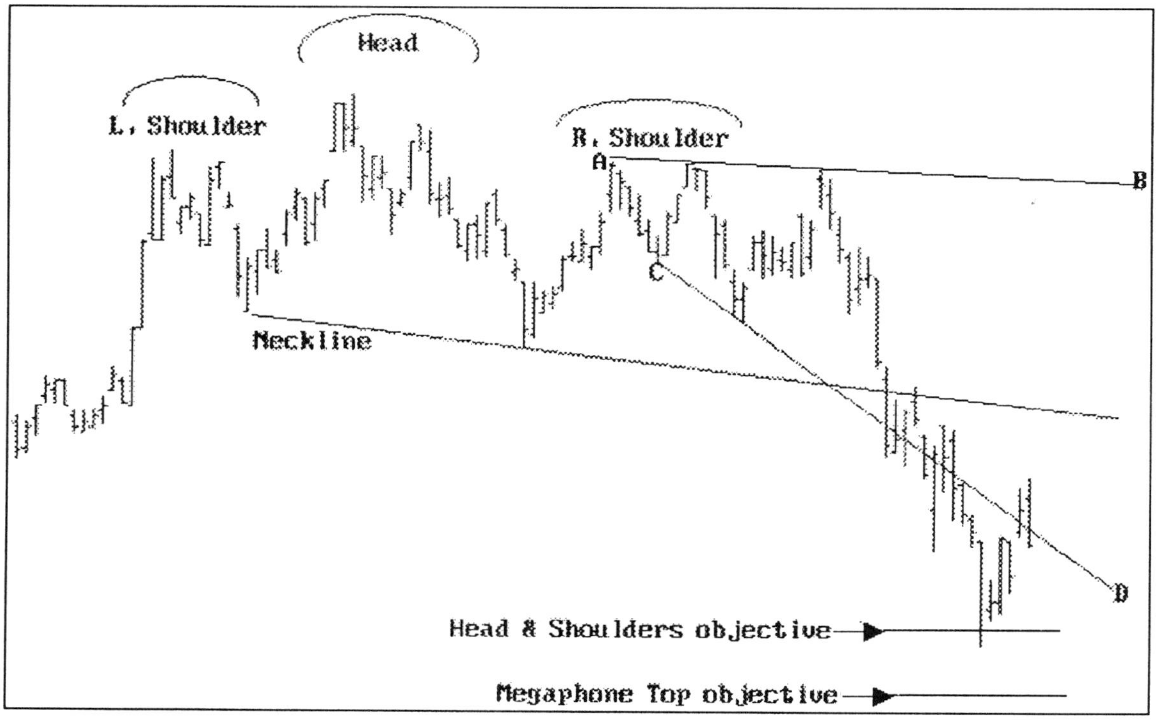

So far so good. In a very similar analysis to the one we've just done, the technician came up within pennies of having the same objectives as the ones we've shown.

Those objectives were based upon what, until that point, could be been seen on the chart. Calling those objectives was an example of trading what you see.

As ***you*** can see, prices went directly down to the objective area and then bounced.

Then the technician we've been referring to decided to play God. We want to quote what he said. See if you can see where he changed from what could be seen to what he began to think.

"IMPLICATIONS FOR PRICES"

"...we see a major head-and-shoulders top whose right shoulder is, in itself, a megaphone top.

"The fact that these two highly reliable topping patterns form together within the same distribution reveals underlying weakness in the price action. Notice that the neckline of the head-and-shoulders top and the lower trend line of the megaphone top are broken at nearly the same price.

"This convergence confirms that the breakout was genuine and that prices are poised to move significantly lower."

“HOW MUCH LOWER?”

The downside objectives of both the head-and-shoulders top and the megaphone top, based on the methods previously described are shown on the chart. Prices set a low that was between the two objectives. (*This paragraph is ours.*)

Continuing with the quote: “With both targets realized, the market may now find support to take prices slightly higher. In fact, prices could rise all the way to retest point without invalidating the technical picture.

“Since both the head-and-shoulders top and the megaphone top typically appear at major trend reversals, prices probably have not seen their lows.

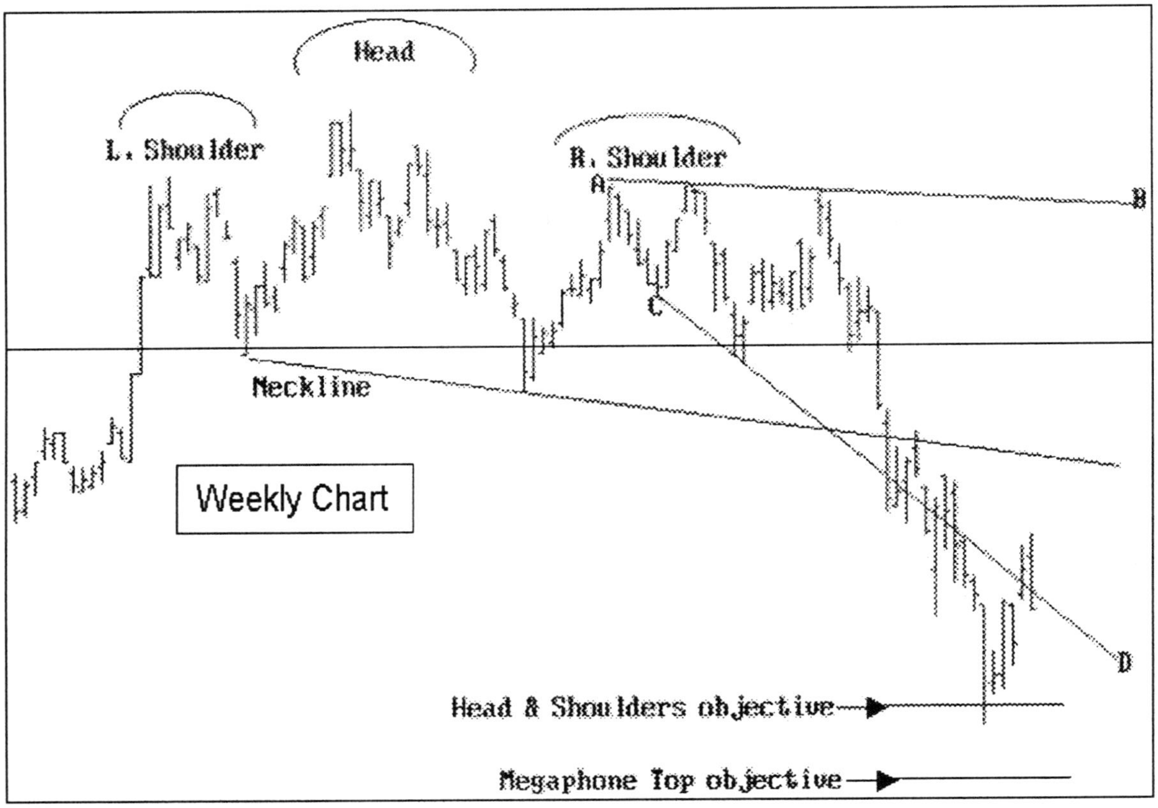

"The price chart reveals a major continuing downtrend and that down trend has actually accelerated, breaking below the lower parallel channel line. After establishing the lowest low you see on the chart and trending higher to the retest high, prices are now poised to retest if not surpass the lowest low shown on the chart."

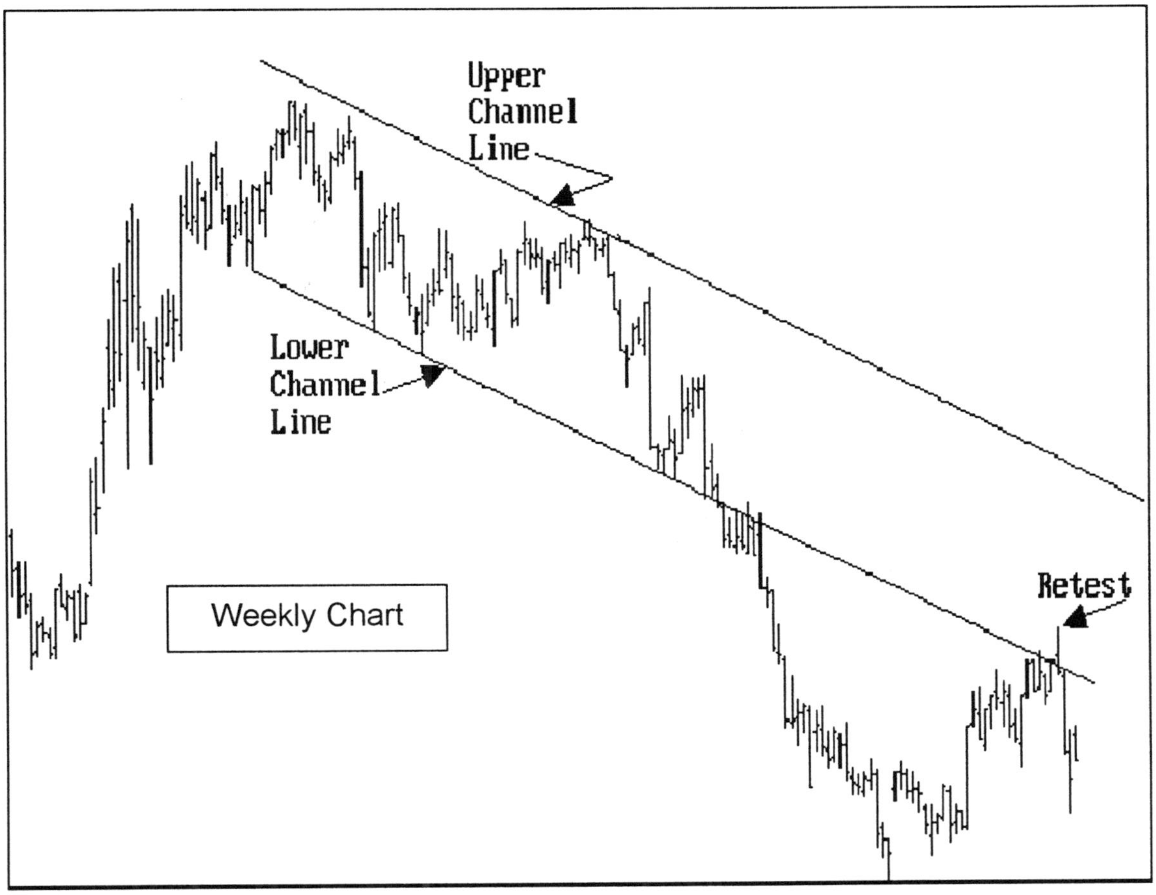

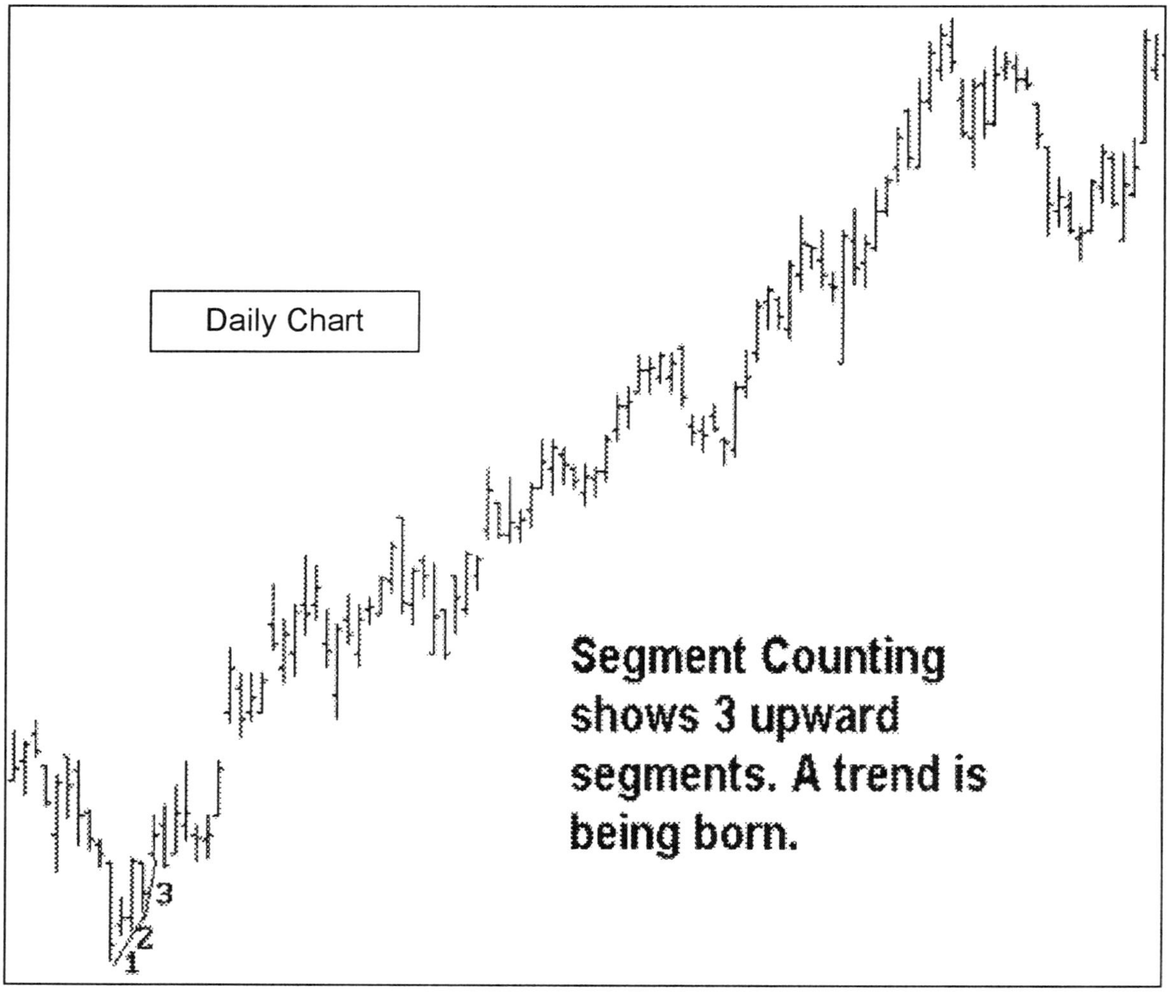

Would not our technician have been a lot better off to accept the fact that prices did as indicated by his technical analysis, and left well enough alone?

All he had to do was start counting. On the chart above we've shown what would have been as simple as counting to three.

He could have traded from a 1-2-3 low formation, as well. We've shown that on the next page.

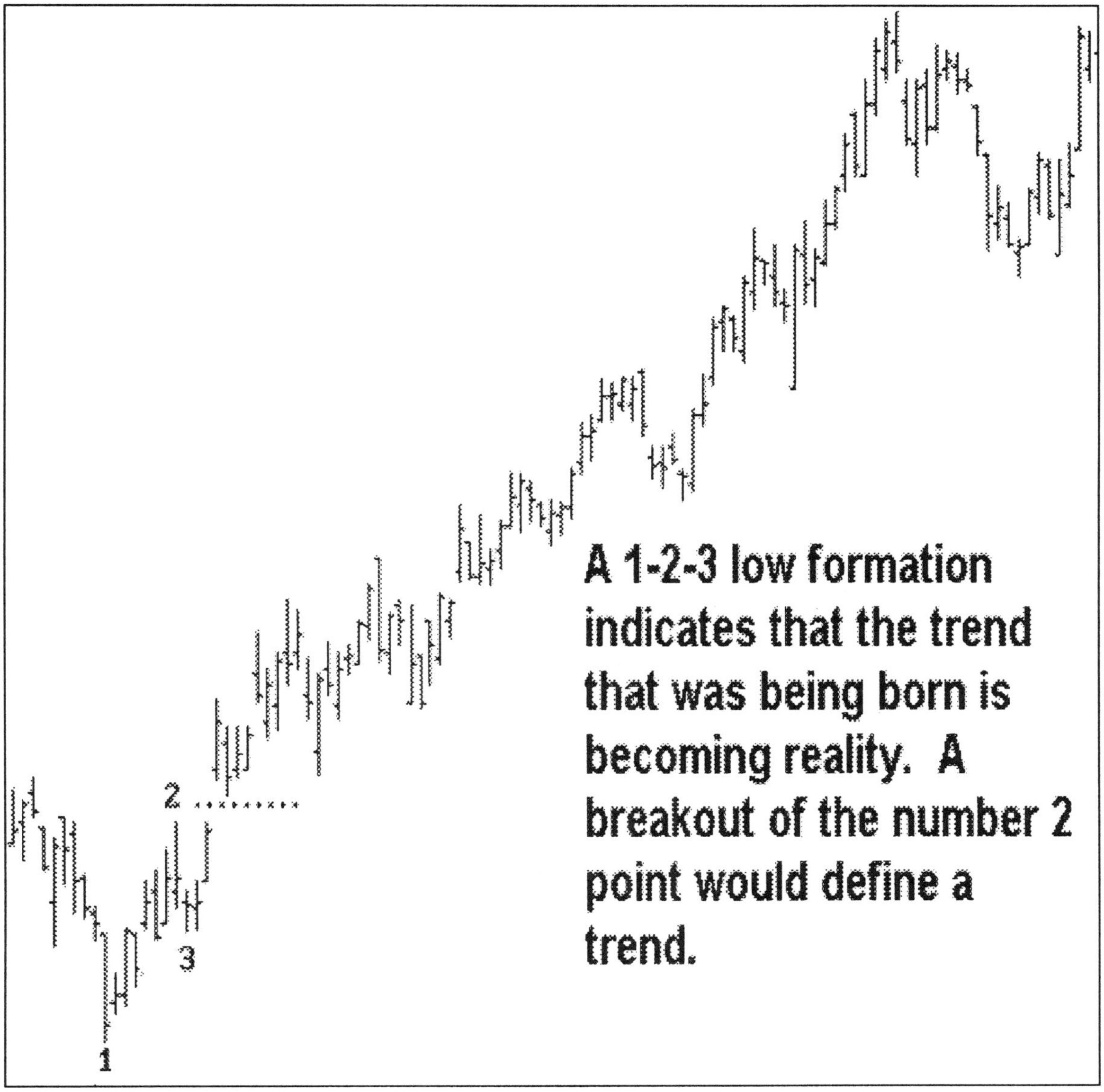

The point is, ultimately the technician went beyond what could be seen to what he thought might happen. By the time he realized that his theory had been violated, there was no basis via pure technical analysis for getting into the trade until the top of the retest bar was violated.

Chapter 24

TRADING GAPS

Hey, what do I do about gap openings?

All right, what do you do about them?!

First of all let's show some gap openings.

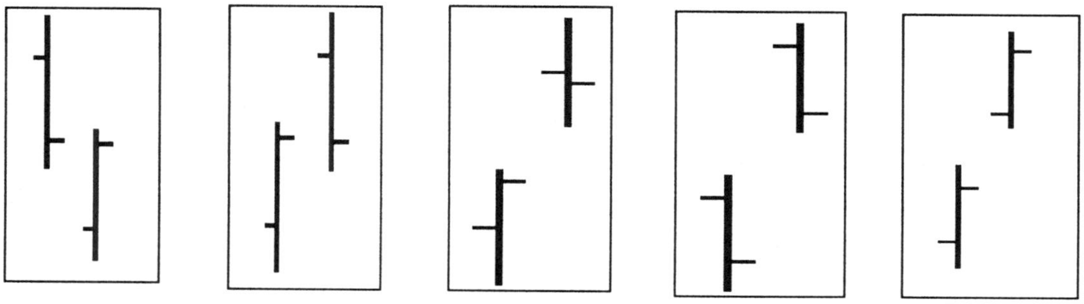

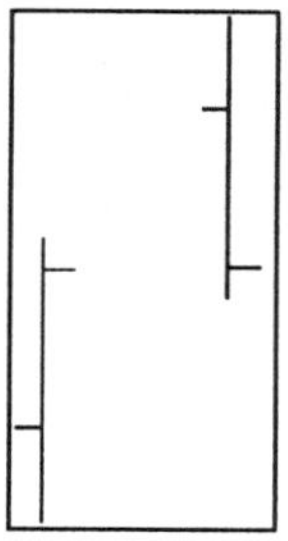

Situation 1: The opening must be higher than the previous bar's high, thereby causing a gap between the previous bar's high and the current bar's open. Go short.

Situation 2: The opening must be lower than the previous bar's low, thereby causing a gap between the previous bar's low and the current bar's open. Go Long.

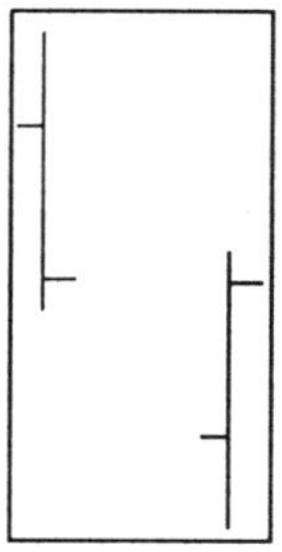

Let's add one more piece of information to our scenario.

LET'S SAY THAT IN THE FIRST INSTANCE, THE SECOND BAR MUST CLOSE IN THE LOWER HALF OF ITS PRICE RANGE, AND IN THE SECOND INSTANCE, THE SECOND BAR MUST CLOSE IN THE UPPER HALF OF ITS PRICE RANGE.

Now, what in the world can you do with this situation?

Obviously, any move on a weekly chart is going to be a lot more significant than a similar move on a one minute chart. Because of that, the following analysis makes a lot more sense on a longer term chart.

WHAT DOES IT MEAN

On the first chart, we have a sell signal, so from now on let's call it the Go Short chart. On the second chart we have buy signal, so from now on let's call it the Go Long chart. Whatever caused the price action we see does not really matter. The truth is the truth and a chart is a chart.

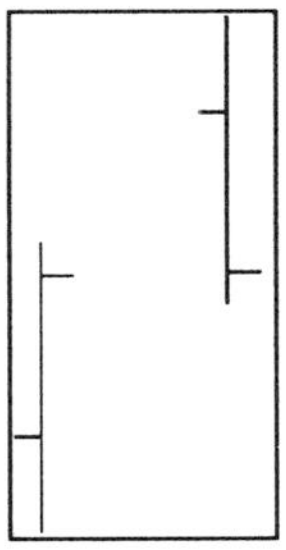

Good chart reading reveals the following information: With the Go Short chart, prices had moved higher on bar one, and there was follow through on the open of bar two, gap open. However, before the bar ended, bearish influences had taken over thereby driving prices to close lower on bar two.

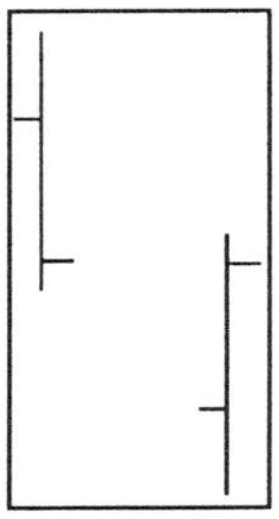

On the Go Long chart prices had moved lower on bar one, and there was follow through on the open of bar two, gap open. However before the bar ended, bullish influences had taken over, thereby driving prices to close higher on bar two.

ANTICIPATION

The anticipation from the Go Short bar is that there will be follow-through on the succeeding bar. Why? Because the bears were clearly in charge at the period of time that the bar ended.

The anticipation from the Go Long bar is just the opposite. There should be follow through to the upside because the bulls were clearly in charge at the close.

Now here is a qualifier. It is best to trade these signals in a trending market. Yes, you can do them in a sideways market, but the risk is much greater that nothing much will happen.

SECOND BAR REVERSAL?

Does the second bar have to be a reversal bar? Absolutely! It is the only way the signal can occur.

HOW FREQUENT IS THE SIGNAL?

The signal does not occur very often. More than that, when it does occur, it often happens in such a way as to preclude entry. Here's why!, see the chart on the next page.

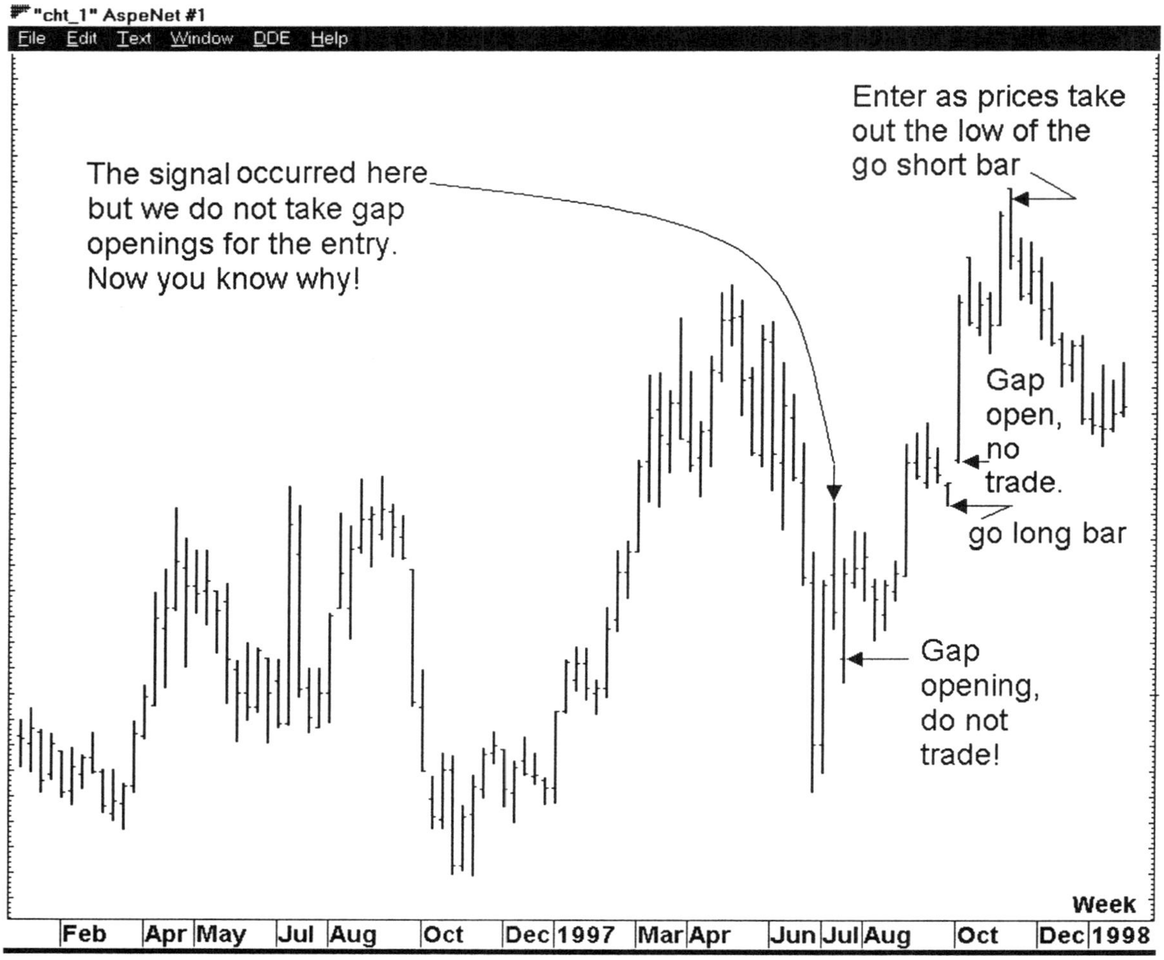

HOW TO ENTER

RULE: DO NOT TRADE GAP OPENINGS.

The best way to take the signal is to enter the market on a buy or sell stop, ***after*** the Open.

Let's say you see the go short signal after the Close on a Friday. On Monday, place a sell stop in the market at a price that represents a breakout of the Low of Friday's bar. You want a trade-through breakout of the low, not a gap opening. Do the opposite for a go long signal, take a trade-through breakout of the previous bar's high.

These trades, when they occur, are excellent profit making scalps. Once you go in, keep as tight a stop on them as you can afford.

"What's that? We can hear it already! You want more action than that. Uh, huh, we might have known."

"Okay, here it comes! You can do a similar trade on any reversal week. ***A reversal is when prices are overall moving down, you get a bar with a close that is higher than the open, and when prices are overall moving up, you get a bar whose close is lower than the open****. We just wanted to whet your appetite. We knew exactly what you would say. Why are you soooo greedy? Here's that chart again on the next page.!"*

The rules will be a little different from before.

On the chart on the next page, we've shown all the instances of the trades being possible. For awhile, we thought we were going to run out of letters. At the very end we saw one we had missed at the beginning. We marked it "x."

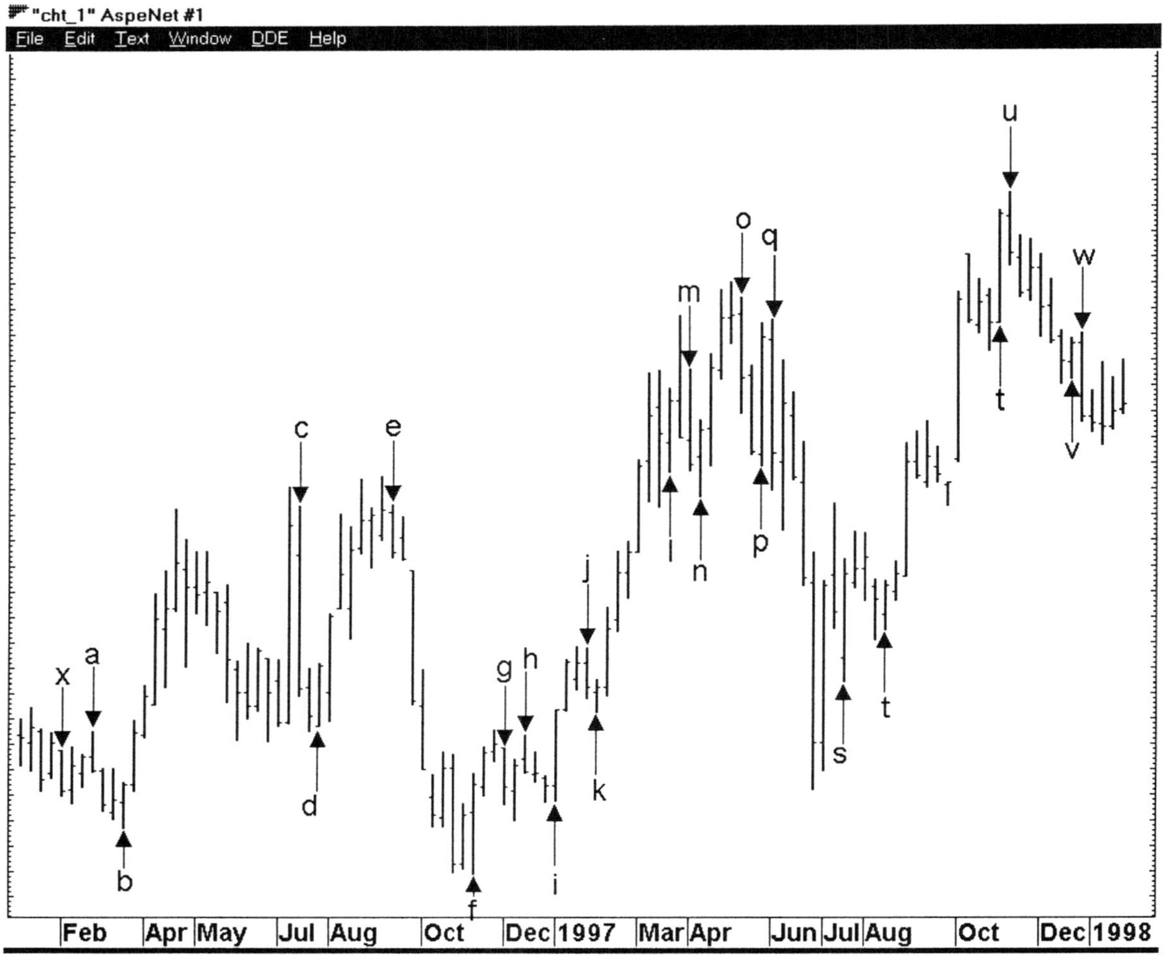

- RULE **1:** THE REVERSAL BAR MUST FINISH IN THE UPPER OR LOWER **1/2** OF ITS RANGE.

- RULE **2:** YOU ENTER ON A TRADE-THROUGH **(**NO GAP**)** BREAKOUT OF THE EXTREME OF THE SIGNAL BAR. **(**THE SIGNAL BARS ARE SHOWN BY ARROWS ON THE CHART.**)**

- RULE **3:** ONCE THE TRADE SHOWS ANY PROFIT AT ALL, YOU PLACE A STOP AT NO WORSE THAN BREAKEVEN.

"What, no more rules? No, no more rules."

If this doesn't pay for the price of this course for the next eleventy-seven years, we don't know what will. Are you telling your friends to buy this course? Please do!

Now for a few comments. The arrows are pointing to the signal (go short or go long) bars. We put all those letters on that chart in case we needed to comment on any of them.

Notice that there were some signals, where a gap opening occurred. We did not count any of those or mark them with an arrow. On the bar following "a" you see one that was very close. We did count it as a trade-through the low of "a," and therefore marked a with an arrow. However the bar before "m" gave a signal but we didn't mark it because "m" itself (besides being a signal bar) gapped open below the low of the signal bar that preceded it.

At "g," "h," "q," "w," and several others, there was only a small gain to be made at some time during the week. That is why you must place a stop at no worse a point than breakeven.

Although you may enter the trade based on the weekly signal, you execute and monitor the trade via the daily chart.

If you are using the daily chart for your entry signal, monitor the trade via an intraday.

If you are using an intraday chart, for example a 60 minute chart, then monitor the trade in some lesser time frame.

Perhaps you never thought of "scalping" in the sense of doing it from a weekly chart, but the reversal signal is truly a scalp trade. Why? Because the duration of the trade is not expected to be long. All we are attempting to do is to take advantage of the thrust and potential follow-through taking place in the price action.

ANOTHER GREAT GAP TRADE

This has proven to be an especially good trade when it comes along. We might mention that there are some real time sophisticated market scanning software packages available that will help to find gaps. If you like to trade gaps we highly recommend their purchase. Now on with the trade.

The gap chart might look like this:

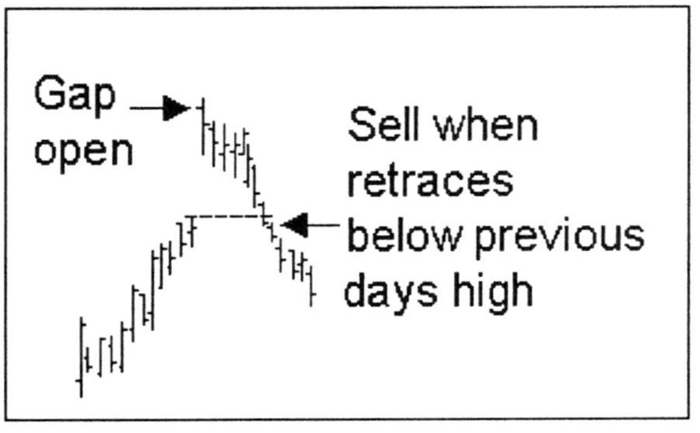

This is a great opportunity to sell short.

or it may look like this.

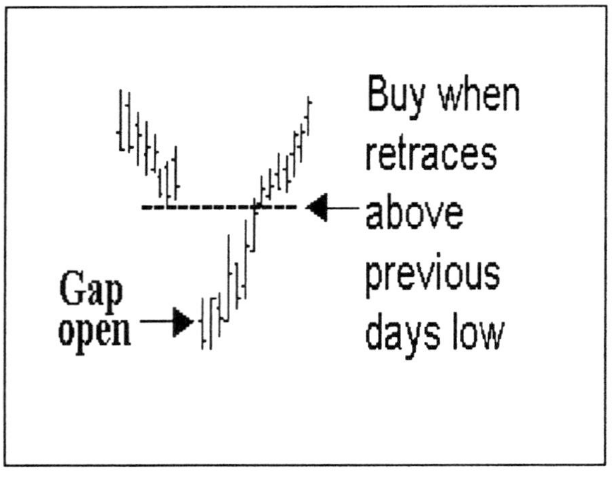

This is a great opportunity to go long.

Chapter 25

SOME FINAL NOTES

THE MARKET HAS TO BE READY

When is a market ready? It is ready when you can perceive that now is the time for you to get on, start paddling, enter that wave, and go for a ride. It is ready when it is doing the things that you expected it to do. It is ready when its behavior is predictable enough for you to feel safe entering it.

If a market is extremely volatile, making large unpredictable swings and moves, you may not feel comfortable entering that market, so you DON'T!

If a market is flat and not giving you the kind of action that you would expect or want for a trade, you stay out. You only enter a market when you are READY and THE MARKET IS READY!

Here is a good analogy. Many times a surfer will let many waves go by looking for the one big one that will yield the longest ride. A lot of fun-type small waves go by. But the surfer will ignore those. Intermediate, strong waves will go by, but the surfer will ignore those. The surfer is looking for the big wave, the one that will carry him all the way up past the water mark.

So, when the smaller waves come along, even though they may be ready, the surfer is not ready. When the good intermediate waves come and are ready to ride, the surfer is still not ready. He wants the big action, the big wave.

This is what it is like to trade long term. If and when we trade long term, we're looking for the big action, bypassing the lesser action.

That doesn't mean that the surfer rides only the long waves. Moods change. On another day, at another time, it's fun to ride the small or the intermediate waves. Sometimes there are not enough big waves to ride, so the surfer might want to master the skill of riding the smaller waves.

When we trade, we do the same thing. Big wave, intermediate wave, or small wave, all are interesting — as long as they are profitable.

When we ride the small waves we have to get in and out of the surf a lot. We pay a price in energy expended and wear and tear on our body. When we trade the short term trend of the market we have to get in and out of the market a lot. That gets expensive, because we have transaction costs and face possible slippage every time we do it. The short term trader has a much higher overhead than the longer term trader, but he does get more action.

We have a friend who is a only a short term trader. He is a day trader. Once we asked him why he day trades. His answer was that he couldn't stand leaving all that money on the table. In other words he couldn't stand watching all of those small waves go by and not taking a ride. Is that OK? Sure, everyone has to trade within his own personality, using his own judgments, based on his own perceptions. If he doesn't he will not be ready! He will lose.

A long term trader may leave 50% of the intraday market move on the table, but that is more than offset by the sizable gains from the daily trend, and the fewer commissions that he pays, and the less slippage that he experiences.

By the way, we should explain here that slippage occurs because we can't always buy at the exact price that we may want, or sell at the exact price that we expect. In other words, our orders are not always filled at the prices we anticipate.

HARMONY

This manual is in part about harmony. One objective is to show how to get in harmony with markets. There are a number of ways to state this concept, none of them are new. Here are some different quaint ways we have heard it expressed: "The trend is your friend." "Ride with the tide." "Go with the flow." The fact is that they are all correct. We cannot emphasize this strongly enough.

No one of us is big enough to resist the forces of the market. We cannot make the market come our way. The very best we can do is to harmonize with the market — get in step with it.

Have you ever tried to surf out to sea? You can for a short time! You can paddle along with, and ride the outward surge until you run into the first incoming wave, and then you have to duck under quickly or be pounded into the sand. The choice is yours to make. If the incoming wave is big enough, it may pick you up and smash you onto the bottom (ouch). Numerous surfers have been injured and even killed trying this stunt. Somehow they get the notion that they are bigger than the relentless and crashing waves.

There are traders who do the same thing. They think they are bigger than the markets. They think they can get in a quick thrill by going against the tide. Sometimes they are badly hurt, and sometimes they are financially killed by the magnitude of a market move that knocks them for a loop. Sooner or later they will be out of the markets, one way or another.

That is why we trade in harmony with the markets. We want the market to clearly tell us which way it is going. Then we hope that, by skill, we can go along for a profitable ride.

When a skillful surfer is waiting for just the right wave, he observes every wave. Unless the wave forms just right for a ride, he will let it pass by.

So it is in the market. Unless the wave comes your way in just the right way, let it go by. There will be plenty of other waves.

If the surf is not up the way it should be at one beach, then a good surfer will go to another beach.

If the stock you're watching is NOT doing the right things, then go to another stock. There are plenty of stocks to choose from.

You can't make the market do what you want it to do. It is relentless. It will do what it will do, and you cannot change that fact.

A IMPORTANT LESSON

We want to reveal a very important lesson. This one concept, if mastered, can make virtually anyone a winner the vast majority of the time.

LEARN TO REVERSE A LOSING POSITION

The best way we can express what we mean is to relate a true story we witnessed recently. We are going to change the names of the person and the stock traded in order to avoid embarrassing anyone, but otherwise every bit of it really happened.

Trader Tom puts out a periodic trade bulletin, and between bulletins he has a regular hot-line. The stock he had recommended had been making new highs and was steady up due to an agreement by the rhinoceros horn cartel to cut production. Finally, the stock made a new high for the year, topped out, and began to go down. The new high was at 30.50 and prices dropped to 22.375 before rallying to 25.125, thus forming a 1-2-3 high. Trader Tom spotted this as such and put out an open sell order to all of his followers to sell the stock at a breakout of the number 2 point at 22.375. Trader Tom and his followers placed their stops at the number 1 point of 30.50, which by this time seemed pretty safe as it was about 5 points away from the current price action.

The next few days saw the stock rally away from the low at 22.375. In fact, prices never got close to it again. On the fourth day there was a reaction, and the stock made a slightly lower low and a slightly lower high.

Surely the market must be going to break now and come on down. However, after that day's close, a report came out from the Rhinoceros Horn Institute that showed a rather large drop in the Asian stocks of powdered rhinoceros horn. The next day, prices resumed their upward climb. Prices moved up for a few days, and then a correction came. Trader Tom felt sure that now the big break was certainly going to come. Prices moved down for a couple of days, but not by much. Then came an announcement that rhinoceros horn grinders outside the cartel had agreed to cut production in order to keep the price of powdered rhinoceros horn at more acceptable (to them) levels. Rhinoceros horn began to move up once more, and at 26 there was no longer any logical resistance except at 30.50 where trader Tom and his followers' stops were neatly bunched together waiting for the axe to fall (or should we say rise?).

Sure enough, within a few days prices climbed up, took out the stops at 30.50, and continued rising well beyond the 30.50 level. Trader Tom and all his followers lost about $5 per share. WHY? Because Tom was too arrogant, stubborn, stupid, vain, and mechanical to reverse his position. This could easily have been done when the institute reported lower than normal stocks were on hand. Again, it could have been done when the producers outside the cartel announced a cut in ground horn production. Certainly it could have been done on a technical basis as prices broke past the number 3 point, and again when it was clear that there was no more resistance between 26 and 30. But Trader Tom was paralyzed. His system was going to have to work, and if it didn't, he and his followers would eat $5.00 per share, which is what they did.

IF THE BASIS FOR A TRADE NO LONGER EXISTS, REVERSE!

If we are trading the breakout of a number 2 point and prices start going the other way, the basis for the trade no longer exists. It is time to exit or reverse.

If we are trading the breakout of a Trading Range and prices turn and go the other way, we must reverse our position. If we are trading from a Ledge, or a Ross Hook, and prices turn and go the other way, we must reverse our position.

NOTICE!!! We did not say close out our position. We said REVERSE our position. Of course, to reverse we have to close out our original position, but the thinking process is different. We are not abandoning this trade, we are engineering a change of mind and reversing. Eight or nine out of ten times that a position is reversed, it will either break even or go on to make money, as opposed to taking an outright loss.

WHAT IT TAKES

It is totally against human nature to reverse a position. It takes complete humility to do it. It is an admission that the market knows where it's going and the trader doesn't.

It takes a cast iron stomach to reverse. It is something to which we had to inure ourselves. We practiced it on paper for a long time. Then we practiced it with real money until we became steeled to doing it. It is unnatural, but it must be done. Anyone who wants to consistently make money in trading must become hardened to the fact of reversals.

Study charts and see how often this situation occurs. Keep accurate records of what happens when you don't reverse and when you do. There is no reason to sit and watch yourself get killed in the markets. No one has to be paralyzed, sitting there waiting in agony for the terrible loss that is bound to come. We used to think that if we were wrong, that we should get out — take the loss and get out. Many books teach this. Sometimes we moved our stop closer, so that the loss would not be so big, and then get stopped out. It was like the chicken running to the butcher and saying, "Please chop my head off."

HOW TO TURN LEMONS INTO LEMONADE

Now, we want to show one of the best trades that can ever come your way. It doesn't matter whether it comes on a one minute chart or a one month chart, or any kind of chart. It amounts to the aggressive use of one of the greatest lessons, and that is the lesson of reversing position.

When a market goes like this:

/VVVVVVV

Whether it be for a few minutes or a few months, and then breaks out like this:

```
               /
/\/\/\/\/\/\/\/
```

And then does this:

```
             /\
/\/\/\/\/\/\/  \
                \
```

Sell it as it breaks the lows of that congestion or range.

The opposite is equally true.

```
                 /
/\/\/\/\/\/\/\  /
             \/
```

Buy as it breaks the highs of the congestion or range.

It doesn't matter how short or long the congestion is, as long as it can be seen to be moving sideways. Normally, this will take a minimum of 3-4 bars on the chart.

```
       /         /\
/\/\  /       \/\/  \
    \/               \
```

What we're doing here is to avoid taking the first breakout of a congestion or range. Instead, we are opting for the situation in which everyone else has gotten burned by the false breakout, and now prices have crossed the sideways area and have broken out on the other side. You will miss many trades this way because many of them never reverse and come back through the congestion. But when they do, it is dynamite, a trade well worth waiting for.

This is particularly effective in daytrading, since you don't have to wait for a long time to see many of these situations happening on a regular basis.

When position trading on hourly, daily or greater (time interval) charts, take the first breakout, and then reverse if your still in the trade as it comes through and breaks out on the other side of the congestion. If you're not still in the trade when the reversal comes, then essentially you have the situation described above and can enter the breakout in the appropriate direction as it occurs.

NATURALLY, IF YOU'RE ALREADY POSITIONED INCORRECTLY DUE TO THE FIRST BREAKOUT, YOU SHOULD HAVE A REVERSING STOP ORDER RESTING IN THE MARKET!

There is no hard and fast rule here. The reversing stop is intuitive, and the feel for it comes with practice. Start practicing immediately!

Before closing this part of the manual, we want to make something very clear. We want to state here and now that we are not all that thrilled with "Technical Trading" in the way that most people engage in it. Why? Because the majority of traders incorrectly use technical analysis for their trading and the majority of traders lose more than they win. Remember that! If you do what the majority does, you will lose right along with them.

No matter what form the technical analysis takes, whether Fibonacci, oscillators, moving averages, or whatever, the only thing we have ever seen work is the concept that we will now explain.

The odds are that whenever prices begin trending, they will continue to trend for some time. Let's call that the major trend. In technical analysis, the important thing is to find the major trend. Next, it is important to find the intermediate trend. Whenever the intermediate trend begins to go counter-trend to the major trend, there is an entry opportunity coming at the point that the intermediate trend reverses and begins again to go in the direction of the major trend. The entry signal will then come from what is considered to be the short term trend. Memorize this concept. We are continually amazed at how few technical traders actually understand it. Yet if technical analysis is to be done, it is mandatory to understand the major trend / counter-trend process.

Lets repeat it once more. If the major trend is up, then wait for the intermediate trend to turn down. When the intermediate trend begins to turn up, then consider entry into the market based upon a signal from a short term indicator, or simply from the fact that prices are correcting. The opposite is true if the major trend is down.

You most certainly do not need an oscillator to tell you which way the market is going. In an uptrend, wait for the intermediate correcting price action. Attempt to buy into this correcting action, short term, at the time the market appears to be resuming the longer term trend.

The easiest trades to take are the hooks. This is because they are so easy to see. All that is required is a correction occurring during a trend. Trade them in trending markets, because, by definition, that is the only place they occur. Look for a minimum objective of profit. Once that is secured, bail out only when you are convinced the trend is coming to an end.

Although we would love to give you exact statistical percentiles for success in each type of trade, we have found that they vary according to the amount of margin available, and the person doing the trading. The less the margin, the more often you will be stopped out because you have to keep your stops close.

Trading with any of our techniques gives a greater dollar won to dollar lost ratio trading with a $50,000 or greater trading account, than it does when trading a $10,000 account. It enables one to gain greater diversification in the markets, and also allows for more skillful trade management. Everything is not riding on a single position. We have found that when scalping, it is much easier to take a few ticks and run with a larger position than with a smaller.

It has been argued that a larger account allows for placing stops further away. In our opinion, this is false reasoning. Stops should be placed the same whether trading 500 shares or 5000 shares. The risk is proportionate for each.

It is important to remember that when trading a breakout, either from congestion or a number two point, to be especially careful trading the breakout into a prior congestion. This is especially true when prices are near a major top or bottom. Even though you may successfully trade that breakout, you will not normally get any mileage out of the trade if it immediately runs into prior support or resistance. To ascertain if this is the case, sometimes it's necessary to look to a chart showing a larger time-frame.

When you trade the daily charts, look to the weekly and even monthly charts to see where prices are in relation to where they have been in the past.

MORE GOOD STUFF

We don't listen to the news when trading, It throws our trading off. When we are contemplating a trade, we avoid CNBC, CNN, PBS, and any other source of opinion on the markets. We do NOT want to know what they or any of their guests think. We want to emphasize that everything you need to know is right there in front of you. The only thing that can mess up your plan is unexpected news, a World incident, or an "act of God." Then you have your stop in place to bail you out as quickly as possible. No human can predict such incidents. You should, however, know when earnings are being released.

We cannot stand to watch the consumer price index, the producer price index, the wholesale price index, the trade balance, the money supply, the discount rate, the prime rate, or any of the host of other reports spewed out by dozens of government agencies and the like. These reports (and they are forever increasing) cause huge blips, gaps, runs-up and runs-down on the intraday charts. It's enough to give anyone ulcers. Hardly a day goes by that someone, somewhere, isn't releasing a report or making a speech that makes the market jump. It's too nerve-wracking. That's why we ignore all these reports, and all the opinions concerning their implications. However, we are aware of them as a matter of safety and self-protection.

We have come to realize that our own opinion of the market is as good as any. One of the advantages of longer term trading is that these reports are not important to the longer term trend. Outside influence serves only to take away the courage of convictions, therefore we ignore such influence as much as possible.

That is not to say that these reports are not valuable. They are important at the right time and in the right place. However, they are of no value to you in trading when you are utilizing the methods that we use to enter and exit the markets.

We are dead set against all prognosticators, prophets, most advisors, and anyone who tells you that they "think" the market will do such and such. We have enough trouble getting rid of our own "I thinks" which invariably lead us into trouble. We don't want to know what they think when we're busy making our own decisions based on our own methods.

We do the best when we follow our methods, diligently working like a good mechanic, being adept at following what we know works. It's like golf. All you have to do is to hit the smaller ball into the larger hole, but few there are who can do it well. Few, too, are the traders who can diligently, with persistence and consistency, follow a trading system or method that works. We hate ourselves when we don't follow our methods. We aggravate, go into self-abasement, call ourselves all kinds of names, feel ashamed, and get terribly depressed. Yet it happens all too often to suit us. If you have the same problem, here is something you can do.

Keep a log of all your trades, why you made them, and what you were thinking about when you made the decision to enter them. You should do this in part to help you with future trades, and in part to keep yourself too busy to overtrade.

THE BUSINESS OF TRADING

TRADING IS A BUSINESS OF PERCENTAGES. TOO MANY TREAT IT AS A GAME, IN FACT THEY CALL IT A GAME. IF YOU WANT TO BE A LOSER, THEN TREAT IT AS A GAME. IF YOU WANT TO WIN, TREAT IT AS A BUSINESS.

Now what do we mean by that? We mean don't "play" the "game" of trading. You want to be like the baseball manager. The players "play" the game, but the manager is all business. He has firmly in mind the percentages for or against making any move that strategy may dictate. Sound management in placing stops says that you can risk no more money on a single trade than is a multiple of the number of successive losses you can expect from the method of trading you use.

If you have a $50,000 trading account and with your methods of trading you expect no more than 10 trading losses in a row, and if you're willing to see it go down to $25,000 before you've had all the pain you can take, then you can afford to risk $2,500 total per trade made.

SYSTEM VS. METHOD

Here is our definition of the difference between a trading system and a trading method.

A system is extremely mechanical, and leaves little room for emotion, personal thought, and intervention. A trading system is something that is traded mechanically. To make it work, one does what the system dictates, and that is all. Deviation from the system results in failure. Judgment is not involved. We promised you something special if you read this far. We feel you are entitled to send for the trading strategy we promised at the front of this manual. To get it absolutely free, please send a self-addressed stamped envelope to the address shown at the front of the manual. You must include proof of purchase, the name of the manual (so we know which gift to send you), your name, address, telephone number, fax number, and email address if you have one. Ask for gift 303. We know you will be pleasantly surprised.

A trading method is different in that it allows for human intervention. Judgment, wisdom, and personal thought are all able to enter into a trade. The allowance for emotion is the weak point in a trading method. It requires self-control. However, the ability to intervene and use wisdom and sound judgment more than makes up for the risks of emotion, provided that a trader has established self-control. The trading methods in this manual all have the necessary win-to-loss and profit ratios needed for success. The methods shown have worked with only small modification since before the turn of the century.

A trading method, of necessity, involves creating a trading plan. We hate to be trite, but one of the wisest sayings is "plan your work and work your plan." This is essential to good trading. Planning and working a trade keeps you from "willy-nilly" trading, trading on whims, and trading from emotion. "Perfect love drives out fear." We love trading enough that we are willing to work our plan and stick with it. With a plan it is possible to have the courage of your convictions. That courage has turned many a loser into a winner. We know where we're going, why we're going there, and when we might get there.

DON'T GET ANGRY AT A MARKET

Never get angry at a market. After all, it's an inanimate although dynamic thing. Do get angry with yourself. It seems as if we make every mistake in the book, and never seem to learn to avoid them. We want so desperately to have our wits about us when we trade — to think of all the possibilities, and to see what's really happening.

Becoming angry with a market very often leads to wanting to take revenge on that market. This is when some of the greatest losses take place, because of the emotional reaction in trying to get even. It is just childish and immature and a poor way to try to make profits.

Being angry with a market can result only in lost opportunity, yet we know traders who will not trade a certain stock because they are angry with the stock due to losses they have had in trading it.

OBJECTIVES

There can be no more important topic that we can discuss in this manual than that of objectives. Until we learned this lesson, it cost many dollars in lost profits. Never, NEVER, never enter a trade unless you have an objective for the trade and are prepared to get out when that objective is reached. We cannot recall how many times we have had profits in the bag, only to lose them because we failed to tell get out.

If the objective is achieved, be happy and content. Don't care what that market does after your objective has been met!

This is the approach you have to a trade when you are trying to scalp a market. Hit the objective and get out!

When scalping, without an objective there is no real reason to trade. Where is this trade going? Are you in business or are you just gambling? If you're in business then you'd better have some sort of goal.

Of course, when not scalping, if the objective is to be stopped out using a trailing stop, you have the benefit of allowing a trade to build profits before having to get out.

Throughout this manual, we have tried to show how we see the price action on charts. But there are some things we cannot show in a manual. These are the things that make up trading sense. A person can learn these only by getting their lumps and bumps in the market place.

RUNS

A very important concept to grasp when trading is that of the run. All markets, in all trading time frames, have runs. Markets have runs up and runs down. In order to take advantage of these runs, one has to be in a position in the market. It's as we explained earlier, one has to be in the water ready for the wave.

AVOID FOOLISH MOVES

Try to avoid what are obviously foolish moves. Don't sell into support and don't buy into resistance. The odds are against it.

Look at the charts that are one magnitude greater than the one on which you are trading. Look for long time support and resistance areas. Look for Fibonacci support and resistance areas. Don't trade into those areas. Just cool it and wait to see how things develop.

One of the biggest mistakes in trading is that people get so wrapped up in their trading that they fail to realize soon enough that prices are in a trading range. Learn to step back and take a broad overview look at different stocks. You want to be trading the ones that are truly trending.

Sometimes that means not trading at all. One good clue to the fact that you are in congestion areas is that all of a sudden you stop making money. Trades stop working out. You find that you are struggling in the markets. You start taking hits. If this starts to happen, stand back, be eclectic. Virtually every time you will see that the market overall is going sideways.

That is the time when you have to have the maturity to stop trading. No one is looking over your shoulder. Be wise. You don't have to trade all the time. Wait for the right times.

We have now completed Volume III of this course. We can't wait to see you again in ELECTRONIC TRADING 'TNT' IV — TIPS-TRICKS AND OTHER TRADING STUFF. This final book in the 'TNT' course is filled with unbelievable trading stuff that no trader should be without.

Joe Ross Mark Cherlin

FOR YOU

In this course, consisting of the four manuals that make up the ELECTRONIC TRADING 'TNT' series: GORILLA TRADING STUFF, HOW-TO-WIN TRADING STUFF, TECHNICAL TRADING STUFF, and TIPS-TRICKS AND OTHER TRADING STUFF, we've revealed the way we trade and conduct a trading business. We've shown what we do day in and day out. We've described the tools we use, and how, where, when, and why we use them. We do make our living as traders, not as authors.

Unlike most authors who secrete themselves behind a publisher's telephone number and address, we will gladly respond to any phone calls, faxes, E mail, or letters that we receive regarding the material presented in these manuals. For more information about other services, books, and seminars which we offer our readers, please continue reading.

SEMINARS

At times a manual is not enough. Some would like more help than we are able to present in a manual. For this reason, we hold seminars regularly for the purposes of tutoring those who want and can afford the additional help.

If you want to learn to run your trading as a profitable business, you will benefit from the two day seminars we give. We give these seminars almost every month. Enrollment is limited. A prerequisite for taking the seminar is that you must have read both ELECTRONIC TRADING 'TNT' I — GORILLA TRADING STUFF and ELECTRONIC TRADING 'TNT' II — HOW-TO-WIN TRADING STUFF.

At our seminars we attempt to answer any and all questions concerning the material in our books. We then go on to expand the material beyond what is contained in the books.

Once you have taken a seminar, you may attend it again for up to two years. There will be no charge other than what it costs you for travel, lodging and meals. The only requirement is that you let us know well in advance that you will be coming.

At the seminar, you will be shown a great many things that are impossible to get into a book. Here are some of the novel things you will be taught:

How to neutralize the advantages the insiders have over you.

Techniques for getting into a stock ahead of everyone else so that their entry pushes along your position.

Techniques for taking the risk out of a trade.

Techniques for buying more time for a trade without getting hurt.

How to safely hold overnight positions in volatile stocks.

How to figure the true risk in a trade.

How to make significant profits over costs from your trading.

And much, much more in the way of tips and tricks to help your trading. To book reservations, contact information is listed at the front of the manual.

Private Training Sessions

We offer three-day private training sessions, one for day traders and one for position traders. These are intensive sessions for a maximum of four persons at $10,000 each. The same sessions are also available on a one-on-one basis for $12,000.

Private Tutoring and Consulting

For those who want one-on-one private tutoring, we are available by appointment only. Fees are:

$400/hour by telephone

$500/hour in person

$4,000/day in person

$4,000/DAY (plus travel, lodging, meals, and expenses if travel on our part is involved.)

Private tutoring sessions involve any or all of the following: You doing the trading while being coached, offered suggestions, and being helped with proper organization; Answering your particular questions; Custom tailoring of the session time to precisely fit your needs; Anything else with which you might require assistance.

Appendix

MARKET MAKERS

ABSB	ALEX BROWN & SONS, INC.
AGIS	AEGIS CAPITAL CORP.
BEST	BEAR STEARNS & CO., INC.
BTSC	BT SECURITIES
CANT	CANTOR FITZGERALD & CO.
CHGO	CHICAGO CORP.
CJDB	J LAWRENCE DEUTSCHE BANK
COST	COASTAL SECURITIES
COWN	COWEN & CO.
DAIN	DAIN BOSWORTH, INC.
DEAN	DEAN WITTER
DLJP	DONALDSON LUFKIN JENRETTE
DOMS	DOMESTIC SECURITIES
EXPO	EXPONENTIAL CAPITAL MKTS.
FACT	FIRST ALBANY CORP.
FAHN	FAHNESTOCK & CO.
FBCO	FIRST BOSTON CORP.
FPKI	FOX-PITT, KELTON, INC.
GRUN	GRUNTAL & CO., INC.
GSCO	GOLDMAN SACHS & CO.
GVRC	GVR CO.
HMQT	HAMBRECHT & QUIST, INC.
HRZG	HERZOG, HEINE, GEDULD, INC.
JEFF	JEFFERIES CO., INC.
JPMS	J.P. MORGAN
KEMP	KEMPER SECURITIES, INC.
LEHM	LEHMAN BROTHERS
MADF	BERNARD MADOFF
MASH	MAYER & SCHWEITZER, INC.
MHMY	M.H. MEYERSON & CO., INC.
MLCO	MERRIL LYNCH
MONT	MONTGOMERY SECURITIES
MSCO	MORGAN STANLEY & CO.

MSWE	MIDWEST STOCK EXCHANGE
NAWE	NASH WEISS & CO.
NEED	NEDDHAM & CO.
NMRA	NOMURA SECURITIES INTL.
OLDE	OLDE DISCOUNT CORP.
OPCO	OPPENHEIMER & CO.
PERT	PERSHING TRADING CO.
PIPR	PIPER JAFFRAY
PRUS	PRUDENTIAL SECURITIES.
PUNK	PUNK ZIEGEL & KNOELL.
PWJC	PAINE WEBBER INC.
RAGN	RAGEN MCKENZIE INC.
RPSC	RAUSCHER PIERCE
RBSF	ROBERTSON STEPHENS & CO.
SALB	SALOMON BROTHERS
SBNY	SANDS BROTHERS & CO., LTD
SELZ	FURMAN SELZ INC.
SHWD	SHERWOOD SECURITIES CORP.
SNDV	SOUNDVIEW FINANCIAL
SWST	SOUTHWEST SECURITIES.
TSCO	TROSTER SINGER CORP.
TUCK	TUCKER ANTHONY, INC.
TVAN	TEEVAN & CO., INC.
UBSS	UBS SECURITIES
WARB	S.G. WARBURG & CO., INC
WEAT	WHEAT FIRST SECURITIES.
WEDB	WEDBRUSH MORGAN SEC.
WEED	WEEDEN & CO. LP
WERT	WORTHEIM,SCHRODER

THIS LIST IS A REPRESENTATION OF SOME CURRENT MARKET MAKERS. BE CAREFUL, IT CAN AND WILL CHANGE.

READING LIST:

BOOKS AND COURSES

ELECTRONIC TRADING 'TNT' I — GORILLA TRADING STUFF
Joe Ross and Mark Cherlin

ELECTRONIC TRADING 'TNT' II — HOW-TO-WIN TRADING STUFF
Joe Ross and Mark Cherlin

ELECTRONIC TRADING 'TNT' III — TECHNICAL TRADING STUFF
Joe Ross and Mark Cherlin

ELECTRONIC TRADING 'TNT' IV — TIPS –TRICKS AND OTHER TRADING STUFF
Joe Ross and Mark Cherlin

WHAT I LEARNED LOSING A MILLION DOLLARS
Jim Paul and Brendan Moynihan

REMINISCENCES OF A STOCK OPERATOR
Edwin Lefevre

MARKET WIZARDS - (Interviews with Top Traders)
Jack D. Schwager

HOW TO MAKE MONEY IN STOCKS
William J. O'Neil

THE DISCIPLINED TRADER
Mark Douglas

THE INNER GAME OF TRADING
Robert Koppel and Howard Abell

THE WINNING EDGE
Adrienne Laris Toghraie

THE WINNING EDGE II
Adrienne Laris Toghraie

PRIVATE AND GROUP SEMINARS

ELECTRONIC TRADING 'TNT'— EXPLOSIVE TRADING STUFF
Joe Ross — Mark Cherlin

Index